Illustrated C# 2010

Daniel M. Solis

apress®

Illustrated C# 2010

ISBN-13 (pbk): 978-1-4302-3282-7

ISBN-13 (electronic): 978-1-4302-3283-4

Printed and bound in the United States of America 9 8 7 6 5 4 3 2 1

Distributed to the book trade worldwide by Springer Science+Business Media, LLC., 233 Spring Street, 6th Floor, New York, NY 10013. Phone 1-800-SPRINGER, fax (201) 348-4505, e-mail orders-ny@springer-sbm.com, or visit www.springeronline.com.

For information on translations, please e-mail rights@apress.com, or visit www.apress.com.

Apress and friends of ED books may be purchased in bulk for academic, corporate, or promotional use. eBook versions and licenses are also available for most titles. For more information, reference our Special Bulk Sales–eBook Licensing web page at www.apress.com/info/bulksales.

The source code for this book is available to readers at www.apress.com.

*I would like to dedicate this book to
Sian; to my parents, Sal and Amy;
and to Sue.*

Contents at a Glance

Contents

About the Author

 **Dan Solis** holds a Bachelor of Arts degree with majors in biology and English. He initially worked in research on the structure of bi- and tri-metal crystals, until he found that he enjoyed programming much more than working in a lab. He also holds a Master of Science degree in computer science from the University of California at Santa Barbara, where he concentrated on programming languages and compiler design.

Dan has been programming professionally for more than 20 years, with more than half that time working as a consultant and contract programmer, including several projects for Microsoft Consulting Services. His consulting projects have ranged from programs for mutual fund analysis and supply chain management to systems for missile tracking. He has also taught courses on various programming languages, Windows programming, UNIX internals, and a number of other topics, in both the United States and Europe.

Dan's first programming language was C, but he soon became intrigued by the journal articles about a new language being developed called "C with Classes." Eventually that language was renamed C++ and released to the world. He began using C++ as soon as he could get access to a compiler, and he eventually started teaching training seminars on the language as well as continuing to code.

With the advent of C#, .NET, and WPF, he has moved on to enjoying the myriad advantages of the new platform and has been working with them enthusiastically ever since.

Acknowledgments

I want to thank Sian for supporting and encouraging me on a daily basis, and I want to thank my parents and brothers and sisters for their continued love and support.

I also want to express my gratitude to the people at Apress who have worked with me to bring this book to fruition. I really appreciate that they understood and appreciated what I was trying to do and worked with me to achieve it. Thanks to all of you.

Introduction

The purpose of this book is to teach you the fundamentals and mechanics of the C# programming language. Most books teach programming primarily using text. That's great for novels, but many of the important concepts of programming languages can best be understood through a combination of words, figures, and tables.

Many of us think visually, and figures and tables can help clarify and crystallize our understanding of a concept. In several years of teaching programming languages, I have found that the pictures I drew on the whiteboards were the things that most quickly helped the students understand the concepts I was trying to convey. Illustrations alone, however, are not sufficient to explain a programming language and platform. The goal of this book is to find the best combination of words and illustrations to give you a thorough understanding of the language and to allow the book to serve as a reference resource as well.

This book is written for anyone who wants an introduction to the C# programming language—from the novice to the seasoned programmer. For those just getting started in programming, I've included the basics. For seasoned programmers, the content is laid out succinctly, in a form that allows you to go directly to the information required without having to wade through oceans of words. For both sets of programmers, the content itself is presented graphically, in a form that should make the language easy to learn.

You can download the source code for all the book's example programs from the Apress web site—apress.com. And although I can't answer specific questions about your code, you can contact me with suggestions or feedback at dansolis@sbcglobal.net. You can also visit my web site—illustratedcsharp.com. Finally, if you're interested in learning to program using Windows Presentation Foundation, please take a look at my book—*Illustrated WPF*, which uses the same style and approach as this book.

I hope this book makes learning C# an enjoyable experience for you! Take care.

Dan Solis

CHAPTER 1

■ ■ ■

C# and the .NET Framework

Before .NET

The C# programming language was designed for developing programs for Microsoft's .NET Framework. This chapter gives a brief look at where .NET came from and its basic architecture. To start off, let's get the name right: C# is pronounced "see sharp."[1]

Windows Programming in the Late 1990s

In the late 1990s, Windows programming using the Microsoft platform had fractured into a number of branches. Most programmers were using Visual Basic (VB), C, or C++. Some C and C++ programmers were using the raw Win32 API, but most were using the Microsoft Foundation Classes (MFC). Others had moved to the Component Object Model (COM).

All these technologies had their own problems. The raw Win32 API was not object-oriented, and using it required a lot more work than MFC. MFC was object-oriented but was inconsistent and getting old. COM, although conceptually simple, was complex in its actual coding and required lots of ugly, inelegant plumbing.

Another shortcoming of all these programming technologies was that they were aimed primarily at developing code for the desktop rather than the Internet. At the time, programming for the Web was an afterthought and seemed very different from coding for the desktop.

Goals for the Next-Generation Platform Services

What we really needed was a new start—an integrated, object-oriented development framework that would bring consistency and elegance back to programming. To meet this need, Microsoft set out to develop a code execution environment and a code development environment that met these goals. Figure 1-1 lists these goals.

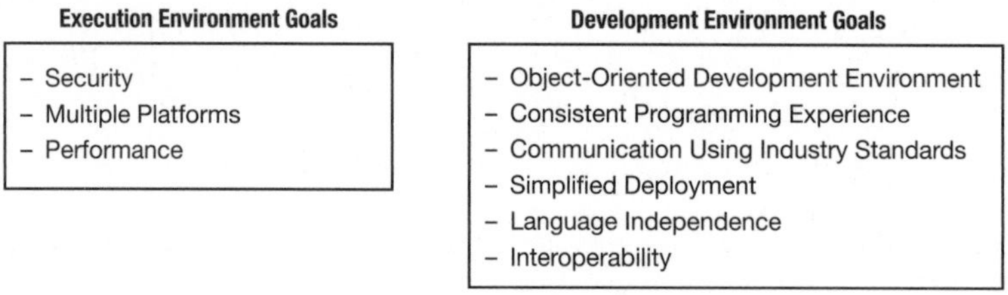

Execution Environment Goals	Development Environment Goals
– Security – Multiple Platforms – Performance	– Object-Oriented Development Environment – Consistent Programming Experience – Communication Using Industry Standards – Simplified Deployment – Language Independence – Interoperability

Figure 1-1. *Goals for the next-generation platform*

Enter Microsoft .NET

In 2002, Microsoft released the first version of the .NET Framework, which promised to address the old problems and meet the goals for the next-generation systems. The .NET Framework is a much more consistent and object-oriented environment than either the MFC or COM programming technology. Some of its features include the following:

---

[1] I was once interviewed for a contract C# position when the Human Resources interviewer asked me how much experience I'd had programming in "see pound" (instead of "see sharp")! It took me a moment to realize what he was talking about.

- *Multiple platforms:* The system runs on a broad range of computers, from servers and desktop machines to PDAs and cell phones.

- *Industry standards:* The system uses industry-standard communication protocols, such as XML, HTTP, SOAP, and WSDL.

- *Security:* The system can provide a much safer execution environment, even in the presence of code obtained from suspect sources.

Components of the .NET Framework

The .NET Framework consists of three components, as shown in Figure 1-2. The execution environment is called the Common Language Runtime (CLR). The CLR manages program execution at run time, including the following:

- Memory management

- Code safety verification

- Code execution, thread management, and exception handling

- Garbage collection

The programming tools include everything you need for coding and debugging, including the following:

- The Visual Studio integrated development environment

- .NET-compliant compilers (e.g., C#, VB .NET, JScript, F#, IronRuby, and managed C++)

- Debuggers

- Web development server-side technologies, such as ASP.NET or WCF

The Base Class Library (BCL) is a large class library used by the .NET Framework and available for you to use in your programs as well.

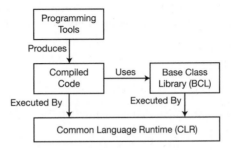

Figure 1-2. *Components of the .NET Framework*

An Improved Programming Environment

The .NET Framework offers programmers considerable improvements over previous Windows programming environments. The following sections give a brief overview of its features and their benefits.

Object-Oriented Development Environment

The CLR, the BCL, and C# are designed to be thoroughly object-oriented and act as a well-integrated environment.

The system provides a consistent, object-oriented model of programming for both local programs and distributed systems. It also provides a software development interface for desktop application programming, mobile application programming, and web development, consistent across a broad range of targets, from servers to cell phones.

Automatic Garbage Collection

The CLR has a service called the garbage collector (GC), which automatically manages memory for you.

- The GC automatically removes objects from memory that your program will no longer access.

- The GC relieves programmers of tasks they have traditionally had to perform, such as deallocating memory and hunting for memory leaks. This is a huge improvement, since hunting for memory leaks can be difficult and time-consuming.

Interoperability

The .NET Framework was designed for interoperability between different .NET languages, the operating system or Win32 DLLs, and COM.

- .NET language interoperability allows software modules written using different .NET languages to interact seamlessly.

    — A program written in one .NET language can use and even inherit from a class written in another .NET language, as long as certain rules are followed.

    — Because of its ability to easily integrate modules produced in different programming languages, the .NET Framework is sometimes described as *language-agnostic*.

- .NET provides a feature called *platform invoke (P/Invoke)*, which allows code written for .NET to call and use code not written for .NET. It can use raw C functions imported from standard Win32 DLLs, such as the Windows APIs.

- The .NET Framework also allows interoperability with COM. The .NET Framework software components can call COM components and COM components can call .NET components as if they were COM components themselves.

No COM Required

The .NET Framework frees the programmer from the COM legacy. As a C# programmer, you don't need to use COM and therefore don't need any of the following:

- *The* IUnknown *interface*: In COM, all objects must implement interface IUnknown. In contrast, all .NET objects derive from a single class called object. Interface programming is still an important part of .NET, but it's no longer the central theme.

- *Type libraries*: In COM, type information is kept in type libraries as .tlb files, which are separate from the executable code. In .NET, a program's type information is kept bundled with the code in the program file.

- *Reference counting*: In COM, the programmer had to keep track of the number of references to an object to make sure it wasn't deleted at the wrong time. In .NET, the GC keeps track of references and removes objects only when appropriate.

- HRESULT: COM used the HRESULT data type to return runtime error codes. .NET doesn't use HRESULTs. Instead, all unexpected runtime errors produce exceptions.

- *The registry*: COM applications had to be registered in the system registry, which holds information about the configurations of the operating system and applications. .NET applications don't need to use the registry. This simplifies the installation and removal of programs. (However, there is something similar called the *global assembly cache*, which I'll cover in Chapter 10.)

Although the amount of COM code that's currently being written is fairly small, there's still quite a number of COM components in systems currently being used, and C# programmers sometimes need to write code that interfaces with those components. C# 4.0 introduces several new features that make that task easier.

Simplified Deployment

Deploying programs written for the .NET Framework can be much easier than it was before, for the following reasons:

- The fact that .NET programs don't need to be registered with the registry means that in the simplest case, a program just needs to be copied to the target machine and it's ready to run.

- .NET offers a feature called *side-by-side execution*, which allows different versions of a DLL to exist on the same machine. This means that every executable can have access to the version of the DLL for which it was built.

Type Safety

The CLR checks and ensures the type safety of parameters and other data objects—even between components written in different programming languages.

The Base Class Library

The .NET Framework supplies an extensive base class library, called, not surprisingly, the *Base Class Library* (*BCL*). (It's also sometimes called the Framework Class Library—FCL). You can use this extensive set of available code when writing your own programs. Some of the categories are the following:

- *General base classes*: Classes that provide you with an extremely powerful set of tools for a wide range of programming tasks, such as file manipulation, string manipulation, security, and encryption

- *Collection classes*: Classes that implement lists, dictionaries, hash tables, and bit arrays

- *Threading and synchronization classes*: Classes for building multithreaded programs

- *XML classes*: Classes for creating, reading, and manipulating XML documents

Compiling to the Common Intermediate Language

The compiler for a .NET language takes a source code file and produces an output file called an assembly. Figure 1-3 illustrates the process.

- An assembly is either an executable or a DLL.

- The code in an assembly isn't native machine code but an intermediate language called the *Common Intermediate Language* (CIL).

- An assembly, among other things, contains the following items:

  — The program's CIL

  — Metadata about the types used in the program

  — Metadata about references to other assemblies

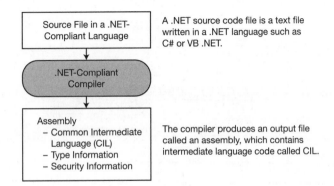

Figure 1-3. *The compilation process*

The acronym for the intermediate language has changed over time, and different references use different terms. Two other terms for the CIL that you might encounter are Intermediate Language (IL) and Microsoft Intermediate Language (MSIL). These terms were frequently used during .NET's initial development and early documentation.

Compiling to Native Code and Execution

The program's CIL isn't compiled to native machine code until it's called to run. At run time, the CLR performs the following steps, as shown in Figure 1-4:

- It checks the assembly's security characteristics.

- It allocates space in memory.

- It sends the assembly's executable code to the just-in-time (JIT) compiler, which compiles portions of it to native code.

The executable code in the assembly is compiled by the JIT compiler only as it's needed. It's then cached in case it's needed for execution again later in the program. Using this process means that code that isn't called during execution isn't compiled to native code, and code that *is* called need only be compiled once.

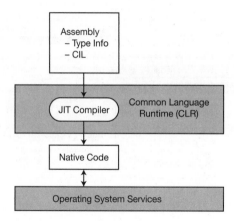

Figure 1-4. *Compilation to native code occurs at run time*

Once the CIL is compiled to native code, the CLR manages it as it runs, performing such tasks as releasing orphaned memory, checking array bounds, checking parameter types, and managing exceptions. This brings up two important terms:

- *Managed code*: Code written for the .NET Framework is called *managed code* and needs the CLR.

- *Unmanaged code*: Code that doesn't run under the control of the CLR, such as Win32 C/C++ DLLs, is called *unmanaged code.*

Microsoft also supplies a tool called the *Native Image Generator*, or *Ngen*, which takes an assembly and produces native code for the current processor. Code that's been run through Ngen avoids the JIT compilation process at run time.

Overview of Compilation and Execution

The same compilation and execution process is followed regardless of the language of the original source files. Figure 1-5 illustrates the entire compilation and run-time processes for three programs written in different languages.

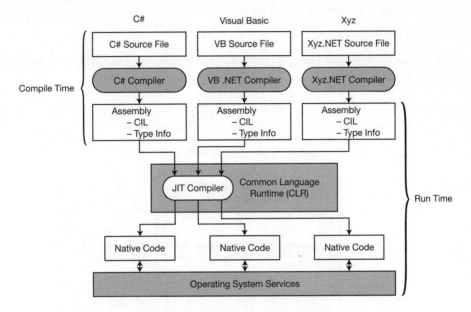

Figure 1-5. *Overview of the compile-time and runtime processes*

The Common Language Runtime

The core component of the .NET Framework is the CLR, which sits on top of the operating system and manages program execution, as shown in Figure 1-6. The CLR also provides the following services:

- Automatic garbage collection

- Security and authentication

- Extensive programming functionality through access to the BCL—including functionality such as web services and data services

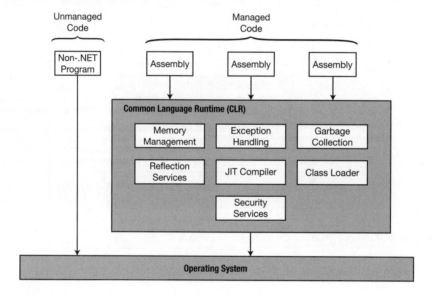

Figure 1-6. *Overview of the CLR*

The Common Language Infrastructure

Every programming language has a set of intrinsic types representing such objects as integers, floating-point numbers, characters, and so on. Historically, the characteristics of these types have varied from one programming language to another and from platform to platform. For example, the number of bits constituting an integer has varied widely depending on the language and platform.

This lack of uniformity, however, makes it difficult if we want programs to play well with other programs and libraries written in different languages. To have order and cooperation, there must be a set of standards.

The Common Language Infrastructure (CLI) is a set of standards that ties all the components of the .NET Framework into a cohesive, consistent system. It lays out the concepts and architecture of the system and specifies the rules and conventions to which all the software must adhere. Figure 1-7 shows the components of the CLI.

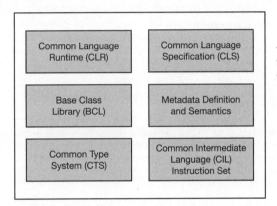

The CLI is a set of specifications that lays out the architecture, rules, and conventions of the system.

Figure 1-7. *Components of the CLI*

Both the CLI and C# have been approved as open international standard specifications by Ecma International. (The name "Ecma" used to be an acronym for the European Computer Manufacturers Association, but it's now just a word in itself.) Ecma members include Microsoft, IBM, Hewlett-Packard, Adobe, and many other corporations associated with computers and consumer electronics.

Important Parts of the CLI

Although most programmers don't need to know the details of the CLI specifications, you should at least be familiar with the meaning and purpose of the Common Type System and the Common Language Specification.

Common Type System (CTS)

The *Common Type System* (*CTS*) defines the characteristics of the types that must be used in managed code. Some important aspects of the CTS are the following:

- The CTS defines a rich set of intrinsic types, with fixed, specific characteristics for each type.

- The types provided by a .NET-compliant programming language generally map to some specific subset of this defined set of intrinsic types.

- One of the most important characteristics of the CTS is that *all* types are derived from a common base class—called object.

Common Language Specification (CLS)

The *Common Language Specification* (*CLS*) specifies the rules, properties, and behaviors of a .NET-compliant programming language. The topics include data types, class construction, and parameter passing.

Review of the Acronyms

This chapter has covered a lot of .NET acronyms, so Figure 1-8 will help you keep them straight.

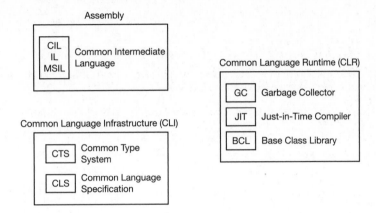

Figure 1-8. *The .NET acronyms*

CHAPTER 2

■ ■ ■

Overview of C# Programming

■ A Simple C# Program

■ Identifiers and Keywords

■ Main: The Starting Point of a Program

■ Whitespace

■ Statements

■ Text Output from a Program

■ Comments: Annotating the Code

A Simple C# Program

This chapter lays the groundwork for studying C#. Since I'll use code samples extensively throughout the text, I first need to show you what a C# program looks like and what its various parts mean.

I'll start by demonstrating a simple program and explaining its components one by one. This will introduce a range of topics, from the structure of a C# program to the method of producing program output to the screen.

With these source code preliminaries out of the way, I can then use code samples freely throughout the rest of the text. So, unlike the following chapters, where one or two topics are covered in detail, this chapter touches on many topics with only a minimum of explanation.

Let's start by looking at a simple C# program. The complete program source is shown in the top, shaded area in Figure 2-1. As shown, the code is contained in a text file called SimpleProgram.cs. As you read through it, don't worry about understanding all the details. Table 2-1 gives a line-by-line description of the code.

- When the code is compiled and executed, it displays the string "Hi there!" in a window on the screen.

- Line 5 contains two contiguous slash characters. These characters—and everything following them on the line—are ignored by the compiler. This is called a *single-line comment*.

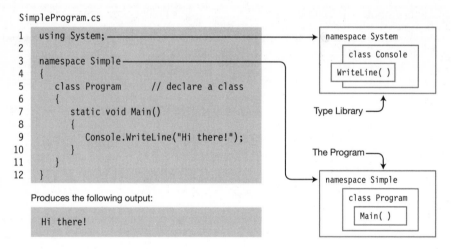

Figure 2-1. *The SimpleProgram program*

Table 2-1. *The SimpleProgram Program, Line by Line*

Line Number	Description
Line 1	Tells the compiler that this program uses types from the System namespace.
Line 3	Declares a new namespace, called Simple.
	• The new namespace starts at the open curly brace on line 4 and extends through the matching curly brace on line 12.
	• Any types declared within this section are members of the namespace.
Line 5	Declares a new class type, called Program.
	• Any members declared between the matching curly braces on lines 6 and 11 are members that make up this class.
Line 7	Declares a method called Main as a member of class Program.
	• In this program, Main is the only member of the Program class.
	• Main is a special function used by the compiler as the starting point of the program
Line 9	Contains only a single, simple statement; this line constitutes the body of Main.
	• Simple statements are terminated by a semicolon.
	• This statement uses a class called Console, in namespace System, to print out the message to a window on the screen
	• Without the using statement in line 1, the compiler wouldn't have known where to look for class Console.

More About SimpleProgram

A C# program consists of one or more type declarations. Much of this book is spent explaining the different types that you can create and use in your programs. The types in a program can be declared in any order. In the SimpleProgram example, only a class type is declared.

A *namespace* is a set of type declarations associated with a name. SimpleProgram uses two namespaces. It creates a new namespace called Simple, in which it declares its type (class Program), and uses the Console class defined in a namespace called System.

To compile the program, you can use Visual Studio or the command-line compiler. To use the command-line compiler, in its simplest form, use the following command in a command window:

```
csc SimpleProgram.cs
```

In this command, `csc` is the name of the command-line compiler, and `SimpleProgram.cs` is the name of the source file.

Identifiers and Keywords

Identifiers are character strings used to name things such as variables, methods, parameters, and a host of other programming constructs that will be covered later.

You can create self-documenting identifiers by concatenating meaningful words into a single descriptive name, using uppercase and lowercase letters (e.g., `CardDeck`, `PlayersHand`, `FirstName`, `SocialSecurityNum`). Certain characters are allowed or disallowed at certain positions in an identifier. Figure 2-2 illustrates these rules.

- The alphabetic and underscore characters (a through z, A through Z, and _) are allowed at any position.

- Digits are not allowed in the first position but are allowed everywhere else.

- The @ character is allowed in the first position of an identifier but not anywhere else. The use of the @ character, although allowed, is discouraged for general use.

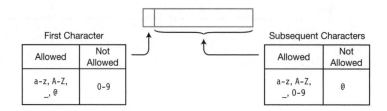

Figure 2-2. *Characters allowed in identifiers*

Identifiers are case-sensitive. For instance, the variable names `myVar` and `MyVar` are different identifiers. It's generally a bad idea, however, to have identifiers that differ only in the case of some of the letters, because they're easily confused.

As an example, in the following code snippet, the variable declarations are all valid and declare different integer variables. But using such similar names will make coding more error-prone and debugging more difficult. Those debugging your code at some later time will not be pleased.

```
// Valid syntactically, but don't do this!
int totalCycleCount;
int TotalCycleCount;
int TotalcycleCount;
```

Naming Conventions

The *C# Language Specification* suggests that certain casing conventions be used in creating identifiers. Table 2-2 summarizes the suggested guidelines for casing.

For most type identifiers, the Pascal casing style is recommended. In this style, each of the words combined to make an identifier is capitalized—for example, FirstName and LastName.

Table 2-2. *Recommended Identifier Naming Styles*

Style Name	Description	Recommended Use	Examples
Pascal casing	Each word in the identifier is capitalized.	Use for type names and member names.	CardDeck, DealersHand
Camel casing	Each word in the identifier, except the first, is capitalized.	Use for local variables and method parameters.	totalCycleCount, randomSeedParam
Uppercase	The identifier is composed of all uppercase letters.	Use only for abbreviations.	IO, DMA, XML

Although these are the suggested guidelines, many organizations use other conventions—particularly in the naming of member fields, which I'll introduce in the next chapter. Two of the common conventions are the following:

- Begin a field name with an underscore: _highTemp, _lowTemp

- Begin a field name with m_: m_highTemp, m_lowTemp

Both of these methods have the advantage of showing you immediately that these identifiers are field names. These forms also allow Visual Studio's IntelliSense feature to group all the fields together in the pop-ups.

Keywords

Keywords are the character string tokens used to define the C# language. Table 2-3 gives a complete list of the C# keywords.

Some important things to know about keywords are the following:

- Keywords cannot be used as variable names or any other form of identifier, unless prefaced with the @ character.

- All C# keywords consist entirely of lowercase letters. (.NET type names, however, use Pascal casing.)

Table 2-3. *The C# Keywords*

abstract	const	extern	int	out	short	typeof
as	continue	false	interface	override	sizeof	uint
base	decimal	finally	internal	params	stackalloc	ulong
bool	default	fixed	is	private	static	unchecked
break	delegate	float	lock	protected	string	unsafe
Byte	do	for	long	public	struct	ushort
case	double	foreach	namespace	readonly	switch	using
catch	else	goto	new	ref	this	virtual
char	enum	if	null	return	throw	void
checked	event	implicit	object	sbyte	true	volatile
class	explicit	in	operator	sealed	try	while

Contextual keywords are identifiers that act as keywords only in certain language constructs. In those positions, they have particular meanings; but unlike keywords, which cannot ever be used as identifiers, contextual keywords can be used as identifiers in other parts of the code. Table 2-4 contains the list of contextual keywords.

Table 2-4. *The C# Contextual Keywords*

add	ascending	by	descending	dynamic	equals	from
get	global	group	into	join	let	on
orderby	partial	remove	select	set	value	var
where	yield					

Main: The Starting Point of a Program

Every C# program must have one class with a method (function) called Main. In the SimpleProgram program shown previously, it was declared in a class called Program.

- The starting point of execution of every C# program is at the first instruction in Main.

- The name Main must be capitalized.

- The simplest form of Main is the following:

```
static void Main( )
{
    Statements
}
```

Whitespace

Whitespace in a program refers to characters that do not have a visible output character. Whitespace in source code is ignored by the compiler, but is used by the programmer to make the code clearer and easier to read. Some of the whitespace characters include the following:

- Space

- Tab

- New line

- Carriage return

For example, the following code fragments are treated exactly the same by the compiler in spite of their differences in appearance.

```
// Nicely formatted
Main()
{
    Console.WriteLine("Hi, there!");
}

// Just concatenated
Main(){Console.WriteLine("Hi, there!");}
```

Statements

The statements in C# are very similar to those of C and C++. This section introduces the general form of statements; the specific statement forms are covered in Chapter 9.

Simple Statements

A *statement* is a source code instruction describing a type or telling the program to perform an action.

- A *simple statement* is *terminated* by a semicolon.

For example, the following code is a sequence of two simple statements. The first statement defines an integer variable named var1 and initializes its value to 5. The second statement prints the value of variable var1 to a window on the screen.

```
int var1 = 5;
System.Console.WriteLine("The value of var1 is {0}", var1);
```

Blocks

A *block* is a sequence of zero or more statements enclosed by a matching set of curly braces; it acts as a single syntactic statement.

You can create a block from the set of two statements in the preceding example by enclosing the statements in matching curly braces, as shown in the following code:

```
{
   int var1 = 5;
   System.Console.WriteLine("The value of var1 is {0}", var1);
}
```

Some important things to know about blocks are the following:

- You can use a block whenever the syntax requires a statement but the action you need requires more than one simple statement.

- Certain program constructs *require* blocks. In these constructs, you cannot substitute a simple statement for the block.

- Although a simple statement is terminated by a semicolon, a block is not followed by a semicolon. (Actually, the compiler will *allow* it—but it's not good style.)

```
{              Terminating semicolon
                      ↓                                      Terminating semicolon
   int var2 = 5;                                                      ↓
   System.Console.WriteLine("The value of var1 is {0}", var1);
}
 ↑ No terminating semicolon
```

Text Output from a Program

A *console window* is a simple command prompt window that allows a program to display text and receive input from the keyboard. The BCL supplies a class called Console (in the System namespace), which contains methods for inputting and outputting data to a console window.

Write

Write is a member of the Console class. It sends a text string to the program's console window. In its simplest form, Write sends a literal string of text to the window. The string must be enclosed in quotation marks—double quotes, not single quotes.

The following line of code shows an example of using the Write member:

```
Console.Write("This is trivial text.");
                    ↑
              Output string
```

This code produces the following output in the console window:

```
This is trivial text.
```

Another example is the following code, which sends three literal strings to the program's console window:

```
System.Console.Write ("This is text1. ");
System.Console.Write ("This is text2. ");
System.Console.Write ("This is text3. ");
```

This code produces the output that follows. Notice that Write does not append a newline character after a string, so the output of the three statements runs together on a single line.

```
This is text1.  This is text2.  This is text3.
     ↑               ↑               ↑
   First           Second           Third
 statement       statement        statement
```

WriteLine

WriteLine is another member of Console, which performs the same functions as Write but appends a newline character to the end of each output string.

For example, if you use the preceding code, substituting WriteLine for Write, the output is on separate lines:

```
System.Console.WriteLine("This is text 1.");
System.Console.WriteLine("This is text 2.");
System.Console.WriteLine("This is text 3.");
```

This code produces the following output in the console window:

```
This is text 1.
This is text 2.
This is text 3.
```

The Format String

The general form of the Write and WriteLine statements takes more than a single parameter.

- If there is more than a single parameter, the parameters are separated by commas.

- The first parameter must always be a string and is called the *format string*.

- The format string can contain *substitution markers*.
  - A substitution marker marks the position in the format string where a value should be substituted in the output string.
  - It consists of an integer enclosed in a set of matching curly braces. The integer is the numeric position of the substitution value to be used.

- The parameters following the format string are called *substitution values*. These substitution values are numbered, starting at 0.

The syntax is as follows:

```
Console.WriteLine( FormatString, SubVal0, SubVal1, SubVal2, ... );
```

For example, the following statement has two substitution markers, numbered 0 and 1, and two substitution values, whose values are 3 and 6, respectively.

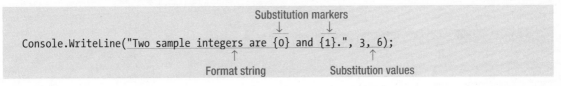

This code produces the following output on the screen:

```
Two sample integers are 3 and 6.
```

Multiple Markers and Values

In C#, you can use any number of markers and any number of values.

- The values can be used in any order.

- The values can be substituted any number of times in the format string.

For example, the following statement uses three markers and only two values. Notice that value 1 is used before value 0 and that value 1 is used twice.

```
Console.WriteLine("Three integers are {1}, {0} and {1}.", 3, 6);
```

This code displays the following on the screen:

```
Three integers are 6, 3 and 6.
```

A marker must not attempt to reference a value at a position beyond the length of the list of substitution values. If it does, it will *not produce a compile error* but a runtime error (called an *exception*).

For example, in the following statement there are two substitution values, with positions 0 and 1. The second marker, however, references position 2—which does not exist. This will produce a runtime error.

```
                                  Position 0   Position 1
                                      ↓            ↓
Console.WriteLine("Two integers are {0} and {2}.", 3    6);    // Error!
                                              ↑
                              There is no position 2 value.
```

Comments: Annotating the Code

You've already seen single-line comments, so here I'll discuss the second type of inline comments—*delimited comments*—and mention a third type called *documentation comments*.

- Delimited comments have a two-character start marker and a two-character end marker.

- Text between the matching markers is ignored by the compiler.

- Delimited comments can span any number of lines.

For example, the following code shows a delimited comment spanning multiple lines.

```
↓ Beginning of comment spanning multiple lines
/*
    This text is ignored by the compiler.
    Unlike single-line comments, delimited comments
    like this one can span multiple lines.
*/
↑ End of comment
```

A delimited comment can also span just part of a line. For example, the following statement shows text commented out of the middle of a line. The result is the declaration of a single variable, var2.

```
Beginning of comment
          ↓
int /*var 1,*/ var2;
                ↑
        End of comment
```

■ **Note** Single-line and delimited comments behave in C# just like they do in C and C++.

More About Comments

There are several other important things you need to know about comments:

- Nested delimited comments are not allowed. Only one comment can be in effect at a time. If you attempt to nest comments, the comment that starts first is in effect until the end of its scope.

- The scope for particularly comment types is as follows:
  - For single-line comments, the comment is in effect until the end of the current line.
  - For delimited comments, the comment is in effect until the *first* end delimiter is encountered.

The following attempts at comments are incorrect:

```
↓ Opens the comment
/* This is an attempt at a nested comment.
    /*  ← Ignored because it's inside a comment
       Inner comment
    */ ←Closes the comment because it's the first end delimiter encountered
*/  ←Syntax error because it has no opening delimiter

↓ Opens the comment          ↓ Ignored because it's inside a comment
// Single-line comment   /* Nested comment?
                    */  ← Incorrect because it has no opening delimiter
```

Documentation Comments

C# also provides a third type of comment: the *documentation comment*. Documentation comments contain XML text that can be used to produce program documentation. Comments of this type look like single-line comments, except that they have three contiguous slashes rather than two. I'll cover documentation comments in Chapter 25.

The following code shows the form of documentation comments:

```
/// <summary>
/// This class does...
/// </summary>
class Program
{
   ...
```

Summary of Comment Types

Inline comments are sections of text that are ignored by the compiler but are included in the code to document it. Programmers insert comments into their code to explain and document it. Table 2-5 summarizes the comment types.

Table 2-5. *Comment Types*

Type	Start	End	Description
Single-line	//		The text from the beginning marker to the end of the current line is ignored by the compiler.
Delimited	/*	*/	The text between the start and end markers is ignored by the compiler.
Documentation	///		Comments of this type contain XML text that is meant to be used by a tool to produce program documentation.

CHAPTER 3

Types, Storage, and Variables

A C# Program Is a Set of Type Declarations

If you were to broadly characterize the source code of C and C++ programs, you might say that a C program is a set of functions and data types and that a C++ program is a set of functions and classes. A C# program, however, is a set of type declarations.

- The source code of a C# program or DLL is a set of one or more type declarations.

- For an executable, one of the types declared must be a class that includes a method called Main.

- A *namespace* is a way of grouping a related set of type declarations and giving the group a name. Since your program is a related set of type declarations, you will generally declare your program type inside a namespace you create.

For example, the following code shows a program that consists of three type declarations. The three types are declared inside a new namespace called MyProgram.

```
namespace MyProgram                      // Create a new namespace.
{
    DeclarationOfTypeA                    // Declare a type.

    DeclarationOfTypeB                    // Declare a type.

    class C                              // Declare a type.
    {
        static void Main()
        {
            ...
        }
    }
}
```

Namespaces are covered in more detail in Chapter 10.

A Type Is a Template

Since a C# program is just a set of type declarations, learning C# consists of learning how to create and use types. So, the first thing you need to do is to look at what a type is.

You can start by thinking of a type as a *template* for creating data structures. It isn't the data structure itself, but it specifies the characteristics of objects constructed from the template.

A type is defined by the following elements:

- A name

- A data structure to contain its data members

- Behaviors and constraints

For example, Figure 3-1 illustrates the components of two types: short and int.

Name	Structure
short	2 Bytes

Behavior	
16-Bit Integer	

Name	Structure
int	4 Bytes

Behavior	
32-Bit Integer	

Figure 3-1. *A type is a template.*

Instantiating a Type

Creating an actual object from the type's template is called *instantiating* the type.

- The object created by instantiating a type is called either an *object* of the type or an *instance* of the type. The terms are interchangeable.

- Every data item in a C# program is an instance of some type—a type either provided by the language, provided by the BCL or another library, or defined by the programmer.

Figure 3-2 illustrates the instantiation of objects of two predefined types.

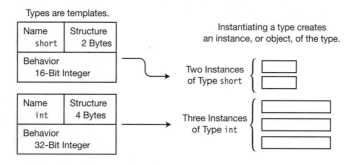

Figure 3-2. *Instantiating a type creates an instance.*

Data Members and Function Members

Some types, such as short, int, and long, are called *simple types* and can store only a single data item.

Other types can store multiple data items. An *array*, for example, is a type that can store multiple items of the same type. The individual items are called *elements* and are referenced by a number, called an *index*. Chapter 14 describes arrays in detail.

Types of Members

Other types, however, can contain data items of many different types. The individual elements in these types are called *members*, and, unlike arrays, in which each member is referred to by a number, these members have distinct names.

There are two types of members: data members and function members.

- *Data members* store data that is relevant to the object of the class or to the class as a whole.

- *Function members* execute code. Function members define how the type can act.

For example, Figure 3-3 shows some of the data members and function members of type XYZ. It contains two data members and two function members.

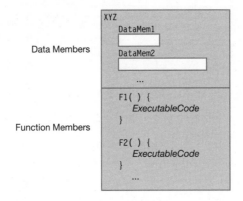

Figure 3-3. *Types specify data members and function members.*

Predefined Types

C# provides 16 predefined types, which are shown in Figure 3-4 and listed in Tables 3-1 and 3-2. They include 13 simple types and 3 nonsimple types.

The names of all the predefined types consist of *all lowercase* characters. The predefined simple types include the following:

- Eleven numeric types, including the following:

    — Various lengths of signed and unsigned integer types.

    — Floating-point types—float and double.

    — A high-precision decimal type called decimal. Unlike float and double, type decimal can represent decimal fractional numbers exactly. It's often used for monetary calculations.

- A Unicode character type, called char.

- A Boolean type, called bool. Type bool represents Boolean values and must be one of two values—either true or false.

■ **Note** Unlike C and C++, numeric values do not have a Boolean interpretation in C#.

The three nonsimple types are the following:

- Type string, which is an array of Unicode characters

- Type object, which is the type on which all other types are based

- Type dynamic, which is used when using assemblies written in dynamic languages

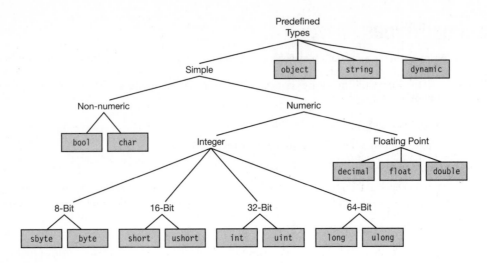

Figure 3-4. *The predefined types*

More About the Predefined Types

All the predefined types are mapped directly to underlying .NET types. The C# type names are just aliases for the .NET types, so using the .NET names works fine syntactically, although this is discouraged. Within a C# program, you should use the C# names rather than the .NET names.

The predefined simple types represent a single item of data. They're listed in Table 3-1, along with the ranges of values they can represent and the underlying .NET types to which they map.

Table 3-1. *The Predefined Simple Types*

Name	Meaning	Range	.NET Framework Type	Default Value
sbyte	8-bit signed integer	-128–127	System.SByte	0
byte	8-bit unsigned integer	0–255	System.Byte	0
short	16-bit signed integer	-32,768–32,767	System.Int16	0
ushort	16-bit unsigned integer	0–65,535	System.UInt16	0
int	32-bit signed integer	-2,147,483,648–2,147,483,647	System.Int32	0
uint	32-bit unsigned integer	0–4,294,967,295	System.UInt32	0
long	64-bit signed integer	-9,223,372,036,854,775,808–9,223,372,036,854,775,807	System.Int64	0
ulong	64-bit unsigned integer	0–18,446,744,073,709,551,615	System.UInt64	0
float	Single-precision float	$1.5 \times 10{-}45$–3.4×1038	System.Single	0.0f
double	Double-precision float	$5 \times 10{-}324$–1.7×10308	System.Double	0.0d
bool	Boolean	true, false	System.Boolean	false
char	Unicode character	U+0000–U+ffff	System.Char	\x0000
decimal	Decimal value with 28-significant-digit precision	$\pm 1.0 \times 1028$–$\pm 7.9 \times 1028$	System.Decimal	0m

The nonsimple predefined types are somewhat more complex. Values of type string contain zero or more Unicode characters. The object type is the base class for all other types in the system, including the predefined, simple types. Table 3-2 shows the predefined nonsimple types.

Table 3-2. *The Predefined Nonsimple Types*

Name	Meaning	.NET Framework Type
object	The base class from which all other types are derived	System.Object
string	A sequence of Unicode characters	System.String
dynamic	A type designed to be used with assemblies written in dynamic languages	

User-Defined Types

Besides the 15 predefined types provided by C#, you can also create your own user-defined types. There are six kinds of types you can create. They are the following:

- class types

- struct types

- array types

- enum types

- delegate types

- interface types

You create a type using a *type declaration*, which includes the following information:

- The kind of type you are creating

- The name of the new type

- A declaration (name and specification) of each of the type's members—except for array and delegate types, which don't have named members

Once you've declared a type, you can create and use objects of the type just as if they were predefined types. Figure 3-5 summarizes the use of predefined and user-defined types. Using predefined types is a one-step process in which you simply instantiate the objects of that type. Using user-defined types is a two-step process. You must first declare the type and then instantiate objects of the type.

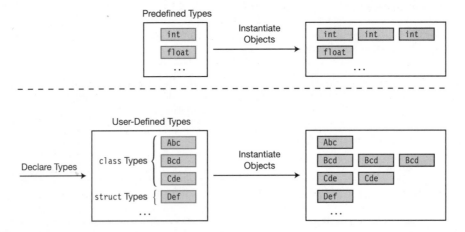

Figure 3-5. *The predefined types require instantiation only. The user-defined types require two steps: declaration and instantiation.*

The Stack and the Heap

While a program is running, its data must be stored in memory. How much memory is required for an item, and where and how it's stored, depends on its type.

A running program uses two regions of memory to store data: the *stack* and the *heap*.

The Stack

The system takes care of all stack manipulation. You, as the programmer, don't need to do anything with it explicitly. But understanding its basic functions will give you a better understanding of what your program is doing when it's running and allow you to better understand the C# documentation and literature.

The stack is an array of memory that acts as a last-in, first-out (LIFO) data structure. It stores several types of data:

- The values of certain types of variables

- The program's current execution environment

- Parameters passed to methods

Facts About Stacks

The general characteristics of stacks are the following:

- Data can be added to and deleted only from the top of the stack.

- Placing a data item at the top of the stack is called *pushing* the item onto the stack.

- Deleting an item from the top of the stack is called *popping* the item from the stack.

Figure 3-6 illustrates the functions and terminology of the stack.

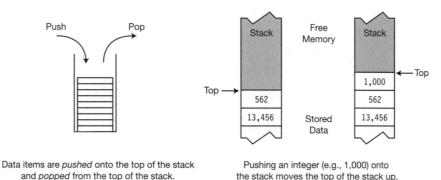

Data items are *pushed* onto the top of the stack   Pushing an integer (e.g., 1,000) onto
and *popped* from the top of the stack.   the stack moves the top of the stack up.

Figure 3-6. *Pushing and popping on the stack*

The Heap

The heap is an area where chunks of memory are allocated to store certain kinds of data objects. Unlike the stack, memory can be stored and removed from the heap in any order. Figure 3-7 shows a program that has stored four items in the heap.

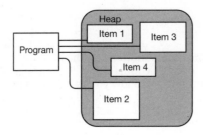

Figure 3-7. *The memory heap*

Although your program can store items in the heap, it cannot explicitly delete them. Instead, the CLR's garbage collector (GC) automatically cleans up orphaned heap objects when it determines that your code is no longer accessing them. This frees you from what in other programming languages can be an error-prone task. Figure 3-8 illustrates the garbage collection process.

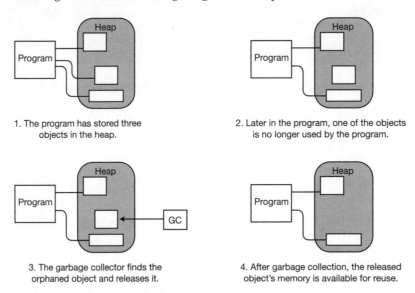

1. The program has stored three objects in the heap.

2. Later in the program, one of the objects is no longer used by the program.

3. The garbage collector finds the orphaned object and releases it.

4. After garbage collection, the released object's memory is available for reuse.

Figure 3-8. *Automatic garbage collection in the heap*

Value Types and Reference Types

The *type* of a data item defines how much memory is required to store it and the data members that comprise it. The type also determines where an object is stored in memory—the stack or the heap.

Types are divided into two categories: value types and reference types. Objects of these types are stored differently in memory.

- *Value types* require only a single segment of memory, which stores the actual data.

- *Reference types* require two segments of memory:

  — The first contains the *actual data*—and is always located in the heap.

  — The second is a reference that points to where in the heap the data is stored.

Data that is not a member of another type is stored as shown in Figure 3-9. For value types, data is stored on the stack. For reference types, the actual data is stored in the heap, and the reference is stored on the stack.

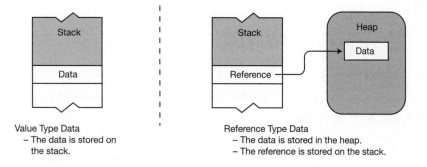

Figure 3-9. *Storing data that is not part of another type*

Storing Members of a Reference Type Object

Figure 3-9 shows how data is stored when it isn't a member of another type. When it's a member of another type, data might be stored a little differently.

- The data portion of a reference type object is *always* stored in the heap, as shown in Figure 3-9.

- A value type object, or the reference part of a reference type, can be stored in either the stack or the heap, depending on the circumstances.

Suppose, for example, that you have an instance of a reference type, called MyType, that has two members—a value type member and a reference type member. How is it stored? Is the value type member stored on the stack and the reference type split between the stack and the heap, as shown in Figure 3-9? The answer is no.

Remember that for a reference type, the data of an instance is *always* stored in the heap. Since both members are part of the object's data, they're both stored in the heap, regardless of whether they are value or reference types. Figure 3-10 illustrates the case of type MyType.

- Even though member A is a value type, it's part of the data of the instance of MyType and is therefore stored with the object's data in the heap.

- Member B is a reference type, and therefore its data portion will always be stored in the heap, as shown by the small box marked "Data." What's different is that its reference is also stored in the heap, inside the data portion of the enclosing MyType object.

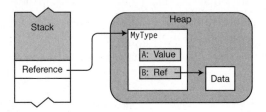

Figure 3-10. *Storage of data as part of a reference type*

■ **Note** For any object of a reference type, all its data members are stored in the heap, regardless of whether they are of value type or reference type.

Categorizing the C# Types

Table 3-3 shows all the types available in C# and what kinds of types they are—value types or reference types. Each reference type is covered later in the text.

Table 3-3. *Value Types and Reference Types in C#*

	Value Types			Reference Types
Predefined types	sbyte short int long bool	byte ushort uint ulong	float double char decimal	object string dynamic
User-defined types	struct enum			class interface delegate array

Variables

A general-purpose programming language must allow a program to store and retrieve data.

- A *variable* is a name that represents data stored in memory during program execution.

- C# provides four categories of variables, each of which will be discussed in detail. These kinds are listed in Table 3-4.

Table 3-4. *The Four Kinds of Variables*

Name	Member of a Type	Description
Local variable	No	Holds temporary data within the scope of a method
Field	Yes	Holds data associated with a type or an instance of a type
Parameter	No	A temporary variable used to pass data from one method to another method
Array element	Yes	One member of a sequenced collection of (usually) homogeneous data items

Variable Declarations

A variable must be declared before it can be used. The variable declaration defines the variable and accomplishes two things:

- It gives the variable a name and associates a type with it.

- It allows the compiler to allocate memory for it.

A simple variable declaration requires at least a type and a name. The following declaration defines a variable named var2, of type int:

```
Type
  ↓
int var2;
      ↑
    Name
```

For example, Figure 3-11 represents the declaration of four variables and their places on the stack.

Figure 3-11. *Value type and reference type variable declarations*

Variable Initializers

Besides declaring a variable's name and type, you can optionally use the declaration to initialize its memory to a specific value.

A *variable initializer* consists of an equals sign followed by the initializing value, as shown here:

```
          Initializer
              ↓
   int var2 = 17;
```

Local variables without initializers have an undefined value and cannot be used until they have been assigned a value. Attempting to use an undefined local variable causes the compiler to produce an error message.

Figure 3-12 shows a number of local variable declarations on the left and the resulting stack configuration on the right. Some of the variables have initializers, and others do not.

```
int     var1;              // Value Type
int     var2 = 17;         // Value Type
float   var3 = 26.843F;    // Value Type
Dealer  dealer1;           // Reference Type
Dealer  dealer2 = null;    // Reference Type
```

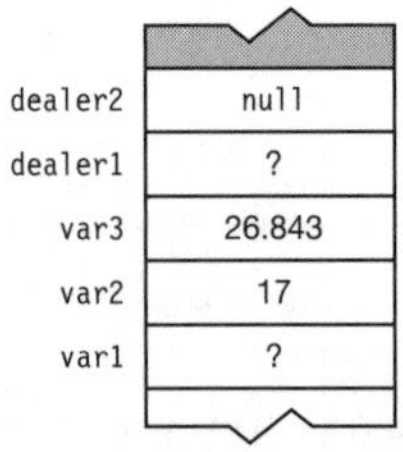

dealer2	null
dealer1	?
var3	26.843
var2	17
var1	?

Figure 3-12. *Variable initializers*

Automatic Initialization

Some kinds of variables are automatically set to default values if they are declared without an initializer, and others are not. Variables that are not automatically initialized to default values contain undefined values until the program assigns them a value. Table 3-5 shows which types of variables are automatically initialized and which are not. I'll cover each of the five variable types later in the text.

Table 3-5. *Types of Variables*

Variable Type	Stored In	Auto-initialized	Use
Local variables	Stack or stack and heap	No	Used for local computation inside a function member
Class fields	Heap	Yes	Members of a class
Struct fields	Stack or heap	Yes	Members of a struct
Parameters	Stack	No	Used for passing values into and out of a method
Array elements	Heap	Yes	Members of an array

Multiple-Variable Declarations

You can declare multiple variables in a single declaration statement.

- The variables in a multiple-variable declaration must all be of the same type.

- The variable names must be separated with commas. Initializers can be included with the variable names.

For example, the following code shows two valid declaration statements with multiple variables. Notice that the initialized variables can be mixed with uninitialized variables as long as they're separated by commas. The last declaration statement shown is invalid because it attempts to declare different types of variables in a single statement.

```
// Variable declarations--some with initializers, some without
int    var3 = 7, var4, var5 = 3;
double var6, var7 = 6.52;

Type       Different type
 ↓              ↓

int var8, float var9;          // Error! Can't mix types (int and float)
```

Using the Value of a Variable

A variable name represents the value stored by the variable. You can use the value by using the variable name.

For example, in the following statement, the value of var2 is retrieved from memory and placed at the position of the variable.

```
Console.WriteLine("{0}", var2);
```

Static Typing and the dynamic Keyword

One thing you'll have noticed is that every variable includes the *type* of the variable, allowing the compiler to determine the amount of memory it will require at runtime and which parts should be stored in the stack and which in the heap. The type of the variable is determined at compile time and cannot be changed at runtime. This is called *static typing*.

Not all languages, though, are statically typed. Many, including such scripting languages as IronPython and IronRuby, are *dynamically typed*. That is, the type of a variable might not be resolved until runtime. Since these are .NET languages, C# programs need to be able to use assemblies written in these languages.

To solve the problem that C# needs to be able to resolve at compile time a type referenced in an assembly that doesn't resolve its types until runtime, the C# language designers added the keyword dynamic to the language. The dynamic keyword represents a specific, actual C# type that knows how to resolve itself at runtime. That is, it's statically typed as dynamic!

This satisfies both constraints. The C# compiler can resolve the keyword to an actual type, and the type object can resolve itself to the target assembly's type at runtime.

Nullable Types

There are situations, particularly when working with databases, where you want to indicate that a variable does not currently hold a valid value. For reference types, you can do this easily, by setting the variable to null. When you define a variable of a value type, however, its memory is allocated whether or not its contents have any valid meaning.

What you would like in this situation is to have a Boolean indicator associated with the variable, so that when the value is valid, the indicator is true, and when the value is not valid, the indicator is false.

Nullable types allow you to create a value type variable that can be marked as valid or invalid so that you can make sure a variable is valid before using it. Regular value types are called *non-nullable types*.

Creating a Nullable Type

A nullable type is always based on another type, called the *underlying type*, that has already been declared.

- You can create a nullable type from any value type, including the predefined, simple types.

- You cannot create a nullable type from a reference type or from another nullable type.

- You do not explicitly declare a nullable type in your code. Instead, you declare a *variable of a nullable type*. The compiler implicitly creates the nullable type for you.

To create a variable of a nullable type, simply add a question mark to the end of the name of the underlying type, in the variable declaration. Unfortunately, this syntax makes it appear that you have a lot of questions about your code.

For example, the following code declares a variable of the nullable int type. Notice that the suffix is attached to the *type* name—not the variable name.

```
    Suffix
      ↓
  int? myNInt = 28;
    ↑
The name of the nullable type includes the suffix.
```

With this declaration statement, the compiler takes care of both producing the nullable type and creating the variable of that type.

Using a nullable type is almost the same as using a variable of any other type. Reading a variable of a nullable type returns its value. You must, however, make sure that the variable is not null. Attempting to read the value of a null variable produces an exception.

- Like any variable, to retrieve its value, you just use its name.

- To check whether a nullable type has a value, you can compare it to null.

```
      Compare to null
            ↓
if ( myInt1 != null )
    Console.WriteLine("{0}", myInt1);
                        ↑
                   Use variable name
```

Both sets of code produce the following output:

15

You can easily convert between a nullable type and its corresponding non-nullable type. We'll go into conversions in detail in Chapter 18, but the important points for nullable types are the following:

- There is an *implicit* conversion between a non-nullable type and its nullable version. That is, no cast is needed.

- There is an *explicit* conversion between a nullable type and its non-nullable version.

For example, the following lines show conversion in both directions. In the first line, a literal of type int is implicitly converted to a value of type int? and is used to initialize the variable of the nullable type. In the second line, the variable is explicitly converted to its non-nullable version.

```
int? myInt1 = 15;               // Implicitly convert int to int?
int  regInt = (int) myInt1;     // Explicitly convert int? to int
```

Assigning to a Nullable Type

You can assign three kinds of values to a variable of a nullable type:

- A value of the underlying type

- A value of the same nullable type

- The value null

The following code shows an example of each of the three types of assignment:

```
int? myI1, myI2, myI3;

myI1 = 28;                              // Value of underlying type
myI2 = myI1;                            // Value of nullable type
myI3 = null;                            // Null

Console.WriteLine("myI1: {0}, myI2: {1}", myI1, myI2);
```

This code produces the following output:

```
myI1: 28, myI2: 28
```

In Chapter 25, when you have a clearer understanding of C#, I'll explain the finer points of nullable types.

CHAPTER 4

■■■

Classes: The Basics

Overview of Classes

In the previous chapter, you saw that C# provides six user-defined types. The most important of these, and the one I'll cover first, is the *class*. Since the topic of classes in C# is a large one, its discussion will be spread over the next several chapters.

A Class Is an Active Data Structure

Before the days of object-oriented analysis and design, programmers thought of a program as just a sequence of instructions. The focus at that time was on structuring and optimizing those instructions. With the advent of the object-oriented paradigm, the focus changed from optimizing instructions to organizing a program's data and functions into encapsulated sets of logically related data items and functions, called classes.

A class is a data structure that can store data and execute code. It contains the following:

- *Data members*, which store data associated with the class or an instance of the class. Data members generally model the attributes of the real-world object the class represents.

- *Function members*, which execute code. Function members generally model the functions and actions of the real-world object the class represents.

A C# class can have any number of data and function members. The members can be any combination of nine possible member types. Table 4-1 shows these member types. The ones I'll cover in this chapter—*fields* and *methods*—are checked in the table.

Table 4-1. *Types of Class Members*

Data Members Store Data	Function Members Execute Code	
✓ Fields	✓ Methods	❑ Operators
❑ Constants	❑ Properties	❑ Indexers
	❑ Constructors	❑ Events
	❑ Destructors	

■ **Note** Classes are encapsulated sets of logically related data items and functions that generally represent objects in the real world or a conceptual world.

Programs and Classes: A Quick Example

A running C# program is a group of interacting type objects, most of which are instances of classes. For example, suppose you have a program simulating a poker game. When it's running, it might have an instance of a class called Dealer, whose job is to run the game, and several instances of a class called Player, which represent the players of the game.

The Dealer object stores such information as the current state of the card deck and the number of players. Its actions include shuffling the deck and dealing the cards.

The Player class is very different. It stores such information as the player's name and the amount of money left to bet, and it performs such actions as analyzing the player's current hand and placing bets. Figure 4-1 illustrates the running program.

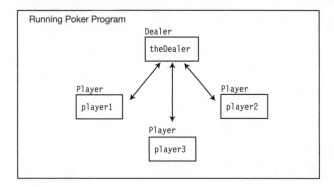

Figure 4-1. *The objects in a running program*

A real program would undoubtedly contain dozens of other classes besides Dealer and Player. These would include classes such as Card and Deck. Each class models some *thing* that is a component of the poker game.

■ **Note** A running program is a set of objects interacting with each other.

Declaring a Class

Although types int, double, and char are defined in the C# language, classes such as Dealer and Player, as you can probably guess, are not defined by the language. If you want to use them in a program, you'll have to define them yourself. You do this by writing a *class declaration*.

A *class declaration* defines the characteristics and members of a new class. It does not create an instance of the class but creates the template from which class instances will be created. The class declaration provides the following:

- The class name

- The members of the class

- The characteristics of the class

The following is an example of the minimum syntax for a class declaration. The curly braces contain the member declarations that make up the *class body*. Class members can be declared in any order inside the class body. This means it's perfectly fine for the declaration of a member to refer to another member that is not yet defined until further down in the class declaration.

```
Keyword     Class name
   ↓            ↓
class   MyExcellentClass
{
    MemberDeclarations
}
```

For example, the following code shows the outlines of two class declarations:

```
class Dealer                              // Class declaration
{
   ...
}

class Player                              // Class declaration
{
   ...
}
```

■ **Note** Since a class declaration "defines" a new class, you will often see a class declaration referred to as a *class definition* both in the literature and in common usage among programmers.

Class Members

Fields and methods are the most important of the class member types. Fields are data members, and methods are function members.

Fields

A *field* is a variable that belongs to a class.

- It can be of any type, either predefined or user-defined.

- Like all variables, fields store data and have the following characteristics:

  — They can be written to.

  — They can be read from.

The minimum syntax for declaring a field is the following:

```
Type
  ↓
Type Identifier;
         ↑
      Field name
```

For example, the following class contains the declaration of field `MyField`, which can store an `int` value:

```
class MyClass
{   Type
      ↓
    int MyField;
         ↑
}       Field name
```

■ **Note** Unlike C and C++, there are *no global variables* (that is, variables or fields) declared outside of a type. All fields belong to a type and must be declared within the type declaration.

Explicit and Implicit Field Initialization

Since a field is a kind of variable, the syntax for a field initializer is the same as that of the variable initializer shown in the previous chapter.

- A *field initializer* is part of the field declaration and consists of an equals sign followed by an expression that evaluates to a value.

- The initialization value *must be determinable at compile time*.

```
class MyClass
{
    int F1 = 17;
}            ↑
        Field initializer
```

- If no initializer is used, the value of a field is set by the compiler to a default value, determined by the type of the field. Table 3-1 (in Chapter 3) gives the default values for the simple types. To summarize them, though, the default value for each type is 0, and false for bool. The default for reference types is null.

For example, the following code declares four fields. The first two fields are initialized implicitly. The second two fields are initialized explicitly with initializers.

```
class MyClass
{
    int    F1;              // Initialized to 0     - value type
    string F2;              // Initialized to null  - reference type

    int    F3 = 25;         // Initialized to 25
    string F4 = "abcd";     // Initialized to "abcd"
}
```

Declarations with Multiple Fields

You can declare multiple fields *of the same type* in the same statement by separating the names with commas. You cannot mix different types in a single declaration. For example, you can combine the four preceding field declarations into two statements, with the exact same semantic result:

```
int    F1, F3 = 25;
string F2, F4 = "abcd";
```

Methods

A method is a named block of executable code that can be executed from many different parts of the program, and even from other programs. (There are also anonymous methods, which aren't named—but I'll cover those in Chapter 15.)

When a method is *called*, or *invoked*, it executes its code and then returns to the code that called it. Some methods return a value to the position from which they were called. Methods correspond to member functions in C++.

The minimum syntax for declaring a method includes the following components:

- *Return type*: This states the type of value the method returns. If a method doesn't return a value, the return type is specified as void.

- *Name*: This is the name of the method.

- *Parameter list*: This consists of at least an empty set of matching parentheses. If there are parameters (which I'll cover in the next chapter), they are listed between the parentheses.

- *Method body*: This consists of a matching set of curly braces, containing the executable code.

For example, the following code declares a class with a simple method called PrintNums. From the declaration, you can tell the following about PrintNums:

- It returns no value; hence, the return type is specified as void.

- It has an empty parameter list.

- It contains two lines of code in its method body.

```
class SimpleClass
{
  Return type      Parameter list
      ↓                  ↓
   void PrintNums( )
   {
      Console.WriteLine("1");
      Console.WriteLine("2");
   }
}
```

■ **Note** Unlike C and C++, there are *no global functions* (that is, methods or functions) declared outside of a type declaration. Also, unlike C and C++, there is no "default" return type for a method. All methods must include a return type or list it as void.

Creating Variables and Instances of a Class

The class declaration is just the blueprint from which instances of the class are created. Once a class is declared, you can create instances of the class.

- Classes are reference types, which, as you will remember from the previous chapter, means that they require memory both for the reference to the data and for the actual data.

- The reference to the data is stored in a variable of the class type. So, to create an instance of the class, you need to start by declaring a variable of the class type. If the variable isn't initialized, its value is undefined.

Figure 4-2 illustrates how to define the variable to hold the reference. At the top of the code on the left is a declaration for class Dealer. Below that is a declaration for class Program, which contains method Main. Main declares variable theDealer of type Dealer. Since the variable is uninitialized, its value is undefined, as shown on the right in the figure.

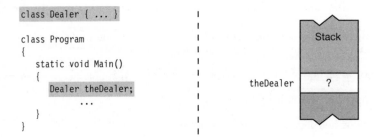

Figure 4-2. *Allocating memory for the reference of a class variable*

Allocating Memory for the Data

Declaring the variable of the class type allocates the memory to hold the reference, but not the memory to hold the actual data of the class object. To allocate memory for the actual data, you use the new operator.

- The new operator allocates and initializes memory for an instance of any specified type. It allocates the memory from either the stack or the heap, depending on the type.

- Use the new operator to form an *object-creation expression*, which consists of the following:

  — The keyword new.

  — The name of the type of the instance for which memory is to be allocated.

  — Matching parentheses, which might or might not include parameters. I'll discuss more about the possible parameters later.

```
   Keyword     Parentheses are required.
      ↓                    ↓
    new  TypeName  ( )
            ↑
          Type
```

- If the memory allocated is for a reference type, the object-creation expression returns a reference to the allocated and initialized instance of the object in the heap.

This is exactly what you need to allocate and initialize the memory to hold the class instance data. Use the new operator to create an object-creation expression, and assign the value returned by it to the class variable. Here's an example:

```
Dealer theDealer;          // Declare variable for the reference.
theDealer = new Dealer();  // Allocate memory for the class object.
              ↑
        Object-creation expression
```

The code on the left in Figure 4-3 shows the new operator used to allocate memory and create an instance of class Dealer, which is then assigned to the class variable. The memory structure is illustrated in the figure, to the right of the code.

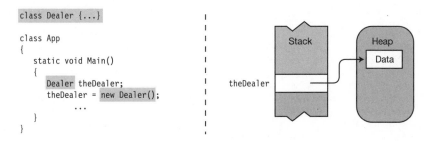

Figure 4-3. *Allocating memory for the data of a class variable*

Combining the Steps

You can combine the two steps by *initializing* the variable with the object-creation expression.

```
    Declare variable.
         ↓
   _____
   Dealer theDealer = new Dealer();                        // Declare and initialize.
                      _____
                         ↑
           Initialize with an object-creation expression.
```

In the case of local variables, but not fields, you can simplify the syntax a bit more by having the compiler infer the type in the declaration part on the left. But I'll cover that in the section on local variables in the next chapter.

Instance Members

A class declaration acts as a blueprint from which you can create as many instances of the class as you like.

- *Instance members*: Each instance of a class is a separate entity that has its own set of data members, distinct from the other instances of the same class. These are called instance members since they are associated with an instance of the class.

- *Static members*: Instance members are the default, but you can also declare members called static members that are associated with the class, rather than the instance. I'll cover these in Chapter 6.

As an example of instance members, the following code shows the poker program with three instances of class Player. Figure 4-4 shows that each instance has a different value for the Name field.

```
class Dealer { ... }                    // Declare class
class Player {                          // Declare class
   string Name;                         // Field
      ...
}

class Program {
   static void Main()
   {
      Dealer theDealer = new Dealer();
      Player player1   = new Player();
      Player player2   = new Player();
      Player player3   = new Player();
         ...
   }
}
```

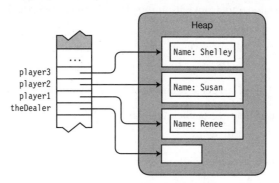

Figure 4-4. *Instance members have distinct values between class objects.*

Access Modifiers

From within a class, any function member can access any other member of the class by simply using that member's name.

The *access modifier* is an optional part of a member declaration that specifies what other parts of the program have access to the member. The access modifier is placed before the simple declaration forms. The following is the syntax for fields and methods:

```
Fields
    AccessModifier Type Identifier

Methods
    AccessModifier ReturnType MethodName ()
    {
       ...
    }
```

The five categories of member access are the following. I'll describe the first two in this chapter and the others in Chapter 7.

- private

- public

- protected

- internal

- protected internal

Private and Public Access

Private members are accessible only from within the class in which they are declared—other classes cannot see or access them.

- Private access is the default access level, so if a member is declared without an access modifier, it is a private member.

- You can also use the `private` access modifier to explicitly declare a member as private.

- There is no semantic difference between declaring a private member implicitly as opposed to explicitly. The forms are equivalent.

For example, the following two declarations both specify `private int` members:

```
        int MyInt1;             // Implicitly declared private
 private int MyInt2;            // Explicitly declared private
    ↑
Access modifier
```

Public members are accessible to other objects in the program. You must use the `public` access modifier to specify public access.

Access modifier
↓

```
public int MyInt;
```

Depicting Public and Private Access

The figures in this text represent classes as labeled boxes, as shown in Figure 4-5.

- The class members are represented as smaller labeled boxes inside the class boxes.

- Private members are represented enclosed entirely within their class box.

- Public members are represented sticking partially outside their class box.

```
class Program
{
            int Member1;
    private int Member2;
    public  int Member3;
}
```

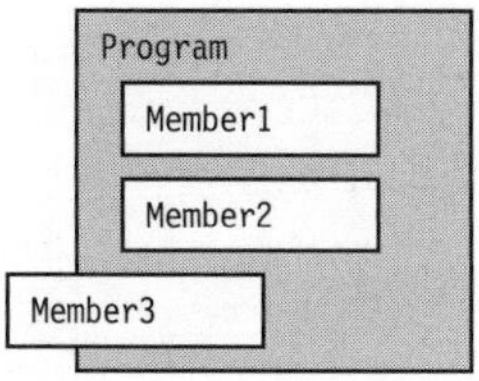

Figure 4-5. *Representing classes and members*

Example of Member Access

Class C1 in the following code declares both public and private fields and methods. Figure 4-6 illustrates the visibility of the members of class C1.

```
class C1
{
    int       F1;              // Implicit private field
    private int F2;            // Explicit private field
    public  int F3;            // Public field

    void DoCalc()              // Implicit private method
    {
        ...
    }

    public int GetVal()        // Public method
    {
        ...
    }
}
```

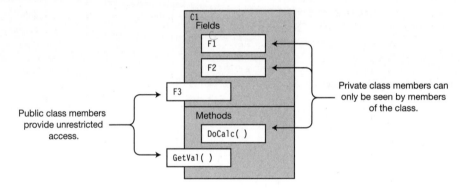

Figure 4-6. *Private and public class members*

Accessing Members from Inside the Class

As mentioned, members of a class can access the other class members by just using their names.

For example, the following class declaration shows the methods of the class accessing the fields and other methods. Even though the fields and two of the methods are declared private, all the members of a class can be accessed by any method (or any function member) of the class. Figure 4-7 illustrates the code.

```
class DaysTemp
{
   // Fields
   private int High = 75;
   private int Low  = 45;

   // Methods
   private int GetHigh()
   {
      return High;                      // Access private field
   }

   private int GetLow()
   {
      return Low;                       // Access private field
   }

   public float Average ()
   {
      return (GetHigh() + GetLow()) / 2;    // Access private methods
   }                ↑            ↑
}            Accessing the private methods
```

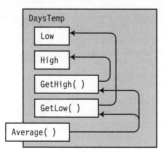

Figure 4-7. *Members within a class can freely access each other.*

Accessing Members from Outside the Class

To access a public instance member from outside the class, you must include the variable name and the member name, separated by a period (dot). This is called dot-syntax notation; it will be discussed in more detail later.

For example, the second line of the following code shows an example of accessing a method from outside the class:

```
DaysTemp myDt = new DaysTemp();      // Create an object of the class.
float fValue  = myDt.Average();      // Access it from outside.
                 ↑      ↑
           Variable name   Member name
```

As an example, the following code declares two classes: DaysTemp and Program.

- The two fields in DaysTemp are declared public, so they can be accessed from outside the class.

- Method Main is a member of class Program. It creates a variable and object of class DaysTemp, and it assigns values to the fields of the object. It then reads the values of the fields and prints them out.

```
class DaysTemp                              // Declare class DaysTemp
{
   public int High = 75;
   public int Low  = 45;
}

class Program                               // Declare class Program.
{
   static void Main()
   {           Variable name
                    ↓
      DaysTemp temp = new DaysTemp();          // Create the object.
   Variable name and field
          ↓
      temp.High = 85;                          // Assign to the fields.
      temp.Low  = 60;            Variable name and field
                                         ↓
      Console.WriteLine("High:  {0}", temp.High );   // Read from fields.
      Console.WriteLine("Low:   {0}", temp.Low  );
   }
}
```

This code produces the following output:

```
High:   85
Low:    60
```

Putting It All Together

The following code creates two instances and stores their references in variables named t1 and t2. Figure 4-8 illustrates t1 and t2 in memory. The code demonstrates the following three actions discussed so far in the use of a class:

- Declaring a class

- Creating instances of the class

- Accessing the class members (that is, writing to a field and reading from a field)

```
class DaysTemp                          // Declare the class.
{
   public int High, Low;                // Declare the instance fields.
   public int Average()                 // Declare the instance method.
   {
      return (High + Low) / 2;
   }
}

class Program
{
   static void Main()
   {
      // Create two instances of DaysTemp.
      DaysTemp t1 = new DaysTemp();
      DaysTemp t2 = new DaysTemp();

      // Write to the fields of each instance.
      t1.High = 76;     t1.Low = 57;
      t2.High = 75;     t2.Low = 53;

      // Read from the fields of each instance and call a method of
      // each instance.
      Console.WriteLine("t1: {0}, {1}, {2}",
                        t1.High, t1.Low, t1.Average() );
      Console.WriteLine("t2: {0}, {1}, {2}",
                        t2.High, t2.Low, t2.Average() );
                          ↑        ↑         ↑
   }                    Field    Field    Method
}
```

This code produces the following output:

```
t1: 76, 57, 66
t2: 75, 53, 64
```

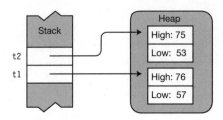

Figure 4-8. *Memory layout of instances t1 and t2*

CHAPTER 5

■■■

Methods

The Structure of a Method

A *method* is a block of code with a name. You can execute the code from somewhere else in the program by using the method's name. You can also pass data into a method and receive data back as output.

As you saw in the previous chapter, a method is a function member of a class. Methods have two major sections, as shown in Figure 5-1—the method header and the method body.

- The *method header* specifies the method's characteristics, including the following:

    — Whether the method returns data and, if so, what type

    — The name of the method

    — What types of data can be passed to and from the method and how that data should be treated

- The *method body* contains the sequence of executable code statements. Execution starts at the first statement in the method body and continues sequentially through the method.

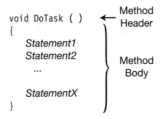

Figure 5-1. *The structure of a method*

The following example shows the form of the method header. I'll cover each part in the following pages.

```
int MyMethod ( int par1, string par2 )
 ↑      ↑              ↑
Return Method      Parameter
 type   name          list
```

For example, the following code shows a simple method called `MyMethod` that, in turn, calls the `WriteLine` method several times:

```
void MyMethod()
{
   Console.WriteLine("First");
   Console.WriteLine("Last");
}
```

Although these first few chapters describe classes, there's another user-defined type called a `struct`, which I'll cover in Chapter 12. Most of what this chapter covers about class methods is also true for struct methods.

Code Execution in the Method Body

The method body is a *block*, which (as you will recall from Chapter 2) is a sequence of statements between curly braces. A block can contain the following items:

- Local variables

- Flow-of-control constructs

- Method invocations

- Blocks nested within it

Figure 5-2 shows an example of a method body and some of its components.

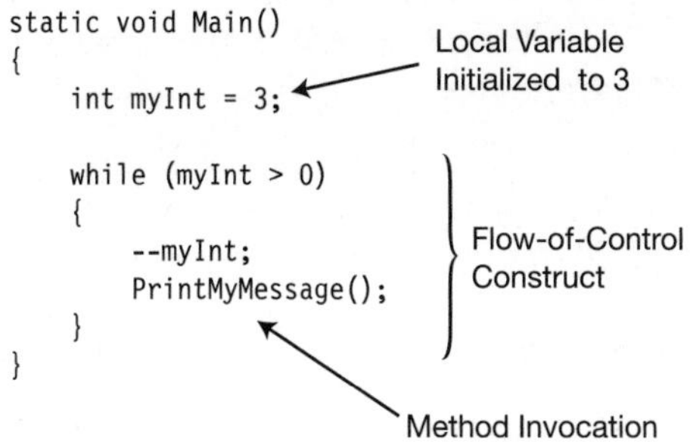

Figure 5-2. *Method body example*

Local Variables

Like fields, local variables store data. While fields usually store data about the state of the object, local variables are usually created to store data for local, or transitory, computations. Table 5-1 compares and contrasts local variables and instance fields.

The following line of code shows the syntax of local variable declarations. The optional initializer consists of the equals sign followed by a value to be used to initialize the variable.

```
              Variable name
                   ↓
                _____
Type Identifier = Value;
                    ↑
              Optional initializer
```

- The existence of a local variable is limited to the block in which it is created and the blocks nested within it.

  — The variable comes into existence at the point at which it is declared.

  — It goes out of existence when the block completes execution.

- You can declare local variables at any position in the method body, but they must be declared before they're used.

The following example shows the declaration and use of two local variables. The first is of type int, and the second is of type SomeClass.

```
static void Main( )
{
   int myInt    = 15;
   SomeClass sc = new SomeClass();
   ...
}
```

Table 5-1. *Instance Fields vs. Local Variables*

	Instance Field	Local Variable
Lifetime	Starts when the class instance is created. Ends when the class instance is no longer accessible.	Starts at the point in the block where it is declared. Ends when the block completes execution.
Implicit initialization	Initialized to a default value for the type.	No implicit initialization. The compiler produces an error message if the variable isn't assigned to before use.
Storage area	All the fields of a class are stored in the heap, regardless of whether they're value types or reference types.	Value type: Stored on the stack. Reference type: Reference stored on the stack and data stored in the heap.

Type Inference and the var Keyword

If you look at the following code, you'll see that when you supply the type name at the beginning of the declaration, you are supplying information that the compiler should already be able to infer from the right side of the initialization.

- In the first variable declaration, the compiler can infer that 15 is an int.

- In the second declaration, the object-creation expression on the right side returns an object of type MyExcellentClass.

So in both cases, including the explicit type name at the beginning of the declaration is redundant.

```
static void Main( )
{
   int total = 15;
   MyExcellentClass mec = new MyExcellentClass();
   ...
}
```

Starting with C# 3.0 you can use the new keyword var in place of the explicit type name at the beginning of the variable declaration, as follows:

```
static void Main( )
{ Keyword
       ↓
   var total = 15;
   var mec   = new MyExcellentClass();
   ...
}
```

The var keyword does *not* signal a special kind of variable. It's just syntactic shorthand for whatever type can be inferred from the initialization on the right side of the statement. In the first declaration, it is shorthand for int. In the second, it is shorthand for MyExcellentClass. The preceding code segment with the explicit type names and the code segment with the var keywords are semantically equivalent.

Some important conditions on using the var keyword are the following:

- You can use it only with local variables—not with fields.

- You can use it only when the variable declaration includes an initialization.

- Once the compiler infers the type of a variable, it is fixed and unchangeable.

■ **Note** The var keyword is *not* like the JavaScript var that can reference different types. It's shorthand for the actual type inferred from the right side of the equals sign. The var keyword *does not change the strongly typed nature of C#.*

Local Variables Inside Nested Blocks

Method bodies can have other blocks nested inside them.

- There can be any number of blocks, and they can be sequential or nested further. Blocks can be nested to any level.

- Local variables can be declared inside nested blocks, and like all local variables, their lifetimes and visibility are limited to the block in which they're declared and the blocks nested within it.

Figure 5-3 illustrates the lifetimes of two local variables, showing the code and the state of the stack. The arrows indicate the line that has just been executed.

- Variable var1 is declared in the body of the method, before the nested block.

- Variable var2 is declared inside the nested block. It exists from the time it's declared, until the end of the block in which it was declared.

- When control passes out of the nested block, its local variables are popped from the stack.

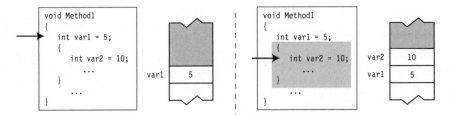

1. Variable var1 is declared before the nested block, and space is allocated for it on the stack.

2. Variable var2 is declared within the nested block, and space is allocated for it on the stack.

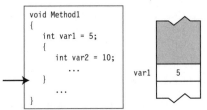

3. When execution passes out of the nested block, var2 is popped from the stack.

Figure 5-3. *The lifetime of a local variable*

■ **Note** In C and C++ you can declare a local variable, and then within a nested block you can declare another local variable with the same name. The inner name masks the outer name while within the inner scope. In C#, however, you cannot declare another local variable with the same name within the scope of the first name regardless of the level of nesting.

Local Constants

A local constant is much like a local variable, except that once it is initialized, its value can't be changed. Like a local variable, a local constant must be declared inside a block.

The two most important characteristics of a constant are the following:

- A constant *must be initialized* at its declaration.

- A constant *cannot be changed* after its declaration.

The core declaration for a constant is shown following. The syntax is the same as that of a field or variable declaration, except for the following:

- The addition of the keyword const before the type.

- The mandatory initializer. The initializer value must be determinable at compile time and is usually one of the predefined simple types or an expression made up of them. It can also be the null reference, but it cannot be a reference to an object, because references to objects are determined at run time.

■ **Note** The keyword const is not a modifier but part of the core declaration. It must be placed immediately before the type.

```
Keyword
  ↓
 const Type Identifier = Value;
                          ↑
              Initializer required
```

A local constant, like a local variable, is declared in a method body or code block, and it goes out of scope at the end of the block in which it is declared. For example, in the following code, local constant PI goes out of scope at the end of method DisplayRadii.

```
void DisplayRadii()
{
   const double PI = 3.1416;                  // Declare local constant

   for (int radius = 1; radius <= 5; radius++)
   {
      double area = radius * radius * PI;     // Read from local constant
      Console.WriteLine
         ("Radius: {0}, Area: {1}" radius, area);
   }
}
```

Flow of Control

Methods contain most of the code for the actions that comprise a program. The remainder is in other function members, such as properties and operators—but the bulk is in methods.

The term *flow of control* refers to the flow of execution through your program. By default, program execution moves sequentially from one statement to the next. The control statements allow you to modify the order of execution.

In this section, I'll just mention some of the available control statements you can use in your code. Chapter 9 covers them in detail.

- *Selection statements*: These statements allow you to select which statement, or block of statements, to execute.

  — if: Conditional execution of a statement

  — if...else: Conditional execution of one statement or another

  — switch: Conditional execution of one statement from a set

- *Iteration statements*: These statements allow you to loop, or iterate, on a block of statements.

  — for: Loop—testing at the top

  — while: Loop—testing at the top

  — do: Loop—testing at the bottom

  — foreach: Execute once for each member of a set

- *Jump statements*: These statements allow you to jump from one place in the block or method to another.

  — break: Exit the current loop.

  — continue: Go to the bottom of the current loop.

  — goto: Go to a named statement.

  — return: Return execution to the calling method.

For example, the following method shows two of the flow-of-control statements. Don't worry about the details.

```
void SomeMethod()
{
    int intVal = 3;
       Equality comparison operator
                 ↓
    if( intVal == 3 )                            // if statement
        Console.WriteLine("Value is 3. ");

    for( int i=0; i<5; i++ )                     // for statement
        Console.WriteLine("Value of i: {0}", i);
}
```

Method Invocations

You can call other methods from inside a method body.

- The phrases *call a method* and *invoke a method* are synonymous.

- You call a method by using its name, along with the parameter list, which I'll discuss shortly.

For example, the following class declares a method called `PrintDateAndTime`, which is called from inside method `Main`:

```
class MyClass
{
   void PrintDateAndTime( )                  // Declare the method.
   {
      DateTime dt = DateTime.Now;            // Get the current date and time.
      Console.WriteLine("{0}", dt);          // Write it out.
   }

   static void Main()                        // Declare the method.
   {
      MyClass mc = new MyClass();
      mc.PrintDateAndTime( );                // Invoke the method.
   }              ↑              ↑
}            Method          Empty
             name       parameter list
```

Figure 5-4 illustrates the sequence of actions when a method is called:

1. Execution of the current method suspends at that point of the invocation.
2. Control transfers to the beginning of the invoked method.
3. The invoked method executes until it completes.
4. Control returns to the calling method.

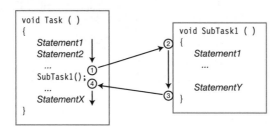

Figure 5-4. *Flow of control when calling a method*

Return Values

A method can return a value to the calling code. The returned value is inserted into the calling code at the position in the expression where the invocation occurred.

- To return a value, the method must declare a *return type* before the method name.

- If a method doesn't return a value, it must declare a return type of void.

The following code shows two method declarations. The first returns a value of type int. The second doesn't return a value.

```
Return type
  ↓
int  GetHour()    { ... }
void DisplayHour() { ... }
  ↑
No value is returned.
```

A method that declares a return type must return a value from the method by using the following form of the return statement, which includes an expression after the keyword return. Every path through the method must end with a return statement of this form.

```
return Expression;                        // Return a value.
        ↑
Evaluates to a value of the return type
```

For example, the following code shows a method called GetHour, which returns a value of type int.

```
Return type
  ↓
int GetHour( )
{
    DateTime dt = DateTime.Now;           // Get the current date and time.
    int hour    = dt.Hour;                // Get the hour.

    return hour;                          // Return an int.
}          ↑
    Return statement
```

You can also return objects of user-defined types. For example, the following code returns an object of type MyClass:

```
Return type -- MyClass
         ↓
MyClass method3( )
{
   MyClass mc = new MyClass();
      ...
   return mc;                              // Return a MyClass object.
}
```

As another example, in the following code, method GetHour is called in the WriteLine statement in Main and returns an int value to that position in the WriteLine statement.

```
class MyClass
{              ↓ Return type
   public int GetHour()
   {
      DateTime dt = DateTime.Now;          // Get the current date and time.
      int hour     = dt.Hour;              // Get the hour.

      return hour;                         // Return an int.
   }              ↑
}           Return value


class Program
{
   static void Main()
   {                            Method invocation
      MyClass mc = new MyClass();          ↓
      Console.WriteLine("Hour: {0}", mc.GetHour());
   }                            ↑      ↑
}                         Instance  Method
                           name     name
```

The Return Statement and Void Methods

In the previous section, you saw that methods that return a value must contain return statements. Void methods do not require return statements. When the flow of control reaches the closing curly brace of the method body, control returns to the calling code, and no value is inserted back into the calling code.

Often, however, you can simplify your program logic by exiting the method early when certain conditions apply.

- You can exit from a void method at any time by using the following form of the return statement, with no parameters:

  ```
  return;
  ```

- This form of the return statement can be used only with methods declared void.

For example, the following code shows the declaration of a void method called SomeMethod, which has three possible places it might return to the calling code. The first two places are in branches called if statements, which are covered in Chapter 9. The last place is the end of the method body.

```
Void return type
     ↓
  void SomeMethod()
  {
     ...
     if ( SomeCondition )          // If ...
        return;                    // return to the calling code.
     ...

     if ( OtherCondition )         // If ...
        return;                    // return to the calling code.


     ...
  }                                // Default return to the calling code.
```

The following code shows an example of a void method with a return statement. The method writes out a message only if the time is after noon. The process, which is illustrated in Figure 5-5, is as follows:

- First the method gets the current date and time. (Don't worry about understanding the details of this right now.)

- If the hour is less than 12 (that is, before noon), the return statement is executed, and control immediately returns to the calling method without writing anything to the screen.

- If the hour is 12 or greater, the return statement is skipped, and the code executes the `WriteLine` statement, which writes an informative message to the screen.

```
class MyClass
{        ↓ Void return type
   void TimeUpdate()
   {
      DateTime dt = DateTime.Now;           // Get the current date and time.
         if (dt.Hour < 12)                  // If the hour is less than 12,
            return;                         // then return.
              ↑
            Return to calling method.
      Console.WriteLine("It's afternoon!");   // Otherwise, print message.
   }

   static void Main()
   {
      MyClass mc = new MyClass();           // Create an instance of the class.
      mc.TimeUpdate();                      // Invoke the method.
   }
}
```

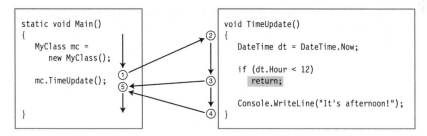

Figure 5-5. *Using a return statement with a void return type*

Parameters

So far, you've seen that methods are named units of code that can be called from many places in a program and can return a single value to the calling code. Returning a single value is certainly valuable, but what if you need to return multiple values? Also, it would be useful to be able to pass data into a method when it starts execution. *Parameters* are special variables that allow you to do both these things.

Formal Parameters

Formal parameters are local variables that are declared in the method declaration's parameter list, rather than in the body of the method.

The following method header shows the syntax of parameter declarations. It declares two formal parameters—one of type int and the other of type float.

```
public void PrintSum( int x, float y )
{                          ↑
    ...           Formal parameter declarations
}
```

- Because formal parameters are variables, they have a data type and a name, and they can be written to and read from.

- Unlike a method's other local variables, the parameters are defined outside the method body and are initialized before the method starts, except for one type, called output parameters, which I'll cover shortly.

- The parameter list can have any number of formal parameter declarations, and the declarations must be separated by commas.

The formal parameters are used throughout the method body, for the most part, just like other local variables. For example, the following declaration of method PrintSum uses two formal parameters, x and y, and a local variable, sum, all of which are of type int.

```
public void PrintSum( int x, int y )
{
    int sum = x + y;
    Console.WriteLine("Newsflash:  {0} + {1} is {2}", x, y, sum);
}
```

Actual Parameters

When your code calls a method, the values of the formal parameters must be initialized before the code in the method begins execution.

- The expressions or variables used to initialize the formal parameters are called the *actual parameters*. They are also sometimes called *arguments*.

- The actual parameters are placed in the parameter list of the method invocation.

- Each actual parameter must match the type of the corresponding formal parameter, or the compiler must be able to implicitly convert the actual parameter to that type. I'll explain the details of conversion from one type to another in Chapter 18.

For example, the following code shows the invocation of method PrintSum, which has two actual parameters of data type int:

```
PrintSum( 5, someInt );
         ↑     ↑
    Expression  Variable of type int
```

When the method is called, the value of each actual parameter is used to initialize the corresponding formal parameter. The method body is then executed. Figure 5-6 illustrates the relationship between the actual parameters and the formal parameters.

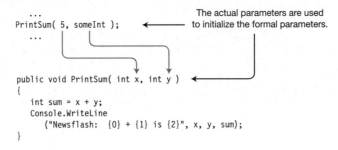

Figure 5-6. *Actual parameters initialize the corresponding formal parameters.*

Notice that in the previous example code, and in Figure 5-6, the number of actual parameters must be the same as the number of formal parameters (with the exception of params parameters, which I'll discuss later). Parameters that follow this pattern are called *positional parameters*. We'll look at some other options shortly.

An Example of Methods with Positional Input Parameters

In the following code, class MyClass declares two methods—one that takes two integers and returns their sum and another that takes two floats and returns their average. In the second invocation, notice that the compiler has implicitly converted the two int values—5 and someInt—to the float type.

```
class MyClass        Formal parameters
{                          ↓
    public int Sum(int x, int y)                    // Declare the method.
    {
        return x + y;                               // Return the sum.
    }                      Formal parameters
                               ↓
    public float Avg(float input1, float input2)    // Declare the method.
    {
        return (input1 + input2) / 2.0F;            // Return the average.
    }
}


class Program
{
    static void Main()
    {
        MyClass myT = new MyClass();
        int someInt = 6;

        Console.WriteLine
           ("Newsflash:  Sum: {0} and {1} is {2}",
                5, someInt, myT.Sum( 5, someInt ));      // Invoke the method.
                                          ↑
        Console.WriteLine          Actual parameters
           ("Newsflash:  Avg: {0} and {1} is {2}",
                5, someInt, myT.Avg( 5, someInt ));      // Invoke the method.
    }                                     ↑
}                              Actual parameters
```

This code produces the following output:

```
Newsflash:  Sum: 5 and 6 is 11
Newsflash:  Avg: 5 and 6 is 5.5
```

Value Parameters

There are several kinds of parameters, which pass data to and from the method in slightly different ways. The kind we've looked at so far is the default type and is called a *value parameter*.

When you use value parameters, data is passed to the method by copying the value of the actual parameter to the formal parameter. When a method is called, the system does the following:

- It allocates space on the stack for the formal parameters.

- It copies the values of the actual parameters to the formal parameters.

An actual parameter for a value parameter doesn't have to be a variable. It can be any expression evaluating to the matching data type. For example, the following code shows two method calls. In the first, the actual parameter is a variable of type float. In the second, it's an expression that evaluates to float.

```
float func1( float val )                        // Declare the method.
{                   ↑
            Float data type
   float j = 2.6F;
   float k = 5.1F;        Variable of type float
                              ↓
   float fValue1 = func1( k );                   // Method call
   float fValue2 = func1( (k + j) / 3 );         // Method call
   ...                         ↑
            Expression that evaluates to a float
```

Before you can use a variable as an actual parameter, that variable must have been assigned a value (except in the case of output parameters, which I'll cover shortly). For reference types, the variable can be assigned either an actual reference or null.

■ **Note** Chapter 3 covered *value types,* which, as you will remember, are types that contain their own data. Don't be confused that I'm now talking about *value parameters*. They're entirely different. *Value parameters* are parameters where the value of the actual parameter is copied to the formal parameter.

For example, the following code shows a method called MyMethod, which takes two parameters—a variable of type MyClass and an int.

- The method adds 5 to both the int type field belonging to the class and to the int.

- You might also notice that MyMethod uses the modifier static, which I haven't explained yet. You can ignore it for now. I'll explain static methods in Chapter 6.

```
class MyClass
{
   public int Val = 20;                          // Initialize the field to 20.
}

class Program                 Formal parameters
{                             ————————————————
                                      ↓
   static void MyMethod( MyClass f1, int f2 )
   {
      f1.Val = f1.Val + 5;                        // Add 5 to field of f1 param.
      f2     = f2 + 5;                            // Add 5 to second param.
   }

   static void Main( )
   {
      MyClass a1 = new MyClass();
      int     a2 = 10;

      MyMethod( a1, a2 );                         // Call the method.
   }          ↑
}          Actual parameters
```

Figure 5-7 illustrates the following about the values of the actual and formal parameters at various stages in the execution of the method:

- Before the method call, variables a1 and a2, which will be used as the actual parameters, are already on the stack.

- By the beginning of the method, the system has allocated space on the stack for the formal parameters and copied the values from the actual parameters.

  — Since a1 is a reference type, the *reference* is copied, resulting in both the actual and formal parameters referring to the same object in the heap.

  — Since a2 is a value type, the *value* is copied, producing an independent data item.

- At the end of the method, both f2 and the field of object f1 have been incremented by 5.

  — After method execution, the formal parameters are popped off the stack.

  — The value of a2, the value type, is *unaffected* by the activity in the method.

  — The value of a1, the reference type, however, *has been changed* by the activity in the method.

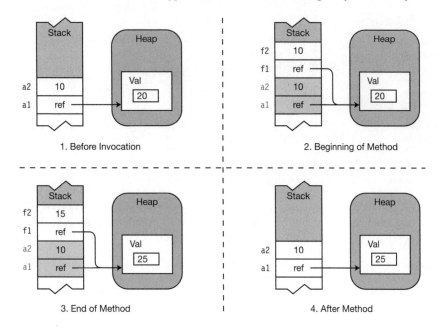

Figure 5-7. *Value parameters*

Reference Parameters

The second type of parameter is called a *reference parameter*.

- When using a reference parameter, you must use the ref modifier in both the declaration and the invocation of the method.

- The actual parameter *must* be a variable, and it must have been assigned to before being used as the actual parameter. If it's a reference type variable, it can be assigned either an actual reference or the value null.

For example, the following code illustrates the syntax of the declaration and invocation:

```
                    Include the ref modifier.
                              ↓
void MyMethod( ref int val )          // Method declaration
{ ... }

int y = 1;                            // Variable for the actual parameter
MyMethod ( ref y );                   // Method call
               ↑
        Include the ref modifier.

MyMethod ( ref 3+5 );                 // Error!
               ↑
        Must use a variable
```

In the previous section you saw that for value parameters, the system allocates memory on the stack for the formal parameters. In contrast, for reference parameters:

- The formal parameter name *acts as if it were an alias for the actual parameter variable*; that is, it acts as if it referred to the same memory location.

Since the formal parameter name and the actual parameter name are acting as if they reference the same memory location, clearly any changes made to the formal parameter during method execution are visible after the method is completed, through the actual parameter variable.

■ **Note** Remember to use the ref keyword in both the method declaration *and* the invocation.

For example, the following code shows method MyMethod again, but this time the parameters are reference parameters rather than value parameters:

```
class MyClass
{
   public int Val = 20;                        // Initialize field to 20.
}

class Program          ref modifier        ref modifier
{                           ↓                   ↓
   static void MyMethod(ref MyClass f1, ref int f2)
   {
       f1.Val = f1.Val + 5;                    // Add 5 to field of f1 param.
       f2     = f2 + 5;                        // Add 5 to second param.
   }

   static void Main()
   {
      MyClass a1 = new MyClass();
      int a2     = 10;

      MyMethod(ref a1, ref a2);                // Call the method.
   }        ↑        ↑
}                ref modifiers
```

Figure 5-8 illustrates the following about the values of the actual and formal parameters at various stages in the execution of the method:

- Before the method call, variables a1 and a2, which will be used as the actual parameters, are already on the stack.

- By the beginning of the method, the names of the formal parameters have been set as if they were aliases for the actual parameters. You can think of variables a1 and f1 as if they referred to the same memory location and a2 and f2 as if they referred to the same memory location.

- At the end of the method, both f2 and the field of the object of f1 have been incremented by 5.

- After method execution, the names of the formal parameters are gone ("out of scope"), but both the value of a2, which is the value type, and the value of the object pointed at by a1, which is the reference type, have been changed by the activity in the method.

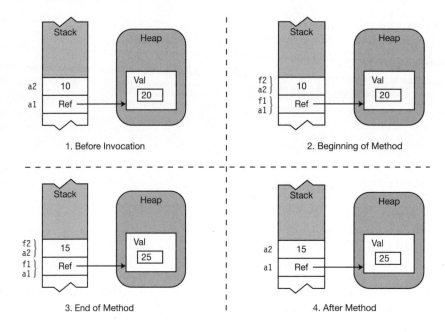

Figure 5-8. *With a reference parameter, the formal parameter behaves as if it were an alias for the actual parameter.*

Output Parameters

Output parameters are used to pass data from inside the method back out to the calling code. Their behavior is very similar to reference parameters. Like reference parameters, output parameters have the following requirements:

- You must use a modifier in both the method declaration and the invocation. With output parameters, the modifier is out, rather than ref.

- Like reference parameters, the actual parameter *must* be a variable—it cannot be another type of expression. This makes sense, since the method needs a memory location to store the value it's returning.

For example, the following code declares a method called MyMethod, which takes a single output parameter.

```
                out modifier
                    ↓
void MyMethod( out int val )          // Method declaration
{ ... }

...
int y = 1;                            // Variable for the actual parameter
MyMethod ( out y );                   // Method call
              ↑
          out modifier
```

Like reference parameters, the formal parameters of output parameters act as if they were aliases for the actual parameters. Any changes made to a formal parameter inside the method are visible through the actual parameter variable after the method completes execution.

Unlike reference parameters, output parameters require the following:

- Inside the method, an output parameter must be assigned to before it can be read from. This means that the initial values of the parameters are irrelevant and that you don't have to assign values to the actual parameters before the method call.

- Inside the method, every possible path through the code must assign a value to every output parameter before the method exits.

Since the code inside the method must write to an output parameter before it can read from it, it is *impossible* to send data *into* a method using output parameters. In fact, if there is any execution path through the method that attempts to read the value of an output parameter before the method has assigned it a value, the compiler produces an error message.

```
public void Add2( out int outValue )
{
   int var1 = outValue + 2;  // Error! Can't read from an output parameter
}                            // before it has been assigned to by the method.
```

For example, the following code again shows method MyMethod, but this time using output parameters:

```
class MyClass
{
   public int Val = 20;                      // Initialize field to 20.
}

class Program          out modifier     out modifier
{                           ↓                ↓
   static void MyMethod(out MyClass f1, out int f2)
   {
      f1 = new MyClass();                    // Create an object of the class.
      f1.Val = 25;                           // Assign to the class field.
      f2     = 15;                           // Assign to the int param.
   }

   static void Main()
   {
      MyClass a1 = null;
      int a2;

      MyMethod(out a1, out a2);              // Call the method.
   }                   ↑       ↑
}                      out modifiers
```

Figure 5-9 illustrates the following about the values of the actual and formal parameters at various stages in the execution of the method.

- Before the method call, variables a1 and a2, which will be used as the actual parameters, are already on the stack.

- At the beginning of the method, the names of the formal parameters are set as aliases for the actual parameters. You can think of variables a1 and f1 as if they referred to the same memory location, and you can think of a2 and f2 as if they referred to the same memory location. The names a1 and a2 are out of scope and cannot be accessed from inside MyMethod.

- Inside the method, the code creates an object of type MyClass and assigns it to f1. It then assigns a value to f1's field and also assigns a value to f2. The assignments to f1 and f2 are both *required*, since they're output parameters.

- After method execution, the names of the formal parameters are out of scope, but the values of both a1, the reference type, and a2, the value type, have been changed by the activity in the method.

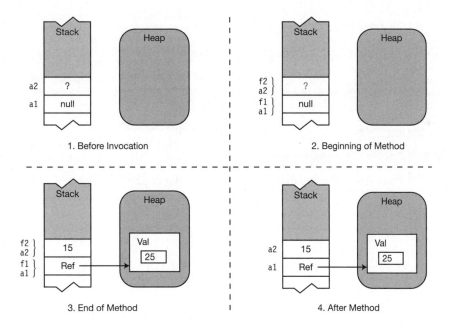

Figure 5-9. *With an output parameter, the formal parameter behaves as if it were an alias for the actual parameter, but with the additional requirement that it must be assigned to inside the method.*

Parameter Arrays

In the parameter types I've covered so far, there must be exactly one actual parameter for each formal parameter. *Parameter arrays* are different in that they allow *zero or more* actual parameters for a particular formal parameter. Important points about parameter arrays are the following:

- There can be only one parameter array in a parameter list.

- If there is one, it must be the last parameter in the list.

To declare a parameter array, you must do the following:

- Use the params modifier before the data type.

- Place a set of empty square brackets after the data type.

The following method header shows the syntax for the declaration of a parameter array of type int. In this example, formal parameter inVals can represent zero or more actual int parameters.

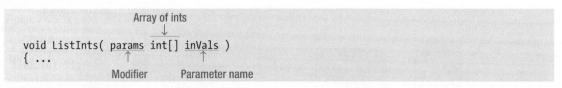

The empty set of square brackets after the type name specifies that the parameter will be an *array* of ints. You don't need to worry about the details of arrays here. They're covered in detail in Chapter 14. For our purposes here, though, all you need to know is the following:

- An array is an ordered set of data items of the same type.

- An array is accessed by using a numerical index.

- An array is a reference type and therefore stores all its data items in the heap.

Method Invocation

You can supply the actual parameters for a parameter array in two ways. The forms you can use are the following:

- A comma-separated list of elements of the data type. All the elements must be of the type specified in the method declaration.

```
ListInts( 10, 20, 30 );              // Three ints
```

- A one-dimensional array of elements of the data type.

```
int[] intArray = {1, 2, 3};
ListInts( intArray );                // An array variable
```

Notice in these examples that you do *not* use the params modifier in the *invocation*. The usage of the modifier in parameter arrays doesn't fit the pattern of the other parameter types.

- The other parameter types are consistent in that they either use a modifier or do not use a modifier.

  — Value parameters take *no* modifier in *either* the declaration or the invocation.

  — Reference and output parameters require the modifier in *both* places.

- The summary for the usage of the params modifier is the following:

  — It is *required* in the *declaration*.

  — It is *not allowed* in the *invocation*.

Expanded Form

The first form of method invocation, where you use separate actual parameters in the invocation, is sometimes called the *expanded form*.

For example, the declaration of method ListInts in the following code matches all the method invocations below it, even though they have different numbers of actual parameters.

```
void ListInts( params int[] inVals ) { ... }     // Method declaration

...
ListInts( );                          // 0 actual parameters
ListInts( 1, 2, 3 );                  // 3 actual parameters
ListInts( 4, 5, 6,  7 );              // 4 actual parameters
ListInts( 8, 9, 10, 11, 12 );         // 5 actual parameters
```

When you use an invocation with separate actual parameters for a parameter array, the compiler does the following:

- It takes the list of actual parameters and uses them to create and initialize an array in the heap.

- It stores the reference to the array in the formal parameter on the stack.

- If there are no actual parameters at the position corresponding to the formal parameter array, the compiler creates an array with zero elements and uses that.

For example, the following code declares a method called ListInts, which takes a parameter array. Main declares three ints and passes them to the array.

```
class MyClass                        Parameter array
{                                         ↓
                              _____
   public void ListInts( params int[] inVals )
   {
      if ( (inVals != null) && (inVals.Length != 0))
         for (int i = 0; i < inVals.Length; i++)      // Process the array.
         {
            inVals[i] = inVals[i] * 10;
            Console.WriteLine("{0}", inVals[i]);    // Display new value.
         }
   }
}

class Program
{
   static void Main()
   {
      int first = 5, second = 6, third = 7;           // Declare three ints.

      MyClass mc = new MyClass();
      mc.ListInts( first, second, third );            // Call the method.
                   ↑
               Actual parameters
      Console.WriteLine("{0}, {1}, {2}", first, second, third);
   }
}
```

This code produces the following output:

```
50
60
70
5, 6, 7
```

Figure 5-10 illustrates the following about the values of the actual and formal parameters at various stages in the execution of the method:

- Before the method call, the three actual parameters are already on the stack.

- By the beginning of the method, the three actual parameters have been used to initialize an array in the heap, and the reference to the array has been assigned to formal parameter `inVals`.

- Inside the method, the code first checks to make sure the array reference is not `null` and then processes the array by multiplying each element in the array by 10 and storing it back.

- After method execution, the formal parameter, `inVals`, is out of scope.

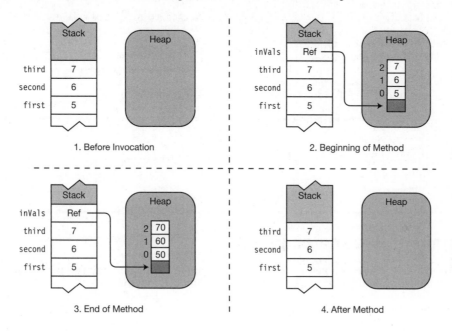

Figure 5-10. *Parameter array*

An important thing to remember about parameter arrays is that when an array is created in the heap, the values of the actual parameters are *copied* to the array. In this way, they're like value parameters.

- If the array parameter is a value type, the *values* are copied, and the actual parameters *cannot be affected* inside the method.

- If the array parameter is a reference type, the *references* are copied, and the objects referenced by the actual parameters *can be affected* inside the method.

Arrays As Actual Parameters

You can also create and populate an array before the method call and pass the single array variable as the actual parameter. In this case, the compiler uses *your* array, rather than creating one.

For example, the following code uses method ListInts, declared in the previous example. In this code, Main creates an array and uses the array variable as the actual parameter, rather than using separate integers.

```
static void Main()
{
   int[] myArr = new int[] { 5, 6, 7 };  // Create and initialize array.

   MyClass mc = new MyClass();
   mc.ListInts(myArr);                    // Call method to print the values.

   foreach (int x in myArr)
      Console.WriteLine("{0}", x);        // Print out each element.
}
```

This code produces the following output:

```
50
60
70
50
60
70
```

Summary of Parameter Types

Since there are four parameter types, it's sometimes difficult to remember their various characteristics. Table 5-2 summarizes them, making it easier to compare and contrast them.

Table 5-2. *Summary of Parameter Type Syntactic Usage*

Parameter Type	Modifier	Used at Declaration?	Used at Invocation?	Implementation
Value	None			The system copies the value of the actual parameter to the formal parameter.
Reference	ref	Yes	Yes	The formal parameter aliases the actual parameter.
Output	out	Yes	Yes	The formal parameter aliases the actual parameter.
Array	params	Yes	No	This allows passing a variable number of actual parameters to a method.

Method Overloading

A class can have more than one method with the same name. This is called *method overloading*. Each method with the same name must have a different *signature* than the others.

- The signature of a method consists of the following information from the method header of the method declaration:
  — The name of the method
  — The number of parameters
  — The data types and order of the parameters
  — The parameter modifiers

- The return type is *not* part of the signature—although it's a common mistake to believe that it is.

- Notice that the *names* of the formal parameters are *not* part of the signature.

```
Not part of signature
       ↓
long AddValues( int a, out int b) { ... }
                    ↑
              Signature
```

For example, the following four methods are overloads of the method name AddValues:

```
class A
{
    long AddValues( int   a, int   b)        { return a + b;         }
    long AddValues( int   c, int   d, int e) { return c + d + e;     }
    long AddValues( float f, float g)        { return (long)(f + g); }
    long AddValues( long  h, long  m)        { return h + m;         }
}
```

The following code shows an illegal attempt at overloading the method name AddValues. The two methods differ only on the return types and the names of the formal parameters. But they still have the same signature, because they have the same method name; and the number, types, and order of their parameters are the same. The compiler would produce an error message for this code.

```
class B               Signature
{                        ↓
    long AddValues( long  a, long  b) { return a+b; }
    int  AddValues( long  c, long  d) { return c+d; } // Error, same signature
}                            ↑
                         Signature
```

Named Parameters

So far in our discussion of parameters we've used positional parameters, which, as you'll remember, means that the position of each actual parameter matches the position of the corresponding formal parameter.

Starting with C# 4.0, you can list the actual parameters in your method invocation in any order, as long as you explicitly specify the names of the parameters. The details are the following:

- Nothing changes in the declaration of the method. The formal parameters already have names.

- In the method invocation, however, you use the formal parameter name, followed by a colon, in front of the actual parameter value or expression, as shown in the following method invocation. Here a, b, and c are the names of the three formal parameters of method Calc:

```
        Actual parameter values
             ↓      ↓      ↓
    c.Calc ( c: 2, a: 4, b: 3);
             ‾T‾   ‾T‾  ‾T‾
          Named parameters
```

Figure 5-11 illustrates the structure of using named parameters.

```
                                              No change in
                                              parameter declarations
    class MyClass
    {
        public int Calc(int a, int b, int c)
        { return (a + b) * c;  }

        static void Main()                    Parameter names
        {                                     used with values
            MyClass mc = new MyClass();

            int result = mc.Calc( c: 2, a: 4, b: 3 );

            Console.WriteLine("{0}", result);
        }
    }
```

Figure 5-11. *When using named parameters, include the parameter name in the method invocation. No changes are needed in the method declaration.*

You can use both positional and named parameters in an invocation, but all the positional parameters must be listed first. For example, the following code shows the declaration of a method called Calc, along with five different calls to the method using different combinations of positional and named parameters:

```
class MyClass
{
   public int Calc( int a, int b, int c )
   { return ( a + b ) * c;  }

   static void Main()
   {
      MyClass mc = new MyClass( );

      int r0 = mc.Calc( 4, 3, 2 );                    // Positional Parameters
      int r1 = mc.Calc( 4, b: 3, c: 2 );              // Positional and Named Parameters
      int r2 = mc.Calc( 4, c: 2, b: 3 );              // Switch order
      int r3 = mc.Calc( c: 2, b: 3, a: 4 );           // All named parameters
      int r4 = mc.Calc( c: 2, b: 1 + 2, a: 3 + 1 );   // Named parameter expressions

      Console.WriteLine("{0}, {1}, {2}, {3}, {4}", r0, r1, r2, r3, r4);
   }
}
```

This code produces the following output:

```
14, 14, 14, 14, 14
```

Named parameters are useful as a means of self-documenting a program, in that they can show, at the position of the method call, what values are being assigned to which formal parameters. For example, in the following two calls to method GetCylinderVolume, the second call is a bit more informative and less prone to error.

```
class MyClass
{
   double GetCylinderVolume( double radius, double height )
   {
      return 3.1416 * radius * radius * height;
   }

   static void Main( string[] args )
   {
      MyClass mc = new MyClass();
      double volume;
                                      ↓     ↓
      volume = mc.GetCylinderVolume( 3.0, 4.0 );
      ...
      volume = mc.GetCylinderVolume( radius: 3.0, height: 4.0 );
      ...                            ‾‾‾‾‾‾‾‾‾   ‾‾‾‾‾‾‾‾‾
   }                                      ↑           ↑
}                                       More informative
```

Optional Parameters

Another feature introduced in C# 4.0, is called *optional parameters*. An optional parameter is a parameter that you can either include or omit when invoking the method.

To specify that a parameter is optional, you need to include a default value for that parameter in the method declaration. The syntax for specifying the default value is the same as that of initializing a local variable, as shown in the method declaration of the following code. In this example:

- Formal parameter b is assigned the default value 3.

- Therefore, if the method is called with only a single parameter, the method will use the value 3 as the initial value of the second parameter.

```
class MyClass                          Optional Parameter
{                                            ↓
    public int Calc( int a, int b = 3 )
    {                                        ⊤
        return a + b;          Default Value Assignment
    }

    static void Main()
    {
        MyClass mc = new MyClass();

        int r0 = mc.Calc( 5, 6 );          // Use explicit values.
        int r1 = mc.Calc( 5 );             // Use default for b.

        Console.WriteLine( "{0}, {1}", r0, r1 );
    }
}
```

This code produces the following output:

```
11, 8
```

There are several important things to know about declaring optional parameters:

- Not all types of parameters can be used as optional parameters.

  — You can use value types as optional parameters as long as the default value is determinable at compile time.

  — You can only use a reference type as an optional parameter if the default value is `null`.

Parameter Types

	Value	ref	out	params
Value Type	Yes	No	No	No
Reference Type	Only null default	No	No	No

Data Types

Figure 5-12. *Optional parameters can only be value parameter types.*

- All required parameters must be declared before any optional parameters are declared. If there is a `params` parameter, it must be declared after all the optional parameters. Figure 5-13 illustrates the required syntactic order.

Required Parameters   Optional Parameters   params Parameter

```
( int x, decimal y,   ...   int op1 = 17, double op2 = 36,   ...   params int[] intVals )
```

Figure 5-13. *In the method declaration, optional parameters must be declared after all the required parameters and before the params parameter, if one exists.*

As you saw in the previous example, you use the default value of an optional parameter by leaving out the corresponding actual parameter from the method invocation. You can't, however, omit just any combination of optional parameters because in many situations it would be ambiguous as to which optional parameters to use. The rules are the following:

- You must omit parameters starting from the end of the list of optional parameters and work toward the beginning.

- That is, you can omit the last optional parameter, or the last *n* optional parameters, but you can't pick and choose to omit any arbitrary optional parameters; they must be taken off the end.

```
class MyClass
{
    public int Calc( int a = 2, int b = 3, int c = 4 )
    {
        return (a + b) * c;
    }

    static void Main( )
    {
        MyClass mc = new MyClass( );
        int r0 = mc.Calc( 5, 6, 7 );    // Use all explicit values.
        int r1 = mc.Calc( 5, 6 );       // Use default for c.
        int r2 = mc.Calc( 5 );          // Use default for b and c.
        int r3 = mc.Calc( );            // Use all defaults.

        Console.WriteLine( "{0}, {1}, {2}, {3}", r0, r1, r2, r3 );
    }
}
```

This code produces the following output:

```
77, 44, 32, 20
```

To omit optional parameters from arbitrary positions within the list of optional parameters, rather than from the end of the list, you must use the names of the optional parameters to disambiguate the assignments. You are therefore using both the named parameters and optional parameters features, as illustrated in the following code:

```
class MyClass
{
    double GetCylinderVolume( double radius = 3.0, double height = 4.0 )
    {
        return 3.1416 * radius * radius * height;
    }

    static void Main( )
    {
        MyClass mc = new MyClass();
        double volume;

        volume = mc.GetCylinderVolume( 3.0, 4.0 );         // Positional
        Console.WriteLine( "Volume = " + volume );

        volume = mc.GetCylinderVolume( radius: 2.0 );      // Use default height
        Console.WriteLine( "Volume = " + volume );

        volume = mc.GetCylinderVolume( height: 2.0 );      // Use default radius
        Console.WriteLine( "Volume = " + volume );

        volume = mc.GetCylinderVolume( );                  // Use both defaults
        Console.WriteLine( "Volume = " + volume );
    }
}
```

This code produces the following output:

```
Volume = 113.0976
Volume = 50.2656
Volume = 56.5488
Volume = 113.0976
```

Stack Frames

So far, you know that local variables and parameters are kept on the stack. Let's look at that organization a little further.

When a method is called, memory is allocated at the top of the stack to hold a number of data items associated with the method. This chunk of memory is called the *stack frame* for the method.

- The stack frame contains memory to hold the following:

  — The return address—that is, where to resume execution when the method exits

  — Those parameters that allocate memory—that is, the value parameters of the method, and the parameter array if there is one

  — Various other administrative data items relevant to the method call

- When a method is called, its entire stack frame is pushed onto the stack.

- When the method exits, its entire stack frame is popped from the stack. Popping a stack frame is sometimes called *unwinding* the stack.

For example, the following code declares three methods. Main calls MethodA, which calls MethodB, creating three stack frames. As the methods exit, the stack unwinds.

```
class Program
{
   static void MethodA( int par1, int par2)
   {
      Console.WriteLine("Enter MethodA: {0}, {1}", par1, par2);
      MethodB(11, 18);                              // Call MethodB.
      Console.WriteLine("Exit  MethodA");
   }

   static void MethodB(int par1, int par2)
   {
      Console.WriteLine("Enter MethodB: {0}, {1}", par1, par2);
      Console.WriteLine("Exit  MethodB");
   }

   static void Main( )
   {
      Console.WriteLine("Enter Main");
      MethodA( 15, 30);                             // Call MethodA.
      Console.WriteLine("Exit  Main");
   }
}
```

This code produces the following output:

```
Enter Main
Enter MethodA: 15, 30
Enter MethodB: 11, 18
Exit  MethodB
Exit  MethodA
Exit  Main
```

Figure 5-14 shows how the stack frames of each method are placed on the stack when the method is called and how the stack is unwound as the methods complete.

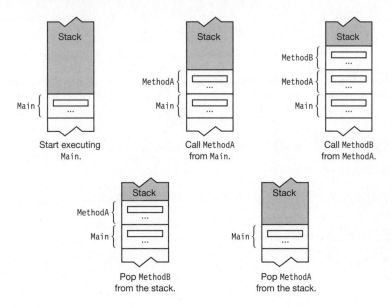

Figure 5-14. *Stack frames in a simple program*

Recursion

Besides calling other methods, a method can also call *itself*. This is called *recursion*.

Recursion can produce some very elegant code, such as the following method for computing the factorial of a number. Notice that inside the method, the method calls itself with an actual parameter of one less than its input parameter.

```
int Factorial(int inValue)
{
    if (inValue <= 1)
        return inValue;
    else
        return inValue * Factorial(inValue - 1);      // Call Factorial again.
                                 ↑
}                        Calls itself
```

The mechanics of a method calling itself are exactly the same as if it had called another, different method. A new stack frame is pushed onto the stack for each call to the method.

For example, in the following code, method Count calls itself with one less than its input parameter and then prints out its input parameter. As the recursion gets deeper, the stack gets larger.

```
class Program
{
    public void Count(int inVal)
    {
        if (inVal == 0)
            return;
        Count(inVal - 1);                 // Invoke this method again.
              ↑
          Calls itself
        Console.WriteLine("{0}", inVal);
    }

    static void Main()
    {
        Program pr = new Program();
        pr.Count(3);
    }
}
```

This code produces the following output:

```
1
2
3
```

Figure 5-15 illustrates the code. Notice that with an input value of 3, there are four different, independent stack frames for method Count. Each has its own value for input parameter inVal.

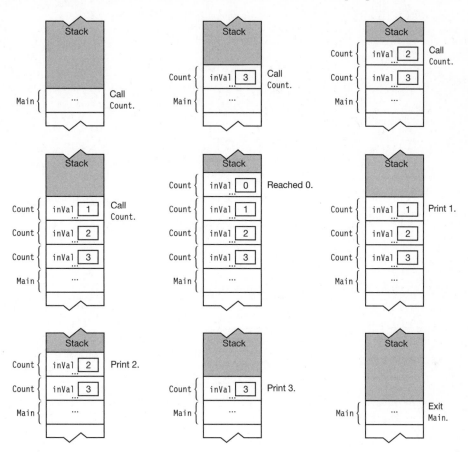

Figure 5-15. *Example of recursion*

CHAPTER 6

■ ■ ■

More About Classes

Class Members

The previous two chapters covered two of the nine types of class members: fields and methods. In this chapter, I'll introduce more types of class members, and explain their features.

Table 6-1 shows a list of the class member types. Those that have already been introduced are marked with diamonds. Those that are covered in this chapter are marked with a check. Those that will be covered later in the text are marked with empty check boxes.

Table 6-1. *Types of Class Members*

Data Members (Store Data)	Function Members (Execute Code)	
♦ Fields	♦ Methods	✓ Operators
✓ Constants	✓ Properties	✓ Indexers
	✓ Constructors	❑ Events
	✓ Destructors	

Order of Member Modifiers

Previously, you saw that the declarations of fields and methods can include modifiers such as `public` and `private`. In this chapter, I'll discuss a number of additional modifiers. Since many of these modifiers can be used together, the question that arises is, what order do they need to be in?

Class member declaration statements consist of the following: the core declaration, an optional set of *modifiers*, and an optional set of *attributes*. The syntax used to describe this structure is the following. The square brackets indicate that the enclosed set of components is optional.

```
[ attributes ] [ modifiers ]  CoreDeclaration
```

The optional components are the following:

- *Modifiers*

  — If there are any modifiers, they must be placed before the core declaration.

  — If there are multiple modifiers, they can be in an order.

- *Attributes*

  — If there are any attributes, they must be placed before the modifiers and core declaration.

  — If there are multiple attributes, they can be in any order.

So far, I've explained only two modifiers: `public` and `private`, and I'll cover attributes in Chapter 24.

For example, public and static are both modifiers that can be used together to modify certain declarations. Since they're both modifiers, they can be placed in either order. The following two lines are semantically equivalent:

```
public static int MaxVal;

static public int MaxVal;
```

Figure 6-1 shows the order of the components as applied to the member types shown so far: fields and methods. Notice that the type of the field and the return type of the method are not modifiers—they're part of the core declaration.

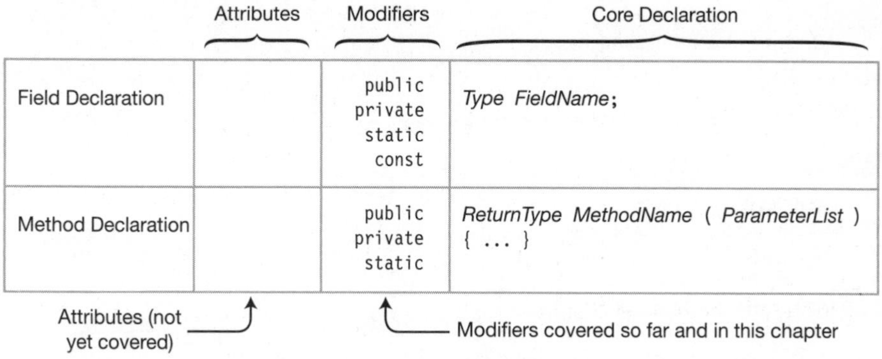

	Attributes	Modifiers	Core Declaration
Field Declaration		public private static const	*Type FieldName*;
Method Declaration		public private static	*ReturnType MethodName (ParameterList)* { ... }

Attributes (not yet covered)

Modifiers covered so far and in this chapter

Figure 6-1. *The order of attributes, modifiers, and core declarations*

Instance Class Members

Class members can be associated with an instance of the class or with the class as a whole. By default, members are associated with an instance. You can think of each instance of a class as having its own copy of each class member. These members are called *instance members*.

Changes to the value of one instance field do not affect the values of the members in any other instance. So far, the fields and methods you've seen have all been instance fields and instance methods.

For example, the following code declares a class D with a single integer field Mem1. Main creates two instances of the class. Each instance has its own copy of field Mem1. Changing the value of one instance's copy of the field doesn't affect the value of the other instance's copy. Figure 6-2 shows the two instances of class D.

```
class D
{
    public int Mem1;
}

class Program
{
    static void Main()
    {
        D d1 = new D();
        D d2 = new D();
        d1.Mem1 = 10; d2.Mem1 = 28;

        Console.WriteLine("d1 = {0}, d2 = {1}", d1.Mem1, d2.Mem1);
    }
}
```

This code produces the following output:

```
d1 = 10, d2 = 28
```

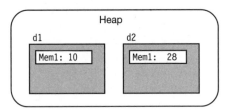

Figure 6-2. *Each instance of class D has its own copy of field Mem1.*

Static Fields

Besides instance fields, classes can have what are called *static fields*.

- A static field is *shared* by *all the instances of the class*, and all the instances access the same memory location. Hence, if the value of the memory location is changed by one instance, the change is visible to all the instances.

- Use the `static` modifier to declare a field static, as follows:

```
class D
{
   int Mem1;                    // Instance field
   static int Mem2;             // Static field
        ↑
}  Keyword
```

For example, the code on the left in Figure 6-3 declares class D with static field Mem2 and instance field Mem1. Main defines two instances of class D. The figure shows that static field Mem2 is stored separately from the storage of any of the instances. The gray fields inside the instances represent the fact that, from inside an instance method, the syntax to access or update the static field is the same as for any other member field.

- Because Mem2 is static, both instances of class D share a single Mem2 field. If Mem2 is changed, that change is seen from both.

- Member Mem1 is not declared `static`, so each instance has its own distinct copy.

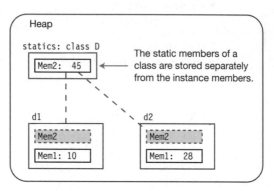

Static field Mem2 is shared by all the instances of class D, whereas each instance has its own copy of instance field Mem1.

Figure 6-3. *Static and instance data members*

Accessing Static Members from Outside the Class

In the previous chapter, you saw that dot-syntax notation is used to access instance members from outside the class. Dot-syntax notation consists of listing the instance name, followed by a dot, followed by the member name.

Static members, like instance members, are also accessed from outside the class using dot-syntax notation. But since there is no instance, you must use the *class name*, as shown here:

```
Class name
  ↓
  D.Mem2 = 5;              // Accessing the static class member
  ↑
 Member name
```

Example of a Static Field

The following code expands the preceding class D by adding two methods:

- One method sets the values of the two data members.

- The other method displays the values of the two data members.

```
class D {
    int        Mem1;
    static int Mem2;

    public void SetVars(int v1, int v2) // Set the values
    { Mem1 = v1; Mem2 = v2; }
                       ↑ Access as if it were an instance field

    public void Display( string str )
    { Console.WriteLine("{0}: Mem1= {1}, Mem2= {2}", str, Mem1, Mem2); }
}                                                              ↑
                                         Access as if it were an instance field
class Program {
    static void Main()
    {
        D d1 = new D(), d2 = new D();   // Create two instances.

        d1.SetVars(2, 4);               // Set d1's values.
        d1.Display("d1");

        d2.SetVars(15, 17);             // Set d2's values.
        d2.Display("d2");

        d1.Display("d1");       // Display d1 again and notice that the
    }                          // value of static member Mem2 has changed!
}
```

This code produces the following output:

```
d1: Mem1= 2, Mem2= 4
d2: Mem1= 15, Mem2= 17
d1: Mem1= 2, Mem2= 17
```

Lifetimes of Static Members

The lifetimes for static members are different from those of instance members.

- As you saw previously, instance members come into existence when the instance is created and go out of existence when the instance is destroyed.

- Static members, however, exist and are accessible *even if there are no instances* of the class.

Figure 6-4 illustrates a class D, with a static field, Mem2. Even though Main doesn't define any instances of the class, it assigns the value 5 to the static field and prints it out with no problem.

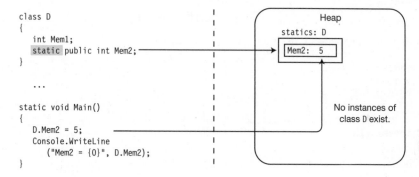

Figure 6-4. *Static fields with no class instances can still be assigned to and read from, because the field is associated with the class, and not an instance.*

The code in Figure 6-4 produces the following output:

```
Mem2 = 5
```

■ **Note** Static members exist even if there are no instances of the class. If a static field has an initializer, the field is initialized before the use of any of the class's static fields but not necessarily at the beginning of program execution.

Static Function Members

Besides static fields, there are also static function members.

- Static function members, like static fields, are independent of any class instance. Even if there are no instances of a class, you can still call a static method.

- Static function members cannot access instance members. They can, however, access other static members.

For example, the following class contains a static field and a static method. Notice that the body of the static method accesses the static field.

```
class X
{
    static public int A;                          // Static field
    static public void PrintValA()                // Static method
    {
        Console.WriteLine("Value of A: {0}", A);
    }                                      ↑
}                                   Accessing the static field
```

The following code uses class X, defined in the preceding code:

```
class Program
{
    static void Main()
    {
        X.A = 10;              // Use dot-syntax notation
        X.PrintValA();         // Use dot-syntax notation
    } ↑
}   Class name
```

This code produces the following output:

```
Value of A: 10
```

Figure 6-5 illustrates the preceding code.

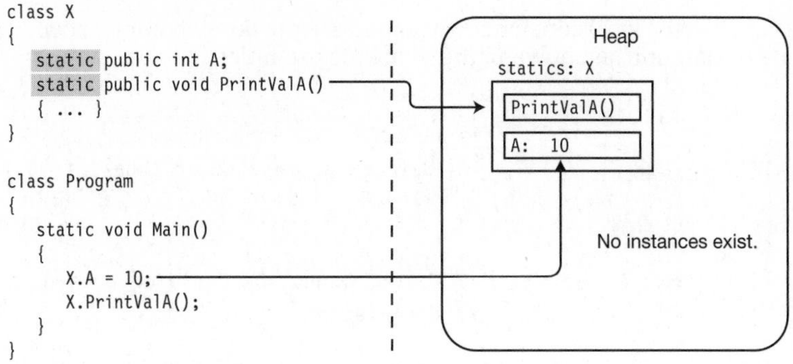
class X
{
static public int A;
static public void PrintValA()
{ ... }
}
class Program
{
static void Main()
{
X.A = 10;
X.PrintValA();
}
}
Heap
statics: X
PrintValA()
A: 10
No instances exist.

Figure 6-5. *Static methods of a class can be called even if there are no instances of the class.*

Other Static Class Member Types

The types of class members that can be declared `static` are shown checked in Table 6-2. The other member types cannot be declared `static`.

Table 6-2. *Class Member Types That Can Be Declared Static*

Data Members (Store Data)	Function Members (Execute Code)
✓ Fields	✓ Methods
Constants	✓ Properties
	✓ Constructors
	✓ Operators
	Indexers
	✓ Events

Member Constants

Member constants are like the local constants covered in the previous chapter, except that they're declared in the class declaration, as shown in the following example:

```
class MyClass
{
    const int IntVal = 100;          // Defines a constant of type int
         ↑            ↑              // with a value of 100.
}        Type        Initializer

const double PI = 3.1416;            // Error: cannot be declared outside a type
                                     // declaration
```

Like local constants, the value used to initialize a member constant must be computable at compile time and is usually one of the predefined simple types or an expression composed of them.

```
class MyClass
{
    const int IntVal1 = 100;
    const int IntVal2 = 2 * IntVal1;  // Fine, since the value of IntVal1
}                                     // was set in the previous line.
```

Like local constants, you cannot assign to a member constant after its declaration.

```
class MyClass
{
    const int IntVal;                 // Error: initialization is required.
    IntVal = 100;                     // Error: assignment is not allowed.
}
```

■ **Note** Unlike C and C++, in C# there are no global constants. Every constant must be declared within a type.

Constants Are Like Statics

Member constants, however, are more interesting than local constants, in that they act like static values. They're "visible" to every instance of the class, and they're available even if there are no instances of the class.

For example, the following code declares class X with constant field PI. Main doesn't create any instances of X, and yet it can use field PI and print its value.

```
class X
{
   public const double PI = 3.1416;
}

class Program
{
   static void Main()
   {
      Console.WriteLine("pi = {0}", X.PI);    // Use static field PI
   }
}
```

This code produces the following output:

```
pi = 3.1416
```

Unlike actual statics, however, constants do not have their own storage locations and are substituted in by the compiler at compile time in a manner similar to #define values in C and C++. This is shown in Figure 6-6, which illustrates the preceding code. Hence, although a constant member acts like a static, you cannot declare a constant as static.

```
static const double PI = 3.14;

Error: can't declare a constant as static
```

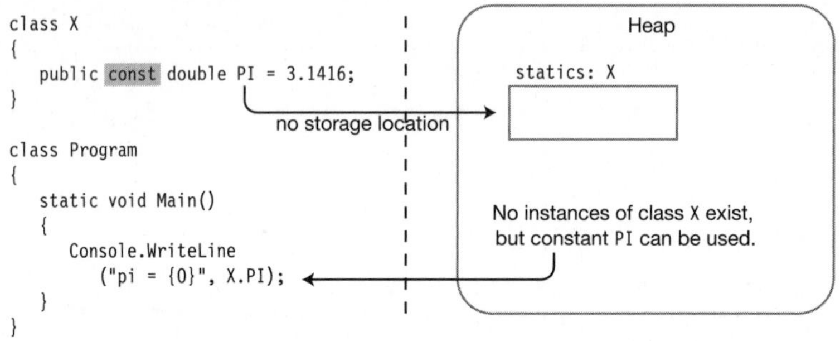

Figure 6-6. *Constant fields act like static fields but do not have a storage location in memory.*

Properties

A property is a member that represents an item of data in a class or class instance. Using a property appears very much like writing to, or reading from, a field. The syntax is the same.

For example, the following code shows the use of a class called `MyClass` that has both a public field and a public property. From their usage, you cannot tell them apart.

```
MyClass mc = new MyClass();

mc.MyField    = 5;                          // Assigning to a field
mc.MyProperty = 10;                         // Assigning to a property

WriteLine("{0} {1}", mc.MyField, mc.MyProperty); // Read field and property
```

A property, like a field, has the following characteristics:

- It is a named class member.

- It has a type.

- It can be assigned to and read from.

Unlike a field, however, a property is a function member.

- It does not necessarily allocate memory for data storage.

- It executes code.

A *property* is a named set of two matching methods called *accessors*.

- The `set` accessor is used for assigning a value to the property.

- The `get` accessor is used for retrieving a value from the property.

Figure 6-7 shows the representation of a property. The code on the left shows the syntax of declaring a property named `MyValue`, of type `int`. The image on the right shows how properties will be represented visually in this text. Notice that the accessors are shown sticking out the back, because, as you will soon see, they're not directly callable.

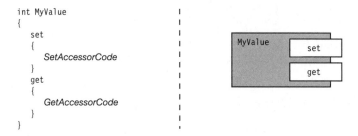

Figure 6-7. *An example property of type int, named MyValue*

Property Declarations and Accessors

The set and get accessors have predefined syntax and semantics. You can think of the set accessor as a method with a single parameter that "sets" the value of the property. The get accessor has no parameters and returns the value the property.

- The set accessor always has the following:

  — A single, implicit value parameter named value, of the same type as the property

  — A return type of void

- The get accessor always has the following:

  — No parameters

  — A return type of the same type as the property

Figure 6-8 shows the structure of a property declaration. Notice in the figure that neither accessor declaration has *explicit* parameter or return type declarations. They don't need them, because they're *implicit* in the type of the property.

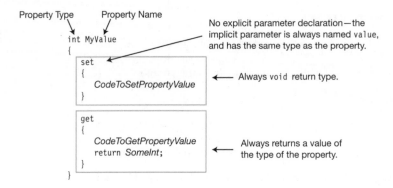

Figure 6-8. *The syntax and structure of a property declaration*

The implicit parameter value in the set accessor is a normal value parameter. Like other value parameters, you can use it to send data into a method body—or in this case, the accessor block. Once inside the block, you can use value like a normal variable, including assigning values to it.

Other important points about accessors are the following:

- All paths through the implementation of a get accessor *must* include a return statement that returns a value of the property type.

- The set and get accessors can be declared in either order, and no methods other than the two accessors are allowed on a property.

A Property Example

The following code shows an example of the declaration of a class called C1 that contains a property named MyValue.

- Notice that the property itself doesn't have any storage. Instead, the accessors determine what should be done with data sent in and what data should be sent out. In this case, the property uses a field called TheRealValue for storage.

- The set accessor takes its input parameter, value, and assigns that value to field TheRealValue.

- The get accessor just returns the value of field TheRealValue.

Figure 6-9 illustrates the code.

```
class C1
{
   private int TheRealValue;              // Field: memory allocated

   public int MyValue                     // Property: no memory allocated
   {
      set
      {
         TheRealValue = value;
      }

      get
      {
         return TheRealValue;
      }
   }
}
```

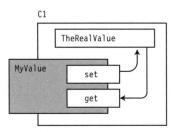

Figure 6-9. *Property accessors often use fields for storage*

Using a Property

As you saw previously, you write to and read from a property in the same way you access a field. The accessors are called implicitly.

- To write to a property, use the property's name on the left side of an assignment statement.

- To read from a property, use the property's name in an expression.

For example, the following code contains an outline of the declaration of a property named MyValue. You write to and read from the property using just the property name, as if it were a field name.

```
int MyValue              // Property declaration
{
    set{ ... }
    get{ ... }
}
...
Property name
      ↓
MyValue = 5;             // Assignment: the set method is implicitly called
z = MyValue;            // Expression: the get method is implicitly called
           ↑
    Property name
```

The appropriate accessor is called implicitly depending on whether you are writing to or reading from the property. You cannot explicitly call the accessors. Attempting to do so produces a compile error.

```
y = MyValue.get();      // Error! Can't explicitly call get accessor.
MyValue.set(5);         // Error! Can't explicitly call set accessor.
```

Properties and Associated Fields

A property is often associated with a field, as shown in the previous two sections. A common practice is to encapsulate a field in a class by declaring it private and declaring a public property to give controlled access to the field from outside the class. The field associated with a property is called the *backing field* or *backing store*.

For example, the following code uses the public property MyValue to give controlled access to private field TheRealValue:

```
class C1
{
   private int TheRealValue = 10;    // Backing Field: memory allocated
   public  int MyValue               // Property: no memory allocated
   {
      set{ TheRealValue = value; }   // Sets the value of field TheRealValue
      get{ return TheRealValue; }    // Gets the value of the field
   }
}

class Program
{
   static void Main()
   {
                                Read from the property as if it were a field.
                                          ↓
      C1 c = new C1();
      Console.WriteLine("MyValue:  {0}", c.MyValue);

      c.MyValue = 20;        ←  Use assignment to set the value of a property.
      Console.WriteLine("MyValue:  {0}", c.MyValue);
   }
}
```

There are several conventions for naming properties and their backing fields. One convention is to use the same string for both names but use camel casing (in which the first letter is lowercase) for the field and Pascal casing for the property. Although this violates the general rule that it is bad practice to have different identifiers that differ only in casing, it has the advantage of tying the two identifiers together in a meaningful way.

Another convention is to use Pascal casing for the property, and then for the field, use the camel case version of the same identifier, with an underscore in front.

The following code shows both conventions:

```
private int firstField;                  // Camel casing
public  int FirstField                   // Pascal casing
{
    get { return firstField; }
    set { firstField = value; }
}

private int _secondField;                // Underscore and camel casing
public  int SecondField
{
    get { return _secondField; }
    set { _secondField = value; }
}
```

Performing Other Calculations

Property accessors are not limited to just passing values back and forth from an associated backing field; the get and set accessors can perform any, or no, computations. The only action *required* is that the get accessor return a value of the property type.

For instance, the following example shows a valid (but probably useless) property that just returns the value 5 when its get accessor is called. When the set accessor is called, it doesn't do anything. The value of implicit parameter value is ignored.

```
public int Useless
{
    set{  /* I'm not setting anything.       */ }
    get{  /* I'm just returning the value 5.  */
        return 5;
    }
}
```

The following code shows a more realistic and useful property, where the set accessor performs filtering before setting the associated field. The set accessor sets field TheRealValue to the input value—unless the input value is greater than 100. In that case, it sets TheRealValue to 100.

```
int TheRealValue = 10;                     // The field
int MyValue                                // The property
{
    set                                    // Sets the value of the field
    {
        TheRealValue = value > 100         // but makes sure it's not > 100
                          ? 100
                          : value;
    }
    get                                    // Gets the value of the field
    {
        return TheRealValue;
    }
}
```

■ **Note** In the preceding code sample, the syntax between the equals sign and the end of the statement might look somewhat strange. That expression uses the *conditional operator*, which will be covered in greater detail in Chapter 8. The conditional operator is a ternary operator that evaluates the expression in front of the question mark, and if the expression evaluates to true, it returns the expression after the question mark. Otherwise, it returns the expression after the colon.

Read-Only and Write-Only Properties

You can leave one or the other (but not both) of a property's accessors undefined by omitting its declaration.

- A property with only a get accessor is called a *read-only* property. A read-only property is a safe way of passing an item of data out from a class or class instance without allowing too much access.

- A property with only a set accessor is called a *write-only* property. A write-only property is a safe way of passing an item of data from outside the class to the class without allowing too much access.

- At least one of the two accessors must be defined, or the compiler will produce an error message.

Figure 6-10 illustrates read-only and write-only properties.

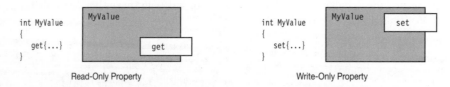

Read-Only Property   Write-Only Property

Figure 6-10. *A property can have one or the other of its accessors undefined.*

An Example of a Computed, Read-Only Property

In most of the examples so far, the property has been associated with a field, and the get and set accessors have referenced that field. However, a property does not have to be associated with a field. In the following example, the get accessor *computes* the return value.

In the following example code, class RightTriangle represents, not surprisingly, a right triangle.

- It has two public fields that represent the lengths of the two right-angle sides of the triangle. These fields can be written to and read from.

- The third side is represented by property Hypotenuse, which is a read-only property whose return value is based on the lengths of the other two sides. It isn't stored in a field. Instead, it computes the correct value, on demand, for the current values of A and B.

Figure 6-11 illustrates read-only property Hypotenuse.

```
class RightTriangle
{
   public double A = 3;
   public double B = 4;
   public double Hypotenuse                      // Read-only property
   {
      get{ return Math.Sqrt((A*A)+(B*B)); }      // Calculate return value
   }
}

class Program
{
   static void Main()
   {
      RightTriangle c = new RightTriangle();
      Console.WriteLine("Hypotenuse:  {0}", c.Hypotenuse);
   }
}
```

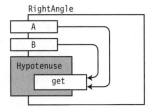

Figure 6-11. *Read-only property Hypotenuse*

Example of Properties and Databases

Another example in which a property is not associated with a field is when the property is associated with a value in a database. In that case, the get accessor makes the appropriate database calls to get the value from the database. The set accessor makes the corresponding calls to the database to set the new value in the database.

For example, the following property is associated with a particular value in some database. The code assumes that there are two other methods in the class to handle the details of the database transactions:

- SetValueInDatabase takes an integer parameter and uses it to set a particular field in a record in some database.

- GetValueFromDatabase retrieves and returns a particular integer field value from a particular record in some database.

```
int MyDatabaseValue
{
    set                         // Sets integer value in the database
    {
        SetValueInDatabase(value);
    }
    get                         // Gets integer value from the database
    {
        return GetValueFromDatabase();
    }
}
```

Properties vs. Public Fields

As a matter of preferred coding practice, properties are preferred over public fields for several reasons:

- Since properties are functional members as opposed to data members, they allow you to process the input and output, which you can't do with public fields.

- The semantics of a compiled variable and a compiled property are different.

The second point has implications when you release an assembly that is accessed by other code. For example, sometimes there's the temptation is to use a public field rather than a property, with the reasoning that if you ever need to add processing to the data held in the field, you can always change it to a property at a later time. This is true, but if you make that change, you will also have to recompile any other assemblies *accessing* that field, because the compiled semantics of fields and properties are different. On the other hand, if you had implemented it as a property and just changed its *implementation*, you wouldn't need to recompile the other assemblies accessing it.

Automatically Implemented Properties

Because properties are so often associated with backing fields, C# 3.0 added *automatically implemented properties*, or *auto-implemented properties*, which allow you to just declare the property, without declaring a backing field. The compiler creates a hidden backing field for you and automatically hooks up the get and set accessors to it.

The important points about auto-implemented properties are the following:

- You do not declare the backing field—the compiler allocates the storage for you, based on the type of the property.

- You cannot supply the bodies of the accessors—they must be declared simply as semicolons. The get acts as a simple read of the memory, and the set as a simple write.

- You cannot access the backing field other than through the accessors. Since you can't access it any other way, it wouldn't make sense to have read-only or write-only auto-implemented properties—so they're not allowed.

The following code shows an example of an automatically implemented property:

```
class C1
{                        ← No declared backing field
    public int MyValue                        // Allocates memory
    {
        set; get;
    }          ↑    ↑
}  The bodies of the accessors are declared as semicolons.

class Program
{
    static void Main()
    {                        Use auto-implemented properties as regular properties.
        C1 c = new C1();                    ↓
        Console.WriteLine("MyValue:  {0}", c.MyValue);

        c.MyValue = 20;
        Console.WriteLine("MyValue:  {0}", c.MyValue);
    }
}
```

This code produces the following output:

```
MyValue:  0
MyValue:  20
```

Besides being convenient, auto-implemented properties allow you to easily insert a property where you might be tempted to declare a public field.

Static Properties

Properties can also be declared static. Accessors of static properties, like all static members

- Cannot access instance members of a class—although they can be accessed by them

- Exist regardless of whether there are instances of the class

- Must be referenced by the class name, rather than an instance name, when being accessed from outside the class

For example, the following code shows a class with an auto-implemented static property called MyValue. In the first three lines of Main, the property is accessed, even though there are no instances of the class. The last line of Main calls an instance method that accesses the property from *inside* the class.

```
class Trivial
{
    public static int MyValue { get;  set; }

    public void PrintValue()                   Accessed from inside the class
    {                                                      ↓
        Console.WriteLine("Value from inside: {0}", MyValue);
    }
}

class Program
{
    static void Main()                         Accessed from outside the class
    {                                                    ↓
        Console.WriteLine("Init Value: {0}", Trivial.MyValue);
        Trivial.MyValue = 10;          ← Accessed from outside the class
        Console.WriteLine("New Value : {0}", Trivial.MyValue);

        Trivial tr = new Trivial();
        tr.PrintValue();
    }
}
```

```
Init Value: 0
New Value : 10
Value from inside: 10
```

Instance Constructors

An *instance constructor* is a special method that is executed whenever a new instance of a class is created.

- A constructor is used to initialize the state of the class instance.

- If you want to be able to create instances of your class from outside the class, you need to declare the constructor public.

Figure 6-12 shows the syntax of a constructor. A constructor looks like the other methods in a class declaration, with the following exceptions:

- The name of the constructor is the same as the name of the class.

- A constructor cannot have a return value.

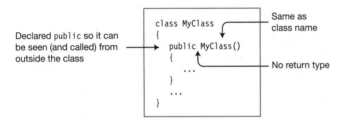

Figure 6-12. *Constructor declaration*

For example, the following class uses its constructor to initialize its fields. In this case, it has a field called TimeOfInstantiation that is initialized with the current date and time.

```
class MyClass
{
    DateTime TimeOfInstantiation;                   // Field
    ...
    public MyClass()                                // Constructor
    {
        TimeOfInstantiation = DateTime.Now;         // Initialize field
    }
    ...
}
```

■ **Note** Having finished the section on static properties, take a closer look at the line that initializes TimeOfInstantiation. The DateTime class is from the BCL, and Now is a *static property* of the DateTime class. The Now property creates a new instance of the DateTime class, initializes it with the current date and time from the system clock, and returns a reference to the new DateTime instance.

Constructors with Parameters

Constructors are like other methods in the following ways:

- A constructor can have parameters. The syntax for the parameters is exactly the same as for other methods.

- A constructor can be overloaded.

When you use an object-creation expression to create a new instance of a class, you use the new operator followed by one of the class's constructors. The new operator uses that constructor to create the instance of the class.

For example, in the following code, Class1 has three constructors: one that takes no parameters, one that takes an int, and another that takes a string. Main creates an instance using each one.

```
class Class1
{
   int Id;
   string Name;

   public Class1()          { Id=28;    Name="Nemo"; }    // Constructor 0
   public Class1(int val)   { Id=val;   Name="Nemo"; }    // Constructor 1
   public Class1(String name) { Name=name;          }    // Constructor 2

   public void SoundOff()
   { Console.WriteLine("Name {0},    Id {1}", Name, Id); }
}

class Program
{
   static void Main()
   {
      Class1 a = new Class1(),                   // Call constructor 0.
             b = new Class1(7),                  // Call constructor 1.
             c = new Class1("Bill");             // Call constructor 2.

      a.SoundOff();
      b.SoundOff();
      c.SoundOff();
   }
}
```

This code produces the following output:

```
Name Nemo,    Id 28
Name Nemo,    Id 7
Name Bill,    Id 0
```

Default Constructors

If no instance constructor is explicitly supplied in the class declaration, then the compiler supplies an implicit, default constructor, which has the following characteristics:

- It takes no parameters.

- It has an empty body.

If you declare any constructors at all for a class, then the compiler does not define a default constructor for the class.

For example, Class2 declares two constructors.

- Because there is at least one explicitly defined constructor, the compiler does not create any additional constructors.

- In Main, there is an attempt to create a new instance using a constructor with no parameters. Since there *is* no constructor with zero parameters, the compiler produces an error message.

```
class Class2
{
   public Class2(int Value)    { ... }    // Constructor 0
   public Class2(String Value) { ... }    // Constructor 1
}

class Program
{
   static void Main()
   {
      Class2 a = new Class2();   // Error! No constructor with 0 parameters
      ...
   }
}
```

Static Constructors

Constructors can also be declared static. While an instance constructor initializes each new instance of a class, a static constructor initializes items at the class level. Generally, static constructors initialize the static fields of the class.

- Class-level items need to be initialized:
  - Before any static member is referenced
  - Before any instance of the class is created

- Static constructors are like instance constructors in the following ways:
  - The name of the static constructor must be the same as the name of the class.
  - The constructor cannot return a value.

- Static constructors are unlike instance constructors in the following ways:
  - Static constructors use the static keyword in the declaration.
  - There can only be a single static constructor for a class, and it cannot have parameters.
  - Static constructors cannot have accessibility modifiers.

The following is an example of a static constructor. Notice that its form is the same as that of an instance constructor, but with the addition of the static keyword.

```
class Class1
{
   static Class1 ()
   {
      ...               // Do all the static initializations.
   }
   ...
```

Other important things you should know about static constructors are the following:

- A class can have both a static constructor and instance constructors.

- Like static methods, a static constructor cannot access instance members of its class and cannot use the this accessor, which we'll cover shortly.

- You cannot explicitly call static constructors from your program. They're called automatically by the system, at some time:
  - Before any instance of the class is created
  - Before any static member of the class is referenced

Example of a Static Constructor

The following code uses a static constructor to initialize a private static field named RandomKey, of type Random. Random is a class provided by the BCL to produce random numbers. It is in the System namespace.

```
class RandomNumberClass
{
    private static Random RandomKey;          // Private static field

    static RandomNumberClass()                // Static constructor
    {
        RandomKey = new Random();             // Initialize RandomKey
    }

    public int GetRandomNumber()
    {
        return RandomKey.Next();
    }
}

class Program
{
    static void Main()
    {
        RandomNumberClass a = new RandomNumberClass();
        RandomNumberClass b = new RandomNumberClass();

        Console.WriteLine("Next Random #: {0}", a.GetRandomNumber());
        Console.WriteLine("Next Random #: {0}", b.GetRandomNumber());
    }
}
```

One execution of this code produced the following output:

```
Next Random #: 47857058
Next Random #: 1124842041
```

Accessibility of Constructors

You can assign access modifiers to instance constructors just as you can to other members. Notice that in the examples, the constructors have been declared public so that you can create instances from outside the class.

You can also create private constructors, which cannot be called from outside the class, but can be used from within the class, as you'll see in the next chapter.

Object Initializers

So far in the text, you've seen that an object-creation expression consists of the keyword new followed by a class constructor and its parameter list. An object initializer extends that syntax by placing a list of member initializations at the end of the expression. This allows you to set the values of fields and properties when creating a new instance of an object.

The syntax has two forms, as shown here. One form includes the constructor's argument list, and the other doesn't. Notice that the first form doesn't even use the parentheses that would enclose the argument list.

```
                                        Object initializer
                                              ↓
new TypeName           { FieldOrProp = InitExpr, FieldOrProp = InitExpr, ...}
new TypeName(ArgList)  { FieldOrProp = InitExpr, FieldOrProp = InitExpr, ...}
                              ↑                        ↑
                         Member initializer       Member initializer
```

For example, for a class named Point with two public integer fields X and Y, you could use the following expression to create a new object:

```
new Point { X = 5, Y = 6 };
             ↑       ↑
           Init X   Init Y
```

Important things to know about object initializers are the following:

- The fields and properties being initialized must be accessible to the code creating the object. For example, in the previous code, X and Y must be public.

- The initialization occurs *after* the constructor has finished execution, so the values might have been set in the constructor and then reset to the same or different value in the object initialize.

The following code shows an example of using an object initializer. In Main, pt1 calls just the constructor, which sets the values of its two fields. For pt2, however, the constructor sets the fields' values to 1 and 2, and the initializer changes them to 5 and 6.

```
public class Point
{
    public int X = 1;
    public int Y = 2;
}

class Program
{
    static void Main( )
    {                                    Object initializer
        Point pt1 = new Point();_____↓_____
        Point pt2 = new Point    { X = 5, Y = 6 };
        Console.WriteLine("pt1: {0}, {1}", pt1.X, pt1.Y);
        Console.WriteLine("pt2: {0}, {1}", pt2.X, pt2.Y);
    }
}
```

This code produces the following output:

```
pt1: 1, 2
pt2: 5, 6
```

Destructors

Destructors perform actions required to clean up or release unmanaged resources after an instance of a class is no longer referenced. The important things to know about destructors are the following:

- You can have only a single destructor per class.

- A destructor cannot have parameters.

- A destructor cannot have accessibility modifiers.

- A destructor has the same name as the class but is preceded by a tilde character (pronounced *TIL-duh*).

- A destructor only acts on *instances* of classes; hence, *there are no static destructors.*

- *You cannot call a destructor explicitly in your code.* Instead, it is called during the garbage collection process, when the garbage collector analyzes your code and determines that there is no longer any path through your code that references the object.

For example, the following code illustrates the syntax for a destructor of a class called `Class1`:

```
Class1
{
    ~Class1()                    // The destructor
    {
        CleanupCode
    }
    ...
}
```

Some important guidelines for using destructors are the following:

- Don't implement a destructor if you don't need one. They can incur performance costs.

- A destructor should only release external resources that the object owns.

- A destructor should not access other objects because you can't assume that those objects haven't already been destroyed.

■ **Note** Before the release of version 3.0 of C#, destructors were sometimes called *finalizers*. You might sometimes still run across this term in the literature and in the .NET API method names.

Calling the Destructor

Unlike a C++ destructor, a C# destructor is not called immediately when an instance goes out of scope. In fact, there is no way of knowing when the destructor will be called. Furthermore, as previously mentioned, you cannot explicitly call a destructor. If your code needs a destructor, you must provide it for the system, which will call it at some point before the object is removed from the managed heap.

If your code contains unmanaged resources that need to be released in a timely manner, you shouldn't leave that task for the destructor, since there is no guarantee that the destructor will run any time soon. Instead, you should adopt the standard pattern where your classes implement what is called the IDisposable interface. (I'll cover interfaces in Chapter 17.) This consists of encapsulating the cleanup code for these resources in a void, parameterless method, which you should call Dispose.

When you're done with the resources and want them released, you need to call Dispose. Notice that it is *you* who needs to call Dispose—not the destructor. The system won't call it for you automatically.

Some guidelines for your Dispose method are the following:

- Implement the code in Dispose in such a way that it is safe for the method to be called more than once. If it has already been called, then on any subsequent invocations it should not raise an exception or do any additional work. (Exceptions are covered in Chapter 11.)

- Write your Dispose method and destructor such that, if for some reason your code doesn't get to call Dispose, your destructor will call it and release the resources.

- Since Dispose is doing the cleanup rather than the destructor, it should call the GC.SuppressFinalize method, which tells the CLR not to call this object's destructor, because it has already been taken care of.

The following code describes the safe disposal process. First, the class needs to declare a Boolean disposed field to keep track of whether the cleanup has occurred. This is initialized to false when the object is created.

Inside the Dispose method, do the following:

- Check the flag to see whether the resources have already been released. If not, then do the following:

  — Call the Dispose methods on any managed resources that require it.

  — Release any unmanaged resources held by the object.

- Now that the disposal has occurred, set the disposed flag to true.

- Finally, call the garbage collector's SuppressFinalize method to tell the garbage collector not to call the class's destructor.

The process in the destructor is similar to but shorter than that in the Dispose method. Just check to see whether the object has already been cleaned up, and if not, then release the unmanaged resources. Notice that in this case you do not call the Dispose methods of any managed resources, because the garbage collector might have already deleted those objects.

```
class MyClass
{
   bool disposed = false;            // Flag indicating disposal status

   ////////////////////////////////////////////////////////
   public void Dispose()             // Public Dispose
   {
      if (disposed == false)         // Check the flag.
      {
         // Call Dispose on managed resources.
         ...

         // Release any unmanaged resources.
         ...
      }
      disposed = true;               // Set the flag to show disposal.
      GC.SuppressFinalize(this);     // Tell GC not to call Finalize.
   }

   ////////////////////////////////////////////////////////
   ~MyClass()                        // Destructor
   {
      if (disposed == false)         // Check the flag.
      {
         // Release any unmanaged resources.
         ...
      }
   }

   ...
}
```

The Standard Dispose Pattern

In the previous section, you saw that the destructor code is essentially a subset of the Dispose code. The standard pattern factors out most of the common code of these two methods into another method called Dispose, which I'll call the *factored Dispose*. It takes a single Boolean parameter that is used to indicate whether the method is being called from the public Dispose method (true) or from the destructor (false).

This standard dispose pattern is shown following and illustrated in Figure 6-13. I'll cover the protected and virtual modifiers in the next chapter.

```
class MyClass : IDisposable
{
   bool disposed = false;                          // Disposal status

   public void Dispose()
   {
      Dispose( true );                              Public Dispose
      GC.SuppressFinalize(this);
   }

   ~MyClass()
   {                                                Destructor
      Dispose(false);
   }

   protected virtual void Dispose(bool disposing)
   {
      if (disposed == false)
      {
         if (disposing == true)
         {
            // Dispose the managed resources.
            ...
         }                                          Factored Dispose

         // Dispose the unmanaged resources.
         ...
      }
      disposed = true;
   }
}
```

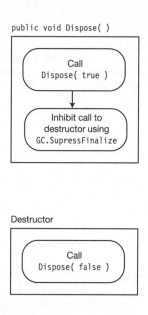

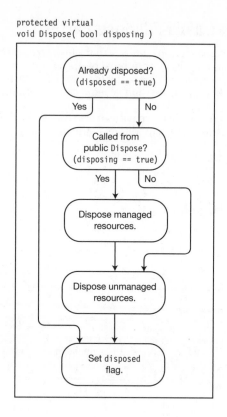

Figure 6-13. *The standard dispose pattern*

Comparing Constructors and Destructors

Table 6-3 provides a summary of when constructors and destructors are called.

Table 6-3. *Constructors and Destructors*

		When and How Often Called
Instance	Constructor	Called once on the creation of each new instance of the class.
	Destructor	Called for each instance of the class, at some point after the program flow can no longer access the instance.
Static	Constructor	Called only once—either before the first access of any static member of the class or before any instances of the class are created, whichever is first.
	Destructor	Does not exist—destructors work only on instances.

The readonly Modifier

A field can be declared with the readonly modifier. The effect is similar to declaring a field as const, in that once the value is set, it cannot be changed.

- While a const field can only be initialized in the field's declaration statement, a readonly field can have its value set in any of the following places:

  — The field declaration statement—like a const.

  — Any of the class constructors. If it's a static field, then it must be done in the static constructor.

- While the value of a const field must be determinable at compile time, the value of a readonly field can be determined at run time. This additional freedom allows you to set different values under different circumstances or in different constructors!

- Unlike a const, which always acts like a static, the following is true of a readonly field:

  — It can be either an instance field or a static field.

  — It has a storage location in memory.

For example, the following code declares a class called Shape, with two readonly fields.

- Field PI is initialized in its declaration.

- Field NumberOfSides is set to either 3 or 4, depending on which constructor is called.

```
class Shape
{   Keyword              Initialized
        ↓                    ↓
    readonly double PI = 3.1416;
    readonly int    NumberOfSides;
        ↑                ↑
      Keyword      Not initialized

    public Shape(double side1, double side2)                // Constructor
    {
        // Shape is a rectangle
        NumberOfSides = 4;
            ↑
        ... Set in constructor
    }

    public Shape(double side1, double side2, double side3)  // Constructor
    {
        // Shape is a triangle
        NumberOfSides = 3;
            ↑
        ... Set in constructor
    }
}
```

The this Keyword

The this keyword, used in a class, is a reference to the current instance. It can be used only in the *blocks* of the following class members:

- Instance constructors.

- Instance methods.

- Instance accessors of properties and indexers. (Indexers are covered in the next section.)

Clearly, since static members are not part of an instance, you cannot use the this keyword inside the code of any static function member. Rather, it is used for the following:

- To distinguish between class members and local variables or parameters

- As an actual parameter when calling a method

For example, the following code declares class MyClass, with an int field and a method that takes a single int parameter. The method compares the values of the parameter and the field and returns the greater value. The only complicating factor is that the names of the field and the formal parameter are the same: Var1. The two names are distinguished inside the method by using the this access keyword to reference the field.

```
class MyClass
{
   int Var1 = 10;
            ↑     Both are called "Var1"    ↓
   public int ReturnMaxSum(int Var1)
   {        Parameter      Field
                   ↓          ↓

      return Var1 > this.Var1
                ? Var1                    // Parameter
                : this.Var1;              // Field
   }
}

class Program
{
   static void Main()
   {
      MyClass mc = new MyClass();

      Console.WriteLine("Max: {0}", mc.ReturnMaxSum(30));
      Console.WriteLine("Max: {0}", mc.ReturnMaxSum(5));
   }
}
```

147

Indexers

Suppose you were to define class Employee, with three fields of type string (as shown in Figure 6-14). You could then access the fields using their names, as shown in the code in Main.

```
class Employee
{
   public string LastName;
   public string FirstName;
   public string CityOfBirth;
}

class Program
{
   static void Main()
   {
      Employee emp1 = new Employee();

      emp1.LastName = "Doe";                              Field Names
      emp1.FirstName = "Jane";
      emp1.CityOfBirth = "Dallas";
      Console.WriteLine("{0}", emp1.LastName);
      Console.WriteLine("{0}", emp1.FirstName);
      Console.WriteLine("{0}", emp1.CityOfBirth);
   }
}
```

Employee

| LastName: Doe |
| FirstName: Jane |
| CityOfBirth: Dallas |

Figure 6-14. *Simple class without indexers*

There are times, however, when it would be convenient to be able to access them with an index, as if the instance were an array of fields. This is exactly what *indexers* allow you to do. If you were to write an indexer for class Employee, method Main might look like the code in Figure 6-15. Notice that instead of using dot-syntax notation, indexers use *index notation*, which consists of an index between square brackets.

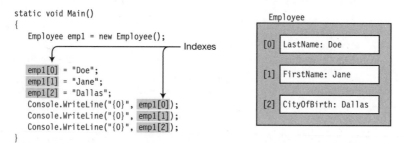

```
static void Main()
{
   Employee emp1 = new Employee();
                                                    Indexes
   emp1[0] = "Doe";
   emp1[1] = "Jane";
   emp1[2] = "Dallas";
   Console.WriteLine("{0}", emp1[0]);
   Console.WriteLine("{0}", emp1[1]);
   Console.WriteLine("{0}", emp1[2]);
}
```

Employee

[0]	LastName: Doe
[1]	FirstName: Jane
[2]	CityOfBirth: Dallas

Figure 6-15. *Using indexed fields*

What Is an Indexer?

An indexer is a pair of get and set accessors, similar to those of properties. Figure 6-16 shows the representation of an indexer for a class that can get and set values of type string.

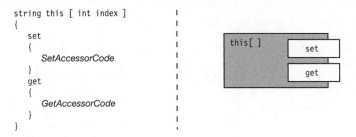

Figure 6-16. *Representations of an indexer*

Indexers and Properties

Indexers and properties are similar in many ways.

- Like a property, an indexer does not allocate memory for storage.

- Both indexers and properties are used primarily for giving access to *other* data members with which they're associated and for which they provide get and set access.

  — A *property* usually represents a *single* data member.

  — An *indexer* usually represents *multiple* data members.

■ **Note** You can think of an *indexer* as a *property* that gives get and set access to *multiple data members* of the class. You select which of the many possible data members by supplying an index, which itself can be of any type—not just numeric.

Some additional points you should know when working with indexers are the following:

- Like a property, an indexer can have either one or both of the accessors.

- Indexers are always instance members; hence, an indexer cannot be declared static.

- Like properties, the code implementing the get and set accessors does not have to be associated with any fields or properties. The code can do anything, or nothing, as long as the get accessor returns some value of the specified type.

Declaring an Indexer

The syntax for declaring an indexer is shown next. Notice the following about indexers:

- An indexer *does not have a name*. In place of the name is the keyword this.

- The parameter list is between *square* brackets.

- There must be at least one parameter declaration in the parameter list.

```
            Keyword      Parameter list
              ↓                ↓
ReturnType this [ Type param1, ... ]
{
    get      Square bracket      Square bracket
    {
        ...
    }
    set
    {
        ...
    }
}
```

Declaring an indexer is similar to declaring a property. Figure 6-17 shows the syntactic similarities and differences.

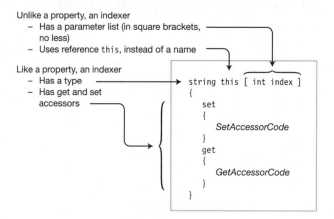

Figure 6-17. *Comparing an indexer declaration to a property declaration*

The Indexer set Accessor

When the indexer is the target of an assignment, the set accessor is called and receives two items of data, as follows:

- An implicit parameter, named value, which holds the data to be stored

- One or more index parameters that represent where it should be stored

```
emp[0] = "Doe";
      ↑       ↑
    Index    Value
  Parameter
```

Your code in the set accessor must examine the index parameters, determine where the data should be stored, and then store it.

Figure 6-18 shows the syntax and meaning of the set accessor. The left side of the figure shows the actual syntax of the accessor declaration. The right side shows the semantics of the accessor if it were written using the syntax of a normal method. The figure on the right shows that the set accessor has the following semantics:

- It has a void return type.

- It uses the same parameter list as that in the indexer declaration.

- It has an implicit value parameter named value, of the same type as the indexer.

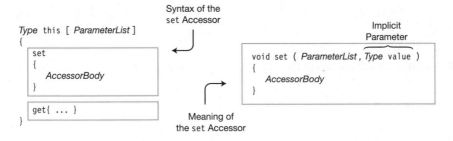

Figure 6-18. *The syntax and meaning of the set accessor declaration*

The Indexer get Accessor

When the indexer is used to retrieve a value, the get accessor is called with one or more index parameters. The index parameters represent which value to retrieve.

```
string s = emp[0];
              ↑
        Index parameter
```

The code in the get accessor body must examine the index parameters, determine which field they represent, and return the value of that field.

Figure 6-19 shows the syntax and meaning of the get accessor. The left side of the figure shows the actual syntax of the accessor declaration. The right side shows the semantics of the accessor if it were written using the syntax of a normal method. The semantics of the get accessor are as follows:

- It has the same parameter list as in the indexer declaration.

- It returns a value of the same type as the indexer.

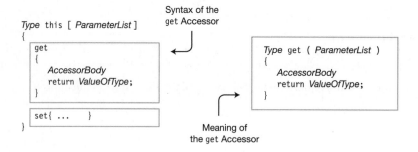

Figure 6-19. *The syntax and meaning of the get accessor declaration*

More About Indexers

As with properties, the get and set accessors cannot be called explicitly. Instead, the get accessor is called automatically when the indexer is used in an expression for a value. The set accessor is called automatically when the indexer is assigned a value with the assignment statement.

When an indexer is "called," the parameters are supplied between the square brackets.

```
  Index   Value
    ↓       ↓
 emp[0] = "Doe";                     // Calls set accessor
 string NewName = emp[0];            // Calls get accessor
                        ↑
                      Index
```

Declaring the Indexer for the Employee Example

The following code declares an indexer for the earlier example: class Employee.

- The indexer must read and write values of type string—so string must be declared as the indexer's type. It must be declared public so that it can be accessed from outside the class.

- The three fields in the example have been arbitrarily indexed as integers 0 through 2, so the formal parameter between the square brackets, named index in this case, must be of type int.

- In the body of the set accessor, the code determines which field the index refers to and assigns the value of implicit variable value to it. In the body of the get accessor, the code determines which field the index refers to and returns that field's value.

```
class Employee
{
    public string LastName;                  // Call this field 0.
    public string FirstName;                 // Call this field 1.
    public string CityOfBirth;               // Call this field 2.

    public string this[int index]           // Indexer declaration
    {
        set                                  // Set accessor declaration
        {
            switch (index)
            {
                case 0: LastName = value;
                    break;
                case 1: FirstName = value;
                    break;
                case 2: CityOfBirth = value;
                    break;

                default:                     // (Exceptions in Ch. 11)
                    throw new ArgumentOutOfRangeException("index");
            }
        }

        get                                  // Get accessor declaration
        {
            switch (index)
            {
                case 0: return LastName;
                case 1: return FirstName;
                case 2: return CityOfBirth;

                default:                     // (Exceptions in Ch. 11)
                    throw new ArgumentOutOfRangeException("index");
            }
        }
    }
}
```

Another Indexer Example

The following is an additional example that indexes the two int fields of class Class1:

```
class Class1
{
    int Temp0;                    // Private field
    int Temp1;                    // Private field
    public int this [ int index ] // The indexer
    {
        get
        {
            return ( 0 == index ) // Return value of either Temp0 or Temp1
                        ? Temp0
                        : Temp1;
        }

        set
        {
            if( 0 == index )
                Temp0 = value;    // Note the implicit variable "value".
            else
                Temp1 = value;    // Note the implicit variable "value".
        }
    }
}

class Example
{
    static void Main()
    {
        Class1 a = new Class1();

        Console.WriteLine("Values -- T0: {0},  T1: {1}", a[0], a[1]);
        a[0] = 15;
        a[1] = 20;
        Console.WriteLine("Values -- T0: {0}, T1: {1}", a[0], a[1]);
    }
}
```

This code produces the following output:

```
Values -- T0: 0,  T1: 0
Values -- T0: 15, T1: 20
```

Indexer Overloading

A class can have any number of indexers, as long as the parameter lists are different; it isn't sufficient for the indexer *type* to be different. This is called *indexer overloading*, because all the indexers have the same "name"—the this access reference.

For example, the following class has three indexers: two of type string and one of type int. Of the two indexers of type string, one has a single int parameter, and the other has two int parameters.

```
class MyClass
{
   public string this [ int index ]
   {
      get { ... }
      set { ... }
   }

   public string this [ int index1, int index2 ]
   {
      get { ... }
      set { ... }
   }

   public int this [ float index1 ]
   {
      get { ... }
      set { ... }
   }

   ...
}
```

■ **Note** Remember that the overloaded indexers of a class must have different parameter lists.

Access Modifiers on Accessors

In this chapter, you've seen two types of function members that have get and set accessors: properties and indexers. By default, both a member's accessors have the same access level as the member itself. That is, if a property has an access level of public, then both its accessors have that same access level. The same is true of indexers.

You can, however, assign different access levels to the two accessors. For example, the following code shows a common and important paradigm of declaring a private set accessor and a public get accessor. The get is public because the access level of the property is public.

Notice in this code that although the property can be read from outside the class, it can only be set from inside the class itself, in this case by the constructor. This is an important tool for encapsulation.

```
class Person
{                              ↓          ↓
   public string Name { get; private set; }
   public Person( string name )
   {
      Name = name;
   }
}

class Program
{
   static public void Main( )
   {
      Person p = new Person( "Capt. Ernest Evans" );
      Console.WriteLine( "Person's name is {0}", p.Name );
   }
}
```

There are several restrictions on the access modifiers of accessors. The most important ones are the following:

- An accessor can have an access modifier only if the member (property or indexer) has both a get accessor and a set accessor.

- Although both accessors must be present, only one of them can have an access modifier.

- The access modifier of the accessor must be *strictly more restrictive* than the access level of the member.

Figure 6-20 shows the hierarchy of access levels. The access level of an accessor must be strictly lower in the chart than the access level of the member.

For example, if a property has an access level of public, you can give any of the four lower access levels on the chart to one of the accessors. But if the property has an access level of protected, the only access modifier you can use on one of the accessors is private.

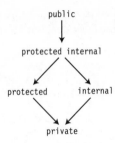

Figure 6-20. *Hierarchy of strictly restrictive accessor levels*

Partial Classes and Partial Types

The declaration of a class can be partitioned among several partial class declarations.

- Each of the partial class declarations contains the declarations of some of the class members.

- The partial class declarations of a class can be in the same file or in different files.

Each partial declaration must be labeled as partial class, in contrast to the single keyword class. The declaration of a partial class looks the same as the declaration of a normal class, other than the addition of the type modifier partial.

```
Type modifier
   ↓
 partial class MyPartClass      // Same class name as following
 {
    member1 declaration
    member2 declaration
        ...
 }

Type modifier
   ↓
 partial class MyPartClass      // Same class name as preceding
 {
    member3 declaration
    member4 declaration
        ...
 }
```

■ **Note** The type modifier partial is not a keyword, so in other contexts you can use it as an identifier in your program. But when used immediately before the keywords class, struct, or interface, it signals the use of a partial type.

For example, the box on the left of Figure 6-21 represents a file with a class declaration. The boxes on the right of the figure represent that same class declaration split into two files.

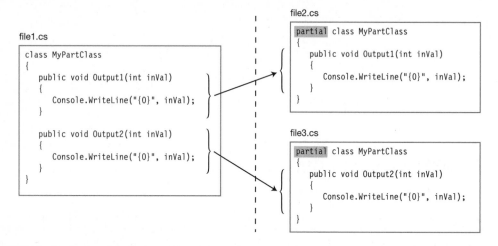

Figure 6-21. *Class split using partial types*

All the partial class declarations comprising a class must be compiled together. A class using partial class declarations has the same meaning as if all the class members were declared within a single class declaration body.

Visual Studio uses this feature in its standard Windows program templates. When you create an ASP.NET project or a Windows Forms project from the standard templates, the templates create two class files for each web page or form:

- One file contains the partial class containing the code generated by Visual Studio, declaring the components on the page. You shouldn't modify the partial class in this file, since it's regenerated by the Visual Studio when you modify the components on the page.

- The other file contains the partial class you use to implement the look and behavior of the components of the page or form.

Besides partial classes, you can also create two other partial types, which are the following:

- Partial structs. (Structs are covered in Chapter 12.)

- Partial interfaces. (Interfaces are covered in Chapter 17.)

Partial Methods

Partial methods are methods that are declared in two parts of a partial class. The two parts of the partial method can be declared in different parts of the partial class or in the same part. The two parts of the partial method are the following:

- The *defining partial method declaration:*

    — Gives the signature and return type.

    — The implementation part of the declaration consists of only a semicolon.

- The *implementing partial method declaration*:

    — Gives the signature and return type.

    — The implementation is in the normal format, which, as you know, is a statement block.

The important things to know about partial methods are the following:

- Both the defining and implementing declaration must match in signature and return type. The signature and return type have the following characteristics:

    — The contextual keyword partial must be included in both the defining and implementing declarations immediately before the keyword void.

    — The signature cannot include access modifiers, *making partial methods implicitly private*.

    — The return type must be void.

    — The parameter list cannot contain out parameters.

- You can have a defining partial method without an implementing partial method. In this case, the compiler removes the declaration and any calls to the method made inside the class. If, however, the class has an implementing partial method, it must also have a defining partial method.

The following code shows an example of a partial method called PrintSum.

- PrintSum is declared in different parts of partial class MyClass: the defining declaration in the first part and the implementing declaration in the second part. The implementation prints out the sum of its two integer parameters.

- Since partial methods are implicitly private, PrintSum cannot be called from outside the class. Method Add is a public method that calls PrintSum.

- Main creates an object of class MyClass and calls public method Add, which calls method PrintSum, which prints out the sum of the input parameters.

```
partial class MyClass
{          Must be void
                ↓
    partial void PrintSum(int x, int y);        // Defining partial method
            ↑                              ↑
    Contextual keyword             No implementation

    public void Add(int x, int y)
    {
        PrintSum(x, y);
    }
}

partial class MyClass
{
    partial void PrintSum(int x, int y)         // Implementing partial method
    {
        Console.WriteLine("Sum is {0}", x + y);      ← Implementation
    }
}

class Program
{
    static void Main( )
    {
        var mc = new MyClass();
        mc.Add(5, 6);
    }
}
```

This code produces the following output:

```
Sum is 11
```

■ ■ ■

Classes and Inheritance

Class Inheritance

Inheritance allows you to define a new class that incorporates and extends an already declared class.

- You can use an existing class, called the *base class*, as the basis for a new class, called the *derived class*. The members of the derived class consist of the following:

  — The members in its own declaration

  — The members of the base class

- To declare a derived class, you add a *class-base specification* after the class name. The class-base specification consists of a colon, followed by the name of the class to be used as the base class. The derived class is said to *directly inherit* from the base class listed.

- A derived class is said to *extend* its base class, because it includes the members of the base class plus any additional functionality provided in its own declaration.

- A derived class *cannot delete* any of the members it has inherited.

For example, the following shows the declaration of a class called OtherClass, which is derived from a class called SomeClass:

```
                    Class-base specification
                            ↓
class OtherClass : SomeClass
{                    ↑      ↑
    ...            Colon  Base class
}
```

Figure 7-1 shows an instance of each of the classes. Class SomeClass, on the left, has one field and one method. Class OtherClass, on the right, is derived from SomeClass and contains an additional field and an additional method.

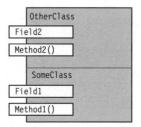
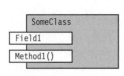

Figure 7-1. *Base class and derived class*

Accessing the Inherited Members

Inherited members are accessed just as if they had been declared in the derived class itself. (Inherited constructors are a bit different—I'll cover them later in the chapter.) For example, the following code declares classes SomeClass and OtherClass, which were shown in Figure 7-1. The code shows that all four members of OtherClass can be seamlessly accessed, regardless of whether they're declared in the base class or the derived class.

- Main creates an object of derived class OtherClass.

- The next two lines in Main call Method1 in the *base class*, using Field1 from the base class and then Field2 from the derived class.

- The subsequent two lines in Main call Method2 in the *derived class*, again using Field1 from the base class and then Field2 from the derived class.

```csharp
class SomeClass                          // Base class
{
   public string Field1 = "base class field ";
   public void Method1( string value ) {
      Console.WriteLine("Base class -- Method1:    {0}", value);
   }
}

class OtherClass: SomeClass              // Derived class
{
   public string Field2 = "derived class field";
   public void Method2( string value ) {
      Console.WriteLine("Derived class -- Method2:  {0}", value);
   }
}

class Program
{
   static void Main() {
      OtherClass oc = new OtherClass();

      oc.Method1( oc.Field1 );        // Base method with base field
      oc.Method1( oc.Field2 );        // Base method with derived field
      oc.Method2( oc.Field1 );        // Derived method with base field
      oc.Method2( oc.Field2 );        // Derived method with derived field
   }
}
```

This code produces the following output:

```
Base class -- Method1:    base class field
Base class -- Method1:    derived class field
Derived class -- Method2: base class field
Derived class -- Method2: derived class field
```

All Classes Are Derived from Class object

All classes, except special class object, are derived classes, even if they don't have a class-base specification. Class object is the only class that is not derived, since it is the base of the inheritance hierarchy.

Classes without a class-base specification are implicitly derived directly from class object. Leaving off the class-base specification is just shorthand for specifying that object is the base class. The two forms are semantically equivalent, as shown in Figure 7-2.

```
class SomeClass                     class SomeClass : object
{                                   {
   ...                                 ...
}                                   }
```

Figure 7-2. *The class declaration on the left implicitly derives from class object, while the one on the right explicitly derives from object. The two forms are semantically equivalent.*

Other important facts about class derivation are the following:

- A class declaration can have only a single class listed in its class-base specification. This is called *single inheritance.*

- Although a class can directly inherit from only a single base class, there is no limit to the *level* of derivation. That is, the class listed as the base class might be derived from another class, which is derived from another class, and so forth, until you eventually reach object.

Base class and *derived class* are relative terms. All classes are derived classes, either from object or from another class—so generally when we call a class a derived class, we mean that it is immediately derived from some class other than object. Figure 7-3 shows a simple class hierarchy. After this, I won't show object in the figures, since all classes are ultimately derived from it.

```
class SomeClass                          | MyNewClass  |
{ ... }                                  |-------------|
                                         | OtherClass  |
class OtherClass: SomeClass              |-------------|
{ ... }                                  | SomeClass   |
                                         |-------------|
class MyNewClass: OtherClass             | object      |
{
   ...
}
```

Figure 7-3. *A class hierarchy*

Hiding Members of a Base Class

Although a derived class cannot delete any of the members it has inherited, it can hide them.

- To hide an inherited data member, declare a new member of the same type and with the same *name*.

- You can *hide*, or *mask*, an inherited function member by declaring in the derived class a new function member with the same signature. Remember that the *signature* consists of the name and parameter list but does not include the return type.

- To let the compiler know that you are purposely hiding an inherited member, use the new modifier. Without it, the program will compile successfully, but the compiler will warn you that you are hiding an inherited member.

- You can also hide static members.

The following code declares a base class and a derived class, each with a string member called Field1. The keyword new is used to explicitly tell the compiler to mask the base class member. Figure 7-4 illustrates an instance of each class.

```
class SomeClass                        // Base class
{
   public string Field1;
   ...
}

class OtherClass : SomeClass           // Derived class
{
   new public string Field1;           // Mask base member with same name
      ↑
   Keyword
```

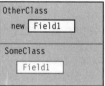

Figure 7-4. *Hiding a member of a base class*

In the following code, OtherClass derives from SomeClass but hides both its inherited members. Note the use of the new modifier. The code is illustrated in Figure 7-5.

```
class SomeClass                                    // Base class
{
   public string Field1 = "SomeClass Field1";
   public void   Method1(string value)
      { Console.WriteLine("SomeClass.Method1:  {0}", value); }
}


class OtherClass : SomeClass                        // Derived class
{ Keyword
   ↓
   new public string Field1 = "OtherClass Field1";  // Mask the base member.
   new public void   Method1(string value)          // Mask the base member.
    ↑   { Console.WriteLine("OtherClass.Method1:  {0}", value); }
} Keyword


class Program
{
   static void Main()
   {
      OtherClass oc = new OtherClass();       // Use the masking member.
      oc.Method1(oc.Field1);                   // Use the masking member.
   }
}
```

This code produces the following output:

OtherClass.Method1: OtherClass Field1

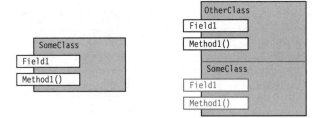

Figure 7-5. *Hiding a field and a method of the base class*

Base Access

If your derived class absolutely must access a hidden inherited member, you can access it by using a *base access* expression. This expression consists of the keyword base, followed immediately by a period and the name of the member, as shown here:

```
Console.WriteLine("{0}", base.Field1);
                           ↑
                       Base access
```

For example, in the following code, derived class OtherClass hides Field1 in its base class but accesses it by using a base access expression.

```
class SomeClass {                                    // Base class
   public string Field1 = "Field1 -- In the base class";
}

class OtherClass : SomeClass {                        // Derived class

   new public string Field1 = "Field1 -- In the derived class";
    ↑                  ↑
   Hides the field in the base class
   public void PrintField1()
   {
      Console.WriteLine(Field1);               // Access the derived class.
      Console.WriteLine(base.Field1);          // Access the base class.
   }                     ↑
}                    Base access

class Program {
   static void Main()
   {
      OtherClass oc = new OtherClass();
      oc.PrintField1();
   }
}
```

This code produces the following output:

```
Field1 -- In the derived class
Field1 -- In the base class
```

If you use this feature frequently, you might want to reevaluate the design of your classes. Generally there are more elegant designs, but the feature is there if there's a situation where nothing else will do.

Using References to a Base Class

An instance of a derived class consists of an instance of the base class, plus the additional members of the derived class. A reference to the derived class points to the whole class object, including the base class part.

If you have a reference to a derived class object, you can get a reference to just the base class part of the object by *casting* the reference to the type of the base class by using the *cast operator*. The cast operator is placed in front of the object reference and consists of a set of parentheses containing the name of the class being cast to. Casting is covered in detail in Chapter 18.

The next few sections cover accessing an object by using a reference to the base class part of the object. We'll start by looking at the two lines of code that follow, which declare references to objects. Figure 7-6 illustrates the code and shows the parts of the object seen by the different variables.

- The first line declares and initializes variable `derived`, which then contains a reference to an object of type `MyDerivedClass`.

- The second line declares a variable of the base class type, `MyBaseClass`, and casts the reference in `derived` to that type, giving a reference to the base class part of the object.

  — The reference to the base class part is stored in variable `mybc`, on the left side of the assignment operator.

  — The reference to the base class part cannot "see" the rest of the derived class object, because it's "looking" at it through a reference to the base type.

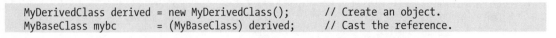

```
MyDerivedClass derived = new MyDerivedClass();      // Create an object.
MyBaseClass mybc       = (MyBaseClass) derived;      // Cast the reference.
```

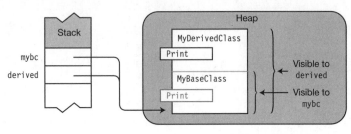

Figure 7-6. *Reference derived can see the entire MyDerivedClass object, while mybc can only see the MyBaseClass part of the object.*

The following code shows the declaration and use of these two classes. Figure 7-7 illustrates the object and references in memory.

Main creates an object of type MyDerivedClass and stores its reference in variable derived. Main also creates a variable of type MyBaseClass and uses it to store a reference to the base class portion of the object. When the Print method is called on each reference, the call invokes the implementation of the method that the reference can see, producing different output strings.

```
class MyBaseClass
{
   public void Print()
   {
      Console.WriteLine("This is the base class.");
   }
}

class MyDerivedClass : MyBaseClass
{
   new public void Print()
   {
      Console.WriteLine("This is the derived class.");
   }
}

class Program
{
   static void Main()
   {
      MyDerivedClass derived = new MyDerivedClass();
      MyBaseClass mybc = (MyBaseClass)derived;
                          ↑
                   Cast to base class
      derived.Print();            // Call Print from derived portion.
      mybc.Print();               // Call Print from base portion.
   }
}
```

This code produces the following output:

```
This is the derived class.
This is the base class.
```

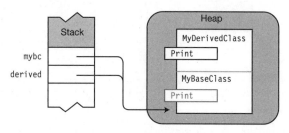

Figure 7-7. *A reference to the derived class and the base class*

Virtual and Override Methods

In the previous section, you saw that when you access an object of a derived class by using a reference to the base class, you get the members from the base class. *Virtual methods* allow a reference to the base class to access "up into" the derived class.

You can use a reference to a base class to call a method in the *derived class*, if the following are true:

- The method in the derived class and the method in the base class each have the same signature and return type.

- The method in the base class is labeled virtual.

- The method in the derived class is labeled override.

For example, the following code shows the virtual and override modifiers on the methods in the base class and derived class:

```
class MyBaseClass                          // Base class
{
   virtual public void Print()
        ↑

   ...
class MyDerivedClass : MyBaseClass         // Derived class
{
   override public void Print()
        ↑
```

Figure 7-8 illustrates this set of virtual and override methods. Notice how the behavior differs from the previous case, where I used new to hide the base class members.

- When the Print method is called by using the reference to the base class (mybc), the method call is passed up to the derived class and executed, because

  — The method in the base class is marked as virtual.

  — There is a matching override method in the derived class.

- Figure 7-8 illustrates this by showing the arrow coming out the back of the virtual Print method and pointing at the override Print method.

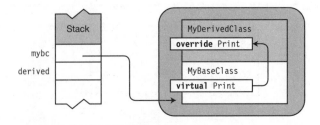

Figure 7-8. *A virtual method and an override method*

The following code is the same as in the previous section, but this time, the methods are labeled virtual and override. This produces a result that is very different from that of the previous example. In this version, calling the method through the base class invokes the method in the derived class.

```
class MyBaseClass
{
   virtual public void Print()
   {
      Console.WriteLine("This is the base class.");
   }
}

class MyDerivedClass : MyBaseClass
{
   override public void Print()
   {
      Console.WriteLine("This is the derived class.");
   }
}

class Program
{
   static void Main()
   {
      MyDerivedClass derived = new MyDerivedClass();
      MyBaseClass mybc        = (MyBaseClass)derived;
                                        ↑
      derived.Print();          Cast to base class
      mybc.Print();
   }
}
```

This code produces the following output:

```
This is the derived class.
This is the derived class.
```

Other important things to know about the virtual and override modifiers are the following:

- The overriding and overridden methods must have the same accessibility. In other words, the overridden method cannot be, for example, private, and the overriding method public.

- You cannot override a method that is static or is nonvirtual.

- Methods, properties, and indexers (which I covered in the preceding chapter), and another member type, called *events* (which I'll cover later in the text), can all be declared virtual and override.

Overriding a Method Marked override

Overriding methods can occur between any levels of inheritance.

- When you use a reference to the base class part of an object to call an overridden method, the method call is passed up the derivation hierarchy for execution to the *most-derived* version of the method marked as override.

- If there are other declarations of the method at higher levels of derivation that are not marked as override—they are not invoked.

For example, the following code shows three classes that form an inheritance hierarchy: MyBaseClass, MyDerivedClass, and SecondDerived. All three classes contain a method named Print, with the same signature. In MyBaseClass, Print is labeled virtual. In MyDerivedClass, it's labeled override. In class SecondDerived, you can declare method Print with either override or new. Let's look at what happens in each case.

```
class MyBaseClass                              // Base class
{
    virtual public void Print()
    { Console.WriteLine("This is the base class."); }
}

class MyDerivedClass : MyBaseClass             // Derived class
{
    override public void Print()
    { Console.WriteLine("This is the derived class."); }
}

class SecondDerived : MyDerivedClass           // Most-derived class
{
    ... // Given in the following pages
}
```

Case 1: Declaring Print with override

If you declare the Print method of SecondDerived as override, then it will override *both the less-derived versions* of the method, as shown in Figure 7-9. If a reference to the base class is used to call Print, it gets passed all the way up the chain to the implementation in class SecondDerived.

The following code implements this case. Notice the code in the last two lines of method Main.

- The first of the two statements calls the Print method by using a reference to the most-derived class—SecondDerived. This is not calling through a reference to the base class portion, so it will call the method implemented in SecondDerived.

- The second statement, however, calls the Print method by using a reference to the base class— MyBaseClass.

```
class SecondDerived : MyDerivedClass
{
   override public void Print() {
      ↑   Console.WriteLine("This is the second derived class.");
   }
}

class Program
{
   static void Main()
   {
      SecondDerived derived = new SecondDerived(); // Use SecondDerived.
      MyBaseClass mybc = (MyBaseClass)derived;      // Use MyBaseClass.

      derived.Print();
      mybc.Print();
   }
}
```

The result is that regardless of whether Print is called through the derived class or the base class, the method in the most-derived class is called. When called through the base class, it's passed up the inheritance hierarchy. This code produces the following output:

```
This is the second derived class.
This is the second derived class.
```

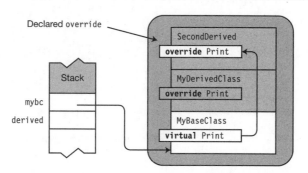

Figure 7-9. *Execution is passed to the top of the chain of multiple levels of override.*

Case 2: Declaring Print with new

If instead you declare the Print method of SecondDerived as new, the result is as shown in Figure 7-10. Main is the same as in the previous case.

```
class SecondDerived : MyDerivedClass
{
   new public void Print()
   {
      Console.WriteLine("This is the second derived class.");
   }
}

class Program
{
   static void Main()                                        // Main
   {
      SecondDerived derived = new SecondDerived();           // Use SecondDerived.
      MyBaseClass mybc = (MyBaseClass)derived;               // Use MyBaseClass.

      derived.Print();
      mybc.Print();
   }
}
```

The result is that when method Print is called through the reference to SecondDerived, the method in SecondDerived is executed, as you would expect. When the method is called through a reference to MyBaseClass, however, the method call is passed up only one level, to class MyDerived, where it is executed. The only difference between the two cases is whether the method in SecondDerived is declared with modifier override or modifier new.

This code produces the following output:

```
This is the second derived class.
This is the derived class.
```

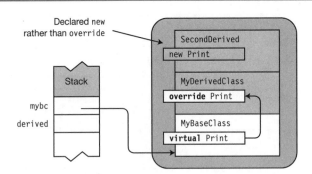

Figure 7-10. *Hiding the overridden methods*

Overriding Other Member Types

In the previous few sections, you've seen how the virtual/override designations work on methods. These work exactly the same way with properties, events, and indexers. For example, the following code shows a read-only property named MyProperty using virtual/override.

```
class MyBaseClass
{
    private int _myInt = 5;
    virtual public int MyProperty
    {
        get { return _myInt; }
    }
}

class MyDerivedClass : MyBaseClass
{
    private int _myInt = 10;
    override public int MyProperty
    {
        get { return _myInt; }
    }
}

class Program
{
    static void Main()
    {
        MyDerivedClass derived = new MyDerivedClass();
        MyBaseClass mybc       = (MyBaseClass)derived;

        Console.WriteLine( derived.MyProperty );
        Console.WriteLine( mybc.MyProperty );
    }
}
```

This code produces the following output:

```
10
10
```

Constructor Execution

In the preceding chapter, you saw that a constructor executes code that prepares a class for use. This includes initializing both the static and instance members of the class. In this chapter, you saw that part of a derived class object is an object of the base class.

- To create the base class part of an object, a constructor for the base class is implicitly called as part of the process of creating the instance.

- Each class in the inheritance hierarchy chain executes its base class constructor before it executes its own constructor body.

For example, the following code shows a declaration of class MyDerivedClass and its constructor. When the constructor is called, it calls the parameterless constructor MyBaseClass() before executing its own body.

```
class MyDerivedClass : MyBaseClass
{
   MyDerivedClass()          // Constructor uses base constructor MyBaseClass().
   {
      ...
   }
}
```

Figure 7-11 shows the order of construction. When an instance is being created, one of the first things that is done is the initialization of all the instance members of the object. After that, the base class constructor is called. Only then is the body of the constructor of the class itself executed.

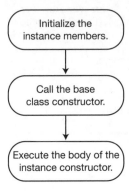

Figure 7-11. *Order of object construction*

For example, in the following code, the values of MyField1 and MyField2 would be set to 5 and 0, respectively, before the base class constructor is called.

```
class MyDerivedClass : MyBaseClass
{
   int MyField1 = 5;                      // 1. Member initialized
   int MyField2;                          //    Member initialized

   public MyDerivedClass()               // 3. Body of constructor executed
   {
      ...
   }
}

class MyBaseClass
{
   public MyBaseClass()                   // 2. Base class constructor called
   {
      ...
   }
}
```

■ **Caution** Calling a virtual method in a constructor is *strongly discouraged*. The virtual method in the base class would call the override method in the derived class while the base class constructor is being executed. But that would be before the derived constructor's body is executed. It would, therefore, be calling up into the derived class before the class is completely initialized.

Constructor Initializers

By default, the parameterless constructor of the base class is called when an object is being constructed. But constructors can be overloaded, so a base class might have more than one. If you want your derived class to use a specific base class constructor other than the parameterless constructor, you must specify it in a *constructor initializer*.

There are two forms of constructor initializer:

- The first form uses the keyword base and specifies which base class constructor to use.

- The second form uses the keyword this and specifies which other constructor from this class should be used.

A base class constructor initializer is placed after a colon following the parameter list in a class's constructor declaration. The constructor initializer consists of the keyword base and the parameter list of the base constructor to call.

For example, the following code shows a constructor for class MyDerivedClass.

- The constructor initializer specifies that the construction process should call the base class constructor with two parameters, where the first parameter is a string and the second parameter is an int.

- The parameters in the base parameter list must match the *intended base constructor's* parameter list, in type and order.

```
                                  Constructor initializer
                                          ↓
    public MyDerivedClass( int x, string s ) : base( s, x )
    {                                           ↑
        ...                              Keyword
```

When you declare a constructor without a constructor initializer, it's a shortcut for the form with a constructor initializer consisting of base(), as illustrated in Figure 7-12. The two forms are semantically equivalent.

```
class MyDerived: MyBase              class MyDerived: MyBase
{                                    {
    MyDerived()                          MyDerived() : base()
    {                                    {
        ...                                  ...
    }                                    }
    ...                                  ...

Constructor implicitly uses base      Constructor explicitly uses base
  constructor MyBase().                  constructor MyBase().
```

Figure 7-12. *Equivalent forms of a constructor*

The other form of constructor initializer instructs the construction process (actually, the compiler) to use a different constructor from the same class. For example, the following shows a constructor with a single parameter for class MyClass. That single-parameter constructor, however, uses a constructor from the same class, but with two parameters, supplying a default parameter as the second one.

```
                                  Constructor initializer
                                           ↓
public MyClass(int x): this(x, "Using Default String")
{                         ↑
    ...                Keyword
}
```

Another situation where this comes in particularly handy is where you have several constructors for a class, and they have common code that should always be performed at the beginning of the object construction process. In this case, you can factor out that common code and place it in a constructor that is used as a constructor initializer by all the other constructors. As a matter of fact, this is a suggested practice since it reduces code duplication.

You might think that you could just declare another method that performs those common initializations and have all the constructors call that method. This isn't as good for several reasons. The first is that the compiler can optimize certain things when it knows a method is a constructor. The second is that there are some things that can be done only in a constructor and not elsewhere. For example, in the previous chapter you learned that readonly fields can be initialized only inside a constructor. You will get a compiler error if you attempt to initialize a readonly field in any other method, even if that method is called by a constructor only.

Going back to that common constructor, if it can stand on its own as a valid constructor that initializes everything in the class that needs to be initialized, then it's perfectly fine to leave it as a public constructor.

What if, however, it doesn't completely initialize an object? In that case, you mustn't allow that constructor to be callable from outside the class, since it would then create incompletely initialized objects. To avoid that problem, you can declare the constructor private instead of public, as shown in the following code:

```
class MyClass
{
   readonly int    firstVar;
   readonly double secondVar;

   public string UserName;
   public int UserIdNumber;

   private MyClass( )            // Private constructor performs initializations
   {                            // common to the other constructors.
      firstVar  = 20;
      secondVar = 30.5;
   }

   public MyClass( string firstName ) : this() // use constructor initializer
   {
      UserName     = firstName;
      UserIdNumber = -1;
   }

   public MyClass( int idNumber ) : this( )    // use constructor initializer
   {
      UserName     = "Anonymous";
      UserIdNumber = idNumber;
   }
}
```

Class Access Modifiers

A class can be seen and accessed by other classes in the system. This section explains the accessibility of classes. Although I'll use classes in the explanations and examples since that's what we've covered so far in the text, the accessibility rules also apply to the other types I'll cover later.

The term *visible* is sometimes used for the term *accessible*. They can be used interchangeably. There are two levels of class accessibility: public and internal.

- A class marked public can be accessed by code from any assembly in the system. To make a class visible to other assemblies, use the public access modifier, as shown here:

```
Keyword
  ↓
public class MyBaseClass
{ ...
```

- A class marked internal can only be seen by classes within its own assembly.

  — This is the default accessibility level, so unless you explicitly specify the modifier public in the class declaration, code outside the assembly cannot access the class.

  — You can explicitly declare a class as internal by using the internal access modifier.

```
Keyword
  ↓
internal class MyBaseClass
{ ...
```

Figure 7-13 illustrates the accessibility of internal and public classes from outside the assembly. Class MyClass is not visible to the classes in the assembly on the left, because it's marked internal. Class OtherClass, however, is visible to the classes on the left, because it's marked public.

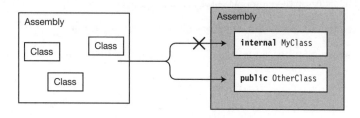

Figure 7-13. *Classes from other assemblies can access public classes but cannot access internal classes.*

Inheritance Between Assemblies

So far, I've been declaring derived classes in the same assembly that contains the base class. But C# also allows you to derive a class from a base class defined in a different assembly. To do this, the following must be true:

- The base class must be declared public so that it can be accessed from outside its assembly.

- You must include a reference in your Visual Studio project to the assembly containing the base class.

To make it easier to refer to the classes and types in the other assembly, without using their fully qualified names, place a using directive at the top of the source file, with the namespace containing the classes or types you want to access.

■ **Note** Adding a reference to the other assembly and adding a using directive are two separate things. Adding the reference to the other assembly tells the compiler where the required types are defined. Adding the using directive allows you to reference other classes without having to use their fully qualified names. Chapter 10 covers this in detail.

For example, the following two code segments, from different assemblies, show how easy it is to inherit a class from another assembly. The first code listing creates an assembly that contains the declaration of a class called MyBaseClass, which has the following characteristics:

- It's declared in a source file called Assembly1.cs and inside a namespace declared as BaseClassNS.

- It's declared public so that it can be accessed from other assemblies.

- It contains a single member, a method called PrintMe, that just writes out a simple message identifying the class.

```
// Source file name Assembly1.cs
using System;
      Namespace containing declaration of base class
                    ↓
namespace BaseClassNS
{ Declare the class public so it can be seen outside the assembly.
     ↓
   public class MyBaseClass {
      public void PrintMe() {
         Console.WriteLine("I am MyBaseClass");
      }
   }
}
```

The second assembly contains the declaration of a class called `DerivedClass`, which inherits from `MyBaseClass`, declared in the first assembly. The source file is named `Assembly2.cs`. Figure 7-14 illustrates the two assemblies.

- `DerivedClass` has an empty body but inherits method `PrintMe` from `MyBaseClass`.

- `Main` creates an object of type `DerivedClass` and calls its inherited method `PrintMe`.

```
// Source file name Assembly2.cs
using System;
using BaseClassNS;
           ↑
Namespace containing declaration of base class
namespace UsesBaseClass
{                          Base class in other assembly
                                      ↓
   class DerivedClass: MyBaseClass {
      // Empty body
   }

   class Program {
      static void Main( )
      {
          DerivedClass mdc = new DerivedClass();
          mdc.PrintMe();
      }
   }
}
```

This code produces the following output:

```
I am MyBaseClass
```

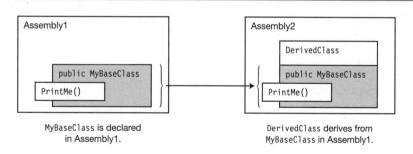

MyBaseClass is declared   DerivedClass derives from
in Assembly1.   MyBaseClass in Assembly1.

Figure 7-14. *Inheriting across assemblies*

Member Access Modifiers

The previous two sections explained class accessibility. With class accessibility, there are only two modifiers—internal and public. This section covers *member accessibility*. Class accessibility describes the visibility of a class; member accessibility describes the visibility of the members of a class object.

Each member declared in a class is visible to various parts of the system, depending on the access modifier assigned to it in its class declaration. You've seen that private members are visible only to other members of the same class, while public members can be visible to classes outside the assembly as well. In this section, we'll look again at the public and private access levels, as well as the three other levels of accessibility.

Before looking at the specifics of member accessibility, there are some general things we need to cover first:

- All members explicitly declared in a class's declaration are visible to each other, regardless of their accessibility specification.

- Inherited members are not explicitly declared in a class's declaration, so, as you'll see, inherited members might or might not be visible to members of a derived class.

- There are five member access levels:
  — public
  — private
  — protected
  — internal
  — protected internal

- You must specify member access levels on a per-member basis. If you don't specify an access level for a member, its implicit access level is private.

- A member cannot be more accessible than its class. That is, if a class has an accessibility level limiting it to the assembly, individual members of the class cannot be seen outside the assembly, regardless of their access modifiers, even public.

Regions Accessing a Member

The member access modifiers in a class's declaration specify which other types can and cannot access which members of the class. For example, the following declaration shows members declared with the five access levels.

```
public class MyClass
{
    public              int Member1;
    private             int Member2;
    protected           int Member3;
    internal            int Member4;
    protected internal  int Member5;
    ...
```

The access levels are based on two characteristics with regard to the class being declared:

- Whether the class is *derived from* the class being declared

- Whether a class is *in the same assembly* as the class being declared

These two characteristics yield four groups, as illustrated in Figure 7-15. In relation to the class being declared, another class can be any of the following:

- In the same assembly and derived from it (bottom right)

- In the same assembly but not derived from it (bottom left)

- In a different assembly and derived from it (top right)

- In a different assembly and not derived from it (top left)

These characteristics are used to define the five access levels.

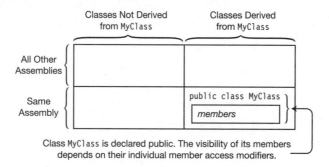

Class MyClass is declared public. The visibility of its members depends on their individual member access modifiers.

Figure 7-15. *Areas of accessibility*

Public Member Accessibility

The public access level is the least restrictive. All classes both inside and outside the assembly have free access to the member. Figure 7-16 illustrates the accessibility of a public class member of MyClass.

To declare a member public, use the public access modifier, as shown.

```
Keyword
   ↓
public int Member1;
```

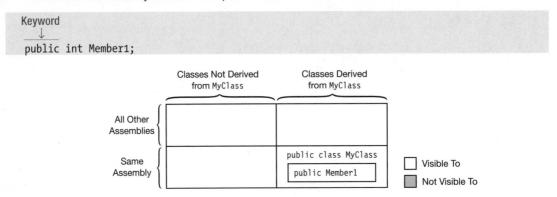

Figure 7-16. *A public member of a public class is visible to all classes in the same assembly or other assemblies.*

Private Member Accessibility

The private access level is the most restrictive.

- A private class member can be accessed only by members of its own class. It cannot be accessed by other classes, including classes that are derived from it.

- A private member can, however, be accessed by members of classes nested in its class. *Nested classes* are covered in Chapter 25.

Figure 7-17 illustrates the accessibility of a private member.

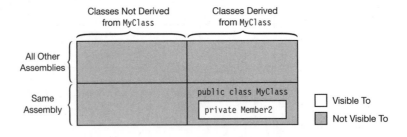

Figure 7-17. *A private member of any class is visible only to members of its own class (or nested classes).*

Protected Member Accessibility

The protected access level is like the private access level, except that it also allows classes derived from the class to access the member. Figure 7-18 illustrates protected accessibility. Notice that even classes outside the assembly that are derived from the class have access to the member.

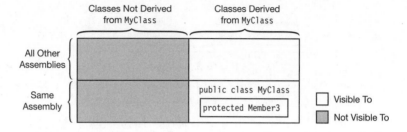

Figure 7-18. *A protected member of a public class is visible to members of its own class or classes derived from it. The derived classes can even be in other assemblies.*

Internal Member Accessibility

Members marked internal are visible to all the classes in the assembly but not to classes outside the assembly, as illustrated in Figure 7-19.

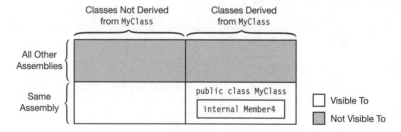

Figure 7-19. *An internal member of a public class is visible to members of any class in the same assembly but not to classes outside the assembly.*

187

Protected Internal Member Accessibility

Members marked protected internal are visible to all the classes that inherit from the class and also to all classes inside the assembly, as shown in Figure 7-20. Notice that the set of classes allowed access is the combined set of classes allowed by the protected modifier plus the set of classes allowed by the internal modifier. Notice that this is the *union* of protected and internal—not the intersection.

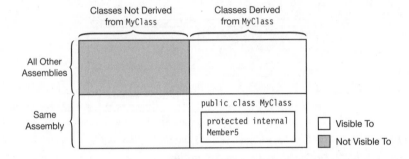

Figure 7-20. *A protected internal member of a public class is visible to members of classes in the same assembly or to members of classes derived from that class. It's not visible to classes in other assemblies that are not derived from the class.*

Summary of Member Access Modifiers

The following two tables summarize the characteristics of the five member access levels. Table 7-1 lists the modifiers and gives an intuitive summary of the effects of the modifier.

Table 7-1. *Member Access Modifiers*

Modifier	Meaning
private	Accessible only within the class
internal	Accessible to all classes within this assembly
protected	Accessible to all classes derived from this class
protected internal	Accessible to all classes that are either derived from this class or declared within this assembly
public	Accessible to any class

Figure 7-21 shows the relative accessibility of the five member access modifiers.

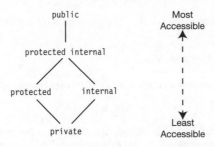

Figure 7-21. *Relative accessibility of the various member access modifiers*

Table 7-2 lists the access modifiers down the left side of the table and the categories of classes across the top. *Derived* refers to classes derived from the class declaring the member. *Nonderived* means classes not derived from the class declaring the member. A check in a cell means that the category of class can access members with the corresponding modifier.

Table 7-2. *Summary of Member Accessibility*

	Classes in Same Assembly		Classes in Different Assembly	
	Non-Derived	Derived	Non-Derived	Derived
private				
internal	✓	✓		
protected		✓		✓
protected internal	✓	✓		✓
public	✓	✓	✓	✓

Abstract Members

An *abstract member* is a function member that is designed to be overridden. An abstract member has the following characteristics:

- It is marked with the abstract modifier.

- It doesn't have an implementation code block. The code blocks of abstract members are represented by semicolons.

For example, the following code from inside a class definition declares two abstract members: an abstract method called PrintStuff and an abstract property called MyProperty. Notice the semicolons in place of the implementation blocks.

```
     Keyword                       Semicolon in place of implementation
       ↓                                      ↓
abstract public void PrintStuff(string s);

abstract public int MyProperty
{
    get;   ← Semicolon in place of implementation
    set;   ← Semicolon in place of implementation
}
```

Abstract members can be declared only in *abstract classes*, which we'll look at in the next section. Four type of member can be declared as abstract:

- Methods

- Properties

- Events

- Indexers

Other important facts about abstract members are the following:

- Abstract members, although they must be overridden by a corresponding member in a derived class, cannot use the `virtual` modifier in addition to the `abstract` modifier.

- As with virtual members, the implementation of an abstract member in a derived class must specify the `override` modifier.

Table 7-3 compares and contrasts virtual members and abstract members.

Table 7-3. *Comparing Virtual and Abstract Members*

	Virtual Member	**Abstract Member**
Keyword	`virtual`	`abstract`
Implementation body	Has an implementation body	No implementation body—semicolon instead
Overridden in a derived class	*Can* be overridden—using override	*Must* be overridden—using override
Types of members	Methods Properties Events Indexers	Methods Properties Events Indexers

Abstract Classes

Abstract classes are designed to be inherited from. An *abstract class* can be used only as the base class of another class.

- You cannot create instances of an abstract class.

- An abstract class is declared using the `abstract` modifier.

```
Keyword
  ↓
abstract class MyClass
{
   ...
}
```

- An abstract class can contain abstract members or regular, nonabstract members. The members of an abstract class can be any combination of abstract members and normal members with implementations.

- An abstract class can itself be derived from another abstract class. For example, the following code shows one abstract class derived from another.

```
abstract class AbClass                  // Abstract class
{
   ...
}

abstract class MyAbClass : AbClass      // Abstract class derived from
{                                       // an abstract class
   ...
}
```

- Any class derived from an abstract class must implement all the abstract members of the class by using the `override` keyword, unless the derived class is itself abstract.

Example of an Abstract Class and an Abstract Method

The following code shows an abstract class called AbClass with two methods.

The first method is a normal method with an implementation that prints out the name of the class. The second method is an abstract method that must be implemented in a derived class. Class DerivedClass inherits from AbClass and implements and overrides the abstract method. Main creates an object of DerivedClass and calls its two methods.

```
Keyword
   ↓
abstract class AbClass                              // Abstract class
{
    public void IdentifyBase()                      // Normal method
    { Console.WriteLine("I am AbClass"); }
     Keyword
        ↓
    abstract public void IdentifyDerived();         // Abstract method
}

class DerivedClass : AbClass                        // Derived class
{    Keyword
         ↓
    override public void IdentifyDerived()          // Implementation of
    { Console.WriteLine("I am DerivedClass"); }     // abstract method
}

class Program
{
    static void Main()
    {
        // AbClass a = new AbClass();               // Error.  Cannot instantiate
        // a.IdentifyDerived();                      // an abstract class.

        DerivedClass b = new DerivedClass(); // Instantiate the derived class.
        b.IdentifyBase();                           // Call the inherited method.
        b.IdentifyDerived();                        // Call the "abstract" method.
    }
}
```

This code produces the following output:

```
I am AbClass
I am DerivedClass
```

Another Example of an Abstract Class

The following code shows the declaration of an abstract class that contains data members as well as function members. Data members cannot be declared as abstract.

```
abstract class MyBase        // Combination of abstract and non-abstract members
{
   public int SideLength        = 10;          // Data member
   const  int TriangleSideCount = 3;           // Data member

   abstract public void PrintStuff( string s );   // Abstract method
   abstract public int  MyInt { get; set; }       // Abstract property

   public int PerimeterLength( )                   // Regular, non-abstract method
   { return TriangleSideCount * SideLength; }
}

class MyClass : MyBase
{
   public override void PrintStuff( string s )    // Override abstract method
   { Console.WriteLine( s ); }

   private int _myInt;
   public override int MyInt                       // Override abstract property
   {
      get { return _myInt; }
      set { _myInt = value; }
   }
}

class Program
{
   static void Main( string[] args )
   {
      MyClass mc = new MyClass( );
      mc.PrintStuff( "This is a string." );
      mc.MyInt = 28;
      Console.WriteLine( mc.MyInt );
      Console.WriteLine( "Perimeter Length: {0}", mc.PerimeterLength( ) );
   }
}
```

This code produces the following output:

```
This is a string.
28
Perimeter Length: 30
```

Sealed Classes

In the previous section, you saw that an abstract class must be used as a base class—it cannot be instantiated as a stand-alone class object. The opposite is true of a *sealed class*.

- A sealed class can be instantiated only as a stand-alone class object—it cannot be used as a base class.

- A sealed class is labeled with the sealed modifier.

For example, the following class is a sealed class. Any attempt to use it as the base class of another class will produce a compile error.

```
Keyword
  ↓
sealed class MyClass
{
    ...
}
```

Static Classes

A static class is a class where all the members are static. Static classes are used to group data and functions that are not affected by instance data. A common use of a static class might be to create a math library containing sets of mathematical methods and values.

The important things to know about static classes are the following:

- The class itself must be marked static.

- All the members of the class must be static.

- The class can have a static constructor, but it cannot have an instance constructor, since you cannot create an instance of the class.

- Static classes are implicitly sealed. That is, you cannot inherit from a static class.

You access the members of a static class just as you would access any static member, by using the class name and the member name.

The following code shows an example of a static class:

```
Class must be marked static
        ↓
  static public class MyMath
  {
     public static float PI = 3.14f;
     public static bool IsOdd(int x)
              ↑            { return x % 2 == 1; }
            Members must be static
                  ↓
     public static int Times2(int x)
                      { return 2 * x; }
  }

  class Program
  {
     static void Main( )
     {                                    Use class name and member name.
        int val = 3;                              ↓
        Console.WriteLine("{0} is odd is {1}.", val,  MyMath.IsOdd(val));
        Console.WriteLine("{0} * 2 = {1}.",     val,  MyMath.Times2(val));
     }
  }
```

This code produces the following output:

```
3 is odd is True.
3 * 2 = 6.
```

Extension Methods

So far in this text, every method you've seen has been associated with the class in which it is declared. The *extension method* feature introduced in C# 3.0 extends that boundary, allowing you to write methods associated with classes *other than the class in which they are declared.*

To see how you might use this feature, take a look at the following code. It contains class MyData, which stores three values of type double, and contains a constructor and a method called Sum, which returns the sum of the three stored values.

```
class MyData
{
   private double D1;                                  // Fields
   private double D2;
   private double D3;

   public MyData(double d1, double d2, double d3)      // Constructor
   {
      D1 = d1; D2 = d2; D3 = d3;
   }

   public double Sum()                                 // Method Sum
   {
      return D1 + D2 + D3;
   }
}
```

This is a pretty limited class, but suppose it would be more useful if it contained another method, which returned the average of the three data points. With what you know so far about classes, there are several ways you might implement the additional functionality:

- If you have the source code and can modify the class, you could, of course, just add the new method to the class.

- If, however, you can't modify the class—for example, if the class is in a third-party class library—then, as long as it isn't sealed, you could use it as a base class and implement the additional method in a class derived from it.

If, however, you don't have access to the code or the class is sealed or there is some other design reason that neither of these solutions will work, then you will have to write a method in another class that uses the publicly available members of the class.

For example, you might write a class like the one in the following code. The code contains a static class called ExtendMyData, which contains a static method called Average, which implements the additional functionality. Notice that the method takes an instance of MyData as a parameter.

```
static class ExtendMyData        Instance of MyData class
{                                          ↓
    public static double Average( MyData md )
    {
        return md.Sum() / 3;
    }               ↑
}    Use the instance of MyData.


class Program
{
    static void Main()
    {                                                    Instance of MyData
        MyData md = new MyData(3, 4, 5);                          ↓
        Console.WriteLine("Average: {0}", ExtendMyData.Average(md));
    }                                              ↑
}                                          Call the static method.
```

This code produces the following output:

```
Average: 4
```

Although this is a perfectly fine solution, it would be more elegant if you could call the method on the class instance itself, rather than creating an instance of another class to act on it. The following two lines of code illustrate the difference. The first uses the method just shown—invoking a static method on an instance of another class. The second shows the form we would like to use—invoking an instance method on the object itself.

```
ExtendMyData.Average( md )          // Static invocation form
md.Average();                       // Instance invocation form
```

Extension methods allow you to use the second form, even though the first form would be the normal way of writing the invocation.

By making a small change in the declaration of method Average, you can use the instance invocation form. The change you need to make is to add the keyword this before the type name in the parameter declaration as shown following. Adding the this keyword to the first parameter of the static method of the static class changes it from a regular method of class ExtendMyData into an *extension method* of class MyData. You can now use both invocation forms.

```
Must be a static class
         ↓
static class ExtendMyData
{   Must be public and static          Keyword and type
                   ↓                          ↓
    public static double Average( this MyData md )
    {
       ...
    )
}
```

The important requirements for an extension method are the following:

- The class in which the extension method is declared must also be declared static.

- The extension method itself must be declared static.

- The extension method must contain as its first parameter type the keyword this, followed by the name of the class it is extending.

Figure 7-22 illustrates the structure of an extension method.

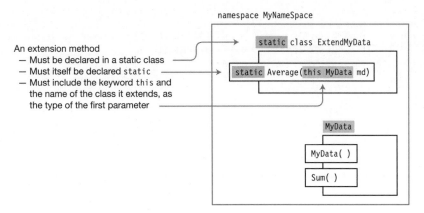

Figure 7-22. *The structure of an extension method*

The following code shows a full program, including class MyData and extension method Average declared in class ExtendMyData. Notice that method Average is invoked exactly as if it were an *instance member* of MyData! Figure 7-22 illustrates the code. Classes MyData and ExtendMyData together act like the desired class, with three methods.

```
namespace ExtensionMethods
{
    sealed class MyData
    {
        private double D1, D2, D3;
        public MyData(double d1, double d2, double d3)
        { D1 = d1; D2 = d2; D3 = d3; }

        public double Sum() { return D1 + D2 + D3; }
    }

    static class ExtendMyData          Keyword and type
    {                                         ↓
        public static double Average(this MyData md)
        {           ↑
            Declared static
            return md.Sum() / 3;
        }
    }

    class Program
    {
        static void Main()
        {
            MyData md = new MyData(3, 4, 5);
            Console.WriteLine("Sum:     {0}", md.Sum());
            Console.WriteLine("Average: {0}", md.Average());
        }                                      ↑
    }                     Invoke as an instance member of the class
}
```

This code produces the following output:

```
Sum:     12
Average: 4
```

CHAPTER 8

■■■

Expressions and Operators

- Expressions
- Literals
- Order of Evaluation
- Simple Arithmetic Operators
- The Remainder Operator
- Relational and Equality Comparison Operators
- Increment and Decrement Operators
- Conditional Logical Operators
- Logical Operators
- Shift Operators
- Assignment Operators
- The Conditional Operator
- Unary Arithmetic Operators
- User-Defined Type Conversions
- Operator Overloading
- The typeof Operator
- Other Operators

Expressions

This chapter defines expressions and describes the operators provided by C#. It also explains how you can define the C# operators to work with your user-defined classes.

An *expression* is a string of operators and operands. The following are some of the constructs that can act as operands:

- Literals

- Constants

- Variables

- Method calls

- Element accessors, such as array accessors and indexers

- Other expressions

The C# operators take one, two, or three operands. An operator does the following:

- Takes its operands as input

- Performs an action

- Returns a value, based on the action

Expressions can be combined, using operators, to create other expressions, as shown in this expression, with three operators and four operands:

$$
\left.
\begin{array}{l}
\underbrace{a + b}_{} \\
\underbrace{expr + c}_{} \\
expr \quad + d
\end{array}
\right\} \quad a + b + c + d
$$

Evaluating an expression is the process of applying each operator to its operands, in the proper sequence, to produce a value.

- The value is returned to the position at which the expression was evaluated. There, it might in turn be an operand in an enclosing expression.

- Besides the value returned, some expressions also have side effects, such as setting a value in memory.

Literals

Literals are numbers or strings typed into the source code that represent a specific, set value of a specific type.

For example, the following code shows literals of six types. Notice, for example, the difference between the double literal and the float literal.

```
static void Main()            Literals
{                                ↓
    Console.WriteLine("{0}", 1024);          // int literal
    Console.WriteLine("{0}", 3.1416);        // double literal
    Console.WriteLine("{0}", 3.1416F);       // float literal
    Console.WriteLine("{0}", true);          // boolean literal
    Console.WriteLine("{0}", 'x');           // character literal
    Console.WriteLine("{0}", "Hi there");    // string literal
}
```

The output of this code is the following:

```
1024
3.1416
3.1416
True
x
Hi there
```

Because literals are written into the source code, their values must be known at compile time. Several of the predefined types have their own forms of literal:

- Type bool has two literals: true and false.

- For reference type variables, literal null means that the variable is not set to a reference in memory.

Integer Literals

Integer literals are the most commonly used literals. They are written as a sequence of decimal digits, with the following:

- No decimal point

- An optional suffix to specify the type of the integer

For example, the following lines show four literals for the integer 236. Each is interpreted by the compiler as a different type of integer, depending on its suffix.

```
236           // int
236L          // long
236U          // unsigned
236UL         // unsigned long
```

Integer type literals can also be written in hexadecimal (hex) form. The digits must be the hex digits (0 through F), and the string must be prefaced with either 0x or 0X (numeral *0*, letter *x*).

Figure 8-1 shows the forms of the integer literal formats. Components with names in square brackets are optional.

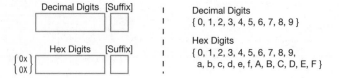

Figure 8-1. *The integer literal formats*

Table 8-1 lists the integer literal suffixes. For a given suffix, the compiler will interpret the string of digits as the smallest of the corresponding integer types that can represent the value without losing data.

For example, take the literals 236 and 5000000000, neither of which has a suffix. Since 236 can be represented with 32 bits, it will be interpreted by the compiler as an int. The larger number, however, won't fit into 32 bits, so the compiler will represent it as a long.

Table 8-1. *Integer Literal Suffixes*

Suffix	Integer Type	Notes
None	int, uint, long, ulong	
U, u	uint, ulong	
L, l	long, ulong	Using the lowercase letter *l* is not recommended, because it is easily mistaken for the digit *1*.
ul, uL, Ul, UL lu, Lu, lU, LU	ulong	Using the lowercase letter *l* is not recommended, because it is easily mistaken for the digit *1*

Real Literals

Literals for real numbers consist of the following:

- Decimal digits

- An optional decimal point

- An optional exponent part

- An optional suffix

For example, the following code shows various formats of literals of the real types:

```
float  f1 = 236F;
double d1 = 236.714;
double d2 = .35192;
double d3 = 6.338e-26;
```

Figure 8-2 shows the valid formats for real literals. Components with names in square brackets are optional. Table 8-2 shows the real suffixes and their meanings.

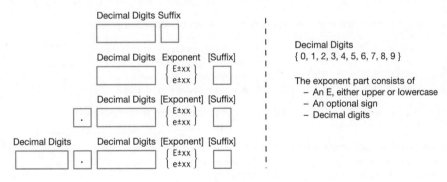

Figure 8-2. *The real literal formats*

Table 8-2. *Suffixes for the Real Literals*

Suffix	Real Type
None	double
F, f	float
D, d	double
M, m	decimal

■ **Note** Real literals without a suffix are of type `double`, not `float`!

Character Literals

A character literal consists of a character representation between two single quote marks. A character representation can be any of the following: a single character, a simple escape sequence, a hex escape sequence, or a Unicode escape sequence.

- The type of a character literal is `char`.

- A *simple escape sequence* is a backslash followed by a single character.

- A hex escape sequence is a backslash, followed by an uppercase or lowercase *x*, followed by up to four hex digits.

- A Unicode escape sequence is a backslash, followed by an uppercase or lowercase *u*, followed by up to four hex digits.

For example, the following code shows various formats of character literals:

```
char c1 = 'd';                  // Single character
char c2 = '\n';                 // Simple escape sequence
char c3 = '\x0061';             // Hex escape sequence
char c4 = '\u005a';             // Unicode escape sequence
```

Table 8-3 shows some of the important special characters and their encodings.

Table 8-3. *Important Special Characters*

Name	Escape Sequence	Hex Encoding
Null	\0	0x0000
Alert	\a	0x0007
Backspace	\b	0x0008
Horizontal tab	\t	0x0009
New line	\n	0x000A
Vertical tab	\v	0x000B
Form feed	\f	0x000C

Name	Escape Sequence	Hex Encoding
Carriage return	\r	0x000D
Double quote	\"	0x0022
Single quote	\'	0x0027
Backslash	\\	0x005C

String Literals

String literals use double quote marks rather than the single quote marks used in character literals. There are two types of string literals:

- Regular string literals

- Verbatim string literals

A regular string literal consists of a sequence of characters between a set of double quotes. A regular string literal can include the following:

- Characters

- Simple escape sequences

- Hex and Unicode escape sequences

Here's an example:

```
string st1 = "Hi there!";
string st2 = "Val1\t5, Val2\t10";
string st3 = "Add\x000ASome\u0007Interest";
```

A verbatim string literal is written like a regular string literal but is prefaced with an @ character. The important characteristics of verbatim string literals are the following:

- Verbatim literals differ from regular string literals in that escape sequences are not evaluated. Everything between the set of double quotes—including what would normally be considered escape sequences—is printed exactly as it is listed in the string.

- The only exception with verbatim literals is sets of contiguous double quotes, which are interpreted as a *single* double quote character.

For example, the following code compares some regular and verbatim string literals:

```
string rst1 = "Hi there!";
string vst1 = @"Hi there!";

string rst2 = "It started, \"Four score and seven...\"";
string vst2 = @"It started, ""Four score and seven...""";

string rst3 = "Value 1 \t 5, Val2 \t 10";     // Interprets tab esc sequence
string vst3 = @"Value 1 \t 5, Val2 \t 10";    // Does not interpret tab

string rst4 = "C:\\Program Files\\Microsoft\\";
string vst4 = @"C:\Program Files\Microsoft\";

string rst5 = " Print \x000A Multiple \u000A Lines";
string vst5 = @" Print
 Multiple
 Lines";
```

Printing these strings produces the following output:

```
Hi there!
Hi there!

It started, "Four score and seven..."
It started, "Four score and seven..."

Value 1         5, Val2         10
Value 1 \t 5, Val2 \t 10

C:\Program Files\Microsoft\
C:\Program Files\Microsoft\

 Print
 Multiple
 Lines

 Print
 Multiple
 Lines
```

■ **Note** The compiler saves memory by having identical string literals share the same memory location in the heap.

Order of Evaluation

An expression can be made up of many nested subexpressions. The order in which the subexpressions are evaluated can make a difference in the final value of the expression.

For example, given the expression 3 * 5 + 2, there are two possible results depending on the order in which the subexpressions are evaluated, as shown in Figure 8-3.

- If the multiplication is performed first, the result is 17.

- If the 5 and the 2 are added together first, the result is 21.

Figure 8-3. *Simple order of evaluation*

Precedence

You know from your grade-school days that in the preceding example, the multiplication must be performed before the addition because multiplication has a higher precedence than addition. But unlike grade-school days, when you had four operators and two levels of precedence, things are a bit more complex with C#, which has more than 45 operators and 14 levels of precedence.

Table 8-4 shows the complete list of operators and their precedences. The table lists the highest precedence operators at the top and continues to the lowest precedence operators at the bottom.

Table 8-4. *Operator Precedence: Highest to Lowest*

Category	Operators
Primary	`a.x, f(x), a[x], x++, x--, new, typeof, checked, unchecked`
Unary	`+, -, !, ~, ++x, --x, (T)x`
Multiplicative	`*, /, %`
Additive	`+, -`
Shift	`<<, >>`
Relational and type	`<, >, <=, >=, is, as`
Equality	`==, !=`
Logical AND	`&`
Logical XOR	`^`

Category	Operators
Logical OR	|
Conditional AND	&&
Conditional OR	||
Conditional	?:
Assignment	=, *=, /=, %=, +=, -=, <<=, >>=, &=, ^=, |=

Associativity

If all the operators in an expression have different levels of precedence, then evaluate each subexpression, starting at the one with the highest level, and work down the precedence scale.

But what if two sequential operators have the same level of precedence? For example, given the expression 2 / 6 * 4, there are two possible evaluation sequences:

$$(2 / 6) * 4 = 4/3$$

or

$$2 / (6 * 4) = 1/12$$

When sequential operators have the same level of precedence, the order of evaluation is determined by *operator associativity*. That is, given two operators of the same level of precedence, one or the other will have precedence, depending on the operators' associativity. Some important characteristics of operator associativity are the following and are summarized in Table 8-5:

- *Left-associative* operators are evaluated from left to right.

- *Right-associative* operators are evaluated from right to left.

- Binary operators, except the assignment operators, are left-associative.

- The assignment operators and the conditional operator are right-associative.

Therefore, given these rules, the preceding example expression should be grouped left to right, giving (2 / 6) * 4, which yields 4/3.

Table 8-5. *Summary of Operator Associativity*

Type of Operator	Associativity
Assignment operators	Right-associative
Other binary operators	Left-associative
The conditional operator	Right-associative

You can explicitly set the order of evaluation of the subexpressions of an expression by using parentheses. Parenthesized subexpressions do the following:

- Override the precedence and associativity rules

- Are evaluated in order from the innermost nested set to the outermost

Simple Arithmetic Operators

The simple arithmetic operators perform the four basic arithmetic operations and are listed in Table 8-6. These operators are binary and left-associative.

Table 8-6. *The Simple Arithmetic Operators*

Operator	Name	Description
+	Addition	Adds the two operands.
-	Subtraction	Subtracts the second operand from the first.
*	Multiplication	Multiplies the two operands.
/	Division	Divides the first operand by the second. Integer division rounds the result toward 0 to the nearest integer.

The arithmetic operators perform the standard arithmetic operations on all the predefined simple arithmetic types.

The following are examples of the simple arithmetic operators:

```
int x1 = 5 + 6;        double d1 = 5.0 + 6.0;
int x2 = 12 - 3;       double d2 = 12.0 - 3.0;
int x3 = 3 * 4;        double d3 = 3.0 * 4.0;
int x4 = 10 / 3;       double d4 = 10.0 / 3.0;

byte b1 = 5 + 6;
sbyte sb1 = 6 * 5;
```

The Remainder Operator

The remainder operator (%) divides the first operand by the second operand, ignores the quotient, and returns the remainder. Table 8-7 gives its description.

The remainder operator is binary and left-associative.

Table 8-7. *The Remainder Operator*

Operator	Name	Description
%	Remainder	Divides the first operand by the second operand and returns the remainder

The following lines show examples of the integer remainder operator:

- 0 % 3 = 0, because 0 divided by 3 is 0 with a remainder of 0.

- 1 % 3 = 1, because 1 divided by 3 is 0 with a remainder of 1.

- 2 % 3 = 2, because 2 divided by 3 is 0 with a remainder of 2.

- 3 % 3 = 0, because 3 divided by 3 is 1 with a remainder of 0.

- 4 % 3 = 1, because 4 divided by 3 is 1 with a remainder of 1.

The remainder operator can also be used with real numbers to give *real remainders*.

```
Console.WriteLine("0.0f % 1.5f is {0}" , 0.0f % 1.5f);
Console.WriteLine("0.5f % 1.5f is {0}" , 0.5f % 1.5f);
Console.WriteLine("1.0f % 1.5f is {0}" , 1.0f % 1.5f);
Console.WriteLine("1.5f % 1.5f is {0}" , 1.5f % 1.5f);
Console.WriteLine("2.0f % 1.5f is {0}" , 2.0f % 1.5f);
Console.WriteLine("2.5f % 1.5f is {0}" , 2.5f % 1.5f);
```

This code produces the following output:

```
0.0f % 1.5f is 0          // 0.0 / 1.5 = 0 remainder 0
0.5f % 1.5f is 0.5        // 0.5 / 1.5 = 0 remainder .5
1.0f % 1.5f is 1          // 1.0 / 1.5 = 0 remainder 1
1.5f % 1.5f is 0          // 1.5 / 1.5 = 1 remainder 0
2.0f % 1.5f is 0.5        // 2.0 / 1.5 = 1 remainder .5
2.5f % 1.5f is 1          // 2.5 / 1.5 = 1 remainder 1
```

Relational and Equality Comparison Operators

The relational and equality comparison operators are binary operators that compare their operands and return a value of type bool. Table 8-8 lists these operators.

The relational and equality operators are binary and left-associative.

Table 8-8. *The Relational and Equality Comparison Operators*

Operator	Name	Description
<	Less than	true if first operand is less than second operand; false otherwise
>	Greater than	true if first operand is greater than second operand; false otherwise
<=	Less than or equal to	true if first operand is less than or equal to second operand; false otherwise
>=	Greater than or equal to	true if first operand is greater than or equal to second operand; false otherwise
==	Equal to	true if first operand is equal to second operand; false otherwise
!=	Not equal to	true if first operand is not equal to second operand; false otherwise

A binary expression with a relational or equality operator returns a value of type bool.

■ **Note** Unlike C and C++, numbers in C# do not have a Boolean interpretation.

```
int x = 5;
if( x )          // Wrong.  x is of type int, not type boolean.
   ...
if( x == 5 )     // Fine, since expression returns a value of type boolean
   ...
```

When printed, the Boolean values true and false are represented by the string output values True and False.

```
int x = 5, y = 4;
Console.WriteLine("x == x is {0}" , x == x);
Console.WriteLine("x == y is {0}" , x == y);
```

The output of this code is the following:

```
x == x is True
x == y is False
```

Comparison and Equality Operations

When comparing most reference types for equality, only the references are compared.

- If the references are equal—that is, if they point to the same object in memory—the equality comparison is true; otherwise, it is false, even if *the two separate objects* in memory are *exactly equivalent* in every other respect.

- This is called a *shallow comparison*.

Figure 8-4 illustrates the comparison of reference types.

- On the left of the figure, the references of both a and b are the same, so a comparison would return true.

- On the right of the figure, the references are not the same, so even if the contents of the two AClass objects were exactly the same, the comparison would return false.

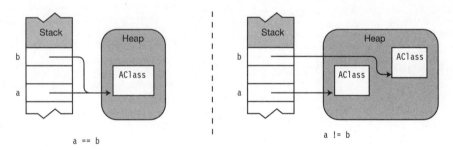

Figure 8-4. *Comparing reference types for equality*

Objects of type string are also reference types but are compared differently. When strings are compared for equality, they are compared in length and case-sensitive content.

- If two strings have the same length and the same case-sensitive content, the equality comparison returns true, even if they occupy different areas of memory.

- This is called a *deep comparison*.

Delegates, which are covered in Chapter 15, are also reference types and also use deep comparison. When delegates are compared for equality, the comparison returns true if both delegates are null or if both have the same number of members in their invocation lists and the invocation lists match.

When comparing numeric expressions, the types and values are compared. When comparing enum types, the comparisons are done on the underlying values of the operands. Enums are covered in Chapter 13.

Increment and Decrement Operators

The increment operator adds 1 to the operand. The decrement operator subtracts 1 from the operand. Table 8-9 lists the operators and their descriptions.

These operators are unary and have two forms, the *pre-* form and the *post-* form, which act differently.

- In the pre-form, the operator is placed before the operand; for example, ++x and --y.

- In the post-form, the operator is placed after the operand; for example, x++ and y--.

Table 8-9. *The Increment and Decrement Operators*

Operator	Name	Description
++	Pre-increment ++var	Increment the value of the variable by 1 and save it back into the variable. Return the new value of the variable.
	Post-increment var++	Increment the value of the variable by 1 and save it back into the variable. Return the old value of the variable before it was incremented.
--	Pre-decrement--var	Decrement the value of the variable by 1 and save it back into the variable. Return the new value of the variable.
	Post-decrement var--	Decrement the value of the variable by 1 and save it back into the variable. Return the old value of the variable before it was decremented.

In comparing the pre- and post-forms of the operators

- The final, stored value of the operand variable after the statement is executed is the same regardless of whether the pre- or post-form of the operator is used.

- The only difference is the value *returned* by the operator to the expression.

Table 8-10 shows an example summarizing the behavior.

Table 8-10. *Behavior of Pre- and Post-Increment and Decrement Operators*

	Expression: x = 10	Value Returned to the Expression	Value of Variable After Evaluation
Pre-increment	++x	11	11
Post-increment	x++	10	11
Pre-decrement	--x	9	9
Post-decrement	x--	10	9

For example, the following is a simple demonstration of the four different versions of the operators. To show the different results on the same input, the value of the operand x is reset to 5 before each assignment statement.

```
int x = 5, y;
y = x++;   // result: y: 5, x: 6
Console.WriteLine("y: {0}, x: {1}" , y, x);

x = 5;
y = ++x;   // result: y: 6, x: 6
Console.WriteLine("y: {0}, x: {1}" , y, x);

x = 5;
y = x--;   // result: y: 5, x: 4
Console.WriteLine("y: {0}, x: {1}" , y, x);

x = 5;
y = --x;   // result: y: 4, x: 4
Console.WriteLine("y: {0}, x: {1}" , y, x);
```

This code produces the following output:

```
y: 5, x: 6
y: 6, x: 6
y: 5, x: 4
y: 4, x: 4
```

Conditional Logical Operators

The logical operators are used for comparing or negating the logical values of their operands and returning the resulting logical value. Table 8-11 lists the operators.

The logical AND and logical OR operators are binary and left-associative. The logical NOT is unary.

Table 8-11. *The Conditional Logical Operators*

Operator	Name	Description
&&	Logical AND	true if both operands are true; false otherwise
||	Logical OR	true if at least one operand is true; false otherwise
!	Logical NOT	true if the operand is false; false otherwise

The syntax for these operators is the following, where *Expr1* and *Expr2* evaluate to Boolean values:

```
Expr1 && Expr2
Expr1 || Expr2
   ! Expr
```

The following are some examples:

```
bool bVal;
bVal = (1 == 1) && (2 == 2);        // True, both operand expressions are true
bVal = (1 == 1) && (1 == 2);        // False, second operand expression is false

bVal = (1 == 1) || (2 == 2);        // True, both operand expressions are true
bVal = (1 == 1) || (1 == 2);        // True, first operand expression is true
bVal = (1 == 2) || (2 == 3);        // False, both operand expressions are false

bVal = true;                        // Set bVal to true.
bVal = !bVal;                       // bVal is now false.
```

The conditional logical operators operate in "short-circuit" mode, meaning that, if after evaluating *Expr1* the result can already be determined, then it skips the evaluation of *Expr2*. The following code shows examples of expressions in which the value can be determined after evaluating the first operand:

```
bool bVal;
bVal = (1 == 2) && (2 == 2);    // False, after evaluating first expression

bVal = (1 == 1) || (1 == 2);    // True, after evaluating first expression
```

Because of the short circuit behavior, do not place expressions with side effects (such as changing a value) in *Expr2*, since they might not be evaluated. In the following code, the post-increment of variable iVal would not be executed, because after executing the first subexpression, it can be determined that the value of the entire expression is false.

```
bool bVal; int iVal = 10;

bVal = (1 == 2) && (9 == iVal++);        // result:  bVal = False, iVal = 10
           ↑                ↑
         False        Never evaluated
```

Logical Operators

The bitwise logical operators are often used to set the bit patterns for parameters to methods. Table 8-12 lists the bitwise logical operators.

These operators, except for bitwise negation, are binary and left-associative. The bitwise negation operator is unary.

Table 8-12. *The Logical Operators*

Operator	Name	Description
&	Bitwise AND	Produces the bitwise AND of the two operands. The resulting bit is 1 only if both operand bits are 1.
|	Bitwise OR	Produces the bitwise OR of the two operands. The resulting bit is 1 if either operand bit is 1.
^	Bitwise XOR	Produces the bitwise XOR of the two operands. The resulting bit is 1 only if one, but not both, operand bits are 1.
~	Bitwise negation	Each bit in the operand is switched to its opposite. This produces the one's complement of the operand.

The binary bitwise operators compare the corresponding bits at each position in each of their two operands, and they set the bit in the return value according to the logical operation.

Figure 8-5 shows four examples of the bitwise logical operations.

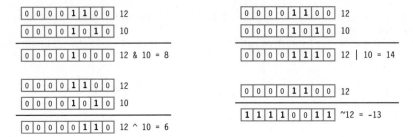

Figure 8-5. *Examples of bitwise logical operators*

The following code implements the preceding examples:

```
const byte x = 12, y = 10;
sbyte a;

a = x & y;          //  a = 8
a = x | y;          //  a = 14
a = x ^ y;          //  a = 6
a = ~x;             //  a = -13
```

Shift Operators

The bitwise shift operators shift the bit pattern either right or left a specified number of positions, with the vacated bits filled with 0s or 1s. Table 8-13 lists the shift operators.

The shift operators are binary and left-associative. The syntax of the bitwise shift operators is shown here. The number of positions to shift is given by *Count*.

```
Operand << Count                    // Left shift
Operand >> Count                    // Right shift
```

Table 8-13. *The Shift Operators*

Operator	Name	Description
<<	Left shift	Shifts the bit pattern left by the given number of positions. The bits shifted off the left end are lost. Bit positions opening up on the right are filled with 0s.
>>	Right shift	Shifts the bit pattern right by the given number of positions. Bits shifted off the right end are lost.

For the vast majority of programming in C#, you don't need to know anything about the hardware underneath. If you're doing bitwise manipulation of signed numbers, however, it can be helpful to know about the numeric representation. The underlying hardware represents signed binary numbers in a form called *two's complement*. In two's-complement representation, positive numbers have their normal binary form. To negate a number, you take the bitwise negation of the number and add 1 to it. This process turns a positive number into its negative representation, and vice versa. In two's complement, all negative numbers have a 1 in the leftmost bit position. Figure 8-6 shows the negation of the number 12.

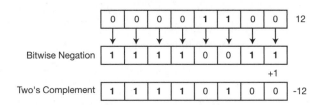

Figure 8-6. *To get the negation of a two's-complement number, take its bitwise negation and add 1.*

The underlying representation is important when shifting signed numbers because the result of shifting an integral value one bit to the left is the same as multiplying it by two. Shifting it to the right is the same as dividing it by two.

If, however, you were to shift a negative number to the right and the leftmost bit were to be filled with a 0, it would produce the wrong result. The 0 in the leftmost position would indicate a positive number. But this is incorrect, because dividing a negative number by 2 doesn't produce a positive number.

To address this situation, when the operand is a signed integer, if the leftmost bit of the operand is a 1 (indicating a negative number), bit positions opening up on the left are filled with 1s rather than 0s. This maintains the correct two's-complement representation. For positive or unsigned numbers, bit positions opening up on the left are filled with 0s.

Figure 8-7 shows how the expression 14 << 3 would be evaluated in a byte. This operation causes the following:

- Each of the bits in the operand (14) is shifted three places to the left.

- The three bit positions vacated on the right end are filled with 0s.

- The resulting value is 112.

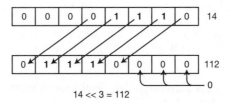

Figure 8-7. *Example of left shift of three bits*

Figure 8-8 illustrates bitwise shift operations.

0	0	0	0	1	1	1	0	14

0	1	1	1	0	0	0	0	14 << 3 = 112

0	0	0	0	1	1	1	0	14

0	0	0	0	0	0	0	1	14 >> 3 = 1

Figure 8-8. *Bitwise shifts*

The following code implements the preceding examples:

```
int a, b, x = 14;

a = x << 3;              // Shift left
b = x >> 3;              // Shift right

Console.WriteLine("{0} << 3 = {1}" , x, a);
Console.WriteLine("{0} >> 3 = {1}" , x, b);
```

This code produces the following output:

```
14 << 3 = 112
14 >> 3 = 1
```

Assignment Operators

The assignment operators evaluate the expression on the right side of the operator and use that value to set the variable expression on the left side of the operator. Table 8-14 lists the assignment operators.

The assignment operators are binary and right-associative.

Table 8-14. *The Assignment Operators*

Operator	Description
=	Simple assignment; evaluate the expression on the right, and assign the returned value to the variable or expression on the left.
*=	Compound assignment; *var* *= *expr* is equal to *var* = *var* * (*expr*).
/=	Compound assignment; *var* /= *expr* is equal to *var* = *var* / (*expr*).
%=	Compound assignment; *var* %= *expr* is equal to *var*= *var* % (*expr*).
+=	Compound assignment; *var* += *expr* is equal to *var* = *var* + (*expr*).
-=	Compound assignment; *var* -= *expr* is equal to *var* = *var*- (*expr*).
<<=	Compound assignment; *var* <<= *expr* is equal to *var* = *var* << (*expr*).
>>=	Compound assignment; *var* >>= *expr* is equal to *var* = *var* >> (*expr*).
&=	Compound assignment; *var* &= *expr* is equal to *var* = *var* & (*expr*).
^=	Compound assignment; *var* ^= *expr* is equal to *var* = *var* ^ (*expr*).
|=	Compound assignment; *var* |= *expr* is equal to *var* = *var* | (*expr*).

The syntax is as follows:

```
VariableExpression Operator Expression
```

For simple assignment, the expression to the right of the operator is evaluated, and its value is assigned to the variable on the left.

```
int x;
x = 5;
x = y * z;
```

The types of objects that can be on the left side of an assignment operator are the following. They are discussed later in the text.

- Variables (local variables, fields, parameters)

- Properties

- Indexers

- Events

Compound Assignment

Frequently, you'll want to evaluate an expression and add the results to the current value of a variable, as shown here:

```
x = x + expr;
```

The compound assignment operators allow a shorthand method for avoiding the repetition of the left-side variable on the right side under certain common circumstances. For example, the following two statements are semantically equivalent, but the second is shorter and just as easy to understand.

```
x = x + (y - z);
x += y - z;
```

The other compound assignment statements are analogous:

```
                         Notice the parentheses.
                            ↓      ↓
x *= y - z;     // Equivalent to x = x * (y - z)
x /= y - z;     // Equivalent to x = x / (y - z)
   ...
```

The Conditional Operator

The conditional operator is a powerful and succinct way of returning one of two values, based on the result of a condition. Table 8-15 shows the operator.

The conditional operator is ternary.

Table 8-15. *The Conditional Operator*

Operator	Name	Description
? :	Conditional operator	Evaluates an expression and returns one of two values, depending on whether the expression returns true or false

The syntax for the conditional operator is shown following. It has a test expression and two result expressions.

- *Condition* must return a value of type bool.

- If *Condition* evaluates to true, then *Expression1* is evaluated and returned. Otherwise, *Expression2* is evaluated and returned.

```
Condition ? Expression1 : Expression2
```

The conditional operator can be compared with the if...else construct. For example, the following if...else construct checks a condition, and if the condition is true, it assigns 5 to variable intVar. Otherwise, it assigns it the value 10.

```
if ( x < y )                              // if...else
   intVar = 5;
else
   intVar = 10;
```

The conditional operator can perform the same operation in a less verbose form, as shown in the following statement:

```
intVar = x < y ? 5 : 10;                  // Conditional operator
```

Placing the condition and each return expression on separate lines, as in the following code, makes the intent very easy to understand.

```
intVar = x < y
         ? 5
         : 10 ;
```

Figure 8-9 compares the two forms shown in the example.

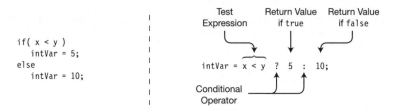

```
if( x < y )
    intVar = 5;
else
    intVar = 10;
```

Figure 8-9. *The conditional operator versus if...else*

For example, the following code uses the conditional operator three times—once in each of the WriteLine statements. In the first instance, it returns either the value of x or the value of y. In the second two instances, it returns either the empty string or the string " not".

```
int x = 10, y = 9;
int highVal = x > y                        // Condition
                ? x                        // Expression 1
                : y;                       // Expression 2
Console.WriteLine("highVal:  {0}\n" , highVal);

Console.WriteLine("x is{0} greater than y" ,
                x > y                      // Condition
                ? ""                       // Expression 1
                : " not" );                // Expression 2
y = 11;
Console.WriteLine("x is{0} greater than y" ,
                x > y                      // Condition
                ? ""                       // Expression 1
                : " not" );                // Expression 2
```

This code produces the following output:

```
highVal:  10

x is greater than y
x is not greater than y
```

■ **Note** The if...else statement is a flow-of-control *statement*. It should be used for doing one or the other of two *actions*. The conditional operator returns an *expression*. It should be used for *returning* one or the other of two *values*.

Unary Arithmetic Operators

The unary operators set the sign of a numeric value. They are listed in Table 8-16.

- The unary positive operator simply returns the value of the operand.

- The unary negative operator returns the value of the operand subtracted from 0.

Table 8-16. *The Unary Operators*

Operator	Name	Description
+	Positive sign	Returns the numeric value of the operand
-	Negative sign	Returns the numeric value of the operand subtracted from 0

For example, the following code shows the use and results of the operators:

```
int x = +10;      // x = 10
int y = -x;       // y = -10
int z = -y;       // z = 10
```

User-Defined Type Conversions

User-defined conversions are discussed in greater detail in Chapter 18, but I'll mention them here as well because they are operators.

- You can define both implicit and explicit conversions for your own classes and structs. This allows you to convert an object of your user-defined type to some other type, and vice versa.

- C# provides implicit and explicit conversions.

  — With an *implicit conversion*, the compiler automatically makes the conversion, if necessary, when it is resolving what types to use in a particular context.

  — With an *explicit conversion*, the compiler will make the conversion only when an explicit cast operator is used.

The syntax for declaring an implicit conversion is the following. The `public` and `static` modifiers are required for all user-defined conversions.

```
          Required                Target            Source
             ↓                      ↓                 ↓
public static implicit operator TargetType ( SourceType Identifier )
{
    ...
    return ObjectOfTargetType;
}
```

The syntax for the explicit conversion is the same, except that `explicit` is substituted for `implicit`.

The following code shows an example of declarations for conversion operators that will convert an object of type `LimitedInt` to type `int`, and vice versa.

```
class LimitedInt                  Target      Source
{                                    ↓           ↓
    public static implicit operator int (LimitedInt li)    // LimitedInt to int
    {
        return li.TheValue;
    }                             Target      Source
                                     ↓           ↓
    public static implicit operator LimitedInt (int x)     // int to LimitedInt
    {
        LimitedInt li = new LimitedInt();
        li.TheValue = x;
        return li;
    }

    private int _theValue = 0;
    public int TheValue{ ... }
}
```

For example, the following code reiterates and uses the two type conversion operators just defined. In `Main`, an `int` literal is converted into a `LimitedInt` object, and in the next line, a `LimitedInt` object is converted into an `int`.

```
class LimitedInt
{
   const int MaxValue = 100;
   const int MinValue = 0;

   public static implicit operator int(LimitedInt li)       // Convert type
   {
      return li.TheValue;
   }

   public static implicit operator LimitedInt(int x)        // Convert type
   {
      LimitedInt li = new LimitedInt();
      li.TheValue = x;
      return li;
   }

   private int _theValue = 0;
   public int TheValue                                      // Property
   {
      get { return _theValue; }
      set
      {
         if (value < MinValue)
            _theValue = 0;
         else
            _theValue = value > MaxValue
                          ? MaxValue
                          : value;
      }
   }
}

class Program
{
   static void Main()                             // Main
   {
      LimitedInt li = 500;                         // Convert 500 to LimitedInt
      int value    = li;                           // Convert LimitedInt to int

      Console.WriteLine("li: {0}, value: {1}" , li.TheValue, value);
   }
}
```

This code produces the following output:

```
li: 100, value: 100
```

Explicit Conversion and the Cast Operator

The preceding example code showed the implicit conversion of the int to a LimitedInt type and the implicit conversion of a LimitedInt type to an int. If, however, you had declared the two conversion operators as explicit, you would have had to explicitly use cast operators when making the conversions.

A *cast operator* consists of the name of the type to which you want to convert the expression, inside a set of parentheses. For example, in the following code, method Main casts the value 500 to a LimitedInt object.

```
                            Cast operator
                                 ↓
        LimitedInt li = (LimitedInt) 500;
```

For example, here is the relevant portion of the code, with the changes marked:

```
                      ↓
public static explicit operator int(LimitedInt li)
{
    return li.TheValue;
}
                      ↓
public static explicit operator LimitedInt(int x)
{
    LimitedInt li = new LimitedInt();
    li.TheValue   = x;
    return li;
}

static void Main()
{                             ↓
    LimitedInt li = (LimitedInt) 500;
    int value     = (int) li;
                        ↑
    Console.WriteLine("li: {0}, value: {1}" , li.TheValue, value);
}
```

In both versions of the code, the output is the following:

```
li: 100, value: 100
```

There are two other operators that take a value of one type and return a value of a different, specified type. These are the is operator and the as operator. These are covered at the end of Chapter 18.

Operator Overloading

The C# operators, as you've seen, are defined to work using the predefined types as operands. If confronted with a user-defined type, an operator simply would not know how to process it. Operator overloading allows you to define how the C# operators should operate on operands of your user-defined types.

- Operator overloading is available only for classes and structs.

- You can overload an operator x for use with your class or struct by declaring a method named operator x that implements the behavior (for example, operator +, operator -, and so on).

  - The overload methods for unary operators take a single parameter of the class or struct type.

  - The overload methods for binary operators take two parameters, at least one of which must be of the class or struct type.

```
public static LimitedInt operator -(LimitedInt x)              // Unary
public static LimitedInt operator +(LimitedInt x, double y)   // Binary
```

The declaration of an operator overload method requires the following:

- The declaration must use both the static and public modifiers.

- The operator must be a member of the class or struct for which it is an operator.

For example, the following code shows two of the overloaded operators of class LimitedInt: the addition operator and the negation operator. You can tell that it is negation and not subtraction because the operator overload method has only a single parameter and is therefore unary; whereas the subtraction operator is binary.

```
class LimitedInt Return
{           Required      type    Keyword Operator      Operand
              ↓            ↓        ↓      ↓               ↓
    public static LimitedInt operator + (LimitedInt x, double y)
    {
        LimitedInt li = new LimitedInt();
        li.TheValue = x.TheValue + (int)y;
        return li;
    }

    public static LimitedInt operator - (LimitedInt x)
    {
        // In this strange class, negating a value just sets its value to 0.
        LimitedInt li = new LimitedInt();
        li.TheValue = 0;
        return li;
    }
    ...
}
```

Restrictions on Operator Overloading

Not all operators can be overloaded, and there are restrictions on the types of overloading that can be done. The important things you should know about the restrictions on operator overloading are described later in the section.

Only the following operators can be overloaded. Prominently missing from the list is the assignment operator.

Overloadable unary operators: +, -, !, ~, ++, --, true, false

Overloadable binary operators: +, -, *, /, %, &, |, ^, <<, >>, ==, !=, >, <, >=, <=

The increment and decrement operators are overloadable. But unlike the predefined versions, there is no distinction between the pre- and post-usage of the overloaded operator.

You *cannot* do the following things with operator overloading:

- Create a new operator

- Change the syntax of an operator

- Redefine how an operator works on the predefined types

- Change the precedence or associativity of an operator

■ **Note** Your overloaded operators should conform to the intuitive meanings of the operators.

Example of Operator Overloading

The following example shows the overloads of three operators for class LimitedInt: negation, subtraction, and addition.

```
class LimitedInt {
   const int MaxValue = 100;
   const int MinValue = 0;

   public static LimitedInt operator -(LimitedInt x)
   {
      // In this strange class, negating a value just sets its value to 0.
      LimitedInt li = new LimitedInt();
      li.TheValue = 0;
      return li;
   }

   public static LimitedInt operator -(LimitedInt x, LimitedInt y)
   {
      LimitedInt li = new LimitedInt();
      li.TheValue = x.TheValue - y.TheValue;
      return li;
   }

   public static LimitedInt operator +(LimitedInt x, double y)
   {
      LimitedInt li = new LimitedInt();
      li.TheValue = x.TheValue + (int)y;
      return li;
   }

   private int _theValue = 0;
   public int TheValue
   {
      get { return _theValue; }
      set
      {
         if (value < MinValue)
            _theValue = 0;
         else
            _theValue = value > MaxValue
                              ? MaxValue
                              : value;
      }
   }
}
```

```
class Program {
    static void Main() {
        LimitedInt li1 = new LimitedInt();
        LimitedInt li2 = new LimitedInt();
        LimitedInt li3 = new LimitedInt();
        li1.TheValue = 10; li2.TheValue = 26;
        Console.WriteLine(" li1: {0}, li2: {1}" , li1.TheValue, li2.TheValue);

        li3 = -li1;
        Console.WriteLine("-{0} = {1}" , li1.TheValue, li3.TheValue);

        li3 = li2 - li1;
        Console.WriteLine(" {0} - {1} = {2}" ,
                li2.TheValue, li1.TheValue, li3.TheValue);

        li3 = li1 - li2;
        Console.WriteLine(" {0} - {1} = {2}" ,
                li1.TheValue, li2.TheValue, li3.TheValue);
    }
}
```

This code produces the following output:

```
li1: 10, li2: 26
-10 = 0
26 - 10 = 16
10 - 26 = 0
```

The typeof Operator

The typeof operator returns the System.Type object of any type given as its parameter. From this object, you can learn the characteristics of the type. (There is only one System.Type object for any given type.) You cannot overload the typeof operator. Table 8-17 lists the operator's characteristics.

The typeof operator is unary.

Table 8-17. *The typeof Operator*

Operator	Description
typeof	Returns the System.Type object of a given type

The following is an example of the syntax of the typeof operator. Type is a class in the System namespace.

```
Type t = typeof ( SomeClass )
```

For example, the following code uses the typeof operator to get information on a class called SomeClass and to print the names of its public fields and methods.

```
using System.Reflection;   // Use the Reflection namespace to take full advantage
                           // of determining information about a type.
class SomeClass
{
   public int  Field1;
   public int  Field2;

   public void Method1() { }
   public int  Method2() { return 1; }
}

class Program
{
   static void Main()
   {
      Type t = typeof(SomeClass);
      FieldInfo[]  fi = t.GetFields();
      MethodInfo[] mi = t.GetMethods();

      foreach (FieldInfo f in fi)
         Console.WriteLine("Field : {0}" , f.Name);
      foreach (MethodInfo m in mi)
         Console.WriteLine("Method: {0}" , m.Name);
   }
}
```

The output of this code is the following:

```
Field : Field1
Field : Field2
Method: Method1
Method: Method2
Method: ToString
Method: Equals
Method: GetHashCode
Method: GetType
```

The typeof operator is also called by the GetType method, which is available for every object of every type. For example, the following code retrieves the name of the type of the object:

```
class SomeClass
{
    ...
}

class Program
{
    static void Main()
    {
        SomeClass s = new SomeClass();

        Console.WriteLine("Type s: {0}" , s.GetType().Name);
    }
}
```

This code produces the following output:

```
Type s: SomeClass
```

Other Operators

The operators covered in this chapter are the standard operators for the built-in types. There are other special usage operators that are dealt with later in the book, along with their operand types. For example, the nullable types have a special operator called the null coalescing operator, which is described in Chapter 25 along with a more in-depth description of nullable types.

CHAPTER 9

■ ■ ■

Statements

What Are Statements?

The statements in C# are very similar to those of C and C++. This chapter covers the characteristics of a C# statement, as well as the flow-of-control statements provided by the language.

- A *statement* is a source code instruction describing a type or telling the program to perform an action.

- There are three major categories of statements:

  — *Declaration statements:* Statements that declare types or variables

  — *Embedded statements:* Statements that perform actions or manage flow of control

  — *Labeled statements:* Statements to which control can jump

Previous chapters have covered a number of different declaration statements, including declarations of local variables, classes, and class members. This chapter covers the embedded statements, which do not declare types, variables, or instances. Instead, they use expressions and flow-of-control constructs to work with the objects and variables that have been declared by the declaration statements.

- A *simple statement* consists of an expression followed by a semicolon.

- A *block* is a sequence of statements enclosed by matching curly braces. The enclosed statements can include the following:

  — Declaration statements

  — Embedded statements

  — Labeled statements

  — Nested blocks

The following code gives examples of each:

```
int x = 10;          // Simple declaration
int z;               // Simple declaration

{                    // Block
   int y = 20;       // Simple declaration
   z = x + y;        // Embedded statement
top: y = 30;         // Labeled statement
   ...
   {                 // Nested block
   ...
   }
}
```

■ **Note** A block counts syntactically as a single embedded statement. Anywhere that an embedded statement is required syntactically, you can use a block.

An *empty statement* consists of just a semicolon. You can use an empty statement at any position where the syntax of the language requires an embedded statement but your program logic does not require any action.

For example, the following code is an example of using the empty statement:

- The second line in the code is an empty statement. It is required because there must be an embedded statement between the if part and the else part of the construct.

- The fourth line is a simple statement, as shown by the terminating semicolon.

```
if( x < y )
    ;                   // Empty statement
else
    z = a + b;          // Simple statement
```

Expression Statements

The previous chapter looked at expressions. Expressions return values, but they can also have *side effects*.

- A side effect is an action that affects the state of the program.

- Many expressions are evaluated only for their side effects.

You can create a statement from an expression by placing a statement terminator (semicolon) after it. Any value returned by the expression is discarded. For example, the following code shows an expression statement. It consists of the assignment expression (an assignment operator and two operands) followed by a semicolon. This does the following two things:

- The expression assigns the value on the right of the operator to the memory location referenced by variable x. Although this is probably the main reason for the statement, *this is considered the side effect.*

- After setting the value of x, the expression returns with the new value of x. But there is nothing to receive this return value, so it is ignored.

```
x = 10;
```

The whole reason for evaluating the expression is to achieve the side effect.

Flow-of-Control Statements

C# provides the flow-of-control constructs common to modern programming languages.

- *Conditional execution* executes or skips a section of code depending on a condition. The conditional execution statements are the following:
  - — `if`
  - — `if...else`
  - — `switch`

- *Looping statements* repeatedly execute a section of code. The looping statements are the following:
  - — `while`
  - — `do`
  - — `for`
  - — `foreach`

- *Jump statements* change the flow of control from one section of code to a specific statement in another section of code. The jump statements are the following:
  - — `break`
  - — `continue`
  - — `return`
  - — `goto`
  - — `throw`

Conditional execution and looping constructs (other than `foreach`) require a test expression, or *condition*, to determine where the program should continue execution.

■ **Note** Unlike C and C++, test expressions must return a value of type `bool`. Numbers do not have a Boolean interpretation in C#.

The if Statement

The `if` statement implements conditional execution. The syntax for the `if` statement is shown here and is illustrated in Figure 9-1.

- *TestExpr* must evaluate to a value of type bool.

- If *TestExpr* evaluates to true, *Statement* is executed.

- If it evaluates to false, *Statement* is skipped.

```
if( TestExpr )
    Statement
```

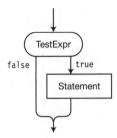

Figure 9-1. *The if statement*

The following code shows examples of `if` statements:

```
// With a simple statement
if( x <= 10 )
    z = x - 1;                  // Single statement – no curly braces needed


// With a block
if( x >= 20 )
{
    x = x - 5;                  // Block – curly braces needed
    y = x + z;
}


int x = 5;
if( x )           // Error: test expression must be a bool, not int
{
    ...
}
```

The if . . . else Statement

The if...else statement implements a two-way branch. The syntax for the if...else statement is shown here and is illustrated in Figure 9-2.

- If *TestExpr* evaluates to true, *Statement1* is executed.

- If it evaluates to false, *Statement2* is executed instead.

```
if( TestExpr )
    Statement1
else
    Statement2
```

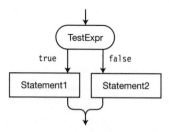

Figure 9-2. *The if . . . else statement*

The following is an example of the if...else statement:

```
if( x <= 10 )
    z = x - 1;                 // Single statement
else
{                             // Multiple statements--block
    x = x - 5;
    y = x + z;
}
```

The switch Statement

The switch statement implements multiway branching. Figure 9-3 shows the syntax and structure of the switch statement.

- The switch statement contains zero or more *switch sections*.

- Each *switch section* starts with one or more *switch labels*.

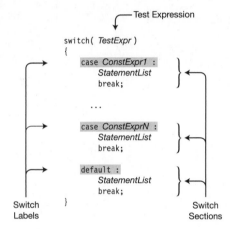

Figure 9-3. *Structure of a switch statement*

Switch labels have the following form:

The flow of control through the structure in Figure 9-3 is the following:

- The test expression, *TestExpr*, is evaluated at the top of the construct.

- Each switch section must end with the break statement or one of the other four jump statements.

  — The jump statements are break, return, continue, goto, and throw, and they are described later in this chapter.

  — Of the five jump statements, the break statement is the most commonly used for ending a switch section. The break statement branches execution to the end of the switch statement. We'll cover all the jump statements later in this chapter.

- If the value of *TestExpr* is equal to the value *ConstExpr1*, the constant expression in the first switch label and then the statements in the *statement list* following the switch label are executed, until the one of the jump statements is encountered.

- The default section is optional, but if it is included, it must end with one of the jump statements.

Figure 9-4 illustrates the general flow of control through a switch statement. You can modify the flow through a switch statement with a goto statement or a return statement.

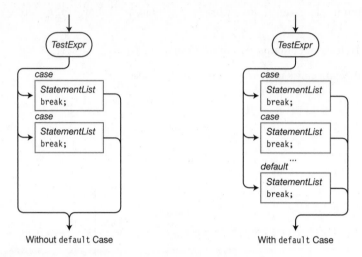

Figure 9-4. *The flow of control through a switch statement*

A Switch Example

The following code executes the switch statement five times, with the value of x ranging from 1 to 5. From the output, you can tell which case section was executed on each cycle through the loop.

```
for( int x=1; x<6; x++ )
{
   switch( x )                          // Evaluate the value of variable x.
   {
     case 2:                                    // If x equals 2
        Console.WriteLine("x is {0} -- In Case 2", x);
        break;                                  // Go to end of switch.


     case 5:                                    // If x equals 5
        Console.WriteLine("x is {0} -- In Case 5", x);
        break;                                  // Go to end of switch.


     default:                                   // If x is neither 2 nor 5
        Console.WriteLine("x is {0} -- In Default case", x);
        break;                                  // Go to end of switch.
   }
}
```

This code produces the following output:

```
x is 1 -- In Default case
x is 2 -- In Case 2
x is 3 -- In Default case
x is 4 -- In Default case
x is 5 -- In Case 5
```

More on the switch Statement

A switch statement can have any number of switch sections, including none. The default section is not required, as shown in the following example. It is, however, generally considered good practice to include it, since it can catch potential errors.

For example, the switch statement in the following code has no default section. The switch statement is inside a for loop, which executes the statement five times, with the value of x starting at 1 and ending at 5.

```
for( int x=1; x<6; x++ )
{
    switch( x )
    {
        case 5:
            Console.WriteLine("x is {0} -- In Case 5", x);
            break;
    }
}
```

This code produces the following output:

```
x is 5 -- In Case 5
```

The following code has only the default section:

```
for( int x=1; x<4; x++ )
{
    switch( x )
    {
        default:
            Console.WriteLine("x is {0} -- In Default case", x);
            break;
    }
}
```

This code produces the following output:

```
x is 1 -- In Default case
x is 2 -- In Default case
x is 3 -- In Default case
```

Switch Labels

The expression following the keyword case in a switch label must be a constant expression and must therefore be completely evaluable by the compiler at *compile* time. It must also be of the same type as the test expression

For example, Figure 9-5 shows three sample switch statements.

```
const string YES = "yes";          const char LetterB = 'b';        const int Five = 5;

string s = "no";                   char c = 'a';                    int x = 5;
switch (s)                         switch (c)                       switch (x)
{                                  {                                {
    case YES:                          case 'a':                        case Five:
        PrintOut("Yes");                   PrintOut("a");                   PrintOut("5");
        break;                             break;                           break;

    case "no":                         case LetterB:                    case 10:
        PrintOut("No");                    PrintOut("b");                   PrintOut("10");
        break;                             break;                           break;
}                                  }                                }
```

Figure 9-5. *Switch statements with different types of switch labels*

■ **Note** Unlike C and C++, each switch section, including the optional default section, must end with one of the jump statements. In C#, you cannot execute the code in one switch section and then *fall through* to the next.

Although C# does not allow falling through from one switch section to another, you can do the following:

- You can attach multiple switch labels to any switch section.

- Following the statement list associated with a case, there must be one of the jump statements before the next switch label, unless there are *no intervening executable statements* between the switch labels.

For example, in the following code, since there are no executable statements between the first three switch labels, it's fine to have one follow the other. Cases 5 and 6, however, have an executable statement between them, so there must be a jump statement before case 6.

```
switch( x )
{
    case 1:                 // Acceptable
    case 2:
    case 3:
        ...                 // Execute this code if x equals 1, 2, or 3.
        break;
    case 5:
        y = x + 1;
    case 6:                 // Not acceptable because there is no break
        ...
```

The while Loop

The while loop is a simple loop construct in which the test expression is performed at the top of the loop. The syntax of the while loop is shown here and is illustrated in Figure 9-6.

- First, *TestExpr* is evaluated.

- If *TestExpr* evaluates to false, then execution continues after the end of the while loop.

- Otherwise, when *TestExpr* evaluates to true, then *Statement* is executed, and *TestExpr* is evaluated again. Each time *TestExpr* evaluates to true, *Statement* is executed another time. The loop ends when *TestExpr* evaluates to false.

```
while( TestExpr )
    Statement
```

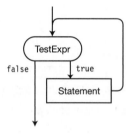

Figure 9-6. *The while loop*

The following code shows an example of the while loop, where the test expression variable starts with a value of 3 and is decremented at each iteration. The loop exits when the value of the variable becomes 0.

```
int x = 3;
while( x > 0 )
{
    Console.WriteLine("x:  {0}", x);
    x--;
}
Console.WriteLine("Out of loop");
```

This code produces the following output:

```
x:  3
x:  2
x:  1
Out of loop
```

The do Loop

The do loop is a simple loop construct in which the test expression is performed at the bottom of the loop. The syntax for the do loop is shown here and illustrated in Figure 9-7.

- First, *Statement* is executed.

- Then, *TestExpr* is evaluated.

- If *TestExpr* returns true, then *Statement* is executed again.

- Each time *TestExpr* returns true, *Statement* is executed again.

- When *TestExpr* returns false, control passes to the statement following the end of the loop construct.

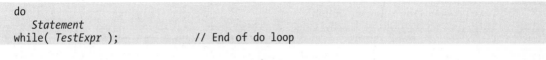

```
do
    Statement
while( TestExpr );           // End of do loop
```

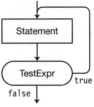

Figure 9-7. *The do loop*

The do loop has several characteristics that set it apart from other flow-of-control constructs. They are the following:

- The body of the loop, *Statement*, is always executed at least once, even if *TestExpr* is initially false.

- The semicolon is required after the closing parenthesis of the test expression.

The following code shows an example of a do loop:

```
int x = 0;
do
   Console.WriteLine("x is {0}", x++);
while (x<3);
            ↑
        Required
```

This code produces the following output:

```
x is 0
x is 1
x is 2
```

The for Loop

The for loop construct executes the body of the loop as long as the test expression returns true when it is evaluated at the top of the loop. The syntax of the for loop is shown here and illustrated in Figure 9-8.

- At the beginning of the for loop, *Initializer* is executed once.

- *TestExpr* is then evaluated.

- If *TestExpr* returns true, *Statement* is executed, followed by *IterationExpr*.

- Control then returns to the top of the loop, and *TestExpr* is evaluated again.

- As long as *TestExpr* returns true, *Statement*, followed by *IterationExpr*, is executed.

- As soon as *TestExpr* returns false, execution continues at the statement following *Statement*.

```
                    Separated by semicolons
                        ↓           ↓
for( Initializer ; TestExpr ; IterationExpr )
    Statement
```

Some parts of the statement are optional.

- *Initializer*, *TestExpr*, and *IterationExpr* are all optional. Their positions can be left blank. If the *TestExpr* position is left blank, the test is *assumed to return* true. Therefore, there must be some other method of exiting the statement if the program is to avoid going into an infinite loop.

- The two semicolons are required as field separators.

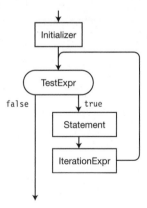

Figure 9-8. *The for loop*

Figure 9-8 illustrates the flow of control through the for statement. You should also know the following about its components:

- *Initializer* is executed only once, before any other part of the for construct. It is usually used to declare and initialize local values to be used in the loop.

- *TestExpr* is evaluated to determine whether *Statement* should be executed or skipped. It must evaluate to a value of type bool.

- *IterationExpr* is executed immediately after *Statement* and before returning to the top of the loop to *TestExpr*.

For example, in the following code:

- Before anything else, the initializer (int i=0) defines a variable called i and initializes its value to 0.

- The condition (i<3) is then evaluated. If it is true, then the body of the loop is executed.

- At the bottom of the loop, after all the loop statements have been executed, the *IterationExpr* statement is executed—in this case, incrementing the value of i.

```
// The body of this for loop is executed three times.
for( int i=0 ; i<3 ; i++ )
    Console.WriteLine("Inside loop.  i:  {0}", i);

Console.WriteLine("Out of Loop");
```

This code produces the following output:

```
Inside loop.  i:  0
Inside loop.  i:  1
Inside loop.  i:  2
Out of Loop
```

The Scope of Variables in a for Statement

Any variables declared in the *initializer* are visible *only within the* for *statement.*

- This is different from C and C++, where the declaration introduces the variable into the enclosing block.

- The following code illustrates this point:

```
Type is needed here for declaration.
   ↓
for(int i=0; i<10; i++ ) // Variable i is in scope here, and also
   Statement;            // here within the statement.
                         // Here, after the statement, i no longer exists.

Type is needed here again because the previous variable i has gone out of existence.
   ↓
for(int i=0; i<10; i++ ) // We need to define a new variable i here,
   Statement;            // the previous one has gone out of existence.
```

The local variables declared within the body of the loop are known only within the loop.

■ **Note** Unlike C and C++, the scope of variables declared in the initializer lasts only for the length of the loop.

Multiple Expressions in the Initializer and Iteration Expression

Both the initializer expression and the iteration expression can contain multiple expressions as long as they are separated by commas.

For example, the following code has two variable declarations in the initializer and two expressions in the iteration expression:

```
static void Main( )
{
   const int MaxI = 5;

                    Two declarations            Two expressions
                          ↓                           ↓
   for (int i = 0, j = 10; i < MaxI; i++, j += 10)
   {
      Console.WriteLine("{0}, {1}", i, j);
   }
}
```

This code produces the following output:

```
0, 10
1, 20
2, 30
3, 40
4, 50
```

Jump Statements

When the flow of control reaches *jump statements,* program execution is unconditionally transferred to another part of the program. The jump statements are the following:

- break

- continue

- return

- goto

- throw

This chapter covers the first four of these statements. The throw statement is explained in Chapter 11.

The break Statement

Earlier in this chapter you saw the break statement used in the switch statement. It can also be used in the following statement types:

- for

- foreach

- while

- do

In the body of one of these statements, break causes execution to exit the *innermost enclosing loop.*
    For example, the following while loop would be an infinite loop if it relied only on its test expression, which is always true. But instead, after three iterations of the loop, the break statement is encountered, and the loop is exited.

```
int x = 0;
while( true )
{
    x++;
    if( x >= 3 )
        break;
}
```

The continue Statement

The continue statement causes program execution to go to the *top* of the *innermost enclosing loop* of the following types:

- while

- do

- for

- foreach

For example, the following for loop is executed five times. In the first three iterations, it encounters the continue statement and goes directly back to the top of the loop, missing the WriteLine statement at the bottom of the loop. Execution only reaches the WriteLine statement during the last two iterations.

```
for( int x=0; x<5; x++ )              // Execute loop five times
{
   if( x < 3 )                        // The first three times
      continue;                       // Go directly back to top of loop

   // This line is only reached when x is 3 or greater.
   Console.WriteLine("Value of x is {0}", x);
}
```

This code produces the following output:

```
Value of x is 3
Value of x is 4
```

The following code shows an example of a continue statement in a while loop. This code produces the same output as the preceding for loop example.

```
int x = 0;
while( x < 5 )
{
   if( x < 3 )
   {
      x++;
      continue;                       // Go back to top of loop
   }

   // This line is reached only when x is 3 or greater.
   Console.WriteLine("Value of x is {0}", x);
   x++;
}
```

Labeled Statements

A *labeled statement* consists of an identifier, followed by a colon, followed by a statement. It has the following form:

```
Identifier: Statement
```

A labeled statement is executed exactly as if the label were not there and consisted of just the *Statement* part.

- Adding a label to a statement allows control to be transferred to the statement from another part of the code.

- Labeled statements are allowed only inside blocks.

Labels

Labels have their own declaration space, so the identifier in a labeled statement can be any valid identifier—including those that might be declared in an overlapping scope, such as local variables or parameter names.

For example, the following code shows the valid use of a label with the same identifier as a local variable:

```
{
    int xyz = 0;                              // Variable xyz
        ...
    xyz: Console.WriteLine("No problem.");    // Label xyz
}
```

There are restrictions, however. The identifier cannot be either

- The same as another label identifier with an overlapping scope

- A keyword

The Scope of Labeled Statements

Labeled statements cannot be seen (or accessed) from *outside* the block in which they are declared. The scope of a labeled statement is

- The block in which it is declared

- Any blocks nested inside that block

For example, the code on the left of Figure 9-9 contains several nested blocks, with their scopes marked. There are two labeled statements declared in scope B of the program: increment and end.

- The shaded portions on the right of the figure show the areas of the code in which the labeled statements are in scope.

- Code in scope B, and all the nested blocks, can see and access the labeled statements.

- Code from any of the inner scopes can jump *out* to the labeled statements.

- Code from outside (scope A, in this case) *cannot jump into* a block with a labeled statement.

```
static void Main( )
{ // Scope A

    { // Scope B

    increment: x++;
        { // Scope C

            { // Scope D
            ...
            }
            { // Scope E
            ...
            }
            ...
        }
    end: Console.WriteLine("Exiting");
    }
}
```

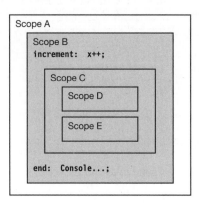

Figure 9-9. *The scope of labels includes nested blocks.*

The goto Statement

The goto statement unconditionally transfers control to a *labeled statement*. Its general form is the following, where *Identifier* is the identifier of a labeled statement:

```
goto Identifier ;
```

For example, the following code shows the simple use of a goto statement:

```
bool thingsAreFine;
while (true)
{
   thingsAreFine = GetNuclearReactorCondition();

   if ( thingsAreFine )
      Console.WriteLine("Things are fine.");
   else
      goto NotSoGood;
}

NotSoGood: Console.WriteLine("We have a problem.");
```

The goto statement must be *within* the scope of the labeled statement.

- A goto statement can jump to any labeled statement within its own block or can jump *out* to any block in which it is nested.

- A goto statement cannot jump *into* any blocks nested within its own block.

■ **Caution** Using the goto statement is strongly discouraged, because it can lead to code that is poorly structured and difficult to debug and maintain. Edsger Dijkstra's 1968 letter to the Communications of the ACM, entitled "Go To Statement Considered Harmful," was an important contribution to computer science; it was one of the first published descriptions of the pitfalls of using the goto statement.

The goto Statement Inside a switch Statement

There are also two other forms of the goto statement, for use inside switch statements. These goto statements transfer control to the correspondingly named switch label in the switch statement.

```
goto case ConstantExpression;
goto default;
```

The using Statement

Certain types of unmanaged objects are limited in number or are expensive with system resources. It's important that when your code is done with them, they be released as soon as possible. The using statement helps simplify the process and ensures that these resources are properly disposed of.

A *resource* is a class or struct that implements the System.IDisposable interface. Interfaces are covered in detail in Chapter 17—but in short, an interface is a collection of unimplemented function members that classes and structs can choose to implement. The IDisposable interface contains a single method named Dispose.

The phases of using a resource are shown in Figure 9-10 and consist of the following:

- Allocating the resource

- Using the resource

- Disposing of the resource

If an unexpected run-time error occurs during the portion of the code using the resource, the code disposing of the resource might not get executed.

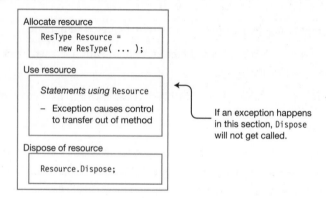

Figure 9-10. *Components of using a resource*

■ **Note** The using statement is different from the using directives. The using directives are covered in Chapter 10.

Packaging Use of the Resource

The using statement helps reduce the potential problem of an unexpected run-time error by neatly packaging the use of a resource.

There are two forms of the using statement. The first form is the following and is illustrated in Figure 9-11.

- The code between the parentheses allocates the resource.

- *Statement* is the code that uses the resource.

- The using statement *implicitly generates* the code to dispose of the resource.

```
using ( ResourceType Identifier = Expression ) Statement
                      ↑                            ↑
              Allocates resource              Uses resource
```

Unexpected run-time errors are called *exceptions* and are covered in Chapter 11. The standard way of handling the possibility of exceptions is to place the code that might cause an exception in a try block and place any code that *must* be executed, whether or not there is an exception, into a finally block.

This form of the using statement does exactly that. It performs the following:

- Allocates the resource

- Places *Statement* in a try block

- Creates a call to the resource's Dispose method and places it in a finally block

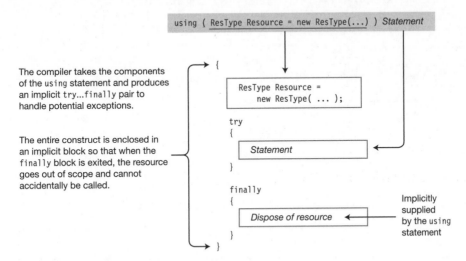

Figure 9-11. *The effect of the using statement*

Example of the using Statement

The following code uses the using statement twice—once with a class called TextWriter and once with a class called TextReader, both from the System.IO namespace. Both classes implement the IDisposable interface, as required by the using statement.

- The TextWriter resource opens a text file for writing and writes a line to the file.

- The TextReader resource then opens the same text file and reads and displays the contents, line by line.

- In both cases, the using statement makes sure that the objects' Dispose methods are called.

- Notice also the difference between the using statements in Main and the using directives on the first two lines.

```
using System;                    // using DIRECTIVE; not using statement
using System.IO;                 // using DIRECTIVE; not using statement

namespace UsingStatement
{
   class Program
   {
      static void Main( )
      {
         // using statement
         using (TextWriter tw = File.CreateText("Lincoln.txt") )
         {
            tw.WriteLine("Four score and seven years ago, ...");
         }

         // using statement
         using (TextReader tr = File.OpenText("Lincoln.txt"))
         {
            string InputString;
            while (null != (InputString = tr.ReadLine()))
               Console.WriteLine(InputString);
         }
      }
   }
}
```

This code produces the following output:

```
Four score and seven years ago, ...
```

Multiple Resources and Nesting

The using statement can also be used with multiple resources of the same type, with the resource declarations separated by commas. The syntax is the following:

```
             Only one type     Resource        Resource
             ‾‾‾‾‾‾‾‾‾‾‾          ‾‾‾‾‾‾           ‾‾‾‾‾‾
                 ↓                 ↓                ↓
using ( ResourceType Id1 = Expr1,  Id2 = Expr2, ... ) EmbeddedStatement
```

For example, in the following code, each using statement allocates and uses two resources:

```
static void Main()
{
   using (TextWriter tw1 = File.CreateText("Lincoln.txt"),
                     tw2 = File.CreateText("Franklin.txt"))
   {
      tw1.WriteLine("Four score and seven years ago, ...");
      tw2.WriteLine("Early to bed; Early to rise ...");
   }

   using (TextReader tr1 = File.OpenText("Lincoln.txt"),
                     tr2 = File.OpenText("Franklin.txt"))
   {
      string InputString;

      while (null != (InputString = tr1.ReadLine()))
         Console.WriteLine(InputString);

      while (null != (InputString = tr2.ReadLine()))
         Console.WriteLine(InputString);
   }
}
```

The using statement can also be nested. In the following code, besides the nesting of the using statements, also note that it is not necessary to use a block with the second using statement because it consists of only a single, simple statement.

```
using ( TextWriter tw1 = File.CreateText("Lincoln.txt") )
{
   tw1.WriteLine("Four score and seven years ago, ...");

   using ( TextWriter tw2 = File.CreateText("Franklin.txt") ) // Nested
      tw2.WriteLine("Early to bed; Early to rise ...");        // Single
}
```

Another Form of the using Statement

Another form of the using statement is the following:

```
Keyword    Resource        Uses resource
   ↓          ↓                 ↓
 using ( Expression ) EmbeddedStatement
```

In this form, the resource is declared before the using statement.

```
TextWriter tw = File.CreateText("Lincoln.txt");          // Resource declared

using ( tw )                                             // using statement
   tw.WriteLine("Four score and seven years ago, ...");
```

Although this form still ensures that the Dispose method will always be called after you finish using the resource, it does not protect you from attempting to use the resource after the using statement has released its unmanaged resources, leaving it in an inconsistent state. It therefore gives less protection and is discouraged. This form is illustrated in Figure 9-12.

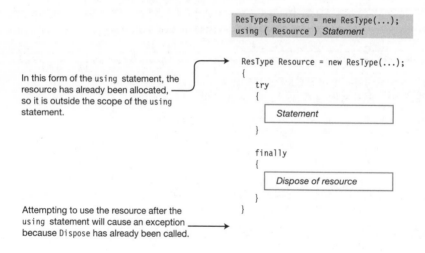

Figure 9-12. *Resource declaration before the using statement*

Other Statements

There are other statements that are associated with particular features of the language. These statements are covered in the sections dealing with those features. The statements covered in other chapters are shown in Table 9-1.

Table 9-1. *Statements Covered in Other Chapters*

Statement	Description	Relevant Chapter
checked, unchecked	These statements control the overflow checking context.	Chapter 18
foreach	This statement iterates through each member of a collection.	Chapters 14 and 20
try, throw, finally	These statements are associated with exceptions.	Chapter 11
return	This statement returns control to the calling function member and can also return a value.	Chapter 5
yield	This statement is used with iterators.	Chapter 20

∎∎∎

CHAPTER 10

Namespaces and Assemblies

Referencing Other Assemblies

In Chapter 1, we took a high-level look at the compilation process. You saw that the compiler takes the source code file and produces an output file called an *assembly*. This chapter takes a closer look at assemblies and how they are produced and deployed. You will also look at how namespaces help organize types.

All the programs you've seen so far have, for the most part, declared and used their own classes. In many projects, however, you will want to use classes or types from other assemblies. These other assemblies might come from the BCL or a third-party vendor, or you might have created them yourself. These are called *class libraries*, and the names of their assembly files generally end with the `.dll` extension rather than the `.exe` extension.

Suppose, for example, that you want to create a class library that contains classes and types that can be used by other assemblies. The source code for a simple library is shown in the following example and is contained in a file called `SuperLib.cs`. The library contains a single public class called `SquareWidget`. Figure 10-1 illustrates the production of the DLL.

```
public class SquareWidget
{
    public double SideLength = 0;
    public double Area
    {
        get { return SideLength * SideLength; }
    }
}
```

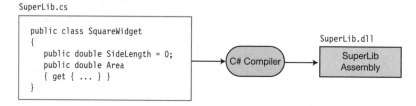

Figure 10-1. *The SuperLib source code and the resulting assembly*

To create a class library using Visual Studio 2010, select the Class Library template from the installed Windows templates. Specifically, when in Visual Studio, do the following:

1. Select File ➤ New ➤ Project, and the New Project window will open.
2. In the left pane in the Installed Templates panel, find the Visual C# node under the Other Languages root, and select the Windows entry.
3. In the right pane, select the Class Library template.

Suppose also that you are writing a program called `MyWidgets`, and you want to use the `SquareWidget` class. The code for the program is in a file called `MyWidgets.cs` and is shown in the following example. The code simply creates an object of type `SquareWidget` and uses the object's members.

```
using System;

class WidgetsProgram
{
   static void Main( )
   {
      SquareWidget sq = new SquareWidget();    // From class library
         ↑
      Not declared in this assembly
      sq.SideLength = 5.0;                      // Set the side length.
      Console.WriteLine(sq.Area);              // Print out the area.
   }       ↑
}     Not declared in this assembly
```

Notice that the code doesn't declare class `SquareWidget`. Instead, you use the class defined in `SuperLib`. When you compile the `MyWidgets` program, however, the compiler must be aware that your code uses assembly `SuperLib` so it can get the information about class `SquareWidget`. To do this, you need to give the compiler a *reference* to the assembly, by giving its name and location.

In Visual Studio, you can add references to a project in the following way:

- Select the Solution Explorer, and find the References folder underneath the project name. The References folder contains a list of the assemblies used by the project.

- Right-click the References folder, and select Add Reference. There are five tabs from which to choose, allowing you to find the class library in different ways.

- For our program, select the Browse tab, browse to the DLL file containing the `SquareWidget` class definition, and select it.

- Click the OK button, and the reference will be added to the project.

After you've added the reference, you can compile MyWidgets. Figure 10-2 illustrates the full compilation process.

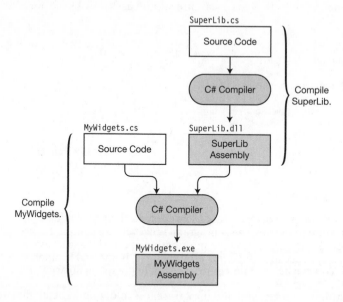

Figure 10-2. *Referencing another assembly*

The mscorlib Library

There's a class library that I've been using in every example in the book so far. It is the one that contains the Console class. The Console class is defined in an assembly called mscorlib in a file called mscorlib.dll. You won't find this assembly listed in the References folder, however. Assembly mscorlib contains the definitions of the C# types and the basic types for most .NET languages. It must always be referenced when compiling a C# program, so Visual Studio doesn't bother showing it in the References folder.

When you take into account mscorlib, the compilation process for MyWidgets looks more like the representation shown in Figure 10-3. After this, I'll assume the use of the mscorlib assembly without representing it again.

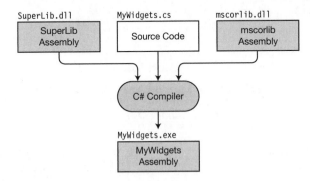

Figure 10-3. *Referencing class libraries*

Now suppose that your program has been working fine with the SquareWidget class, but you want to expand its capabilities to use a class called CircleWidget, which is defined in a different assembly called UltraLib. The MyWidgets source code now looks like the following. It creates a SquareWidget object as defined in SuperLib and a CircleWidget object as defined in UltraLib.

```
class WidgetsProgram
{
   static void Main( )
   {
      SquareWidget sq = new SquareWidget();        // From SuperLib
      ...

      CircleWidget circle = new CircleWidget();    // From UltraLib
      ...
   }
}
```

The source code for class library UltraLib is shown in the following example. Notice that besides class CircleWidget, like library SuperLib, it also declares a class called SquareWidget. You can compile UltraLib to a DLL and add it to the list of references in project MyWidgets.

```
public class SquareWidget
{
   ...
}

public class CircleWidget
{
   public double Radius = 0;
   public double Area
   {
      get { ... }
   }
}
```

Since both libraries contain a class called SquareWidget, when you attempt to compile program MyWidgets, the compiler produces an error message because it doesn't know which version of class SquareWidget to use. Figure 10-4 illustrates this *name clash*.

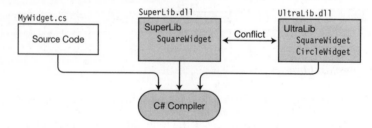

Figure 10-4. *Since assemblies SuperLib and UltraLib both contain declarations for a class called SquareWidget, the compiler doesn't know which one to instantiate.*

Namespaces

In the MyWidgets example, since you have the source code, you can solve the name clash by just changing the name of the SquareWidget class in either the SuperLib source code or the UltraLib source code. But what if these libraries had been developed by separate companies, and you didn't have the source code? Suppose that SuperLib was produced by a company called MyCorp, and UltraLib was produced by the ABCCorp company. In that case, you wouldn't be able to use them together if you used any classes or types where there was a clash.

As you can imagine, with your development machine containing assemblies produced by dozens, if not hundreds, of different companies, there is likely to be a certain amount of duplication in the names of classes. It would be a shame if you couldn't use two assemblies in the same program just because they happened to have type names in common.

Suppose, however, that MyCorp had a policy of prefacing all their classes with a string that consisted of the company name followed by the product name followed by the descriptive class name. Suppose further that ABCCorp had the same policy. In that case, the three class names in our example would be named MyCorpSuperLibSquareWidget, ABCCorpUltraLibSquareWidget, and ABCCorpUltraLibCircleWidget, as shown in Figure 10-5. These are perfectly valid class names, and there's little chance of the classes in one company's library conflicting with those of another company.

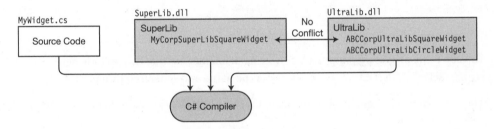

Figure 10-5. *With disambiguating strings prefaced to the class names, there is no conflict between the libraries.*

Our example program, however, would need to use these long names and would look like the following:

```
class WidgetsProgram
{
   static void Main( )
   {
      MyCorpSuperLibSquareWidget sq
            = new MyCorpSuperLibSquareWidget();       // From SuperLib
      ...

      ABCCorpUltraLibCircleWidget circle
            = new ABCCorpUltraLibCircleWidget();      // From UltraLib
      ...
   }
}
```

Although this solves the conflict problem, these new, disambiguated names are harder to read and clumsy to work with, even with IntelliSense.

Suppose, however, that in addition to the characters normally allowed in an identifier, you could also use the period character within the string—although still not at the beginning or at the end of the class name. In this case, we could make the names more understandable, such as `MyCorp.SuperLib.SquareWidget`, `ABCCorp.UltraLib.SquareWidget`, and `ABCCorp.UltraLib.CircleWidget`. Now the code would look like the following:

```
class WidgetsProgram
{
   static void Main( )
   {
      MyCorp.SuperLib.SquareWidget sq
              = new MyCorp.SuperLib.SquareWidget();        // From SuperLib
      ...

      ABCCorp.UltraLib.CircleWidget circle
              = new ABCCorp.UltraLib.CircleWidget();        // From UltraLib
      ...
   }
}
```

This brings us to the concept of the namespace name and a namespace.

- You can think of a *namespace name* as a string of characters (that can include periods inside the string) tacked on to the front of the class or type name and separated by a period.

- The full string including the namespace name, separating period, and the class name is called the class's *fully qualified name*.

- A *namespace* is the *set of classes and types* that share that namespace name.

Figure 10-6 illustrates these definitions.

Figure 10-6. *A namespace is the set of type definitions that share the same namespace name.*

You can use namespaces to group a set of types together and give them a name. Generally, you want namespace names to be descriptive of the types contained by the namespace and to be distinct from other namespace names.

You create a namespace by declaring the namespace in the source file that contains your type declarations. The following shows the syntax for declaring a namespace. You then declare all your classes and other types between the curly braces of the namespace declaration. These are then the *members* of the namespace.

```
  Keyword    Namespace name
     ↓            ↓
namespace NamespaceName
{
    TypeDeclarations
}
```

The following code shows how the programmers at MyCorp could create the `MyCorp.SuperLib` namespace and declare the SquareWidget class inside it.

```
  Company name   Period
              ↓  ↓
namespace MyCorp.SuperLib
{
    public class SquareWidget
    {
        public double SideLength = 0;
        public double Area
        {
            get { return SideLength * SideLength; }
        }
    }
}
```

Now, when the MyCorp company ships you the new updated assembly, you can use it by modifying your MyWidgets program, as shown here:

```
class WidgetsProgram
{
    static void Main( )
    {            Fully qualified name                              Fully qualified name
                          ↓                                                  ↓
        MyCorp.SuperLib.SquareWidget sq = new MyCorp.SuperLib.SquareWidget();
                 ↑              ↑

        Namespace name     Class name

        CircleWidget circle = new CircleWidget();
        ...
```

Now that you have explicitly specified the SuperLib version of SquareWidget in your code, the compiler will no longer have a problem distinguishing the classes. The fully qualified name is a bit long to type, but at least you can now use both libraries. A little later in the chapter, we'll cover the using alias directive to solve the inconvenience of having to repeatedly type in the fully qualified name.

If the UltraLib assembly is also updated with a namespace by the company that produces it (ABCCorp), then the compile process would be as shown in Figure 10-7.

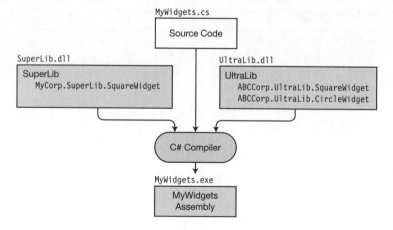

Figure 10-7. *Class libraries with namespaces*

Namespace Names

As you saw, the name of a namespace can contain the name of the company that created the assembly. Besides identifying the company, the name is also used to help programmers get a quick idea of the kinds of types defined in the namespace.

Some important points about the names of namespaces are the following:

- A namespace name can be any valid identifier, as described in Chapter 2.

- Additionally, a namespace name can include any number of period characters. You can use this to organize types into hierarchies.

For example, Table 10-1 gives the names of some of the namespaces in the .NET BCL.

Table 10-1. *Sample Namespaces from the BCL*

System	System.IO
System.Data	Microsoft.CSharp
System.Drawing	Microsoft.VisualBasic

Namespace naming guidelines suggest the following:

- Start namespace names with the company name.

- Follow the company name with the technology name.

- Do not name a namespace with the same name as a class or type.

For example, the software development department of the Acme Widget Company develops software in the following three namespaces, as shown in the following code:

- AcmeWidgets.SuperWidget

- AcmeWidgets.Media

- AcmeWidgets.Games

```
namespace AcmeWidgets.SuperWidget
{
   class SPDBase ...
   ...
}
```

More About Namespaces

There are several other important points you should know about namespaces:

- Every type name in a namespace must be different from all the others.

- The types in a namespace are called *members* of the namespace.

- A source file can contain any number of namespace declarations, either sequentially or nested.

Figure 10-8 shows a source file on the left that declares two namespaces sequentially, with several types in each one. Notice that even though the namespaces contain several class names in common, they are differentiated by their namespace names, as shown in the assembly at the right of the figure.

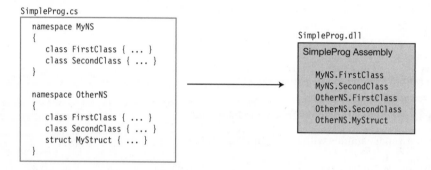

Figure 10-8. *Multiple namespaces in a source file*

The .NET Framework BCL offers thousands of defined classes and types to choose from in building your programs. To help organize this vast array of available functionality, types with related functionality are declared in the same namespace. The BCL uses more than 100 namespaces to organize its types.

Namespaces Spread Across Files

A namespace is not closed. This means you can add more type declarations to it by declaring it again either later in the source file or in another source file.

For example, Figure 10-9 shows the declaration of three classes, all in the same namespace but declared in separate source files. The source files can be compiled into a single assembly, as shown in Figure 10-9, or into separate assemblies, as shown in Figure 10-10.

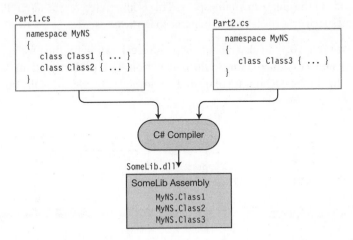

Figure 10-9. *A namespace can be spread across source files and compiled to a single assembly.*

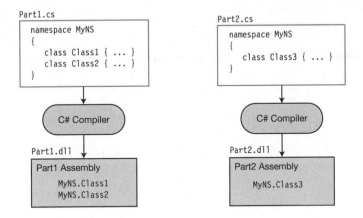

Figure 10-10. *A namespace can be spread across source files and compiled to separate assemblies.*

Nesting Namespaces

Namespaces can be nested, producing a *nested namespace*. Nesting namespaces allows you to create a conceptual hierarchy of types.

There are two ways you can declare a nested namespace:

- *Textual nesting*: You can create a nested namespace by placing its declaration inside the declaration body of the enclosing namespace. This is illustrated on the left in Figure 10-11. In this example, namespace OtherNs is nested in namespace MyNamespace.

- *Separate declaration*: You can also create a separate declaration for the nested namespace, but you must use its fully qualified name in the declaration. This is illustrated on the right in Figure 10-11. Notice that in the declaration of nested namespace OtherNs, the fully qualified name MyNamespace.OtherNS is used.

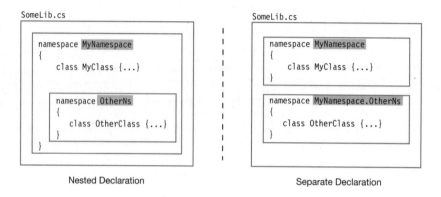

Figure 10-11. *The two forms of declaring a nested namespace are equivalent.*

Both forms of the nested namespace declarations shown in Figure 10-11 produce the same assembly, as illustrated in Figure 10-12. The figure shows the two classes declared in file SomeLib.cs, with their fully qualified names.

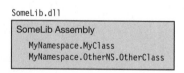

Figure 10-12. *Nested namespace structure*

Although the nested namespace is inside the enclosing namespace, its members are *not* members of the enclosing namespace. A common misconception is that since the nested namespace is inside the enclosing namespace, the members of the nested namespace must be a subset of the enclosing namespace. This is not true; the namespaces are separate.

The using Directives

Fully qualified names can be quite long, and using them throughout your code can become quite cumbersome. There are two compiler directives, however, that allow you to avoid having to use fully qualified names—the using *namespace directive* and the using *alias directive*.

Two important points about the using directives are the following:

- They must be placed at the top of the source file, *before any type declarations*.

- They apply for all the namespaces in the current source file.

The using Namespace Directive

You saw in the MyWidgets example several sections back that you can specify a class by using the fully qualified name. You can avoid having to use the long name by placing using *namespace* directives at the top of the source file.

The using namespace directive instructs the compiler that you will be using types from certain specific namespaces. You can then go ahead and use the simple class names without having to fully qualify them.

When the compiler encounters a name that is not in the current namespace, it checks the list of namespaces given in the using namespace directives and appends the unknown name to the first namespace in the list. If the resulting fully qualified name matches a class in this assembly or a referenced assembly, the compiler uses that class. If it does not match, it tries the next namespace in the list.

The using namespace directive consists of the keyword using, followed by a namespace identifier.

```
Keyword
  ↓
using System ;
           ↑
     Name of namespace
```

One method I have been using throughout the text is the WriteLine method, which is a member of class Console, in the System namespace. Rather than use its fully qualified name throughout the code, I simplified our work just a bit, by the use of the using namespace directive at the top of the code.

For example, the following code uses the using namespace directive in the first line to state that the code uses classes or other types from the System namespace.

```
using System;                              // using namespace directive
   ...
System.Console.WriteLine("This is text 1"); // Use fully qualified name
Console.WriteLine("This is text 2");        // Use directive
```

The using Alias Directive

The using *alias directive* allows you to assign an alias for either of the following:

- A namespace

- A type in a namespace

For example, the following code shows the use of two using alias directives. The first directive instructs the compiler that identifier Syst is an alias for namespace System. The second directive says that identifier SC is an alias for class System.Console.

```
Keyword Alias   Namespace
   ↓      ↓         ↓
 using Syst = System;
 using SC   = System.Console;
   ↑    ↑            ↑
Keyword Alias      Class
```

The following code uses these aliases. All three lines of code in Main call the System.Console.WriteLine method.

- The first statement in Main uses the alias for a *namespace*—System.

- The second statement uses the *fully qualified name* of the method.

- The third statement uses the alias for a *class*—Console.

```
using Syst = System;                     // using alias directive
using SC   = System.Console;             // using alias directive

namespace MyNamespace
{
   class SomeClass
   {
      static void Main()
      { Alias for namespace
             ↓
         Syst.Console.WriteLine  ("Using the namespace alias.");
         System.Console.WriteLine("Using fully qualified name.");
         SC.WriteLine            ("Using the type alias");
           ↑
      } Alias for class
   }
}
```

The Structure of an Assembly

As you saw in Chapter 1, an assembly does not contain native machine code, but Common Intermediate Language (CIL) code. It also contains everything needed by the Just-in-Time (JIT) compiler to convert the CIL into native code at run time, including references to other assemblies it references. The file extension for an assembly is generally .exe or .dll.

Most assemblies are composed of a single file. Figure 10-13 illustrates the four main sections of an assembly.

- The assembly *manifest* contains the following:

  — The identity of the assembly

  — A list of the files that make up the assembly

  — A map of where things are in the assembly

  — Information about other assemblies that are referenced

- The *type metadata* section contains the information about all the types defined in the assembly. This information contains everything there is to know about each type.

- The *CIL* section contains all the intermediate code for the assembly.

- The *resources* section is optional but can contain graphics or language resources.

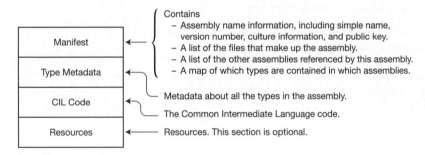

Figure 10-13. *The structure of a single-file assembly*

Although most assemblies comprise a single file, some have more. For an assembly with multiple modules, one file is the *primary module*, and the others are *secondary modules*.

- The primary module contains the manifest of the assembly and references to the secondary modules.

- The file names of secondary modules end with the extension .netmodule.

- Multiple-file assemblies are considered a single unit. They are deployed together and versioned together.

Figure 10-14 illustrates a multifile assembly with secondary modules.

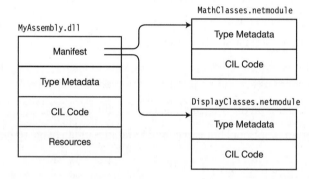

Figure 10-14. *A multifile assembly*

The Identity of an Assembly

In the .NET Framework, the file names of assemblies are not as important as in other operating systems and environments. What is much more important is the *identity* of an assembly.

The identity of an assembly has four components that together should uniquely identify it. These four components are the following:

- *Simple name*: This is just the file name without the file extension. Every assembly has a simple name. It is also called the *assembly name* or the *friendly name*.

- *Version number*: This consists of a string of four period-separated integers, in the form `MajorVersion.MinorVersion.Build.Revision`—for example, `2.0.35.9`.

- *Culture information*: This is a string that consists of two to five characters representing a language, or a language and a country or region. For example, the culture name for English as used in the United States is `en-US`. For German as used in Germany, it is `de-DE`.

- *Public key*: This 128-byte string should be unique to the company producing the assembly.

The public key is part of a public/private key pair, which is a set of two very large, specially chosen numbers that can be used to create secure digital signatures. The public key, as its name implies, can be made public. The private key must be guarded by the owner. The public key is part of the assembly's identity. We will look at the use of the private key later in the chapter.

The components of an assembly's name are embedded in the assembly's manifest. Figure 10-15 illustrates this section of the manifest.

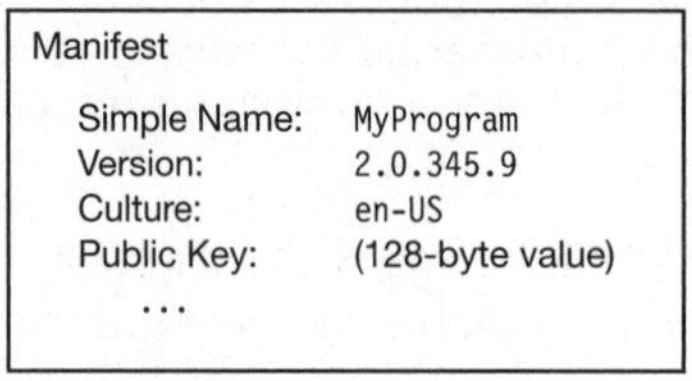

Manifest
Simple Name: MyProgram
Version: 2.0.345.9
Culture: en-US
Public Key: (128-byte value)
...

Figure 10-15. *The components of an assembly identity in the manifest*

Figure 10-16 shows some of the terms used in the .NET documentation and literature regarding the identity of an assembly.

Identity: All four of the components listed at the right together constitute the identity of an assembly.
Fully qualified name: A textual listing of the simple name, version, culture, and the public key, represented by a 16-byte public key token.
Display name: Same as fully qualified name.
Simple Name
Version
Culture
Public Key

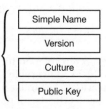

Figure 10-16. *Terms for an assembly's identity*

Strongly Named Assemblies

A *strongly named* assembly is one that has a unique digital signature attached to it. Strongly named assemblies are much more secure than assemblies that do not have strong names, for the following reasons:

- A strong name uniquely identifies an assembly. No one else can create an assembly with the same strong name, so the user can be sure that the assembly came from the claimed source.

- The contents of an assembly with a strong name cannot be altered without the security components of the CLR catching the modification.

A *weakly named* assembly is one that is not strongly named. Since a weakly named assembly does not have a digital signature, it is inherently insecure. Because a chain is only as strong as its weakest link, by default, strongly named assemblies can only access other strongly named assemblies. (There's also a way to allow "partially trusted callers," but I won't be covering that topic.)

The programmer does not produce the strong name. The compiler produces it by taking information about the assembly and hashing it to create a unique digital signature that it attaches to the assembly. The pieces of information it uses in the hash process are the following:

- The sequence of bytes composing the assembly

- The simple name

- The version number

- The culture information

- The public/private key pair

■ **Note** There is some diversity in the nomenclature surrounding strong names. What I'm calling "strongly named" is often referred to as "strong-named." What I'm calling "weakly named" is sometimes referred to as "not strong-named" or "assembly with a simple name."

Creating a Strongly Named Assembly

To strongly name an assembly using Visual Studio 2010, you must have a copy of the public/private key pair file. If you don't have a key file, you can have Visual Studio generate one for you. You can then do the following:

1. Open the properties of the project.
2. Select the Signing tab.
3. Select the Sign the Assembly check box, and enter the location of the key file or create a new one.

When you compile the code, the compiler will produce a strongly named assembly. Figure 10-17 illustrates the inputs and output of the compiler.

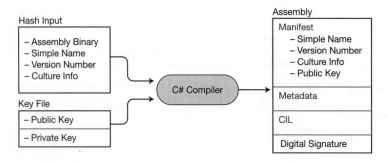

Figure 10-17. *Creating a strongly named assembly*

Private Deployment of an Assembly

Deploying a program on a target machine can be as simple as creating a directory on the machine and copying the application to it. If the application doesn't need other assemblies (such as DLLs) or if the required DLLs are in the same directory, the program should work just fine where it is. Programs deployed this way are called *private assemblies*, and this method of deployment is called *xcopy* deployment.

Private assemblies can be placed in almost any directory and are self-sufficient as long as all the files on which they depend are in the same directory or a subdirectory. In fact, you could have several directories in various parts of the file system, each with the identical set of assemblies, and they would all work fine in their various locations.

Some important things to know about private assembly deployment are the following:

- The directory in which the private assemblies are placed is called the *application directory*.

- A private assembly can be either strongly named or weakly named.

- There is no need to register components in the registry.

- To uninstall a private assembly, just delete it from the file system.

Shared Assemblies and the GAC

Private assemblies are very useful, but sometimes you'll want to put a DLL in a central place so that a single copy can be shared by other assemblies on the system. .NET has such a repository, called the *global assembly cache* (GAC). An assembly placed into the GAC is called a *shared assembly*.

Some important facts about the GAC are the following:

- Only strongly named assemblies can be added to the GAC.

- Although earlier versions of the GAC accepted only files with the `.dll` extension, you can now add assemblies with the `.exe` extension as well.

- The GAC is located in a subdirectory named `Assembly`, of the Windows system directory.

Installing Assemblies into the GAC

When you attempt to install an assembly into the GAC, the security components of the CLR must first verify that the digital signature on the assembly is valid. If there is no digital signature or if it is invalid, the system will not install it into the GAC.

This is a one-time check, however. After an assembly is in the GAC, no further checks are required when it is referenced by a running program.

The `gacutil.exe` command-line utility allows you to add and delete assemblies from the GAC and list the assemblies it contains. The three most useful flags are the following:

- `/i`: Inserts an assembly into the GAC

- `/u`: Uninstalls an assembly from the GAC

- `/l`: Lists the assemblies in the GAC

Side-by-Side Execution in the GAC

After an assembly is deployed to the GAC, it can be used by other assemblies in the system. Remember, however, that an assembly's identity consists of all four parts of the fully qualified name. So, if the version number of a library changes or if it has a different public key, these differences specify different assemblies.

The result is that there can be many different assemblies in the GAC that have the same file name. Although they have the same file name, *they are different assemblies* and coexist perfectly fine together in the GAC. This makes it easy for different applications to use different versions of the same DLL at the same time, since they are different assemblies with different identities. This is called *side-by-side execution*.

Figure 10-18 illustrates four different DLLs in the GAC that all have the same file name—`MyLibrary.dll`. Looking at the figure, you can see that the first three come from the same company, because they have the same public key, and the fourth comes from a different source, since it has a different public key. These versions differ as follows:

- An English version 1.0.0.0, from company A

- An English version 2.0.0.0, from company A

- A German version 1.0.0.0, from company A

- An English version 1.0.0.0, from company B

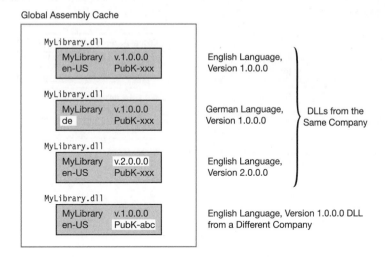

Figure 10-18. *Four different side-by-side DLLs in the GAC*

Configuration Files

Configuration files contain information about the application, for use by the CLR at run time. They can instruct the CLR to do such things as use a different version of a DLL or to look in additional directories when searching for a DLL referenced by the program.

Configuration files consist of XML code and don't contain C# code. The details of writing the XML code are beyond the scope of this text, but you should understand the purpose of configuration files and how they are used. One way they are used is to update an application assembly to use the new version of a DLL.

Suppose, for example, that you have an application that references a DLL in the GAC. The identity of the reference in the application's manifest must exactly match the identity of the assembly in the GAC. If a new version of the DLL is released, it can be added to the GAC, where it can happily coexist with the old version.

The application, however, still has embedded in its manifest the identity of the old version of the DLL. Unless you recompile the application and make it reference the new version of the DLL, it will continue to use the old version. That's fine, if that's what you want.

If, however, you do not want to recompile the application but want it to use the new DLL, then you can create a configuration file telling the CLR to use the new version rather than the old version. The configuration file is placed in the application directory.

Figure 10-19 illustrates objects in the run-time process. The MyProgram.exe application on the left calls for version 1.0.0.0 of the MyLibrary.dll, as indicated by the dashed arrow. But the application has a configuration file, which instructs the CLR to load version 2.0.0.0 instead. Notice that the name of the configuration file consists of the full name of the executable file including the extension, plus the additional extension .config.

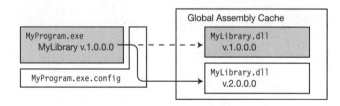

Figure 10-19. *Using a configuration file to bind to a new version*

Delayed Signing

It is important that companies carefully guard the private key of their official public/private key pair. Otherwise, if untrustworthy people were to obtain it, they could publish code masquerading as the company's code. To avoid this, companies clearly cannot allow free access to the file containing their public/private key pair. In large companies, the final strong naming of an assembly is often performed at the very end of the development process, by a special group with access to the key pair.

This can cause problems, though, in the development and testing processes, for several reasons. First, since the public key is one of the four components of an assembly's identity, it can't be set until the public key is supplied. Also, a weakly named assembly cannot be deployed to the GAC. Both the developers and testers need to be able to compile and test the code in the way it will be deployed on release, including its identity and location in the GAC.

To allow for this, there is a modified form of assigning a strong name, called *delayed signing*, or *partial signing*, that overcomes these problems, but without releasing access to the private key.

In delayed signing, the compiler uses only the public key of the public/private key pair. The public key can then be placed in the manifest to complete the assembly's identity. Delayed signing also uses a block of 0s to reserve space for the digital signature.

To create a delay-signed assembly, you must do two things. First, create a copy of the key file that has only the public key, rather than the public/private key pair. Next, add an additional attribute called `DelaySignAttribute` to the assembly scope of the source code and set its value to `true`.

Figure 10-20 shows the input and output for producing a delay-signed assembly. Notice the following in the figure:

- In the input, the `DelaySignAttribute` is located in the source files, and the key file contains only the public key.

- In the output, there is space reserved for the digital signature at the bottom of the assembly.

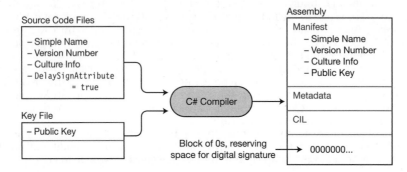

Figure 10-20. *Creating a delay-signed assembly*

If you try to deploy the delay-signed assembly to the GAC, the CLR will not allow it, because it's not strongly named. To deploy it on a particular machine, you must first issue a command-line command that disables the GAC's signature verification on that machine, for this assembly only, and allows it to be installed in the GAC. To do this, issue the following command from the Visual Studio command prompt.

```
sn -vr MyAssembly.dll
```

You've now looked at weakly named assemblies, delay-signed assemblies, and strongly named assemblies. Figure 10-21 summarizes the differences in their structures.

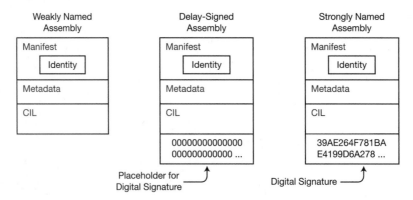

Figure 10-21. *The structures of different assembly signing stages*

CHAPTER 11

Exceptions

What Are Exceptions?

An *exception* is a run-time error in a program that violates a system or application constraint, or a condition that is not expected to occur during normal operation. Examples are when a program tries to divide a number by zero or tries to write to a read-only file. When these occur, the system catches the error and *raises* an exception.

If the program has not provided code to handle the exception, the system will halt the program. For example, the following code raises an exception when it attempts to divide by zero:

```
static void Main()
{
   int x = 10, y = 0;
   x /= y;                  // Attempt to divide by zero--raises an exception
}
```

When this code is run, the system displays the following error message:

```
Unhandled Exception: System.DivideByZeroException: Attempted to divide by zero.
        at Exceptions_1.Program.Main() in C:\Progs\Exceptions\Program.cs:line 12
```

The try Statement

The try statement allows you to designate blocks of code to be guarded for exceptions and to supply code to handle them if they occur. The try statement consists of three sections, as shown in Figure 11-1.

- The try *block* contains the code that is being guarded for exceptions.

- The catch *clauses section* contains one or more catch *clauses*. These are blocks of code to handle the exceptions. They are also known as *exception handlers*.

- The finally *block* contains code to be executed under all circumstances, whether or not an exception is raised.

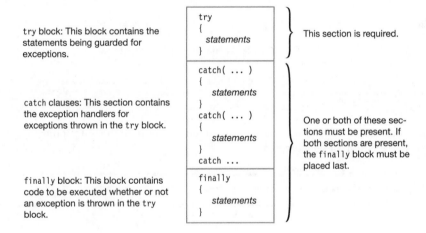

Figure 11-1. *Structure of the try statement*

Handling the Exception

The previous example showed that attempting to divide by zero causes an exception. You can modify the program to handle that exception by placing the code inside a try block and supplying a simple catch clause. When the exception is raised, it is caught and handled in the catch block.

```
static void Main()
{
   int x = 10;

   try
   {
      int y = 0;
      x /= y;                    // Raises an exception
   }
   catch
   {
      ...                        // Code to handle the exception

      Console.WriteLine("Handling all exceptions - Keep on Running");
   }
}
```

This code produces the following message. Notice that, other than the output message, there is no indication that an exception has occurred.

```
Handling all exceptions - Keep on Running
```

The Exception Classes

There are many different types of exceptions that can occur in a program. The BCL defines a number of exception classes, each representing a specific type. When one occurs, the CLR does the following:

- It creates an exception object for the type.

- It looks for an appropriate catch clause to handle it.

All exception classes are ultimately derived from the System.Exception class. Figure 11-2 shows a portion of the exception inheritance hierarchy.

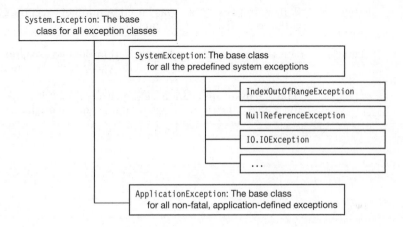

Figure 11-2. *Structure of the exception hierarchy*

An exception object contains read-only properties with information about the exception that caused it. Table 11-1 shows some of these properties.

Table 11-1. *Selected Properties of an Exception Object*

Property	Type	Description
Message	string	This property contains an error message explaining the cause of the exception.
StackTrace	string	This property contains information describing where the exception occurred.
InnerException	Exception	If the current exception was raised by another exception, this property contains a reference to the previous exception.
HelpLink	string	This property can be set by application-defined exceptions to give a URN or URL for information on the cause of the exception.
Source	string	If not set by an application-defined exception, this property contains the name of the assembly where the exception originated.

The catch Clause

The catch clause handles exceptions. There are three forms, allowing different levels of processing. Figure 11-3 shows the forms.

```
catch                                  General catch Clause
{                                        – Does not have a parameter list after the catch keyword.
   Statements                            – Matches any type of exception raised in the try block.
}
- - - - - - - - - - - - - - - - - - - - - - - - - - - - - - - - - - - - - - - - - - - - -
catch( ExceptionType )                 Specific catch Clause
{                                        – Takes the name of an exception class as a single parameter.
   Statements                            – Matches any exception of the named type.
}
- - - - - - - - - - - - - - - - - - - - - - - - - - - - - - - - - - - - - - - - - - - - -
                                       Specific catch Clause with Object
catch( ExceptionType  ExceptionVariable )  – Includes an identifier after the name of the exception class.
{                                        – The identifier acts as a local variable in the block of the catch
   Statements                              clause, and is called the exception variable.
}                                        – The exception variable references the exception object, and
                                           can be used to access information about the object.
```

Figure 11-3. *The three forms of the catch clause*

The *general* catch clause can accept any exception but can't determine the type of exception that caused it. This allows only general processing and cleanup for whatever exception might occur.

The *specific* catch clause form takes the name of an exception class as a parameter. It matches exceptions of the specified class or exception classes derived from it.

The *specific* catch *clause with object* form gives you the most information about the exception. It matches exceptions of the specified class, or exception classes derived from it. It gives you a reference to the exception object created by the CLR, by assigning it to the *exception variable.* You can access the exception variable's properties within the block of the catch clause to get specific information about the exception raised.

For example, the following code handles exceptions of type IndexOutOfRangeException. When one occurs, a reference to the actual exception object is passed into the code with parameter name e. The three WriteLine statements each read a string field from the exception object.

```
                  Exception type     Exception variable
                        ↓                   ↓
catch ( IndexOutOfRangeException   e )
{                                         Accessing the exception variable
                                                     ↓
    Console.WriteLine( "Message: {0}", e.Message );
    Console.WriteLine( "Source:  {0}", e.Source );
    Console.WriteLine( "Stack:   {0}", e.StackTrace );
```

Examples Using Specific catch Clauses

Going back to our divide-by-zero example, the following code modifies the previous catch clause to specifically handle exceptions of the DivideByZeroException class. While in the previous example, the catch clause would handle any exception raised in the try block, the current example will only handle those of the DivideByZeroException class.

```
int x = 10;
try
{
    int y = 0;
    x /= y;                      // Raises an exception
}                    Exception type
                         ↓
catch ( DivideByZeroException )
{
    ...
    Console.WriteLine("Handling an exception.");
}
```

You could further modify the catch clause to use an exception variable. This allows you to access the exception object inside the catch block.

```
int x = 10;
try
{
    int y = 0;
    x /= y;                      // Raises an exception
}          Exception type    Exception variable
                  ↓                 ↓
catch ( DivideByZeroException  e )
{                              Accessing the exception variable
                                        ↓
    Console.WriteLine("Message: {0}", e.Message );
    Console.WriteLine("Source:  {0}", e.Source );
    Console.WriteLine("Stack:   {0}", e.StackTrace );
}
```

This code produces the following output:

```
Message: Attempted to divide by zero.
Source:  Exceptions 1
Stack:      at Exceptions_1.Program.Main() in C:\Progs\Exceptions 1\
Exceptions 1\Program.cs:line 14
```

The catch Clauses Section

The purpose of a catch clause is to allow you to handle an exception in an elegant way. If your catch clause is of the form that takes a parameter, then the system has set that exception variable to a reference to the exception object, which you can inspect to determine the cause of the exception. If the exception was the result of a previous exception, you can get a reference to that previous exception's exception object from the exception variable's InnerException property.

The catch clauses section can contain multiple catch clauses. Figure 11-4 shows a summary of the catch clauses section.

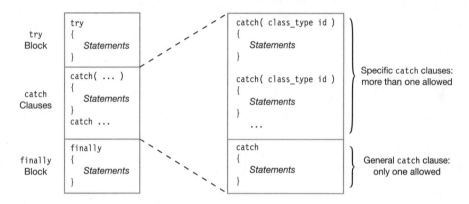

Figure 11-4. *Structure of the catch clauses section of a try statement*

When an exception is raised, the system searches the list of catch clauses in order, and the first catch clause that matches the type of the exception object is executed. Because of this, there are two important rules in ordering the catch clauses. They are the following:

- The specific catch clauses must be ordered with the most specific exception types first, progressing to the most general. For example, if you declare an exception class *derived from* NullReferenceException, the catch clause for your derived exception type should be listed before the catch clause for NullReferenceException.

- If there is a general catch clause, it must be last, after all specific catch clauses. Using the general catch clause is discouraged. You should use one of the specific catch clauses if at all possible. The general catch clause hides bugs by allowing the program to continue execution and can leave the program in an unknown state.

The finally Block

If a program's flow of control enters a try statement that has a finally block, the finally block is *always* executed. Figure 11-5 shows the flow of control.

- If no exception occurs inside the try block, then at the end of the try block, control skips over any catch clauses and goes to the finally block.

- If an exception occurs inside the try block, then the appropriate catch clause in the catch clauses section is executed, followed by execution of the finally block.

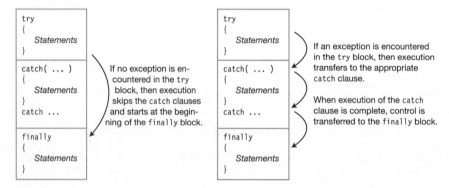

Figure 11-5. *Execution of the finally block*

The finally block will always be executed before returning to the calling code, even if a try block has a return statement or an exception is thrown in the catch block. For example, in the following code, there is a return statement in the middle of the try block that is executed under certain conditions. This does not allow it to bypass the finally statement.

```
try
{
    if (inVal < 10) {
        Console.Write("First Branch  - ");
        return;
    }
    else
        Console.Write("Second Branch - ");
}
finally
{ Console.WriteLine("In finally statement"); }
```

This code produces the following output when variable inVal has the value 5:

```
First Branch  - In finally statement
```

Finding a Handler for an Exception

When a program raises an exception, the system checks to see whether the program has provided a handler for it. Figure 11-6 shows the flow of control.

- If the exception occurred inside a try block, the system will check to see whether any of the catch clauses can handle the exception.

- If an appropriate catch clause is found, the one of the following happens:

  — The catch clause is executed.

  — If there is a finally block, it is executed.

  — Execution continues after the end of the try statement (that is, after the finally block, or after the last catch clause if there is no finally block).

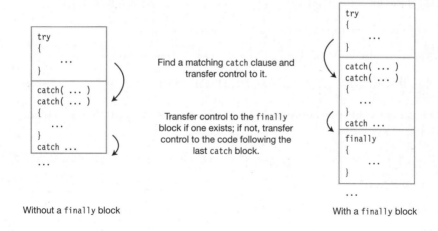

Figure 11-6. *Exception with handler in current try statement*

Searching Further

If the exception was raised in a section of code that was not guarded by a `try` statement or if the try statement does not have a matching exception handler, the system will have to look further for a matching handler. It will do this by searching down the call stack, in sequence, to see whether there is an enclosing `try` block with a matching handler.

Figure 11-7 illustrates the search process. On the left of the figure is the calling structure of the code, and on the right is the call stack. The figure shows that `Method2` is called from inside the `try` block of `Method1`. If an exception occurs inside the `try` block in `Method2`, the system does the following:

- First, it checks to see whether `Method2` has exception handlers that can handle the exception.

  — If so, `Method2` handles it, and program execution continues.

  — If not, the system continues down the call stack to `Method1`, searching for an appropriate handler.

- If `Method1` has an appropriate `catch` clause, the system does the following:

  — Goes back to the top of the call stack—which is `Method2`

  — Executes `Method2`'s `finally` block and pops `Method2` off the stack

  — Executes `Method1`'s `catch` clause and its `finally` block

- If `Method1` doesn't have an appropriate `catch` clause, the system continues searching down the call stack.

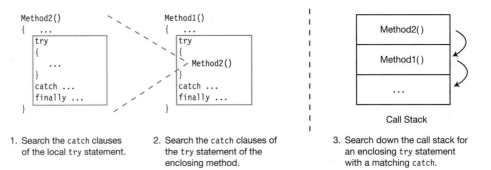

Figure 11-7. *Searching down the call stack*

General Algorithm

Figure 11-8 shows the general algorithm for handling an exception.

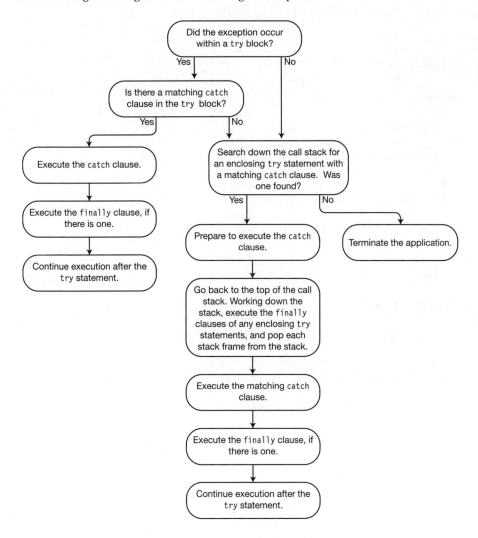

Figure 11-8. *The general algorithm for handling an exception*

Example of Searching Down the Call Stack

In the following code, Main starts execution and calls method A, which calls method B. A description and diagram of the process are given after the code and in Figure 11-9.

```
class Program
{
   static void Main()
   {
      MyClass MCls = new MyClass();
      try
         { MCls.A(); }
      catch (DivideByZeroException e)
         { Console.WriteLine("catch clause in Main()"); }
      finally
         { Console.WriteLine("finally clause in Main()"); }
      Console.WriteLine("After try statement in Main.");
      Console.WriteLine("              -- Keep running.");
   }
}

class MyClass
{
   public void A()
   {
      try
         { B(); }
      catch (System.NullReferenceException)
         { Console.WriteLine("catch clause in A()"); }
      finally
         { Console.WriteLine("finally clause in A()"); }
   }

   void B()
   {
      int x = 10, y = 0;
      try
         { x /= y; }
      catch (System.IndexOutOfRangeException)
         { Console.WriteLine("catch clause in B()"); }
      finally
         { Console.WriteLine("finally clause in B()"); }
   }
}
```

This code produces the following output:

```
finally clause in B()
finally clause in A()
catch clause in Main()
finally clause in Main()
After try statement in Main.
           -- Keep running.
```

1. Main calls A, which calls B, which encounters a DivideByZeroException exception.
2. The system checks B's catch section for a matching catch clause. Although it has one for IndexOutOfRangeException, it doesn't have one for DivideByZeroException.
3. The system then moves down the call stack and checks A's catch section, where it finds that A also doesn't have a matching catch clause.
4. The system continues down the call stack and checks Main's catch clause section, where it finds that Main *does* have a DivideByZeroException catch clause.
5. Although the matching catch clause has now been located, *it is not executed yet*. Instead, the system goes back to the top of the stack, executes B's finally clause, and pops B from the call stack.
6. The system then moves to A, executes its finally clause, and pops A from the call stack.
7. Finally, Main's matching catch clause is executed, followed by its finally clause. Execution then continues after the end of Main's try statement.

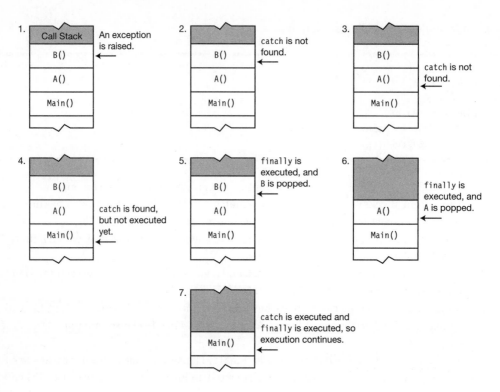

Figure 11-9. *Searching the stack for an exception handler*

Throwing Exceptions

You can make your code explicitly raise an exception by using the throw statement. The syntax for the throw statement is the following:

```
throw ExceptionObject;
```

For example, the following code defines a method called PrintArg, which takes a string argument and prints it out. Inside the try block, it first checks to make sure the argument is not null. If it is, it creates an ArgumentNullException instance and throws it. The exception instance is caught in the catch statement, and the error message is printed. Main calls the method twice: once with a null argument and then with a valid argument.

```
class MyClass
{
   public static void PrintArg(string arg)
   {
      try
      {
         if (arg == null)                                    Supply name of null argument
         {                                                              ↓
            ArgumentNullException myEx = new ArgumentNullException("arg");
            throw myEx;
         }
         Console.WriteLine(arg);
      }
      catch (ArgumentNullException e)
      {
         Console.WriteLine("Message:  {0}", e.Message);
      }
   }
}
class Program
{
   static void Main()
   {
      string s = null;
      MyClass.PrintArg(s);
      MyClass.PrintArg("Hi there!");
   }
}
```

This code produces the following output:

```
Message:  Value cannot be null.
Parameter name: arg
Hi there!
```

313

Throwing Without an Exception Object

The throw statement can also be used without an exception object, inside a catch block.

- This form rethrows the current exception, and the system continues its search for additional handlers for it.

- This form can be used only inside a catch statement.

For example, the following code rethrows the exception from inside the first catch clause:

```
class MyClass
{
   public static void PrintArg(string arg)
   {
      try
      {
         try
         {
            if (arg == null)                              Supply name of null argument
            {                                                      ↓
               ArgumentNullException myEx = new ArgumentNullException("arg");
               throw myEx;
            }
            Console.WriteLine(arg);
         }
         catch (ArgumentNullException e)
         {
            Console.WriteLine("Inner Catch:  {0}", e.Message);
            throw;
         }     ↑
      }     Rethrow the exception, with no additional parameters
      catch
      {
         Console.WriteLine("Outer Catch:  Handling an Exception.");
      }
   }
}

class Program {
   static void Main() {
      string s = null;
      MyClass.PrintArg(s);
   }
}
```

This code produces the following output:

```
Inner Catch:  Value cannot be null.
Parameter name: arg
Outer Catch:  Handling an Exception.
```

CHAPTER 12

■ ■ ■

Structs

What Are Structs?

Structs are programmer-defined data types, very similar to classes. They have data members and function members. Although similar to classes, there are a number of important differences. The most important ones are the following:

- Classes are reference types, and structs are value types.

- Structs are implicitly sealed, which means they cannot be derived from.

The syntax for declaring a struct is similar to that of declaring a class:

```
Keyword
   ↓
struct StructName
{
    MemberDeclarations
}
```

For example, the following code declares a struct named Point. It has two public fields, named X and Y. In Main, three variables of struct type Point are declared, and their values are assigned and printed out.

```
struct Point
{
    public int X;
    public int Y;
}

class Program
{
    static void Main()
    {
        Point first, second, third;

        first.X  = 10; first.Y = 10;
        second.X = 20; second.Y = 20;
        third.X  = first.X + second.X;
        third.Y  = first.Y + second.Y;

        Console.WriteLine("first:   {0}, {1}", first.X,  first.Y);
        Console.WriteLine("second:  {0}, {1}", second.X, second.Y);
        Console.WriteLine("third:   {0}, {1}", third.X,  third.Y);
    }
}
```

Structs Are Value Types

As with all value types, a variable of a struct type contains its own data. Consequently:

- A variable of a struct type cannot be null.

- Two structs variables cannot refer to the same object.

For example, the following code declares a class called CSimple, a struct called Simple, and a variable of each. Figure 12-1 shows how the two would be arranged in memory.

```
class CSimple
{
   public int X;
   public int Y;
}

struct Simple
{
   public int X;
   public int Y;
}

class Program
{
   static void Main()
   {
      CSimple cs = new CSimple();
      Simple  ss = new Simple();

         ...
```

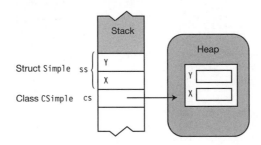

Figure 12-1. *Memory arrangement of a class versus a struct*

Assigning to a Struct

Assigning one struct to another copies the values from one to the other. This is quite different from copying from a class variable, where only the reference is copied.

Figure 12-2 shows the difference between the assignment of a class variable and a struct variable. Notice that after the class assignment, cs2 is pointing at the same object in the heap as cs1. But after the struct assignment, the values of ss2's members are copies of those in ss1.

```
class CSimple
{ public int X; public int Y; }

struct Simple
{ public int X; public int Y; }

class Program
{
   static void Main()
   {
      CSimple cs1 = new CSimple(), cs2 = null;        // Class instances
      Simple  ss1 = new Simple(),  ss2 = new Simple(); // Struct instances

      cs1.X = ss1.X = 5;                   // Assign 5 to ss1.X and cs1.X
      cs1.Y = ss1.Y = 10;                  // Assign 10 to ss1.Y and cs1.Y

      cs2 = cs1;                           // Assign class instance
      ss2 = ss1;                           // Assign struct instance
   }
}
```

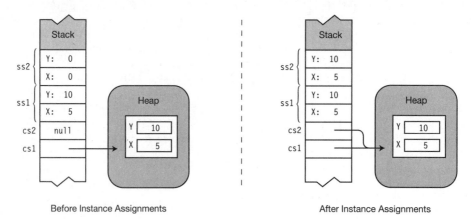

Figure 12-2. *Assigning a class variable and a struct variable*

Constructors and Destructors

Structs can have instance and static constructors, but destructors are not allowed.

Instance Constructors

The language implicitly supplies a parameterless constructor for every struct. This constructor sets each of the struct's members to the default value for that type. Value members are set to their default values. Reference members are set to null.

The predefined parameterless constructor exists for every struct—and you cannot delete or redefine it. You can, however, create additional constructors, as long as they have parameters. Notice that this is different from classes. For classes, the compiler will supply an implicit parameterless constructor only if no other constructors are declared.

To call a constructor, including the implicit parameterless constructor, use the new operator. Notice that the new operator is used even though the memory is not allocated from the heap.

For example, the following code declares a simple struct with a constructor that takes two int parameters. Main creates two instances of the struct—one using the implicit parameterless constructor and the second with the declared two-parameter constructor.

```
struct Simple
{
   public int X;
   public int Y;

   public Simple(int a, int b)                // Constructor with parameters
   {
      X = a;
      Y = b;
   }
}

class Program
{
   static void Main()
   {                       Call implicit constructor
                                    ↓
      Simple s1 = new Simple();
      Simple s2 = new Simple(5, 10);
                                    ↑
                      Call constructor
      Console.WriteLine("{0},{1}", s1.X, s1.Y);
      Console.WriteLine("{0},{1}", s2.X, s2.Y);
   }
}
```

You can also create an instance of a struct without using the new operator. If you do this, however, there are some restrictions, which are the following:

- You cannot use the value of a data member until you have explicitly set it.

- You cannot call *any* function member of the struct until *all* the data members have been assigned.

For example, the following code shows two instances of struct Simple created without using the new operator. When there is an attempt to access s1 without explicitly setting the data member values, the compiler produces an error message. There are no problems reading from s2 after assigning values to its members.

```
struct Simple
{
    public int X;
    public int Y;
}

class Program
{
    static void Main()
    {       No constructor calls
                ↓      ↓
        Simple s1, s2;
        Console.WriteLine("{0},{1}", s1.X, s1.Y);              // Compiler error
                                      ↑      ↑
        s2.X = 5;                  Not yet assigned
        s2.Y = 10;
        Console.WriteLine("{0},{1}", s2.X, s2.Y);              // OK
    }
}
```

Static Constructors

As with classes, the static constructors of structs create and initialize the static data members and cannot reference instance members. Static constructors for structs follow the same rules as those for classes.

A static constructor is called before the first of either of the following two actions:

- A call to an explicitly declared constructor

- A reference to a static member of the struct

Summary of Constructors and Destructors

Table 12-1 summarizes the use of constructors and destructors with structs.

Table 12-1. *Summary of Constructors and Destructors*

Type	Description
Instance constructor (parameterless)	Cannot be declared in the program. An implicit constructor is supplied by the system for all structs. It cannot be deleted or redefined by the program.
Instance constructor (with parameters)	Can be declared in the program.
Static constructor	Can be declared in the program.
Destructor	Cannot be declared in the program. Destructors are not allowed.

Field Initializers Are Not Allowed

Field initializers are not allowed in struct declarations, as shown in the following code:

```
struct Simple
{                   Not allowed
                      ↓
   public int x = 0;               // Compile error
   public int y = 10;              // Compile error
}                     ↑
                   Not allowed
```

Structs Are Sealed

Structs are always implicitly sealed, and hence you cannot derive other structs from them.

Since structs do not support inheritance, the use of several of the class member modifiers with struct members would not make sense; thus, they cannot be used in their declarations. The modifiers that cannot be used with structs are the following:

- protected

- internal

- abstract

- virtual

Structs themselves are, under the covers, derived from System.ValueType, which is derived from object.

The two inheritance-associated keywords you *can* use with struct members are the new and override modifiers, when creating a member with the same name as a member of base class System.ValueType, from which all structs are derived.

Boxing and Unboxing

As with other value type data, if you want to use a struct instance as a reference type object, you must make a boxed copy. Boxing and unboxing are explained in Chapter 18.

Structs As Return Values and Parameters

Structs can be used as return values and parameters.

- *Return value*: When a struct is a return value, a copy is created and returned from the function member.

- *Value parameter*: When a struct is used as a value parameter, a copy of the actual parameter struct is created. The copy is used in the execution of the method.

- ref *and* out *parameters*: If you use a struct as a ref or out parameter, a reference to the struct is passed into the method so that the data members can be changed.

Additional Information About Structs

Allocating structs requires less overhead than creating instances of a class, so using structs instead of classes can sometimes improve performance—but beware of the high cost of boxing and unboxing.
Finally, some last things you should know about structs are the following:

- The predefined simple types (int, short, long, and so on), although considered primitives in .NET and C#, are all actually implemented under the covers in .NET as structs.

- You can declare partial structs in the same way as partial classes, as described in Chapter 6.

Structs, like classes, can implement interfaces, which will be covered in Chapter 17.

Enumerations

Enumerations

An enumeration, or enum, is a programmer-defined type, like a class or a struct.

- Like structs, enums are value types and therefore store their data directly, rather than separately, with a reference and data.

- Enums have only one type of member: named constants with integral values.

The following code shows an example of the declaration of a new enum type called TrafficLight, which contains three members. Notice that the list of member declarations is a comma-separated list; there are no semicolons in an enum declaration.

```
Keyword     Enum name
   ↓            ↓
 enum TrafficLight
 {
    Green,    ←  Comma separated—no semicolons
    Yellow,   ←  Comma separated—no semicolons
    Red
 }
```

Every enum type has an underlying integral type, which by default is int.

- Each enum member is assigned a constant value of the underlying type.

- By default, the compiler assigns 0 to the first member and assigns each subsequent member the value one more than the previous member.

For example, in the TrafficLight type, the compiler assigns the int values 0, 1, and 2 to members Green, Yellow, and Red, respectively. In the output of the following code, you can see the underlying member values by casting them to type int. Figure 13-1 illustrates their arrangement on the stack.

```
TrafficLight t1 = TrafficLight.Green;
TrafficLight t2 = TrafficLight.Yellow;
TrafficLight t3 = TrafficLight.Red;

Console.WriteLine("{0},\t{1}",   t1, (int) t1);
Console.WriteLine("{0},\t{1}",   t2, (int) t2);
Console.WriteLine("{0},\t{1}\n", t3, (int) t3);
                                      ↑
                                  Cast to int
```

This code produces the following output:

```
Green,  0
Yellow, 1
Red,    2
```

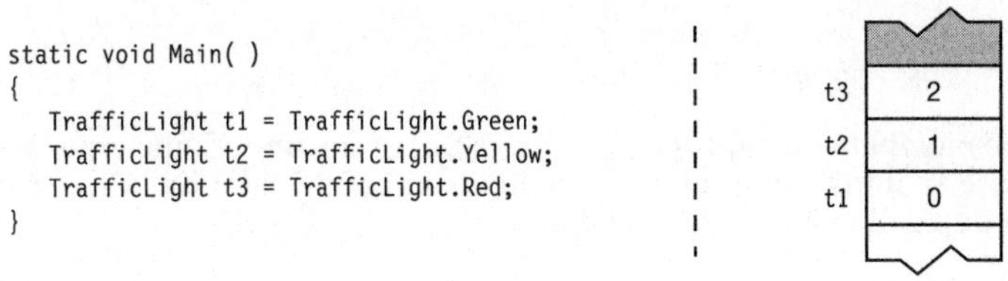

```
static void Main( )
{
    TrafficLight t1 = TrafficLight.Green;
    TrafficLight t2 = TrafficLight.Yellow;
    TrafficLight t3 = TrafficLight.Red;
}
```

```
t3    2
t2    1
t1    0
```

Figure 13-1. *The member constants of an enum are represented by underlying integral values.*

You can assign enum values to variables of the enum type. For example, the following code shows the declaration of three variables of type TrafficLight. Notice that you can assign member literals to variables, or you can copy the value from another variable of the same type.

```
class Program
{
    static void Main()
    {        Type   Variable      Member
             ↓       ↓              ↓
        TrafficLight t1 = TrafficLight.Red;      // Assign from member
        TrafficLight t2 = TrafficLight.Green;    // Assign from member
        TrafficLight t3 = t2;                    // Assign from variable

        Console.WriteLine(t1);
        Console.WriteLine(t2);
        Console.WriteLine(t3);
    }
}
```

This code produces the following output. Notice that the member names are printed as strings.

```
Red
Green
Green
```

Setting the Underlying Type and Explicit Values

You can use an integral type other than int by placing a colon and the type name after the enum name. The type can be any integer type. All the member constants are of the enum's underlying type.

```
                     Colon
                       ↓
enum TrafficLight : ulong
{                     ↑
   ...          Underlying type
```

The values of the member constants can be any values of the underlying type. To explicitly set the value of a member, use an initializer after its name in the enum declaration. There can be duplicate values, although not duplicate names, as shown here:

```
enum TrafficLight
{
   Green  = 10,
   Yellow = 15,             // Duplicate values
   Red    = 15              // Duplicate values
}
```

For example, the code in Figure 13-2 shows two equivalent declarations of enum TrafficLight.

- The code on the left accepts the default type and numbering.

- The code on the right explicitly sets the underlying type to int and the members to values corresponding to the default values.

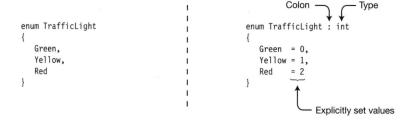

Figure 13-2. *Equivalent enum declarations*

Implicit Member Numbering

You can explicitly assign the values for any of the member constants. If you don't initialize a member constant, the compiler implicitly assigns it a value. Figure 13-3 illustrates the rules the compiler uses for assigning those values.

- The values associated with the member names do not need to be distinct.

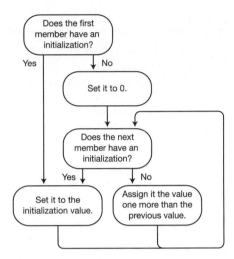

Figure 13-3. *The algorithm for assigning member values*

For example, the following code declares two enumerations. CardSuit accepts the implicit numbering of the members, as shown in the comments. FaceCards sets some members explicitly and accepts implicit numbering of the others.

```
enum CardSuit
{
    Hearts,                     // 0  - Since this is first
    Clubs,                      // 1  - One more than the previous one
    Diamonds,                   // 2  - One more than the previous one
    Spades,                     // 3  - One more than the previous one
    MaxSuits                    // 4  - A common way to assign a constant
}                               //        to the number of listed items.

enum FaceCards
{
    // Member                   // Value assigned
    Jack              = 11,     // 11 - Explicitly set
    Queen,                      // 12 - One more than the previous one
    King,                       // 13 - One more than the previous one
    Ace,                        // 14 - One more than the previous one
    NumberOfFaceCards = 4,      // 4  - Explicitly set
    SomeOtherValue,             // 5  - One more than the previous one
    HighestFaceCard   = Ace     // 14 - Ace is defined above
}
```

Bit Flags

Programmers have long used the different bits in a single word as a compact way of representing a set of on/off flags. Enums offer a convenient way to implement this.

The general steps are the following:

1. Determine how many bit flags you need, and choose an unsigned integral type with enough bits to hold them.

2. Determine what each bit position represents, and give it a name. Declare an enum of the chosen integral type, with each member represented by a bit position.

3. Use the bitwise OR operator to set the appropriate bits in a word holding the bit flags.

4. Unpack the bit flags by using the bitwise AND operator, or the HasFlag method.

For example, the following code shows the enum declaration representing the options for a card deck in a card game. The underlying type, uint, is more than sufficient to hold the four bit flags needed. Notice the following about the code:

- The members have names that represent binary options.

    — Each option is represented by a particular bit position in the word. Bit positions hold either a 0 or a 1.

    — Since a bit flag represents a set of bits that are either on or off, you do not want to use 0 as a member value. It already has a meaning—that all the bit flags are off.

- Hexadecimal representation is often used when working with bit patterns because there is a more direct correlation between a bit pattern and its hexadecimal representation than with its decimal representation.

- Decorating the enum with the Flags attribute is not actually necessary but gives some additional convenience, which I'll discuss shortly. Attributes are covered in Chapter 24.

```
[Flags]
enum CardDeckSettings : uint
{
    SingleDeck    = 0x01,        // Bit 0
    LargePictures = 0x02,        // Bit 1
    FancyNumbers  = 0x04,        // Bit 2
    Animation     = 0x08         // Bit 3
}
```

Figure 13-4 illustrates this enumeration.

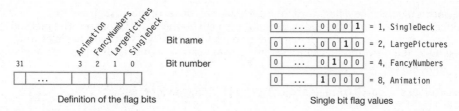

Definition of the flag bits   Single bit flag values

Figure 13-4. *Definition of the flag bits, and their individual representations*

To create a word with the appropriate bit flags, declare a variable of the enum type, and use the bitwise OR operator to set the required bits. For example, the following code sets three of the four options:

```
      Enum type    Flag word          Bit flags ORed together
          ↓            ↓                        ↓
CardDeckSettings ops = CardDeckSettings.SingleDeck
                     | CardDeckSettings.FancyNumbers
                     | CardDeckSettings.Animation ;
```

Prior to C# 4.0, to determine whether a particular bit was set, you would use the bitwise AND operator with the flag word and the bit flag.

For example, the following code checks a value to see whether the FancyNumbers bit flag is set. It does this by ANDing that value with the bit flag and then comparing that result with the bit flag. If the bit was set in the original value, then the result of the AND operation will have the same bit pattern as the bit flag.

```
bool useFancyNumbers =
    (ops & CardDeckSettings.FancyNumbers) == CardDeckSettings.FancyNumbers;
      ↑              ↑
  Flag word      Bit flag
```

Figure 13-5 illustrates the process of creating the flag word and then checking whether a particular bit is set.

Produce flag word representing the states of the flag bits.

Check whether the FancyNumbers bit is set.

Figure 13-5. *Producing a flag word and checking it for a particular bit flag*

This process of checking a flag word for a particular bit or set of bits is such a common task that C# 4.0 introduced a new instance method to the enum type to do the process for you. The method is called HasFlag. You use it on an instance of a flag word and pass it the bit flag you want to check for.

For example, the previous check for useFancyNumbers can be significantly shortened and simplified to the following statement:

```
UseFancyNumbers = ops.HasFlag(CardDeckSettings.FancyNumbers);
                       ↑                        ↑
                   Flag word                 Bit flag
```

The HasFlag method can also check for multiple bit flags. For example, the following code checks whether the flag word, ops, has both the Animation and FancyNumbers bits set. The code does the following:

- The first statement creates a test word instance, called testFlags, with the Animation and FancyNumbers bits set.

- It then passes testFlags as the parameter to the HasFlags method.

- HasFlags checks whether *all* the flags that are set in the test word are also set in the flag word, ops. If they are, then HasFlag returns true. Otherwise, it returns false.

```
CardDeckSettings testFlags =
            CardDeckSettings.Animation | CardDeckSettings.FancyNumbers;

UseAnimationAndFancyNumbers = ops.HasFlag( testFlags );
                                  ↑            ↑
                              Flag word     Test word
```

The Flags Attribute

We'll cover attributes in Chapter 24, but it's worth mentioning the Flags attribute here. An attribute appears as a string between square brackets placed on the line above a class declaration. The Flags attribute does not change the calculations at all. It does, however, provide several convenient features.

First, it informs the compiler, object browsers, and other tools looking at the code that the members of the enum are meant to be combined as bit flags, rather than used only as separate values. This allows the browsers to interpret variables of the enum type more appropriately.

Second, it allows the ToString method of an enum to provide more appropriate formatting for the values of bit flags. The ToString method takes an enum value and compares it to the values of the constant members of the enum. If it matches one of the members, ToString returns the string name of the member.

Suppose, for example, that you have used the enum declaration for CardDeckSettings (given in the preceding code) and have *not* used the Flags attribute. The first line of the following code creates a variable (named ops) of the enum type and sets the value of a single flag bit. The second line uses ToString to get the string name of the member represented by that value.

```
CardDeckSettings ops = CardDeckSettings.FancyNumbers;   // Set the bit flag.
Console.WriteLine( ops.ToString() );                    // Print its name.
```

This code produces the following output:

```
FancyNumbers
```

That's all well and good, but suppose you set two bit flags instead of one, as in the following code. Suppose also that you didn't use the Flags attribute on the enum declaration.

```
// Set two bit flags.
ops = CardDeckSettings.FancyNumbers | CardDeckSettings.Animation;
Console.WriteLine( ops.ToString() );        // Print what?
```

The resulting value of ops is 12, where 4 is from the FancyNumbers flag and 8 is from the Animation flag. In the second line, when ToString attempts to look up the value in the list of enum members, it finds that there is no member with the value 12—so it just returns the string representing 12. The resulting output is the following:

```
12
```

If, however, you change your code to use the Flags attribute before the declaration of the enum, this tells the ToString method that the bits can be considered separately. In looking up the value, it would find that 12 corresponds to the two bit flag members FancyNumbers and Animation. It would then return the string containing their names, separated by a comma and space, as shown here:

```
FancyNumbers, Animation
```

Example Using Bit Flags

The following code puts together all the pieces of using bit flags:

```
[Flags]
enum CardDeckSettings : uint
{
    SingleDeck     = 0x01,       // bit 0
    LargePictures  = 0x02,       // bit 1
    FancyNumbers   = 0x04,       // bit 2
    Animation      = 0x08        // bit 3
}

class MyClass
{
    bool UseSingleDeck            = false,
         UseBigPics               = false,
         UseFancyNumbers          = false,
         UseAnimation             = false,
         UseAnimationAndFancyNumbers = false;

    public void SetOptions( CardDeckSettings ops )
    {
        UseSingleDeck    = ops.HasFlag( CardDeckSettings.SingleDeck );
        UseBigPics       = ops.HasFlag( CardDeckSettings.LargePictures );
        UseFancyNumbers  = ops.HasFlag( CardDeckSettings.FancyNumbers );
        UseAnimation     = ops.HasFlag( CardDeckSettings.Animation );

        CardDeckSettings testFlags =
                    CardDeckSettings.Animation | CardDeckSettings.FancyNumbers;
        UseAnimationAndFancyNumbers = ops.HasFlag( testFlags );
    }

    public void PrintOptions( )
    {
        Console.WriteLine( "Option settings:" );
        Console.WriteLine( "  Use Single Deck            - {0}", UseSingleDeck );
        Console.WriteLine( "  Use Large Pictures         - {0}", UseBigPics );
        Console.WriteLine( "  Use Fancy Numbers          - {0}", UseFancyNumbers );
        Console.WriteLine( "  Show Animation             - {0}", UseAnimation );
        Console.WriteLine( "  Show Animation and FancyNumbers - {0}",
                                                UseAnimationAndFancyNumbers );
    }
}
```

```
class Program
{
   static void Main( string[] args )
   {
      MyClass mc = new MyClass( );
      CardDeckSettings ops = CardDeckSettings.SingleDeck
                             | CardDeckSettings.FancyNumbers
                             | CardDeckSettings.Animation;
      mc.SetOptions( ops );
      mc.PrintOptions( );
   }
}
```

This code produces the following output:

```
Option settings:
   Use Single Deck                    - True
   Use Large Pictures                 - False
   Use Fancy Numbers                  - True
   Show Animation                     - True
   Show Animation and FancyNumbers - True
```

More About Enums

Enums have only a single member type: the declared member constants.

- You cannot use modifiers with the members. They all implicitly have the same accessibility as the enum.

- Since the members are static, they are accessible even if there are no variables of the enum type. Use the enum type name, followed by a dot and the member name.

For example, the following code does not create any variables of the enum TrafficLight type, but the members are accessible and can be printed using WriteLine.

```
static void Main()
{
   Console.WriteLine("{0}", TrafficLight.Green);
   Console.WriteLine("{0}", TrafficLight.Yellow);
   Console.WriteLine("{0}", TrafficLight.Red);
}
                            ↑             ↑
                        Enum name    Member name
```

An enum is a distinct type. Comparing enum members of different enum types results in a compile-time error. For example, the following code declares two enum types.

- The first if statement is fine because it compares different members from the same enum type.

- The second if statement produces an error because it compares members from different enum types, even though their structures and member names are exactly the same.

```csharp
enum FirstEnum                          // First enum type
{
    Mem1,
    Mem2
}

enum SecondEnum                         // Second enum type
{
    Mem1,
    Mem2
}

class Program
{
    static void Main()
    {
        if (FirstEnum.Mem1 < FirstEnum.Mem2)  // OK--members of same enum type
            Console.WriteLine("True");

        if (FirstEnum.Mem1 < SecondEnum.Mem1) // Error--different enum types
            Console.WriteLine("True");
    }
}
```

■■■

Arrays

Arrays

An array is a set of uniform data elements, represented by a single variable name. The individual elements are accessed using the variable name together with one or more indexes between square brackets, as shown here:

Definitions

Let's start with some important definitions having to do with arrays in C#.

- *Elements*: The individual data items of an array are called *elements*. All elements of an array must be of the same type or derived from the same type.

- *Rank/dimensions*: Arrays can have any positive number of dimensions. The number of dimensions an array has is called its *rank*.

- *Dimension length*: Each dimension of an array has a *length*, which is the number of positions in that direction.

- *Array length*: The total number of elements contained in an array, in *all* dimensions, is called the *length* of the array.

Important Details

The following are some important general facts about C# arrays:

- Once an array is created, its size is fixed. C# does not support dynamic arrays.

- Array indexes are *0-based*. That is, if the length of a dimension is *n*, the index values range from 0 to *n* – 1. For example, Figure 14-1 shows the dimensions and lengths of two example arrays. Notice that for each dimension, the indexes range from 0 to *length* – 1.

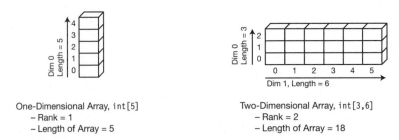

Figure 14-1. *Dimensions and sizes*

Types of Arrays

C# provides two kinds of arrays:

- One-dimensional arrays can be thought of as a single line, or *vector*, of elements.

- Multidimensional arrays are composed such that each position in the primary vector is itself an array, called a *subarray*. Positions in the subarray vectors can themselves be subarrays.

Additionally, there are two types of multidimensional arrays, *rectangular arrays* and *jagged arrays*, which have the following characteristics:

- Rectangular arrays

    — Are multidimensional arrays where all the subarrays in a particular dimension have the same length

    — Always use a single set of square brackets, regardless of the number of dimensions

    ```
    int x = myArray2[4, 6, 1]          // One set of square brackets
    ```

- Jagged arrays

    — Are multidimensional arrays where each subarray is an independent array

    — Can have subarrays of *different* lengths

    — Use a separate set of square brackets for each dimension of the array

    ```
    jagArray1[2][7][4]                  // Three sets of square brackets
    ```

Figure 14-2 shows the kinds of arrays available in C#.

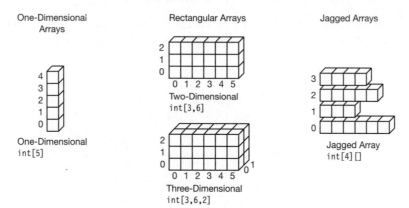

Figure 14-2. *One-dimensional, rectangular, and jagged arrays*

An Array As an Object

An array instance is an object whose type derives from class System.Array. Since arrays are derived from this BCL base class, they inherit a number of useful members from it, such as the following:

- Rank: A property that returns the number of dimensions of the array

- Length: A property that returns the length (the total number of elements) of the array

Arrays are reference types, and as with all reference types, they have both a reference to the data and the data object itself. The reference is in either the stack or the heap, and the data object itself will always be in the heap. Figure 14-3 shows the memory configuration and components of an array.

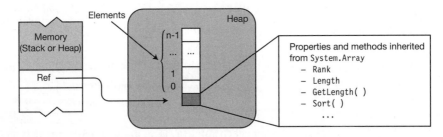

Figure 14-3. *Structure of an array*

Although an array is always a reference type, the elements of the array can be either value types or reference types.

- An array is called a *value type array* if the elements stored are value types.

- An array is called a *reference type array* if the elements stored in the array are references of reference type objects.

Figure 14-4 shows a value type array and a reference type array.

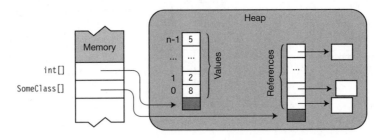

Figure 14-4. *Elements can be values or references.*

One-Dimensional and Rectangular Arrays

Syntactically, one-dimensional arrays and rectangular arrays are very similar, so I'll treat them together. I'll then treat jagged arrays separately.

Declaring a One-Dimensional Array or a Rectangular Array

To declare a one-dimensional or rectangular array, use a single set of square brackets between the type and the variable name.

The *rank specifiers* are commas between the brackets. They specify the number of dimensions the array will have. The rank is the number of commas, plus one. For example, no commas indicates a one-dimensional array, one comma indicates a two-dimensional array, and so forth.

The base type, together with the rank specifiers, is the *type* of the array. For example, the following line of code declares a one-dimensional array of longs. The type of the array is long[], which is read as "an array of longs."

```
Rank specifiers = 1
         ↓
long[ ]  secondArray;
  ↑
Array type
```

The following code shows examples of declarations of rectangular arrays. Notice the following:

- You can have as many rank specifiers as you need.

- You cannot place array dimension lengths in the array type section. The rank is part of the array's type, but the lengths of the dimensions are *not* part of the type.

- When an array is declared, the *number* of dimensions is fixed. The *length* of the dimensions, however, is not determined until the array is instantiated.

```
Rank specifiers
      ↓
int[,,]   firstArray;        // Array type: 3-D array of int
int[,]    arr1;              // Array type: 2-D array of int
long[,,]  arr3;              // Array type: 3-D array of long
  ↑
Array type

long[3,2,6] SecondArray;     // Wrong!  Compile error
    ↑ ↑ ↑
Dimension lengths not allowed!
```

■ **Note** Unlike C/C++, the brackets follow the base type, not the variable name.

Instantiating a One-Dimensional or Rectangular Array

To instantiate an array, you use an *array-creation expression*. An array-creation expression consists of the new operator, followed by the base type, followed by a pair of square brackets. The length of each dimension is placed in a comma-separated list between the brackets.

The following are examples of one-dimensional array declarations:

- Array arr2 is a one-dimensional array of four ints.

- Array mcArr is a one-dimensional array of four MyClass references.

- Figure 14-5 shows their layouts in memory.

```
                     Four elements
                          ↓
int[]      arr2  = new int[4];
MyClass[] mcArr = new MyClass[4];
                      ↑
            Array-creation expression
```

The following is an example of a rectangular array. Array arr3 is a three-dimensional array.

- The length of the array is 3 * 6 * 2 = 36.

- Figure 14-5 shows its layout in memory.

```
              Lengths of the dimensions
                          ↓
int[,,] arr3 = new int[3,6,2] ;
```

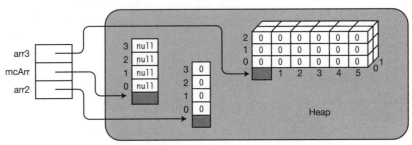

Figure 14-5. *Declaring and instantiating arrays*

■ **Note** Unlike object-creation expressions, array-creation expressions do not contain parentheses—even for reference type arrays.

Accessing Array Elements

An array element is accessed using an integer value as an index into the array.

- Each dimension uses 0-based indexing.

- The index is placed between square brackets following the array name.

The following code shows examples of declaring, writing to, and reading from a one-dimensional and a two-dimensional array:

```
int[]  intArr1 = new int[15];        // Declare 1-D array.
intArr1[2]     = 10;                 // Write to element 2 of the array.
int var1       = intArr1[2];         // Read from element 2 of the array.


int[,] intArr2 = new int[5,10];      // Declare 2-D array.
intArr2[2,3]   = 7;                  // Write to the array.
int var2       = intArr2[2,3];       // Read from the array.
```

The following code shows the full process of creating and accessing a one-dimensional array:

```
int[] myIntArray;                           // Declare the array.

myIntArray = new int[4];                    // Instantiate the array.

for( int i=0; i<4; i++ )                    // Set the values.
   myIntArray[i] = i*10;

// Read and display the values of each element.
for( int i=0; i<4; i++ )
   Console.WriteLine("Value of element {0} = {1}", i, myIntArray[i]);
```

This code produces the following output:

```
Value of element 0 is 0
Value of element 1 is 10
Value of element 2 is 20
Value of element 3 is 30
```

Initializing an Array

Whenever an array is created, each of the elements is automatically initialized to the default value for the type. The default values for the predefined types are 0 for integer types, 0.0 for floating-point types, false for Booleans, and null for reference types.

For example, the following code creates an array and initializes its four elements to the value 0. Figure 14-6 illustrates the layout in memory.

```
int[] intArr = new int[4];
```

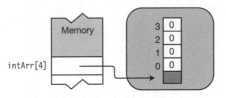

Figure 14-6. *Automatic initialization of a one-dimensional array*

Explicit Initialization of One-Dimensional Arrays

For a one-dimensional array, you can set explicit initial values by including an *initialization list* immediately after the array-creation expression of an array instantiation.

- The initialization values must be separated by commas and enclosed in a set of curly braces.

- The dimension lengths are optional, since the compiler will infer the lengths from the number of initializing values.

- Notice that nothing separates the array-creation expression and the initialization list. That is, there is no equals sign or other connecting operator.

For example, the following code creates an array and initializes its four elements to the values between the curly braces. Figure 14-7 illustrates the layout in memory.

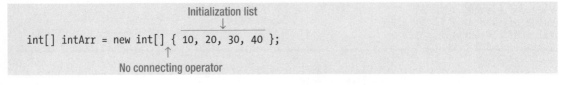

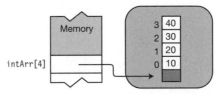

Figure 14-7. *Explicit initialization of a one-dimensional array*

Explicit Initialization of Rectangular Arrays

To explicitly initialize a rectangular array, you need to follow these rules:

- Each *vector of initial values* must be enclosed in curly braces.

- Each *dimension* must also be nested and enclosed in curly braces.

- In addition to the initial values, the initialization lists and components of each dimension must also be separated by commas.

For example, the following code shows the declaration of a two-dimensional array with an initialization list. Figure 14-8 illustrates the layout in memory.

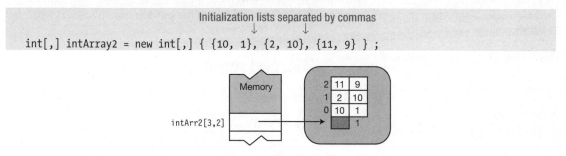

Figure 14-8. *Initializing a rectangular array*

Syntax Points for Initializing Rectangular Arrays

Rectangular arrays are initialized with nested, comma-separated initialization lists. The initialization lists are nested in curly braces. This can sometimes be confusing, so to get the nesting, grouping, and commas right, the following tips might be helpful:

- Commas are used as *separators* between all *elements* and *groups*.

- Commas are *not* placed between left curly braces.

- Commas are *not* placed before a right curly brace.

- Read the rank specifications from left to right, designating the last number as "elements" and all the others as "groups."

For example, read the following declaration as "intArray has four groups of three groups of two elements."

```
                                    Initialization lists, nested and separated by commas
int[,,] intArray = new int[4,3,2] {      ↓          ↓          ↓
                                    { {8, 6},   {5,  2}, {12, 9} },
                                    { {6, 4},  {13, 9}, {18, 4} },
                                    { {7, 2},   {1, 13}, {9,  3} },
                                    { {4, 6},   {3,  2}, {23, 8} }
                                  };
```

Shortcut Syntax

When combining declaration, array creation, and initialization in a single statement, you can omit the array-creation expression part of the syntax entirely and provide just the initialization portion. Figure 14-9 shows this shortcut syntax.

```
int[] arr1 = new int[3] {10, 20, 30};   }
int[] arr1 =              {10, 20, 30};  } Equivalent


int[,] arr = new int[2,3] {{0, 1, 2}, {10, 11, 12}};  }
int[,] arr =              {{0, 1, 2}, {10, 11, 12}};  } Equivalent
```

Figure 14-9. *Shortcut for array declaration, creation, and initialization*

Implicitly Typed Arrays

So far, we've explicitly specified the array types at the beginnings of all our array declarations. But, like other local variables, your arrays can also be implicitly typed. This means the following:

- When initializing an array, you can let the compiler infer the array's type from the type of the initializers. This is allowed as long as all the initializers can be implicitly converted to a single type.

- Just as with implicitly typed local variables, use the keyword var instead of the array type.

The following code shows explicit and implicit versions of three array declarations. The first set is a one-dimensional array of ints. The second is a two-dimensional array of ints. The third is an array of strings. Notice that in the declaration of implicitly typed intArr4 you still need to include the rank specifier in the initialization.

```
    Explicit            Explicit
      ↓                   ↓
  int [] intArr1 = new int[] { 10, 20, 30, 40 };
  var    intArr2 = new    [] { 10, 20, 30, 40 };
   ↑                    ↑
Keyword             Inferred
  int[,] intArr3 = new int[,] { { 10, 1 }, { 2, 10 }, { 11, 9 } };
  var    intArr4 = new    [,] { { 10, 1 }, { 2, 10 }, { 11, 9 } };
                        ↑
                  Rank specifier
  string[] sArr1 = new string[] { "life", "liberty", "pursuit of happiness" };
  var      sArr2 = new      [] { "life", "liberty", "pursuit of happiness" };
```

Putting It All Together

The following code puts together all the pieces we've looked at so far. It creates, initializes, and uses a rectangular array.

```
// Declare, create, and initialize an implicitly typed array.
var arr = new int[,] {{0, 1, 2}, {10, 11, 12}};

// Print the values.
for( int i=0; i<2; i++ )
   for( int j=0; j<3; j++ )
      Console.WriteLine("Element [{0},{1}] is {2}", i, j, arr[i,j]);
```

This code produces the following output:

```
Element [0,0] is 0
Element [0,1] is 1
Element [0,2] is 2
Element [1,0] is 10
Element [1,1] is 11
Element [1,2] is 12
```

Jagged Arrays

A jagged array is an array of arrays. Unlike rectangular arrays, the subarrays of a jagged array can have different numbers of elements.

For example, the following code declares a two-dimensional jagged array. Figure 14-10 shows the array's layout in memory.

- The length of the first dimension is 3.

- The declaration can be read as "jagArr is an array of three arrays of ints."

- Notice that the figure shows *four* array objects—one for the top-level array and three for the subarrays.

```
int[][] jagArr = new int[3][];   // Declare and create top-level array.
        ...                      // Declare and create subarrays.
```

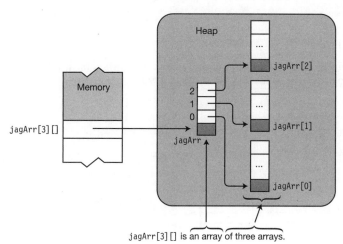

Figure 14-10. *A jagged array is an array of arrays.*

Declaring a Jagged Array

The declaration syntax for jagged arrays requires a separate set of square brackets for each dimension. The number of sets of square brackets in the declaration of the array variable determines the rank of the array.

- A jagged array can be of any number of dimensions greater than one.

- As with rectangular arrays, dimension lengths cannot be included in the array type section of the declaration.

```
Rank specifiers
     ↓
int[][]   SomeArr;              // Rank = 2
int[][][] OtherArr;            // Rank = 3
    ↑         ↑
Array type  Array name
```

Shortcut Instantiation

You can combine the jagged array declaration with the creation of the first-level array using an array-creation expression, such as in the following declaration. Figure 14-11 shows the result.

```
                   Three subarrays
                         ↓
int[][] jagArr = new int[3][];
```

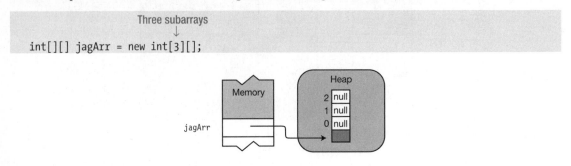

Figure 14-11. *Shortcut first-level instantiation*

You cannot instantiate more than the first-level array in the declaration statement.

```
                     Allowed
                       ↓
int[][] jagArr = new int[3][4];              // Wrong! Compile error
                       ↑
                  Not allowed
```

Instantiating a Jagged Array

Unlike other types of arrays, you cannot fully instantiate a jagged array in a single step. Since a jagged array is an array of independent arrays, each array must be created separately. Instantiating a full jagged array requires the following steps:

1. Instantiate the top-level array.
2. Instantiate each subarray separately, assigning the reference of the newly created array to the appropriate element of its containing array.

For example, the following code shows the declaration, instantiation, and initialization of a two-dimensional jagged array. Notice in the code that the reference to each subarray is assigned to an element in the top-level array. Steps 1 through 4 in the code correspond to the numbered representations in Figure 14-12.

```
int[][] Arr = new int[3][];                  // 1. Instantiate top level

Arr[0] = new int[] {10, 20, 30};             // 2. Instantiate subarray
Arr[1] = new int[] {40, 50, 60, 70};         // 3. Instantiate subarray
Arr[2] = new int[] {80, 90, 100, 110, 120};  // 4. Instantiate subarray
```

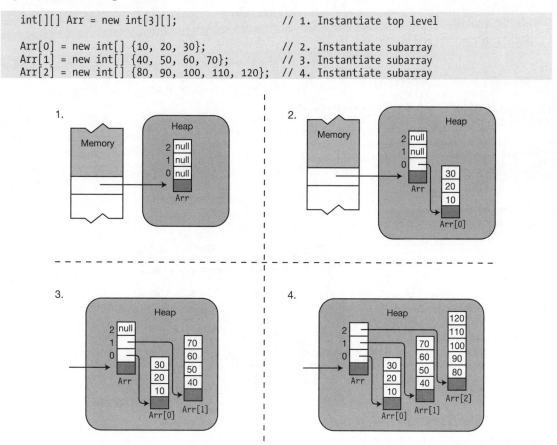

Figure 14-12. *Creating a two-dimensional jagged array*

Subarrays in Jagged Arrays

Since the subarrays in a jagged array are themselves arrays, It's possible to have rectangular arrays inside jagged arrays. For example, the following code creates a jagged array of three two-dimensional rectangular arrays and initializes them with values. It then displays the values.

- Figure 14-13 illustrates the structure.

- The code uses the GetLength(int n) method of arrays, inherited from System.Array, to get the length of the specified dimension of the array.

```
int[][,] Arr;        // An array of 2-D arrays
Arr = new int[3][,]; // Instantiate an array of three 2-D arrays.

Arr[0] = new int[,] { { 10, 20 },       { 100, 200 }          };
Arr[1] = new int[,] { { 30, 40, 50 },   { 300, 400, 500 }     };
Arr[2] = new int[,] { { 60, 70, 80, 90 }, { 600, 700, 800, 900 } };

                         ↓ Get length of dimension 0 of Arr
for (int i = 0; i < Arr.GetLength(0); i++)
{                              ↓ Get length of dimension 0 of Arr[ i ]
   for (int j = 0; j < Arr[i].GetLength(0); j++)
   {                              ↓ Get length of dimension 1 of Arr[ i ]
      for (int k = 0; k < Arr[i].GetLength(1); k++) {
         Console.WriteLine
               ("[{0}][{1},{2}] = {3}", i, j, k, Arr[i][j, k]);
      }
      Console.WriteLine("");
   }
   Console.WriteLine("");
}
```

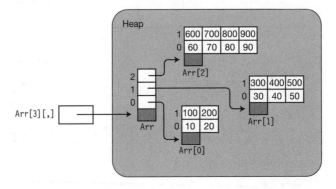

Figure 14-13. *Jagged array of three two-dimensional arrays*

Comparing Rectangular and Jagged Arrays

The structure of rectangular and jagged arrays is significantly different. For example, Figure 14-14 shows the structure of a rectangular three-by-three array, as well as a jagged array of three one-dimensional arrays of length 3.

- Both arrays hold nine integers, but as you can see, their structures are quite different.

- The rectangular array has a single array object, while the jagged array has four array objects.

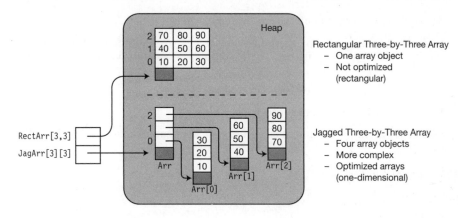

Figure 14-14. *Comparing the structure of rectangular and jagged arrays*

One-dimensional arrays have specific instructions in the CIL that allow them to be optimized for performance. Rectangular arrays do not have these instructions and are not optimized to the same level. Because of this, it can sometimes be more efficient to use jagged arrays of one-dimensional arrays—which can be optimized—than rectangular arrays, which cannot.

On the other hand, the programming complexity can be less for a rectangular array because it can be treated as a single unit, rather than an array of arrays.

The foreach Statement

The foreach statement allows you to sequentially access each element in an array. It's actually a more general construct in that it also works with other collection types as well—but this section only discusses its use with arrays. Chapter 20 covers its use with other collection types.

The important points of the foreach statement are the following:

- The *iteration variable* is a temporary variable of the same type as the elements of the array. The foreach statement uses the iteration variable to sequentially represent each element in the array.

- The syntax of the foreach statement is shown here, where

   — *Type* is the type of the elements of the array. You can explicitly supply its type, or you can let it be implicitly typed and inferred by the compiler, since the compiler knows the type of the array.

   — *Identifier* is the name of the iteration variable.

   — *ArrayName* is the name of the array to be processed.

   — *Statement* is a simple statement or a block that is executed once for each element in the array.

```
    Explicitly typed iteration variable declaration
                     ↓
foreach( Type Identifier in ArrayName )
     Statement


            Implicitly typed iteration variable declaration
                     ↓
foreach( var Identifier in ArrayName )
     Statement
```

In the following text, I'll sometimes use implicit typing, and other times I'll use explicit typing so that you can see the exact type being used. But the forms are semantically equivalent.

The foreach statement works in the following way:

- It starts with the first element of the array and assigns that value to the *iteration variable*.

- It then executes the body of the statement. Inside the body, you can use the iteration variable as a read-only alias for the array element.

- After the body is executed, the foreach statement selects the next element in the array and repeats the process.

In this way, it cycles through the array, allowing you to access each element one by one. For example, the following code shows the use of a foreach statement with a one-dimensional array of four integers:

- The WriteLine statement, which is the body of the foreach statement, is executed once for each of the elements of the array.

- The first time through the loop, iteration variable item has the value of the first element of the array. Each successive time, it has the value of the next element in the array.

```
int[] arr1 = {10, 11, 12, 13};
Iteration variable declaration
            ↓                                Iteration variable use
foreach( int item in arr1 )                         ↓
    Console.WriteLine("Item Value: {0}", item);
```

This code produces the following output:

```
Item Value: 10
Item Value: 11
Item Value: 12
Item Value: 13
```

The Iteration Variable Is Read-Only

Since the value of the iteration variable is read-only, clearly it cannot be changed. But this has different effects on value type arrays and reference type arrays.

For value type arrays, this means you cannot change the data of the array. For example, in the following code, the attempt to change the data in the iteration variable produces a compile-time error message:

```
int[] arr1 = {10, 11, 12, 13};

foreach( int item in arr1 )
   item++;      // Compilation error. Changing variable value is not allowed.
```

For reference type arrays, you still cannot change the iteration variable, but the iteration variable only holds the reference to the data, not the data itself. So although you cannot change the reference, you can change the *data* through the iteration variable.

The following code creates an array of four MyClass objects and initializes them. In the first foreach statement, the data in each of the objects is changed. In the second foreach statement, the changed data is read from the objects.

```
class MyClass
{
   public int MyField = 0;
}

class Program  {
   static void Main() {
      MyClass[] mcArray = new MyClass[4];             // Create array
      for (int i = 0; i < 4; i++)
      {
         mcArray[i] = new MyClass();                  // Create class objects
         mcArray[i].MyField = i;                      // Set field
      }
      foreach (MyClass item in mcArray)
         item.MyField += 10;                          // Change the data.

      foreach (MyClass item in mcArray)
         Console.WriteLine("{0}", item.MyField);      // Read the changed data.
   }
}
```

This code produces the following output:

```
10
11
12
13
```

The foreach Statement with Multidimensional Arrays

In a multidimensional array, the elements are processed in the order in which the rightmost index is incremented fastest. When the index has gone from 0 to length – 1, the next index to the left is incremented, and the indexes to the right are reset to 0.

Example with a Rectangular Array

The following example shows the foreach statement used with a rectangular array:

```
class Program
{
    static void Main()
    {
        int total = 0;
        int[,] arr1 = { {10, 11}, {12, 13} };

        foreach( var element in arr1 )
        {
            total += element;
            Console.WriteLine
                    ("Element: {0}, Current Total: {1}", element, total);
        }
    }
}
```

This code produces the following output:

```
Element: 10, Current Total: 10
Element: 11, Current Total: 21
Element: 12, Current Total: 33
Element: 13, Current Total: 46
```

Example with a Jagged Array

Since jagged arrays are arrays of arrays, you must use separate foreach statements for each dimension in the jagged array. The foreach statements must be nested properly to make sure that each nested array is processed properly.

For example, in the following code, the first foreach statement cycles through the top-level array—arr1—selecting the next subarray to process. The inner foreach statement processes the elements of that subarray.

```
class Program
{
   static void Main( )
   {
      int total = 0;
      int[][] arr1 = new int[2][];
      arr1[0] = new int[] { 10, 11 };
      arr1[1] = new int[] { 12, 13, 14 };

      foreach (int[] array in arr1)        // Process the top level.
      {
         Console.WriteLine("Starting new array");
         foreach (int item in array)       // Process the second level.
         {
            total += item;
            Console.WriteLine("  Item: {0}, Current Total: {1}", item, total);
         }
      }
   }
}
```

This code produces the following output:

```
Starting new array
   Item: 10, Current Total: 10
   Item: 11, Current Total: 21
Starting new array
   Item: 12, Current Total: 33
   Item: 13, Current Total: 46
   Item: 14, Current Total: 60
```

Array Covariance

Under certain conditions, you can assign an object to an array element even if the object is not of the array's base type. This property of arrays is called *array covariance*. You can use array covariance if the following are true:

- The array is a reference type array.

- There is an implicit or explicit conversion between the type of the object you are assigning and the array's base type.

Since there is always an implicit conversion between a derived class and its base class, you can always assign an object of a derived class to an array declared for the base class.

For example, the following code declares two classes, A and B, where class B derives from class A. The last line shows covariance by assigning objects of type B to array elements of type A. Figure 14-15 shows the memory layout for the code.

```
class A { ... }                                    // Base class
class B : A { ... }                                // Derived class

class Program {
   static void Main() {
      // Two arrays of type A[]
      A[] AArray1 = new A[3];
      A[] AArray2 = new A[3];

      // Normal--assigning objects of type A to an array of type A
      AArray1[0] = new A(); AArray1[1] = new A(); AArray1[2] = new A();

      // Covariant--assigning objects of type B to an array of type A
      AArray2[0] = new B(); AArray2[1] = new B(); AArray2[2] = new B();
   }
}
```

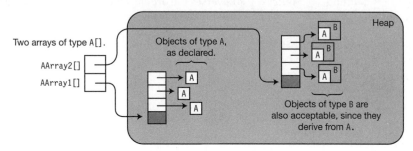

Figure 14-15. *Arrays showing covariance*

■ **Note** There is no covariance for value type arrays.

Useful Inherited Array Members

I mentioned earlier that C# arrays are derived from class System.Array. From that base class they inherit a number of useful properties and methods. Table 14-1 lists some of the most useful ones.

Table 14-1. *Some Useful Members Inherited by Arrays*

Member	Type	Lifetime	Meaning
Rank	Property	Instance	Gets the number of dimensions of the array
Length	Property	Instance	Gets the total number of elements in all the dimensions of the array
GetLength	Method	Instance	Returns the length of a particular dimension of the array
Clear	Method	Static	Sets a range of elements to 0 or null
Sort	Method	Static	Sorts the elements in a one-dimensional array
BinarySearch	Method	Static	Searches a one-dimensional array for a value, using binary search
Clone	Method	Instance	Performs a shallow copy of the array—copying only the elements, both for arrays of value types and reference types
IndexOf	Method	Static	Returns the index of the first occurrence of a value in a one-dimensional array
Reverse	Method	Static	Reverses the order of the elements of a range of a one-dimensional array
GetUpperBound	Method	Instance	Gets the upper bound at the specified dimension

For example, the following code uses some of these properties and methods:

```
public static void PrintArray(int[] a)
{
    foreach (var x in a)
        Console.Write("{0}  ", x);

    Console.WriteLine("");
}

static void Main()
{
    int[] arr = new int[] { 15, 20, 5, 25, 10 };
    PrintArray(arr);

    Array.Sort(arr);
    PrintArray(arr);

    Array.Reverse(arr);
    PrintArray(arr);

    Console.WriteLine();
    Console.WriteLine("Rank = {0}, Length = {1}",arr.Rank, arr.Length);
    Console.WriteLine("GetLength(0)     = {0}",arr.GetLength(0));
    Console.WriteLine("GetType()        = {0}",arr.GetType());
}
```

This code produces the following output:

```
15   20   5   25   10
5    10   15   20   25
25   20   15   10   5

Rank = 1, Length = 5
GetLength(0)       = 5
GetType()          = System.Int32[]
```

The Clone Method

The Clone method performs a shallow copy of an array. This means that it only creates a clone of the array itself. If it is a reference type array, it does *not* copy the objects referenced by the elements. This has different results for value type arrays and reference type arrays.

- Cloning a value type array results in two independent arrays.

- Cloning a reference type array results in two arrays pointing at the same objects.

The Clone method returns a reference of type object, which must be cast to the array type.

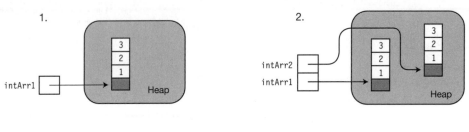

```
int[] intArr1 = { 1, 2, 3 };
                Array type        Returns an object
                    ↓                   ↓
int[] intArr2 = ( int[] ) intArr1.Clone();
```

For example, the following code shows an example of cloning a value type array, producing two independent arrays. Figure 14-16 illustrates the steps shown in the code.

```
static void Main()
{
   int[] intArr1 = { 1, 2, 3 };                            // Step 1
   int[] intArr2 = (int[]) intArr1.Clone();                // Step 2

   intArr2[0] = 100; intArr2[1] = 200; intArr2[2] = 300;   // Step 3
}
```

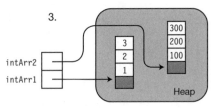

Figure 14-16. *Cloning a value type array produces two independent arrays.*

Cloning a reference type array results in two arrays *pointing at the same objects*. The following code shows an example. Figure 14-17 illustrates the steps shown in the code.

```
class A
{
   public int Value = 5;
}

class Program
{
   static void Main()
   {
      A[] AArray1 = new A[3] { new A(), new A(), new A() };    // Step 1
      A[] AArray2 = (A[]) AArray1.Clone();                     // Step 2

      AArray2[0].Value = 100;
      AArray2[1].Value = 200;
      AArray2[2].Value = 300;                                  // Step 3
   }
}
```

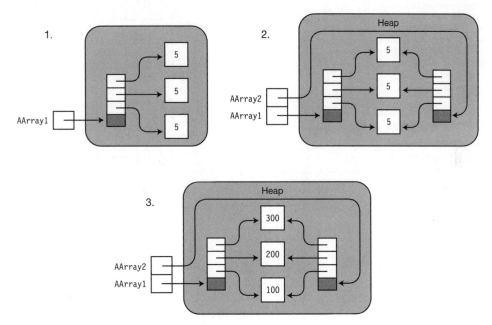

Figure 14-17. *Cloning a reference type array produces two arrays referencing the same objects.*

Comparing Array Types

Table 14-2 summarizes some of the important similarities and differences between the three types of arrays.

Table 14-2. *Summary Comparing Array Types*

| Array Type | Array Objects | Syntax | | Shape |
		Brackets	Commas	
One-dimensional • Has optimizing instructions in CIL.	1	Single set	No	One-Dimensional `int[3]`
Rectangular • Multidimensional. • All subarrays in a multidimensional array must be of the same length.	1	Single set	Yes	Two-Dimensional `int[3,6]` Three-Dimensional `int[3,6,2]`
Jagged • Multidimensional. • Subarrays can be of different lengths.	Multiple	Multiple sets	No	Jagged `int[4][]`

CHAPTER 15

■ ■ ■

Delegates

What Is a Delegate?

A delegate is a user-defined type, like a class. But whereas a class represents a collection of data, a delegate keeps track of one or more methods. You use a delegate by doing the following. We'll go through each of these steps in detail in the following sections.

1. Declare a new delegate type with a particular signature and return type. A delegate declaration looks like a method declaration, except that it doesn't have an implementation block.
2. Declare a delegate variable of the new delegate type.
3. Create an object of the delegate type, and assign it to the delegate variable. The new delegate object includes a reference to a method with the same signature as defined in the first step.
4. Add additional methods into the delegate object. These methods must have the same signature and return type as the delegate type defined in the first step.
5. Throughout your code you can then invoke the delegate, just as it if it were a method. When you invoke the delegate, each of the methods it contains is executed.

In looking at the previous steps, you might have noticed that they're similar to the steps in creating and using a class. Figure 15-1 compares the processes of creating and using classes and delegates.

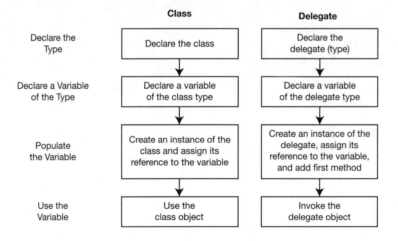

Figure 15-1. *A delegate is a user-defined reference type, like a class.*

■ **Note** If you're coming from a C++ background, the fastest way for you to understand delegates is to think of them as type-safe, object-oriented *C++ function pointers* on steroids.

You can think of a *delegate* as an object that contains an ordered list of methods with the same signature and return type, as illustrated in Figure 15-2.

- The list of methods is called the *invocation list*.

- Methods held by a delegate *can be from any class or struct*, as long as they match *both* the delegate's

  — Return type

  — Signature (including ref and out modifiers)

- Methods in the invocation list can be either instance methods or static methods.

- When a delegate is invoked, each method in its invocation list is executed.

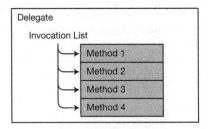

Figure 15-2. *A delegate as a list of methods*

Declaring the Delegate Type

Delegates are types, just as classes are types. And as with classes, a *delegate* type must be declared before you can use it to create variables and objects of the type. The following example code declares a delegate type.

- Even though the delegate type declaration looks like a method declaration, it does not need to be declared inside a class because it is a type declaration.

```
Keyword      Delegate type name
   ↓              ↓
 delegate void MyDel ( int x );
```

The declaration of a delegate type looks much like the declaration of a method, in that it has both a *return type* and a *signature*. The return type and signature specify the form of the methods that the delegate will accept.

For example, the following code declares delegate type `MyDel`. This declaration specifies that delegates of this type will only accept methods that have a single `int` parameter and that have no return value. Figure 15-3 shows a representation of the delegate type on the left and the delegate object on the right.

```
          Delegate type name
                 ↓
 delegate void MyDel( int x );
            ↑           ↑
        Return type  Signature
```

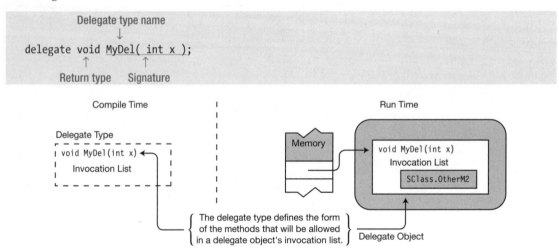

Figure 15-3. *Delegate type and object*

The delegate type declaration differs from a method declaration in two ways. The delegate type declaration

- Is prefaced with the keyword `delegate`

- Does not have a method body

Creating the Delegate Object

A delegate is a reference type and therefore has both a reference and an object. After a delegate type is declared, you can declare variables and create objects of the type. The following code shows the declaration of a variable of a delegate type:

```
Delegate type   Variable
     ↓            ↓
    MyDel    delVar;
```

There are two ways you can create a delegate object. The first is to use an object-creation expression with the new operator, as shown in the following code. The operand of the new operator consists of the following:

- The delegate type name.

- A set of parentheses containing the name of a method to use as the first member in the invocation list. *The method can be either an instance method or a static method.*

```
                        Instance method
                             ↓
delVar = new MyDel( myInstObj.MyM1 );        // Create delegate and save ref.
dVar   = new MyDel( SClass.OtherM2 );        // Create delegate and save ref.
                         ↑
                    Static method
```

You can also use the shortcut syntax, which consists of just the method specifier, as shown in the following code. This code and the preceding code are equivalent. Using the shortcut syntax works because there is an implicit conversion between a method name and a compatible delegate type.

```
delVar = myInstObj.MyM1;        // Create delegate and save reference.
dVar   = SClass.OtherM2;        // Create delegate and save reference.
```

For example, the following code creates two delegate objects—one with an instance method and the other with a static method. Figure 15-4 shows the instantiations of the delegates. This code assumes that there is an object called myInstObj, which is an instance of a class that has defined a method called MyM1 returning no value and taking an int as a parameter. It also assumes that there is a class called SClass, which has a static method OtherM2 with a return type and signature matching those of delegate MyDel.

```
delegate void MyDel(int x);            // Declare delegate type.
MyDel delVar, dVar;                    // Create two delegate variables.
                    Instance method
                         ↓
delVar = new MyDel( myInstObj.MyM1 );  // Create delegate and save ref.
dVar   = new MyDel( SClass.OtherM2 );  // Create delegate and save ref.
                         ↑
                    Static method
```

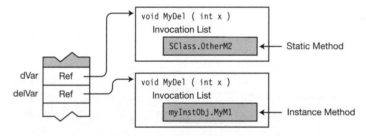

Figure 15-4. *Instantiating the delegates*

Besides allocating the memory for the delegate, creating a delegate object also places the first method in the delegate's invocation list.

You can also create the variable and instantiate the object in the same statement, using the initializer syntax. For example, the following statements also produce the same configuration shown in Figure 15-4:

```
MyDel delVar = new MyDel( myInstObj.MyM1 );
MyDel dVar   = new MyDel( SClass.OtherM2 );
```

The following statements use the shortcut syntax but again produce the results shown in Figure 15-4:

```
MyDel delVar = myInstObj.MyM1;
MyDel dVar   = SClass.OtherM2;
```

Assigning Delegates

Because delegates are reference types, you can change the reference contained in a delegate variable by assigning to it. The old delegate object will be disposed of by the garbage collector (GC) when it gets around to it.

For example, the following code sets and then changes the value of delVar. Figure 15-5 illustrates the code.

```
MyDel delVar;
delVar = myInstObj.MyM1;     // Create and assign the delegate object.

  ...
delVar = SClass.OtherM2;     // Create and assign the new delegate object.
```

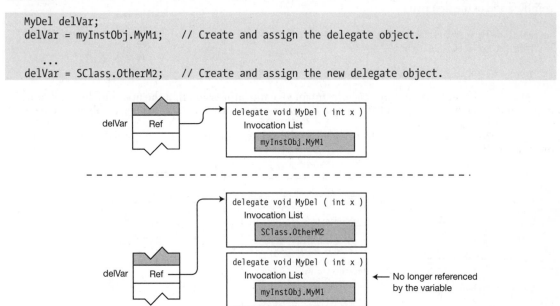

Figure 15-5. *Assigning to a delegate variable*

Combining Delegates

All the delegates you've seen so far have had only a single method in their invocation lists. Delegates can be "combined" by using the addition operator. The result of the operation is the creation of a new delegate, with an invocation list that is the concatenation of copies of the invocation lists of the two operand delegates.

For example, the following code creates three delegates. The third delegate is created from the combination of the first two.

```
MyDel delA = myInstObj.MyM1;
MyDel delB = SClass.OtherM2;

MyDel delC = delA + delB;                    // Has combined invocation list
```

Although the term *combining delegates* might give the impression that the operand delegates are modified, they are not changed at all. In fact, *delegates are immutable*. After a delegate object is created, it cannot be changed.

Figure 15-6 illustrates the results of the preceding code. Notice that the operand delegates remain unchanged.

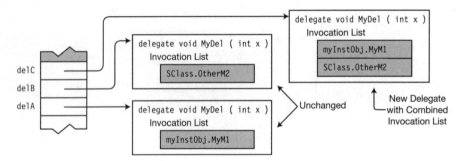

Figure 15-6. *Combining delegates*

Adding Methods to Delegates

Although you saw in the previous section that delegates are, in reality, immutable, C# provides syntax for making it appear that you can add a method to a delegate, using the += operator.

For example, the following code "adds" two methods to the invocation list of the delegate. The methods are added to the bottom of the invocation list. Figure 15-7 shows the result.

```
MyDel delVar  = inst.MyM1;    // Create and initialize.
delVar       += SC1.m3;       // Add a method.
delVar       += X.Act;        // Add a method.
```

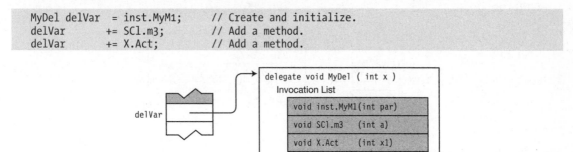

Figure 15-7. *Result of "adding" methods to a delegate. In reality, because delegates are immutable, the resulting delegate with three methods in its invocation list is an entirely new delegate pointed at by the variable.*

What is actually happening, of course, is that when the += operator is used, a new delegate is created, with an invocation list that is the combination of the delegate on the left plus the method listed on the right. This new delegate is then assigned to the delVar variable.

Removing Methods from a Delegate

You can also remove a method from a delegate, using the -= operator. The following code shows the use of the operator. Figure 15-8 shows the result of this code when applied to the delegate illustrated in Figure 15-7.

```
delVar -= SC1.m3;                // Remove the method from the delegate.
```

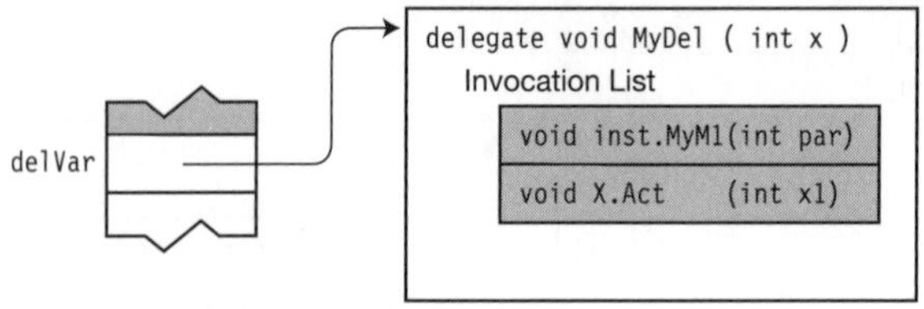

Figure 15-8. *Result of removing a method from a delegate*

As with adding a method to a delegate, the resulting delegate is actually a new delegate. The new delegate is a copy of the old delegate—but its invocation list no longer contains the reference to the method that was removed.

The following are some things to remember when removing methods:

- If there are multiple entries for a method in the invocation list, the -= operator *starts searching at the bottom of the list* and removes the first instance of the matching method it finds.

- Attempting to delete a method that is not in the delegate has no effect.

- Attempting to invoke an empty delegate throws an exception.

- You can check whether a delegate's invocation list is empty by comparing the delegate to null. If the invocation list is empty, the delegate is null.

Invoking a Delegate

You invoke a delegate by calling it, as if it were simply a method. The parameters used to invoke the delegate are used to invoke each of the methods on the invocation list (unless one of the parameters is an output parameter, which we'll cover shortly).

For example, the delegate delVar, as shown in the following code, takes a single integer input value. Invoking the delegate with a parameter causes it to invoke each of the members in its invocation list with the same parameter value (55, in this case). Figure 15-9 illustrates the invocation.

```
MyDel delVar  = inst.MyM1;
delVar        += SC1.m3;
delVar        += X.Act;
   ...
delVar( 55 );                            // Invoke the delegate.
   ...
```

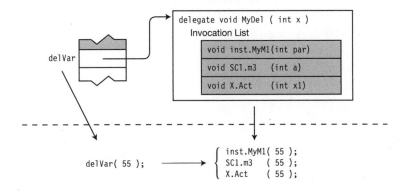

Figure 15-9. *When the delegate is invoked, it executes each of the methods in its invocation list, with the same parameters with which it was called.*

A method can be in the invocation list more than once. If it's in the list more than once, then when the delegate is invoked, the method will be called each time it is encountered in the list.

Delegate Example

The following code defines and uses a delegate with no parameters and no return value. Note the following about the code:

- Class Test defines two print functions.

- Method Main creates an instance of the delegate and then adds three more methods.

- The program then invokes the delegate, which calls its methods. Before invoking the delegate, however, it checks to make sure it's not null.

```
// Define a delegate type with no return value and no parameters.
delegate void PrintFunction();

class Test
{
    public void Print1()
    { Console.WriteLine("Print1 -- instance"); }

    public static void Print2()
    { Console.WriteLine("Print2 -- static"); }
}

class Program
{
    static void Main()
    {
        Test t = new Test();     // Create a test class instance.
        PrintFunction pf;        // Create a null delegate.

        pf = t.Print1;           // Instantiate and initialize the delegate.

        // Add three more methods to the delegate.
        pf += Test.Print2;
        pf += t.Print1;
        pf += Test.Print2;
        // The delegate now contains four methods.

        if( null != pf )         // Make sure the delegate isn't null.
            pf();                // Invoke the delegate.
        else
            Console.WriteLine("Delegate is empty");
    }
}
```

This code produces the following output:

```
Print1 -- instance
Print2 -- static
Print1 -- instance
Print2 -- static
```

Invoking Delegates with Return Values

If a delegate has a return value and more than one method in its invocation list, the following occurs:

- The value returned by the last method in the invocation list is the value returned from the delegate invocation.

- The return values from all the other methods in the invocation list are ignored.

For example, the following code declares a delegate that returns an int value. Main creates an object of the delegate and adds two additional methods. It then calls the delegate in the WriteLine statement and prints its return value. Figure 15-10 shows a graphical representation of the code.

```
delegate int MyDel( );                   // Declare method with return value.
class MyClass {
    int IntValue = 5;
    public int Add2() { IntValue += 2; return IntValue;}
    public int Add3() { IntValue += 3; return IntValue;}
}

class Program {
    static void Main( ) {
        MyClass mc = new MyClass();
        MyDel mDel = mc.Add2;           // Create and initialize the delegate.
        mDel += mc.Add3;                // Add a method.
        mDel += mc.Add2;                // Add a method.
        Console.WriteLine("Value: {0}", mDel() );
    }                                          ↑
}                          Invoke the delegate and use the return value.
```

This code produces the following output:

```
Value: 12
```

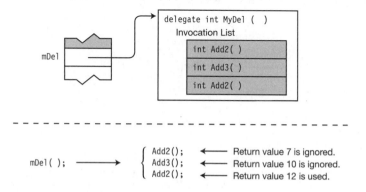

Figure 15-10. *The return value of the last method executed is the value returned by the delegate.*

Invoking Delegates with Reference Parameters

If a delegate has a reference parameter, the value of the parameter can change upon return from one or more of the methods in the invocation list.

- When calling the next method in the invocation list, the *new value of the parameter—not the initial value*—is the one passed to the next method.

For example, the following code invokes a delegate with a reference parameter. Figure 15-11 illustrates the code.

```csharp
delegate void MyDel( ref int X );

class MyClass
{
    public void Add2(ref int x) { x += 2; }
    public void Add3(ref int x) { x += 3; }
    static void Main()
    {
        MyClass mc = new MyClass();

        MyDel mDel = mc.Add2;
        mDel += mc.Add3;
        mDel += mc.Add2;

        int x = 5;
        mDel(ref x);

        Console.WriteLine("Value: {0}", x);
    }
}
```

This code produces the following output:

```
Value: 12
```

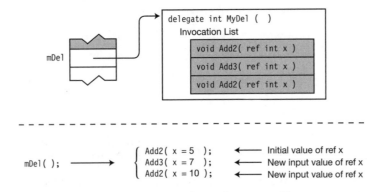

Figure 15-11. *The value of a reference parameter can change between calls.*

Anonymous Methods

So far, you've seen that you can use either static methods or instance methods to instantiate a delegate. In either case, the method itself can be called explicitly from other parts of the code and, of course, must be a member of some class or struct.

What if, however, the method is used only one time—to instantiate the delegate? In that case, other than the syntactic requirement for creating the delegate, there is no real need for a separate, named method. Anonymous methods allow you to dispense with the separate, named method.

- An *anonymous method* is a method that is declared inline, at the point of instantiating a delegate.

For example, Figure 15-12 shows two versions of the same class. The version on the left declares and uses a method named Add20. The version on the right uses an anonymous method instead. The nonshaded code of both versions is identical.

```
class Program                                          class Program
{                                                      {
    public static int Add20(int x)
    {
      return x + 20;
    }

    delegate int OtherDel(int InParam);                    delegate int OtherDel(int InParam);
    static void Main()                                     static void Main()
    {                                                      {
        OtherDel del = Add20;                                  OtherDel del = delegate(int x)
                                                                             {
                                                                               return x + 20;
                                                                             };
        Console.WriteLine("{0}", del(5));                     Console.WriteLine("{0}", del(5));
        Console.WriteLine("{0}", del(6));                     Console.WriteLine("{0}", del(6));
    }                                                      }
}                                                      }
             Named Method                                        Anonymous Method
```

Figure 15-12. *Comparing a named method and an anonymous method*

Both sets of code in Figure 15-12 produce the following output:

```
25
26
```

Using Anonymous Methods

You can use an anonymous method in the following places:

- As an initializer expression when declaring a delegate variable.

- On the right side of an assignment statement when combining delegates.

- On the right side of an assignment statement adding a delegate to an event. Chapter 16 covers events.

Syntax of Anonymous Methods

The syntax of an anonymous method expression includes the following components:

- The type keyword delegate

- The *parameter list*, which can be omitted if the statement block doesn't use any parameters

- The *statement block*, which contains the code of the anonymous method

```
              Parameter
Keyword        list           Statement block
   ↓            ↓                    ↓
delegate ( Parameters )   { ImplementationCode }
```

Return Type

An anonymous method does not explicitly declare a return type. The behavior of the implementation code itself, however, must match the delegate's return type by returning a value of that type. If the delegate has a return type of void, then the anonymous method code cannot return a value.

For example, in the following code, the delegate's return type is int. The implementation code of the anonymous method must therefore return an int on all pathways through the code.

```
      Return type of delegate type
             ↓
delegate int OtherDel(int InParam);

static void Main()
{
    OtherDel del = delegate(int x)
            {
                return x + 20 ;                 // Returns an int
            };
        ...
}
```

Parameters

Except in the case of array parameters, the parameter list of an anonymous method must match that of the delegate in the following three characteristics:

- Number of parameters

- Types and positions of the parameters

- Modifiers

You can simplify the parameter list of an anonymous method by leaving the parentheses empty or omitting them altogether, but only if *both* of the following are true:

- The delegate's parameter list does not contain any out parameters.

- The anonymous method does not use *any* parameters.

For example, the following code declares a delegate that does not have any out parameters and an anonymous method that does not use any parameters. Since both conditions are met, you can omit the parameter list from the anonymous method.

```
delegate void SomeDel ( int X );                // Declare the delegate type.

SomeDel SDel = delegate                         // Parameter list omitted
               {
                    PrintMessage();
                    Cleanup();
               };
```

params Parameters

If the delegate declaration's parameter list contains a params parameter, then the params keyword is omitted from the parameter list of the anonymous method. For example, in the following code, this happens:

- The delegate type declaration specifies the last parameter as a params type parameter.

- The anonymous method parameter list, however, must omit the params keyword.

```
                    params keyword used in delegate type declaration
                                       ↓
delegate void SomeDel( int X, params int[] Y);

                         params keyword omitted in matching anonymous method
                                       ↓
SomeDel mDel = delegate (int X, int[] Y)
          {
               ...
          };
```

Scope of Variables and Parameters

The scopes of parameters and local variables declared inside an anonymous method are limited to the body of the implementation code, as illustrated in Figure 15-13.

For example, the following anonymous method defines parameter y and local variable z. After the close of the body of the anonymous method, y and z are no longer in scope. The last line of the code would produce a compile error.

```
delegate void MyDel( int x );
...

MyDel mDel = delegate ( int y )
             {
                 int z = 10;                            Scope of y and z
                 Console.WriteLine("{0}, {1}", y, z);
             };

Console.WriteLine("{0}, {1}", y, z);   // Compile error.

                              Out of Scope
```

Figure 15-13. *Scope of variables and parameters*

Outer Variables

Unlike the named methods of a delegate, anonymous methods have access to the local variables and environment of the scope surrounding them.

- Variables from the surrounding scope are called *outer variables*.

- An outer variable used in the implementation code of an anonymous method is said to be *captured* by the method.

For example, the code in Figure 15-14 shows variable x defined outside the anonymous method. The code in the method, however, has access to x and can print its value.

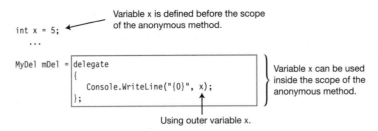

```
                                   Variable x is defined before the scope
int x = 5;                         of the anonymous method.
    ...

MyDel mDel = delegate
             {                                       Variable x can be used
                 Console.WriteLine("{0}", x);        inside the scope of the
             };                                      anonymous method.

                    Using outer variable x.
```

Figure 15-14. *Using an outer variable*

Extension of Captured Variable's Lifetime

A captured outer variable remains alive as long as its capturing method is part of the delegate, even if the variable would have normally gone out of scope.

For example, the code in Figure 15-15 illustrates the extension of a captured variable's lifetime.

- Local variable x is declared and initialized inside a block.

- Delegate mDel is then instantiated, using an anonymous method that captures outer variable x.

- When the block is closed, x goes out of scope.

- If the WriteLine statement following the close of the block were to be uncommented, it would cause a compile error, because it references x, which is now out of scope.

- The anonymous method inside delegate mDel, however, maintains x in its environment and prints its value when mDel is invoked.

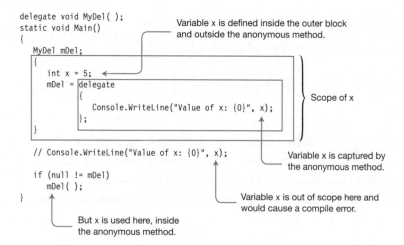

Figure 15-15. *Variable captured in an anonymous method*

The code in the figure produces the following output:

```
Value of x: 5
```

Lambda Expressions

C# 2.0 introduced anonymous methods, which allowed you to include short bits of inline code when creating or adding to delegates. The syntax for anonymous methods, however, is somewhat verbose and requires information that the compiler itself already knows. Rather than requiring you to include this redundant information, C# 3.0 introduced *lambda expressions*, which pare down the syntax of anonymous methods. You'll probably want to use lambda expressions instead of anonymous methods. In fact, if lambda expressions had been introduced first, there never would have been anonymous methods.

In the anonymous method syntax, the `delegate` keyword is redundant because the compiler can already see that you're assigning the method to a delegate. You can easily transform an anonymous method into a lambda expression by doing the following:

- Delete the `delegate` keyword.

- Place the lambda operator, =>, between the parameter list and the body of the anonymous method. The lambda operator is read as "goes to."

The following code shows this transformation. The first line shows an anonymous method being assigned to variable del. The second line shows the same anonymous method after having been transformed into a lambda expression, being assigned to variable le1.

```
MyDel del = delegate(int x)    { return x + 1; } ;    // Anonymous method
MyDel le1 =          (int x) => { return x + 1; } ;    // Lambda expression
```

■ **Note** The term *lambda expression* comes from the *lambda calculus*, which was developed in the 1920s and 1930s by mathematician Alonzo Church and others. The lambda calculus is a system for representing functions and uses the Greek letter lambda (λ) to represent a nameless function. More recently, functional programming languages such as Lisp and its dialects use the term to represent expressions that can be used to directly describe the definition of a function, rather than using a name for it.

This simple transformation is less verbose and looks cleaner, but it only saves you six characters. There's more, however, that the compiler can infer, allowing you to simplify the lambda expression further, as shown in the following code.

- From the delegate's declaration, the compiler also knows the types of the delegate's parameters, so the lambda expression allows you to leave out the parameter types, as shown in the assignment to le2.

  — Parameters listed with their types are called *explicitly typed*.

  — Those listed without their types are called *implicitly typed*.

- If there's only a single, implicitly typed parameter, you can leave off the parentheses surrounding it, as shown in the assignment to le3.

- Finally, lambda expressions allow the body of the expression to be either a statement block or an expression. If the statement block contains a single return statement, you can replace the statement block with just the expression that follows the return keyword, as shown in the assignment to le4.

```
MyDel del = delegate(int x)    { return x + 1; } ;     // Anonymous method
MyDel le1 =          (int x) => { return x + 1; } ;     // Lambda expression
MyDel le2 =              (x) => { return x + 1; } ;     // Lambda expression
MyDel le3 =               x  => { return x + 1; } ;     // Lambda expression
MyDel le4 =               x  =>         x + 1    ;     // Lambda expression
```

The final form of the lambda expression has about one-fourth the characters of the original anonymous method and is cleaner and easier to understand.

The following code shows the full transformation. The first line of Main shows an anonymous method being assigned to variable del. The second line shows the same anonymous method, after having been transformed into a lambda expression, being assigned to variable le1.

```
delegate double MyDel(int par);

static void Main()
{
   MyDel del = delegate(int x)    { return x + 1; } ;   // Anonymous method

   MyDel le1 =         (int x) => { return x + 1; } ;   // Lambda expression
   MyDel le2 =             (x) => { return x + 1; } ;
   MyDel le3 =              x  => { return x + 1; } ;
   MyDel le4 =              x  =>         x + 1    ;

   Console.WriteLine("{0}", del (12));
   Console.WriteLine("{0}", le1 (12));  Console.WriteLine("{0}", le2 (12));
   Console.WriteLine("{0}", le3 (12));  Console.WriteLine("{0}", le4 (12));
}
```

Some important points about lambda expression parameter lists are the following:

- The parameters in the parameter list of a lambda expression must match that of the delegate in number, type, and position.

- The parameters in the parameter list of an expression do not have to include the type (that is, *implicitly typed*) unless the delegate has either ref or out parameters—in which case the types are required (that is, *explicitly typed*).

- If there is only a single parameter and it is implicitly typed, the surrounding parentheses can be omitted. Otherwise, they are required.

- If there are no parameters, you must use an empty set of parentheses.

Figure 15-16 shows the syntax for lambda expressions.

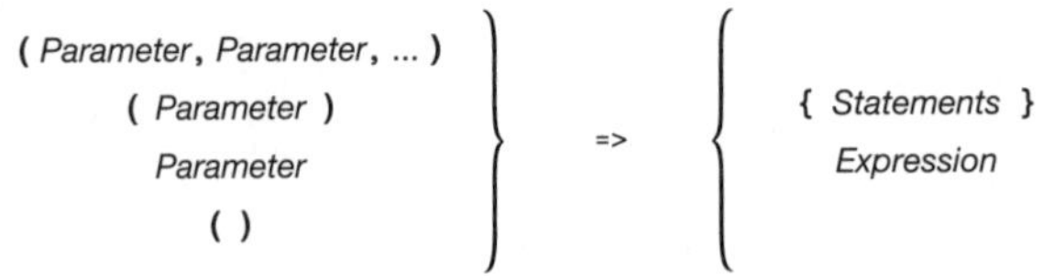

Figure 15-16. *The syntax for lambda expressions consists of the lambda operator with the parameter section on the left and the lambda body on the right.*

CHAPTER 16

■ ■ ■

Events

Events Are Like Delegates

The preceding chapter covered delegates. Many aspects of events are similar to those of delegates. In fact, an event is like a simpler delegate that is specialized for a particular use. Figure 16-1 illustrates that, like a delegate, an event has methods registered with it and invokes those methods when it is invoked.

The following are some important terms related to events:

- *Raising an event*: The term for *invoking* or *firing* an event. When an event is raised, all the methods registered with it are invoked—in order.

- *Publisher:* A class or struct that makes an event available to other classes or structs for their use.

- *Subscriber*: A class or struct that registers methods with a publisher.

- *Event handler*: A method that is registered with an event. It can be declared in the same class or struct as the event or in a different class or struct.

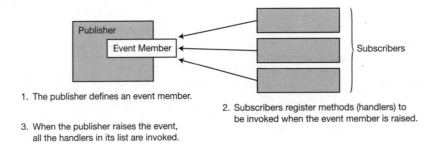

1. The publisher defines an event member.

2. Subscribers register methods (handlers) to be invoked when the event member is raised.

3. When the publisher raises the event, all the handlers in its list are invoked.

Figure 16-1. *Publishers and subscribers*

An Event Has a Private Delegate

There's good reason for the similarities in the behaviors of delegates and events. An event contains a private delegate, as illustrated in Figure 16-2. The important things to know about an event's private delegate are the following:

- An *event* gives structured access to its privately controlled delegate.

- Unlike the many operations available with a delegate, with an event you can only add, remove, and invoke event handlers.

- When an event is raised, it invokes the delegate, which sequentially calls the methods in the invocation list.

Notice in Figure 16-2 that only the += and -= operators are sticking out to the left of the event. This is because they are the only operations allowed on an event.

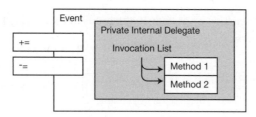

Figure 16-2. *An event has an encapsulated delegate*

Figure 16-3 illustrates the runtime view of a publisher class with an event called Elapsed. ClassA and ClassB, on the right, each has an event handler registered with Elapsed. Inside the event you can see the delegate referencing the two event handlers. Besides the event, the publisher also contains the code that raises the event.

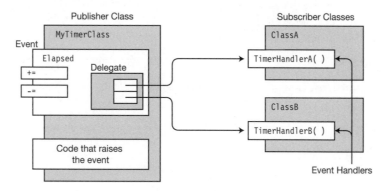

Figure 16-3. *Structure and terminology of a class with a timer event*

Overview of Source Code Components

Five components of code need to be in place to use events. I'll cover each of them in the following sections, and they are illustrated in Figure 16-4. These components are the following:

- *Delegate type declaration*: The event and the event handlers must have a common signature and return type, which is described by the delegate type declaration.

- *Event handler declarations*: These are the declarations in the subscriber classes of the methods (event handlers) to be executed when the event is raised. These do not have to be separate methods. They can be anonymous methods or lambda expressions.

- *Event declaration:* This is the declaration in the publisher class of the event that holds and invokes the event handlers.

- *Event registration*: This is the code that connects the event handlers to the event.

- *Code that raises the event*: This is the code in the publisher that calls the event, causing it to invoke its event handlers.

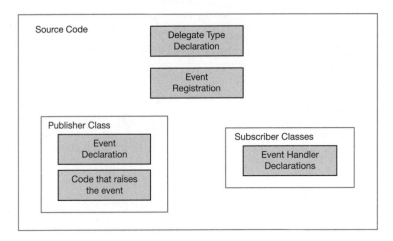

Figure 16-4. *The five source code components of using an event*

Declaring an Event

The publisher must provide the event and often provides the code to raise the event.

Creating an event is simple—it requires only a delegate type and a name. The syntax for an event declaration is shown in the following code, which declares an event called Elapsed. Notice the following about event Elapsed:

- It is declared inside a class called MyTimerClass.

- It accepts event handlers with the return type and signature matching the delegate type EventHandler.

- It is declared public so that other classes and structs can register event handlers with it.

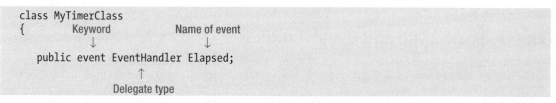

You can declare more than one event in a declaration statement by using a comma-separated list. For example, the following statement declares three events:

```
                                        Three events
                                            ↑
public event EventHandler MyEvent1, MyEvent2, OtherEvent;
```

You can also make events static, by including the static keyword, as shown in the following declaration:

```
public static event EventHandler Elapsed;
          ↑
       Keyword
```

An Event Is a Member

A common error is to think of an event as a type, which it is not. An event is a *member*, and there are several important ramifications to this:

- Because a member is not a type, you do not use an object-creation expression (a new expression) to create its object.

- Because an event is a member

  — It must be declared in a class or struct, with the other members.

  — You cannot declare an event in a block of executable code.

- An event member is implicitly and automatically initialized to null with the other members.

The Delegate Type and EventHandler

An event declaration requires the name of a *delegate type*. You can either declare one or use one that already exists. If you declare a delegate type, it must specify the signature and return type of the methods that will be stored by the event.

A better idea is to use the EventHandler delegate, which is a predefined delegate type used by the .NET BCL and designated as the standard for use with events. You are strongly encouraged to use it. The following code shows what EventHandler's declaration looks like in the BCL. The EventHandler delegate is covered in more detail later in this chapter.

```
public delegate void EventHandler( object sender, EventArgs e );
```

Raising an Event

The event member itself just holds the event handlers that need to be invoked. Nothing happens with them unless the event is raised. You need to make sure there is code to do just that, at the appropriate times.

For example, the following code raises event Elapsed. Notice the following about the code:

- Before raising the event, the code compares it to null, to see whether it contains any event handlers. If the event is null, it is empty.

- Raising the event itself is like invoking a function.

  — Use the name of the event, followed by the parameter list enclosed in parentheses.

  — The parameter list must match the delegate type of the event.

```
if (Elapsed != null)              // Make sure there are methods to execute.
   Elapsed (source, args);        // Raise the event.
        ↑            ↑
   Event name    Parameter list
```

Putting together the event declaration and the code to raise the event gives the following class declaration for the publisher. The code contains two members: the event and a method called OnOneSecond, which raises the event.

```
public class MyTimerClass
{
   public event EventHandler Elapsed;    // Declare the event.

   private void OnOneSecond(object source, EventArgs args)
   {
      if (Elapsed != null)        // Make sure there are methods to execute.
         Elapsed(source, args);
   }                  ↑
                Raise the event.

   // The following code makes sure that method OnOneSecond is called every
   // 1,000 milliseconds.
   ...
}
```

For now, I'll let method OnOneSecond be somehow, mysteriously, called once every second. Later in the chapter I'll show you how to make this happen. But for now, remember these important points:

- The publisher class has an event as a member.
- The class contains the code to raise the event.

Subscribing to an Event

To add an event handler to an event, the handler must have the same return type and signature as the event's delegate.

- Use the += operator to add an event handler to an event, as shown in the following code.

- The method can be any of the following:

  — An instance method

  — A static method

  — An anonymous method

  — A lambda expression

For example, the following code adds three methods to event Elapsed. The first is an instance method using the method form. The second is a static method using the method form. The third is an instance method using the delegate form.

```
Class instance          Instance method
     ↓                        ↓
  mc.Elapsed += ca.TimerHandlerA;                     // Method reference form
  mc.Elapsed += ClassB.TimerHandlerB;                 // Method reference form
         ↑              ↑
  Event member     Static method
  mc.Elapsed += new EventHandler(cc.TimerHandlerC);   // Delegate form
```

Just as with delegates, you can use anonymous methods and lambda expressions to add event handlers. For example, the following code first uses a lambda expression and then uses an anonymous method.

```
mc.Elapsed += (source, args) =>                       // Lambda expression
   {
       Console.WriteLine("Lambda expression.");
   };


mc.Elapsed += delegate(object source, EventArgs args) // Anonymous method
   {
       Console.WriteLine("Anonymous method.");
   };
```

The following program uses the `MyTimerClass` class declared in the previous section. The code performs the following:

- It registers two event handlers from two different class instances.

- After registering the event handlers, it sleeps for two seconds. During that time, the timer class raises the event two times, and both event handlers are executed each time.

```
public class MyTimerClass { ... }

class ClassA
{
   public void TimerHandlerA(object source, EventArgs args)      // Event handler
   {
      Console.WriteLine("Class A handler called");
   }
}

class ClassB
{
   public static void TimerHandlerB(object source, EventArgs args)   // Static
   {
      Console.WriteLine("Class B handler called");
   }
}

class Program
{
   static void Main( )
   {
      ClassA ca = new ClassA();                 // Create the class object.
      MyTimerClass mc = new MyTimerClass();     // Create the timer object.

      mc.Elapsed += ca.TimerHandlerA;           // Add handler A -- instance.
      mc.Elapsed += ClassB.TimerHandlerB;       // Add handler B -- static.

      Thread.Sleep(2250);
   }
}
```

When supplied with the code for `MyTimerClass`, this code produces the following output:

```
Class A handler called
Class B handler called
Class A handler called
Class B handler called
```

Removing Event Handlers

When you're done with an event handler, you should remove it from the event, to allow the garbage collector to free up that memory. You remove an event handler from an event by using the -= operator, as shown here:

```
mc.Elapsed -= ca.TimerHandlerA;          // Remove handler A.
```

For example, the following code removes the event handler for ClassB after the first two times the event is raised and then lets the program run for another two seconds.

```
...
mc.Elapsed += ca.TimerHandlerA;          // Add instance handler A.
mc.Elapsed += ClassB.TimerHandlerB;      // Add static handler B.

Thread.Sleep(2250);                      // Sleep more than 2 seconds.

mc.Elapsed -= ClassB.TimerHandlerB;      // Remove static handler B.
Console.WriteLine("Class B event handler removed");

Thread.Sleep(2250);                      // Sleep more than 2 seconds.
```

This code produces the following output. The first four lines are the result of both handlers being called twice, in the first two seconds. After the handler for ClassB is removed, only the handler for the instance of ClassA is called, during the last two seconds.

```
Class A handler called
Class B handler called
Class A handler called
Class B handler called
Class B event handler removed
Class A handler called
Class A handler called
```

Standard Event Usage

GUI programming is event driven, which means that while the program is running, it can be interrupted at any time by events such as button clicks, key presses, or system timers. When this happens, the program needs to handle the event and then continue on its course.

Clearly, this asynchronous handling of program events is the perfect situation to use C# events. Windows GUI programming uses events so extensively that there is a standard .NET Framework pattern for using them, which you are strongly encouraged to follow.

The foundation of the standard pattern for event usage is the EventHandler delegate type, which is declared in the System namespace. The declaration of the EventHandler delegate type is shown in the following code:

- The first parameter is meant to hold a reference to the object that raised the event. It is of type object and can, therefore, match any instance of any type.

- The second parameter is meant to hold state information of whatever type is appropriate for the application.

- The return type is void.

```
public delegate void EventHandler(object sender, EventArgs e);
```

Using the EventArgs Class

The second parameter in the EventHandler delegate type is an object of class EventArgs, which is declared in the System namespace. You might be tempted to think that, since the second parameter is meant for passing data, an EventArgs class object would be able to store data of some sort. You would be wrong.

- The EventArgs class is designed to carry no data. It is used for event handlers that do not need to pass data—and is generally ignored by them.

- If you want to pass data, you must declare a class *derived* from EventArgs, with the appropriate fields to hold the data you want to pass.

Even though the EventArgs class does not actually pass data, it is an important part of the pattern of using the EventHandler delegate. Class object and class EventArgs are the base classes for whatever actual types are used as the parameters. This allows EventHandler to provide a signature that is the lowest common denominator for all events and event handlers, allowing them to have exactly two parameters, rather than having different signatures for each case.

Passing Data by Extending EventArgs

To pass data in the second parameter of your event handler and adhere to the standard conventions, you need to declare a custom class derived from EventArgs that can store the data you need passed. The name of the class should end in *EventArgs*. For example, the following code declares a custom class that can store a string in a field called Message:

```
              Custom class name      Base class
                    ↓                    ↓
public class MyTCEventArgs: EventArgs
{
    public string Message;                // Stores a message
    public MyTCEventArgs(string s)        // The constructor sets the message.
    {
        Message = s;
    }
}
```

Using the Custom Delegate

Now that you have a custom class for passing data in the second parameter of your event handlers, you need a delegate type that uses the new custom class. There are two ways you can do this:

- The first way is to use a nongeneric delegate. To do this, do the following:

  — Create a new custom delegate using your custom class type, as shown in the following code.

  — Use the new delegate name throughout the four other sections of the event code.

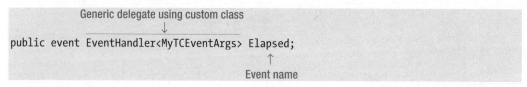

```
                    Custom delegate name                    Custom class
                            ↓                                    ↓
    public delegate void MyTCEventHandler (object sender, MyTCEventArgs e);
```

- The second way was introduced with C# 2.0 and uses the generic delegate EventHandler<>. Chapter 19 covers C# generics. To use the generic delegate, do the following, as shown in the code following:

  — Place the name of the custom class between the angle brackets.

  — Use the entire string wherever you would have used the name of your custom delegate type. For example, this is what the event declaration would look like:

```
                Generic delegate using custom class
                            ↓
    public event EventHandler<MyTCEventArgs> Elapsed;
                                                  ↑
                                             Event name
```

Use the custom class and the custom delegate, either nongeneric or generic, in the other four sections of code dealing with the event.

For example, the following code updates the MyTimerClass code to use a custom EventArgs class called MyTCEventArgs and the generic EventHandler<> delegate.

```
public class MyTCEventArgs: EventArgs
{
   public string Message;

   public MyTCEventArgs(string s) {
      Message = s;
   }
}
```
                                              Declaration of custom class

```
public class MyTimerClass      Generic delegate
{                                  ↓
   public event EventHandler<MyTCEventArgs> Elapsed;      // Event declaration

   private void OnOneSecond(object source, EventArgs args)
   {
      if (Elapsed != null)
      {
         MyTCEventArgs mtcea =
            new MyTCEventArgs("Message from OnOneSecond");
         Elapsed(source, mtcea);
      }
   }
```
                                                          Code to raise event

```
   ...    // This code is given at the end of the chapter.
}

class ClassA
{
   public void TimerHandlerA(object source, MyTCEventArgs args)
   {
      Console.WriteLine("Class A Message:  {0}", args.Message);
   }
}
```
                                                          Event handler

```
class Program
{
   static void Main()
   {
      ClassA ca = new ClassA();
      MyTimerClass mc = new MyTimerClass();

      mc.Elapsed +=                                    // Register handler.
         new EventHandler<MyTCEventArgs> (ca.TimerHandlerA);

      Thread.Sleep(3250);
   }
}
```

This code produces the following output:

```
Class A Message:  Message from OnOneSecond
Class A Message:  Message from OnOneSecond
Class A Message:  Message from OnOneSecond
```

The MyTimerClass Code

Now that you've seen all five components of code that need to be implemented to use an event, I can show you the full MyTimerClass class that the code has been using.

Most things about the class have been pretty clear—it has an event called Elapsed that can be subscribed to and a method called OnOneSecond that is called every second and raises the event. The one question remaining about it is, "What causes OnOneSecond to be called every second?"

The answer is that I've created method OnOneSecond and subscribed it as an event handler to an event in a class called Timer, in the System.Timers namespace. The event in Timer is raised every 1,000 milliseconds and calls event handler OnOneSecond, which in turn raises event Elapsed in class MyTimerClass. Figure 16-5 shows the structure of the code.

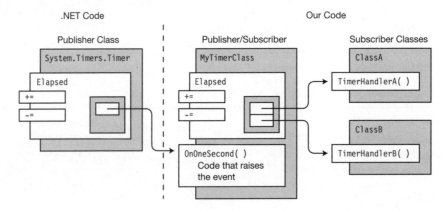

Figure 16-5. *The code structure of MyTimerClass*

The Timer class is a useful tool, so I'll mention a little more about it. First, it has a public event called Elapsed. If that sounds familiar, it's because I named the event in MyTimerClass after it. The names have no other connection than that. I could have named the event in MyTimerClass anything.

One of the properties of Timer is Interval, which is of type double, and specifies the number of milliseconds between raising the event. The other property the code uses is Enabled, which is of type bool, and starts and stops the timer.

The actual code is the following. The only things I haven't shown previously are the private timer field, called MyPrivateTimer, and the constructor for the class. The constructor does the work of setting up the internal timer and attaching it to event handler OnOneSecond.

```
public class MyTimerClass
{
   public event EventHandler Elapsed;

   private void OnOneSecond(object source, EventArgs args)
   {
      if (Elapsed != null)
         Elapsed(source, args);
   }

   //------------
   private System.Timers.Timer MyPrivateTimer;    // Private timer

   public MyTimerClass()                          // Constructor
   {
      MyPrivateTimer = new System.Timers.Timer(); // Create the private timer.


      // The following statement sets our OnOneSecond method above as an event
      // handler to the Elapsed event of class Timer. It is completely
      // unrelated to our event Elapsed, declared above.
      MyPrivateTimer.Elapsed += OnOneSecond;        // Attach our event handler.


      // Property Interval is of type double, and specifies the number of
      // milliseconds between when its event is raised.
      MyPrivateTimer.Interval = 1000;               // 1 second interval.


      // Property Enabled is of type bool, and turns the timer on and off.
      MyPrivateTimer.Enabled = true;                // Start the timer.
   }
}
```

Event Accessors

The last topic to cover in this chapter is event accessors. I mentioned earlier that the += and -= operators were the only operators allowed for an event. These operators have the well-defined behavior that you've seen so far in this chapter.

You can, however, change these operators' behavior and have the event perform whatever custom code you like when they are used. You can do this by defining event accessors for the event.

- There are two accessors: add and remove.

- The declaration of an event with accessors looks similar to the declaration of a property.

The following example shows the form of an event declaration with accessors. Both accessors have an implicit value parameter called value that takes a reference to either an instance method or a static method.

```
public event EventHandler Elapsed
{
   add
   {
      ...                         // Code to implement the =+ operator
   }
   remove
   {
      ...                         // Code to implement the -= operator
   }
}
```

When event accessors are declared, the event does not contain an embedded delegate object. You must implement your own storage mechanism for storing and removing the methods registered with the event.

The event accessors act as void methods, meaning that they cannot use return statements that return a value.

CHAPTER 17

■ ■ ■

Interfaces

What Is an Interface?

An *interface* is a reference type that specifies a set of function members but does not implement them. Other types—classes or structs—can implement interfaces.

To get a feeling for interfaces, I'll start by showing one that is already defined. The BCL declares an interface called IComparable, the declaration of which is shown in the following code. Notice that the interface body contains the declaration of a single method, CompareTo, which takes a single parameter of type object. Although the method has a name, parameters, and a return type, there is no implementation. Instead, the implementation is replaced by a semicolon.

```
          Keyword    Interface name
             ↓          ↓
  public interface IComparable
  {
     int CompareTo( object obj );
  }                              ↑
              Semicolon in place of method implementation
```

Figure 17-1 illustrates interface IComparable. The CompareTo method is shown in gray to illustrate that it doesn't contain an implementation.

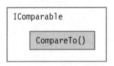

Figure 17-1. *Representation of interface IComparable*

Although the interface declaration doesn't provide an implementation for method CompareTo, the .NET documentation of interface IComparable describes what the method should do, in case you create a class or struct that implements the interface. It says that when method CompareTo is called, it should return one of the following values:

- A negative value, if the current object is less than the parameter object

- A positive value, if the current object is greater than the parameter object

- Zero, if the two objects are considered equal in the comparison

Example Using the IComparable Interface

To understand what this means and why it's useful, let's start by taking a look at the following code, which takes an unsorted array of integers and sorts them in ascending order.

- The first line creates an array of five integers that are in no particular order.

- The second line uses the Array class's static Sort method to sort the elements.

- The foreach loop prints them out, showing that the integers are now in ascending order.

```
var myInt = new [] { 20, 4, 16, 9, 2 };      // Create an array of ints.

Array.Sort(myInt);                           // Sort elements by magnitude.

foreach (var i in myInt)                      // Print them out.
   Console.Write("{0} ", i);
```

This code produces the following output:

```
2 4 9 16 20
```

The Array class's Sort method works great on an array of ints, but what would happen if you were to try to use it on one of your own classes, as shown here?

```
class MyClass                                // Declare a simple class.
{
   public int TheValue;
}
   ...
MyClass[] mc = new MyClass[5];                // Create an array of five elements.
   ...                                       // Create and initialize the elements.

Array.Sort(mc);                              // Try to use Sort--raises exception
```

When you try to run this code, it raises an exception instead of sorting the elements. The reason Sort doesn't work with the array of MyClass objects is that it doesn't know how to compare user-defined objects and how to rank their order.

The algorithm used by Sort depends on the fact that it can use the element's CompareTo method to determine the order of two elements. The int type implements IComparable, but MyClass does not, so when Sort tries to call the nonexistent CompareTo method of MyClass, it raises an exception.

You can make the Sort method work with objects of type MyClass by making the class implement IComparable. To implement an interface, a class or struct must do two things:

- It must list the interface name in its base class list.

- It must provide an implementation for each of the interface's members.

For example, the following code updates MyClass to implement interface IComparable. Notice the following about the code:

- The name of the interface is listed in the base class list of the class declaration.

- The class implements a method called CompareTo, whose parameter type and return type match those of the interface member.

- Method CompareTo is implemented to satisfy the definition given in the interface's documentation. That is, it returns a negative 1, positive 1, or 0, depending on its value compared to the object passed into the method.

```
                 Interface name in base class list
                          ↓
class MyClass : IComparable
{
    public int TheValue;

    public int CompareTo(object obj)    // Implementation of interface method
    {
        MyClass mc = (MyClass)obj;
        if (this.TheValue < mc.TheValue) return -1;
        if (this.TheValue > mc.TheValue) return  1;
        return 0;
    }
}
```

Figure 17-2 illustrates the updated class. The arrow from the grayed interface method to the class method indicates that the interface method doesn't contain code but is implemented by the class-level method.

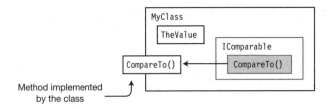

Figure 17-2. *Implementing IComparable in MyClass*

Now that `MyClass` implements `IComparable`, `Sort` will work on it just fine. It would not, by the way, have been sufficient to just declare the `CompareTo` method—it must be part of implementing the interface, which means placing the interface name in the base class list.

The following shows the complete updated code, which can now use the `Sort` method to sort an array of `MyClass` objects. `Main` creates and initializes an array of `MyClass` objects and then prints them out. It then calls `Sort` and prints them out again to show that they've been sorted.

```
class MyClass : IComparable                    // Class implements interface.
{
   public int TheValue;
   public int CompareTo(object obj)            // Implement the method.
   {
      MyClass mc = (MyClass)obj;
      if (this.TheValue < mc.TheValue) return -1;
      if (this.TheValue > mc.TheValue) return 1;
      return 0;
   }
}

class Program
{
   static void PrintOut(string s, MyClass[] mc)
   {
      Console.Write(s);
      foreach (var m in mc)
         Console.Write("{0} ", m.TheValue);
      Console.WriteLine("");
   }

   static void Main()
   {
      var myInt = new [] { 20, 4, 16, 9, 2 };

      MyClass[] mcArr = new MyClass[5];        // Create array of MyClass objs.
      for (int i = 0; i < 5; i++)              // Initialize the array.
      {
         mcArr[i] = new MyClass();
         mcArr[i].TheValue = myInt[i];
      }
      PrintOut("Initial Order:  ", mcArr); // Print the initial array.
      Array.Sort(mcArr);                       // Sort the array.
      PrintOut("Sorted Order:   ", mcArr); // Print the sorted array.
   }
}
```

This code produces the following output:

```
Initial Order:  20 4 16 9 2
Sorted Order:   2 4 9 16 20
```

Declaring an Interface

The previous section used an interface that was already declared in the BCL. In this section, you'll see how to declare interfaces.

The important things to know about declaring an interface are the following:

- An interface declaration *cannot contain data members*.

- An interface declaration can contain only declarations of the following kinds of *nonstatic* function members:
    — Methods
    — Properties
    — Events
    — Indexers

- The declarations of these function members cannot contain any implementation code. Instead, a semicolon must be used for the body of each member declaration.

- By convention, interface names begin with an uppercase *I* (for example, ISaveable).

- Like classes and structs, interface declarations can also be split into partial interface declarations, as described in the "Partial Classes" section of Chapter 6.

The following code shows an example of declaring an interface with two method members:

```
Keyword    Interface name
   ↓            ↓
interface IMyInterface1                        Semicolon in place of body
{                                                      ↓
    int    DoStuff      ( int nVar1, long lVar2 );
    double DoOtherStuff( string s, long x );
}                                                 ↑
                              Semicolon in place of body
```

There is an important difference between the accessibility of an interface and the accessibility of interface members:

- An interface declaration can have any of the access modifiers public, protected, internal, or private.

- *Members* of an interface, however, are implicitly public, and *no* access modifiers, including public, are allowed.

```
Access modifiers are allowed on interfaces.
     ↓
  public interface IMyInterface2
  {
      private int Method1( int nVar1, long lVar2 );            // Error
  }      ↑
Access modifiers are NOT allowed on interface members.
```

Implementing an Interface

Only classes or structs can implement an interface. As shown in the Sort example, to implement an interface, a class or struct must

- Include the name of the interface in its base class list

- Supply implementations for each of the interface's members

For example, the following code shows a new declaration for class MyClass, which implements interface IMyInterface1, declared in the previous section. Notice that the interface name is listed in the base class list after the colon and that the class provides the actual implementation code for the interface members.

```
          Colon   Interface name
            ↓          ↓
class MyClass: IMyInterface1
{
   int    DoStuff     ( int nVar1, long lVar2 )
   { ... }                                        // Implementation code

   double DoOtherStuff( string s, long x )
   { ... }                                        // Implementation code
}
```

Some important things to know about implementing interfaces are the following:

- If a class implements an interface, it must implement *all* the members of that interface.

- If a class is derived from a base class and also implements interfaces, the name of the base class must be listed in the base class list *before* any interfaces, as shown here:

```
          Base class must be first      Interface names
                    ↓                         ↓
class Derived : MyBaseClass, IIfc1, IEnumerable, IComparable
{
   ...
}
```

Example with a Simple Interface

The following code declares an interface named IIfc1, which contains a single method named PrintOut. Class MyClass implements interface IIfc1 by listing it in its base class list and supplying a method named PrintOut that matches the signature and return type of the interface member. Main creates an object of the class and calls the method from the object.

```
interface IIfc1    Semicolon in place of body                  // Declare interface
{                           ↓
   void PrintOut(string s);
}
                Implement interface
                       ↓
class MyClass : IIfc1                                // Declare class
{
   public void PrintOut(string s)                   // Implementation
   {
      Console.WriteLine("Calling through:  {0}", s);
   }
}

class Program
{
   static void Main()
   {
      MyClass mc = new MyClass();                    // Create instance
      mc.PrintOut("object");                         // Call method
   }
}
```

This code produces the following output:

```
Calling through:  object
```

An Interface Is a Reference Type

An interface is more than just a list of members for a class or struct to implement. It is a reference type.

You cannot access an interface directly through the class object's members. You can, however, get a *reference to the interface* by casting the class object reference to the type of the interface. Once you have a reference to the interface, you can use dot-syntax notation with the reference to call interface members.

For example, the following code shows an example of getting an interface reference from a class object reference.

- In the first statement, variable mc is a reference to a class object that implements interface IIfc1. The statement casts that reference to a reference to the interface and assigns it to variable ifc.

- The second statement uses the reference to the interface to call the implementation method.

```
      Interface    Cast to interface
          ↓            ↓
   IIfc1 ifc = (IIfc1) mc;              // Get ref to interface
          ↑            ↑
      Interface ref    Class object ref
   ifc.PrintOut ("interface");          // Use ref to interface to call member
       ↑
   Use dot-syntax notation to call through the interface reference.
```

For example, the following code declares an interface and a class that implements it. The code in Main creates an object of the class and calls the implementation method through the class object. It also creates a variable of the interface type, casts the reference of the class object to the interface type, and calls the implementation method through the reference to the interface. Figure 17-3 illustrates the class and the reference to the interface.

```
interface IIfc1
{
   void PrintOut(string s);
}

class MyClass: IIfc1
{
   public void PrintOut(string s)
   {
      Console.WriteLine("Calling through:  {0}", s);
   }
}

class Program
{
   static void Main()
   {
      MyClass mc = new MyClass();  // Create class object
      mc.PrintOut("object");       // Call class object implementation method

      IIfc1 ifc = (IIfc1)mc;       // Cast class object ref to interface ref
      ifc.PrintOut("interface");   // Call interface method
   }
}
```

This code produces the following output:

```
Calling through:  object
Calling through:  interface
```

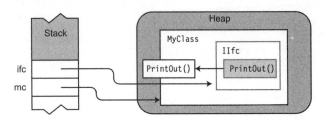

Figure 17-3. *A reference to the class object and a reference to the interface*

Using the as Operator with Interfaces

In the previous section, you saw that you can use the cast operator to get a reference to an object's interface. An even better idea is to use the as operator. The as operator is covered in detail in Chapter 18, but I'll mention it here as well, since it's a good choice to use with interfaces.

If you attempt to cast a class object reference to a reference of an interface that the class doesn't implement, the cast operation will raise an exception. You can avoid this problem by using the as operator instead. It works as follows:

- If the class implements the interface, the expression returns a reference to the interface.

- If the class doesn't implement the interface, the expression returns null rather than raising an exception.

The following code demonstrates the use of the as operator. The first line uses the as operator to obtain an interface reference from a class object. The result of the expression sets the value of b either to null or to a reference to an ILiveBirth interface.

The second line checks the value of b and, if it is not null, executes the command that calls the interface member method.

```
       Class object ref    Interface name
              ↓                 ↓
  ILiveBirth b = a as ILiveBirth;          // Acts like cast: (ILiveBirth)a
              ↑        ↑
        Interface   Operator
          ref
  if (b != null)
     Console.WriteLine("Baby is called: {0}", b.BabyCalled());
```

Implementing Multiple Interfaces

In the examples shown so far, the classes have implemented a single interface.

- A class or struct can implement any number of interfaces.

- All the interfaces implemented must be listed in the base class list and separated by commas (following the base class name, if there is one).

For example, the following code shows class MyData, which implements two interfaces: IDataStore and IDataRetrieve. Figure 17-4 illustrates the implementation of the multiple interfaces in class MyData.

```
interface IDataRetrieve { int GetData(); }          // Declare interface
interface IDataStore { void SetData( int x ); }     // Declare interface
                 Interface        Interface
                    ↓                ↓
class MyData: IDataRetrieve, IDataStore             // Declare class
{
   int Mem1;                                        // Declare field
   public int  GetData()        { return Mem1; }
   public void SetData( int x ) { Mem1 = x;    }
}

class Program
{
   static void Main()                               // Main
   {
      MyData data = new MyData();
      data.SetData( 5 );
      Console.WriteLine("Value = {0}", data.GetData());
   }
}
```

This code produces the following output:

```
Value = 5
```

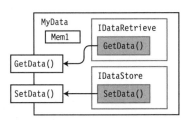

Figure 17-4. *Class implementing multiple interfaces*

Implementing Interfaces with Duplicate Members

Since a class can implement any number of interfaces, it's possible that two or more of the interface members might have the same signature and return type. So, how does the compiler handle that situation?

For example, suppose you had two interfaces—IIfc1 and IIfc2—as shown following. Each interface has a method named PrintOut, with the same signature and return type. If you were to create a class that implemented both interfaces, how should you handle these duplicate interface methods?

```
interface IIfc1
{
   void PrintOut(string s);
}

interface IIfc2
{
   void PrintOut(string t);
}
```

The answer is that if a class implements multiple interfaces, where several of the interfaces have members with the same signature and return type, the class can implement a single member that satisfies all the interfaces containing that duplicated member.

For example, the following code shows the declaration of class MyClass, which implements both IIfc1 and IIfc2. Its implementation of method PrintOut satisfies the requirement for both interfaces.

```
class MyClass : IIfc1, IIfc2              // Implement both interfaces.
{
   public void PrintOut(string s)         // Single implementation for both
   {
      Console.WriteLine("Calling through:  {0}", s);
   }
}

class Program
{
   static void Main()
   {
      MyClass mc = new MyClass();
      mc.PrintOut("object");
   }
}
```

This code produces the following output:

```
Calling through:  object
```

Figure 17-5 illustrates the duplicate interface methods being implemented by a single class-level method implementation.

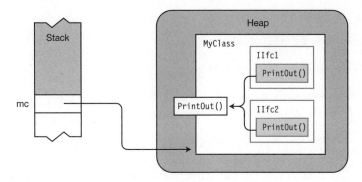

Figure 17-5. *Multiple interfaces implemented by the same class member*

References to Multiple Interfaces

You saw previously that interfaces are reference types and that you can get a reference to an interface by using the as operator or by casting an object reference to the interface type. If a class implements multiple interfaces, you can get separate references for each one.

For example, the following class implements two interfaces with the single method PrintOut. The code in Main calls method PrintOut in three ways:

- Through the class object

- Through a reference to the IIfc1 interface

- Through a reference to the IIfc2 interface

Figure 17-6 illustrates the class object and references to IIfc1 and IIfc2.

```
interface IIfc1                          // Declare interface
{
   void PrintOut(string s);
}

interface IIfc2                          // Declare interface
{
   void PrintOut(string s);
}

class MyClass : IIfc1, IIfc2             // Declare class
{
   public void PrintOut(string s)
   {
      Console.WriteLine("Calling through: {0}", s);
   }
}
```

```
class Program
{
   static void Main()
   {
      MyClass mc = new MyClass();

      IIfc1 ifc1 = (IIfc1) mc;              // Get ref to IIfc1
      IIfc2 ifc2 = (IIfc2) mc;              // Get ref to IIfc2

      mc.PrintOut("object");               // Call through class object

      ifc1.PrintOut("interface 1");        // Call through IIfc1
      ifc2.PrintOut("interface 2");        // Call through IIfc2
   }
}
```

This code produces the following output:

```
Calling through:   object
Calling through:   interface 1
Calling through:   interface 2
```

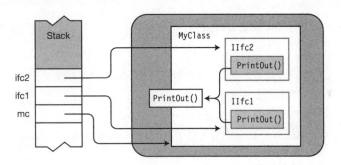

Figure 17-6. *Separate references to different interfaces in the class*

An Inherited Member As an Implementation

A class implementing an interface can inherit the code for an implementation from one of its base classes. For example, the following code illustrates a class inheriting implementation code from a base class.

- IIfc1 is an interface with a method member called PrintOut.

- MyBaseClass contains a method called PrintOut that matches IIfc1's method.

- Class Derived has an empty declaration body but derives from class MyBaseClass and contains IIfc1 in its base class list.

- Even though Derived's declaration body is empty, the code in the base class satisfies the requirement to implement the interface method.

```csharp
interface IIfc1 { void PrintOut(string s); }

class MyBaseClass                               // Declare base class.
{
    public void PrintOut(string s)              // Declare the method.
    {
        Console.WriteLine("Calling through: {0}", s);
    }
}

class Derived : MyBaseClass, IIfc1              // Declare class.
{
}

class Program {
    static void Main()
    {
        Derived d = new Derived();              // Create class object
        d.PrintOut("object.");                  // Call method
    }
}
```

Figure 17-7 illustrates the preceding code. Notice that the arrow from IIfc1 goes down to the code in the base class.

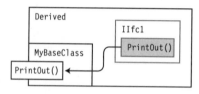

Figure 17-7. *Implementation in the base class*

Explicit Interface Member Implementations

You saw in a previous section that a single class can implement all the members required by multiple interfaces, as illustrated in Figures 17-5 and 17-6.

But what if you want separate implementations for each interface? In this case, you can create what are called *explicit interface member implementations*. An explicit interface member implementation has the following characteristics:

- Like all interface implementations, it is placed in the class or struct implementing the interface.

- It is declared using a *qualified interface name*, which consists of the interface name and member name, separated by a dot.

The following code shows the syntax for declaring explicit interface member implementations. Each of the two interfaces implemented by MyClass implements its own version of method PrintOut.

```
class MyClass : IIfc1, IIfc2
{          Qualified interface name
              ↓
   void IIfc1.PrintOut (string s)            // Explicit implementation
   { ... }

   void IIfc2.PrintOut (string s)            // Explicit implementation
   { ... }
}
```

Figure 17-8 illustrates the class and interfaces. Notice that the boxes representing the explicit interface member implementations are not shown in gray, since they now represent actual code.

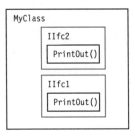

Figure 17-8. *Explicit interface member implementations*

For example, in the following code, class `MyClass` declares explicit interface member implementations for the members of the two interfaces. Notice that in this example there are only explicit interface member implementations. There is no class-level implementation.

```
interface IIfc1 { void PrintOut(string s); }   // Declare interface
interface IIfc2 { void PrintOut(string t); }   // Declare interface

class MyClass : IIfc1, IIfc2
{       Qualified interface name
              ↓
   void IIfc1.PrintOut(string s)                // Explicit interface member
   {                                            //    implementation
      Console.WriteLine("IIfc1: {0}", s);
   }

            Qualified interface name
                  ↓
   void IIfc2.PrintOut(string s)                // Explicit interface member
   {                                            //    implementation
      Console.WriteLine("IIfc2: {0}", s);
   }
}

class Program
{
   static void Main()
   {
      MyClass mc = new MyClass();               // Create class object

      IIfc1 ifc1 = (IIfc1) mc;                   // Get reference to IIfc1
      ifc1.PrintOut("interface 1");             // Call explicit implementation

      IIfc2 ifc2 = (IIfc2) mc;                   // Get reference to IIfc2
      ifc2.PrintOut("interface 2");             // Call explicit implementation
   }
}
```

This code produces the following output:

```
IIfc1:  interface 1
IIfc2:  interface 2
```

Figure 17-9 illustrates the code. Notice in the figure that the interface methods are not pointing at class-level implementations but contain their own code.

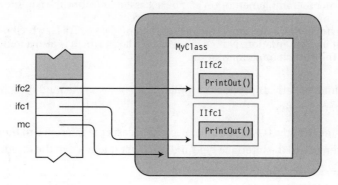

Figure 17-9. *References to interfaces with explicit interface member implementations*

When there is an explicit interface member implementation, a class-level implementation is allowed but not required. The explicit implementation satisfies the requirement that the class or struct must implement the method. You can therefore have any of the following three implementation scenarios:

- A class-level implementation

- An explicit interface member implementation

- Both a class-level and an explicit interface member implementation

Accessing Explicit Interface Member Implementations

An explicit interface member implementation can be accessed *only* through a reference to the interface. This means that even other class members can't directly access them.

For example, the following code shows the declaration of class MyClass, which implements interface IIfc1 with an explicit implementation. Notice that even Method1, which is also a member of MyClass, can't directly access the explicit implementation.

- The first two lines of Method1 produce compile errors because the method is trying to access the implementation directly.

- Only the last line in Method1 will compile, because it casts the reference to the current object (this) to a reference to the interface type and uses that reference to the interface to call the explicit interface implementation.

```csharp
class MyClass : IIfc1
{
    void IIfc1.PrintOut(string s)           // Explicit interface implementation
    {
        Console.WriteLine("IIfc1");
    }

    public void Method1()
    {
        PrintOut("...");               // Compile error
        this.PrintOut("...");          // Compile error

        ((IIfc1)this).PrintOut("...");  // OK, call method
    }               ↑
}     Cast to a reference to the interface
```

This restriction has an important ramification for inheritance. Since other fellow class members can't directly access explicit interface member implementations, members of classes derived from the class clearly can't directly access them either. They must always be accessed through a reference to the interface.

Interfaces Can Inherit Interfaces

You saw earlier that interface *implementations* can be inherited from base classes. But an interface itself can inherit from one or more other interfaces.

- To specify that an interface inherits from other interfaces, place the names of the base interfaces in a comma-separated list after a colon following the interface name in the interface declaration, as shown here:

```
                  Colon          Base interface list
                    ↓                    ↓
      interface IDataIO : IDataRetrieve, IDataStore
      { ...
```

- Unlike a class, which can have only a single class name in its base class list, an interface can have any number of interfaces in its base interface list.

  — The interfaces in the list can themselves have inherited interfaces.

  — The resulting interface contains all the members it declares, as well as all those of its base interfaces.

The code in Figure 17-10 shows the declaration of three interfaces. Interface IDataIO inherits from the first two. The figure on the right shows IDataIO encompassing the other two interfaces.

```
interface IDataRetrieve
{ int GetData( ); }

interface IDataStore
{ void SetData( int x ); }

// Derives from the first two interfaces
interface IDataIO: IDataRetrieve, IDataStore
{
}

class MyData: IDataIO {
   int nPrivateData;
   public int GetData( )
         { return nPrivateData; }
   public void SetData( int x )
         { nPrivateData = x; }
}

class Program {
   static void Main( ) {
      MyData data = new MyData ();
      data.SetData( 5 );
      Console.WriteLine("{0}", data.GetData());
   }
}
```

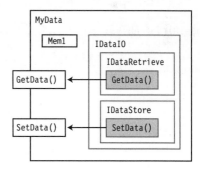

Figure 17-10. *Class with interface inheriting multiple interfaces*

Example of Different Classes Implementing an Interface

The following code illustrates several aspects of interfaces that have been covered. The program declares a class called Animal, which is used as a base class for several other classes that represent various types of animals. It also declares an interface named ILiveBirth.

Classes Cat, Dog, and Bird all derive from base class Animal. Cat and Dog both implement the ILiveBirth interface, but class Bird does not.

In Main, the program creates an array of Animal objects and populates it with a class object of each of the three types of animal classes. The program then iterates through the array and, using the as operator, retrieves references to the ILiveBirth interface of each object that has one and calls its BabyCalled method.

```
interface ILiveBirth                            // Declare interface
{
   string BabyCalled();
}

class Animal { }                                // Base class Animal

class Cat : Animal, ILiveBirth                  // Declare class Cat
{
   string ILiveBirth.BabyCalled()
   { return "kitten"; }
}

class Dog : Animal, ILiveBirth                  // Declare class Dog
{
   string ILiveBirth.BabyCalled()
   { return "puppy"; }
}

class Bird : Animal                             // Declare class Bird
{
}
```

```
class Program
{
   static void Main()
   {
      Animal[] animalArray = new Animal[3];      // Create Animal array
      animalArray[0] = new Cat();                // Insert Cat class object
      animalArray[1] = new Bird();               // Insert Bird class object
      animalArray[2] = new Dog();                // Insert Dog class object
      foreach( Animal a in animalArray )         // Cycle through array
      {
         ILiveBirth b = a as ILiveBirth;         // if implements ILiveBirth...
         if (b != null)
            Console.WriteLine("Baby is called: {0}", b.BabyCalled());
      }
   }
}
```

This code produces the following output:

```
Baby is called: kitten
Baby is called: puppy
```

Figure 17-11 illustrates the array and the objects in memory.

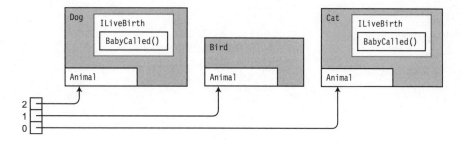

Figure 17-11. *Different object types of base class Animal are interspersed in the array.*

■■■

CHAPTER 18

Conversions

What Are Conversions?

To get an understanding of what conversions are, let's start by considering the simple case in which you declare two variables of different types and then assign the value of one (the *source*) to the other (the *target*). Before the assignment can occur, the source value must be converted to a value of the target type. Figure 18-1 illustrates type conversion.

- *Conversion* is the process of taking a value of one type and *using it as* the equivalent value of another type.

- The value resulting from the conversion should be the same as the source value—but in the target type.

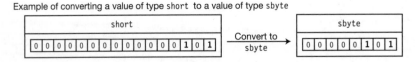

Figure 18-1. *Type conversion*

For example, the code in Figure 18-2 shows the declaration of two variables of different types.

- var1 is of type short, a 16-bit signed integer that is initialized to 5. var2 is of type sbyte, an 8-bit signed integer that is initialized to the value 10.

- The third line of the code assigns the value of var1 to var2. Since these are two different types, the value of var1 must be converted to a value of the same type as var2 before the assignment can be performed. This is performed using the cast expression, which you'll see shortly.

- Notice also that the value and type of var1 are unchanged. Although it is called a conversion, this only means that the source value is used as the target type—not that the source is changed into the target type.

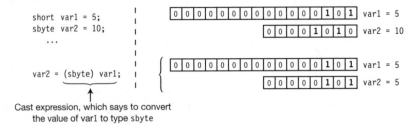

Figure 18-2. *Converting from a short to an sbyte*

Implicit Conversions

For certain types of conversions, there is no possibility of loss of data or precision. For example, it's easy to stuff an 8-bit value into a 16-bit type with no loss of data.

- The language will do these conversions for you automatically. These are called *implicit conversions.*

- When converting from a source type with fewer bits to a target type with more bits, the extra bits in the target need to be filled with either 0s or 1s.

- When converting from a smaller unsigned type to a larger unsigned type, the extra, most significant bits of the target are filled with 0s. This is called *zero extension.*

Figure 18-3 shows an example of the zero extension of an 8-bit value of 10 converted to a 16-bit value of 10.

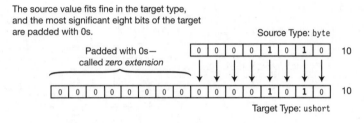

Figure 18-3. *Zero extension in unsigned conversions*

For conversion between signed types, the extra most significant bits are filled with the sign bit of the source expression.

- This maintains the correct sign and magnitude for the converted value.

- This is called *sign extension* and is illustrated in Figure 18-4, first with 10 and then with –10.

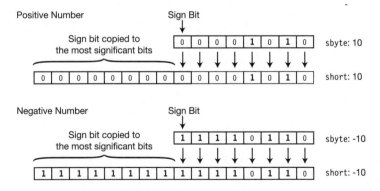

Figure 18-4. *Sign extension in signed conversions*

Explicit Conversions and Casting

When converting from a shorter type to a longer type, it's easy for the longer type to hold all the bits of the shorter type. In other situations, however, the target type might not be able to accommodate the source value without loss of data.

For example, suppose you want to convert a ushort value to a byte.

- A ushort can hold any value between 0 and 65,535.

- A byte can only hold a value between 0 and 255.

- As long as the ushort value you want to convert is less than 256, there won't be any loss of data. If it is greater, however, the most significant bits will be lost.

For example, Figure 18-5 shows an attempt to convert a ushort with a value of 1,365 to a byte, resulting in a loss of data.

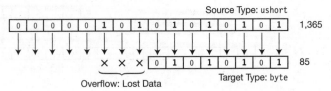

Figure 18-5. *Attempting to convert a ushort to a byte*

Clearly, only a relatively small number (0.4 percent) of the possible unsigned 16-bit ushort values can be safely converted to an unsigned 8-bit byte type without loss of data. The rest result in data *overflow,* yielding different values.

Casting

For the predefined types, C# will automatically convert from one data type to another—but only between those types for which there is no possibility of data loss between the source type and the target type. That is, the language does not provide automatic conversion between two types if there is *any* value of the source type that would lose data if it were converted to the target type. If you want to make a conversion of this type, you must use an *explicit conversion*, called a *cast expression*.

The following code shows an example of a cast expression. It converts the value of var1 to type sbyte. A cast expression consists of the following:

- A set of matching parentheses containing the name of the target type

- The source expression, following the parentheses

```
      Target type
          ↓
      (sbyte) var1;
              ↑
          Source expression
```

When you use a cast expression, you are explicitly taking responsibility for performing the operation that might lose data. Essentially, you are saying, "In spite of the possibility of data loss, I know what I'm doing, so make this conversion anyway." (Make sure, however, that you *do* know what you're doing.)

For example, Figure 18-6 shows cast expressions converting two values of type ushort to type byte. In the first case, there is no loss of data. In the second case, the most significant bits are lost, giving a value of 85—which is clearly not equivalent to the source value, 1,365.

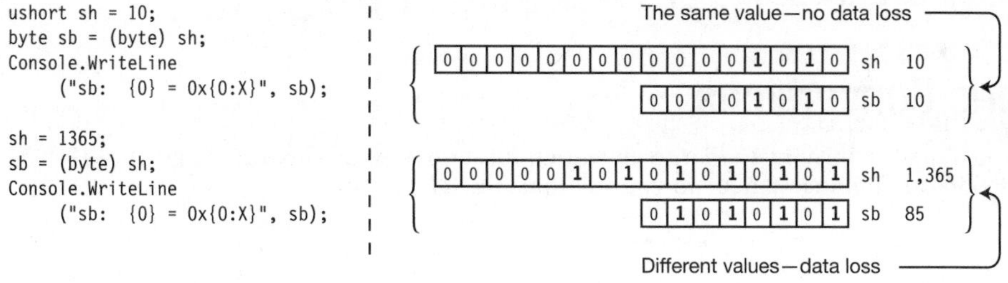

Figure 18-6. *Casting a ushort to a byte*

The output of the code in the figure is the following:

```
sb:  10 = 0xA

sb:  85 = 0x55
```

Types of Conversions

There are a number of standard, predefined conversions for the numeric and reference types. The categories are illustrated in Figure 18-7.

- Beyond the standard conversions, you can also define both implicit and explicit conversions for your user-defined types.

- There is also a predefined type of conversion called *boxing,* which converts any value type to either of these:

  — Type object

  — Type System.ValueType

- Unboxing converts a boxed value back to its original type.

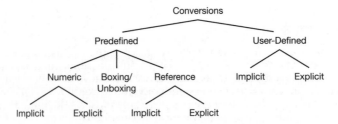

Figure 18-7. *Types of conversions*

Numeric Conversions

Any numeric type can be converted into any other numeric type, as illustrated in Figure 18-8. Some of the conversions are implicit conversions, and others must be explicit.

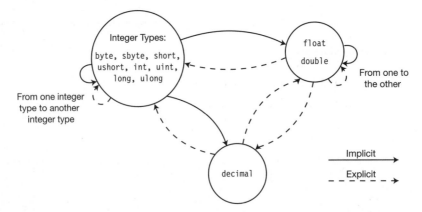

Figure 18-8. *Numeric conversions*

Implicit Numeric Conversions

The implicit numeric conversions are shown in Figure 18-9.

- There is an *implicit conversion* from the source type to the target type if there is a path, following the arrows, from the source type to the target type.

- Any numeric conversion for which there is not a path following the arrows from the source type to the target type must be an *explicit conversion*.

The figure demonstrates that, as you would expect, there is an implicit conversion between numeric types that occupy fewer bits to those that occupy more bits.

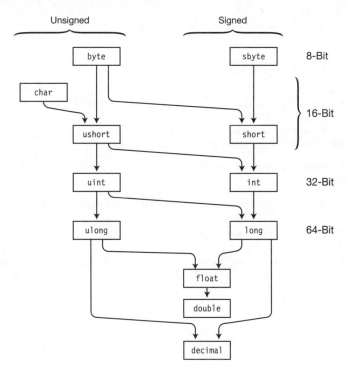

Figure 18-9. *The implicit numeric conversions*

Overflow Checking Context

You've seen that explicit conversions have the possibility of losing data and not being able to represent the source value equivalently in the target type. For integral types, C# provides you with the ability to choose whether the runtime should check the result for overflow when making these types of conversions. It does this through the checked operator and the checked statement.

- Whether a segment of code is checked or not is called its *overflow checking context*.
  - If you designate an expression or segment of code as checked, the CLR will raise an OverflowException exception if the conversion produces an overflow.
  - If the code is not checked, the conversion will proceed regardless of whether there is an overflow.
- The default overflow checking context is not checked.

The checked and unchecked Operators

The checked and unchecked operators control the overflow checking context of an expression, which is placed between a set of parentheses. The expression cannot be a method. The syntax is the following:

```
checked   ( Expression )
unchecked ( Expression )
```

For example, the following code executes the same conversion—first in a checked operator and then in an unchecked operator.

- In the unchecked context, the overflow is ignored, resulting in the value 208.
- In the checked context, an OverflowException exception is raised.

```
ushort sh = 2000;
byte    sb;

sb = unchecked ( (byte) sh );         // Most significant bits lost
Console.WriteLine("sb: {0}", sb);

sb =   checked ( (byte) sh );         // OverflowException raised
Console.WriteLine("sb: {0}", sb);
```

This code produces the following output:

```
sb: 208

Unhandled Exception: System.OverflowException: Arithmetic operation resulted in an overflow.
at Test1.Test.Main() in C:\Programs\Test1\Program.cs:line 21
```

The checked and unchecked Statements

The checked and unchecked *operators* that you just saw act on the single expression between the parentheses. The checked and unchecked *statements* perform the same function but control all the conversions in a block of code, rather than in a single expression.

The checked and unchecked statements can be nested to any level.

For example, the following code uses checked and unchecked statements and produces the same results as the previous example, which uses checked and unchecked expressions. In this case, however, blocks of code are affected, rather than just expressions.

```
byte   sb;
ushort sh = 2000;

unchecked                                           // Set unchecked
{
   sb = (byte) sh;
   Console.WriteLine("sb: {0}", sb);

   checked                                          // Set checked
   {
      sb = (byte) sh;
      Console.WriteLine("sb: {0}", sh);
   }
}
```

Explicit Numeric Conversions

You've seen that the implicit conversions automatically convert from the source expression to the target type because there is no possible loss of data. With the explicit conversions, however, there is the possibility of losing data—so it's important for you as the programmer to know how a conversion will handle that loss if it occurs.

In this section, you will look at each of the various types of explicit numeric conversions. Figure 18-10 shows the subset of explicit conversions shown in Figure 18-8.

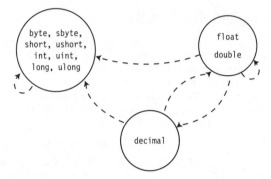

Figure 18-10. *The explicit numeric conversions*

Integral to Integral

Figure 18-11 shows the behavior of the integral-to-integral explicit conversions. In the checked case, if the conversion loses data, the operation raises an OverflowException exception. In the unchecked case, any lost bits go unreported.

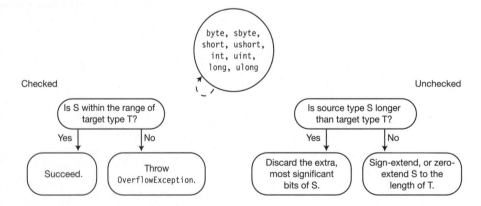

Figure 18-11. *Integer type to integer type explicit conversions*

float or double to Integral

When converting a floating-point type to an integer type, the value is rounded toward 0 to the nearest integer. Figure 18-12 illustrates the conversion conditions. If the rounded value is not within the range of the target type, then

- The CLR raises an OverflowException exception if the overflow checking context is checked.

- C# does not define what its value should be if the context is unchecked.

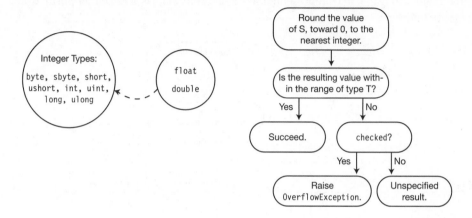

Figure 18-12. *Converting a float or a double to an integer type*

decimal to Integral

When converting from decimal to the integer types, the CLR raises an OverflowException exception if the resulting value is not within the target type's range. Figure 18-13 illustrates the conversion conditions.

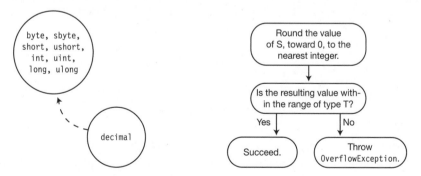

Figure 18-13. *Converting a decimal to an integer type*

double to float

Values of type float occupy 32 bits, and values of type double occupy 64 bits. When a double is rounded to a float, the double type value is rounded to the nearest float type value. Figure 18-14 illustrates the conversion conditions.

- If the value is too small to be represented by a float, the value is set to either positive or negative 0.

- If the value is too large to be represented by a float, the value is set to either positive or negative infinity.

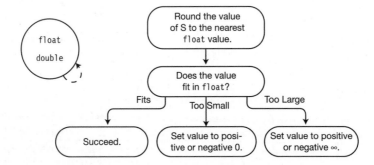

Figure 18-14. *Converting a double to a float*

float or double to decimal

Figure 18-15 shows the conversion conditions for converting from floating-point types to decimal.

- If the value is too small to be represented by the decimal type, the result is set to 0.

- If the value is too large, the CLR raises an OverflowException exception.

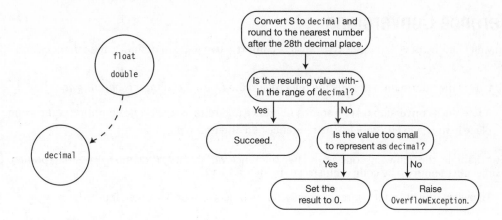

Figure 18-15. *Converting a float or double to a decimal*

decimal to float or double

Conversions from decimal to the floating-point types always succeed. There might, however, be a loss of precision. Figure 18-16 shows the conversion conditions.

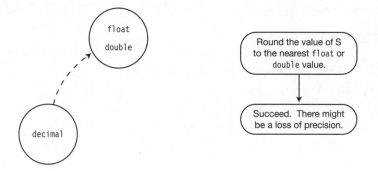

Figure 18-16. *Converting a decimal to a float or double*

Reference Conversions

As you well know by now, reference type objects comprise two parts in memory: the reference and the data.

- Part of the information held by the reference is the *type of the data it is pointing at.*

- A reference conversion takes a source reference and returns a reference pointing at the same place in the heap but "labels" the reference as a different type.

For example, the following code shows two reference variables, myVar1 and myVar2, that point to the same object in memory. The code is illustrated in Figure 18-17.

- To myVar1, the object it references looks like an object of type B—which it is.

- To myVar2, the same object looks like an object of type A.

  — Even though it is actually pointing at an object of type B, it cannot see the parts of B that extend A and therefore cannot see Field2.

  — The second WriteLine statement would therefore cause a compile error.

Notice that the "conversion" does not change myVar1.

```
class A     { public int Field1; }

class B: A { public int Field2; }

class Program
{
    static void Main( )
    {
        B myVar1 = new B();
```
Return the reference to myVar1 as a reference to a class A.
↓
```
        A myVar2 = (A) myVar1;

        Console.WriteLine("{0}", myVar2.Field1);        // Fine
        Console.WriteLine("{0}", myVar2.Field2);        // Compile error!
    }                                          ↑
}                              myVar2 can't see Field2.
```

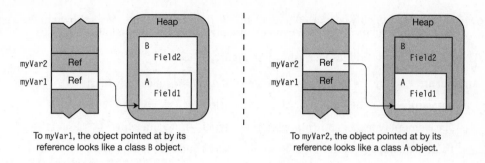

To `myVar1`, the object pointed at by its reference looks like a class B object.

To `myVar2`, the object pointed at by its reference looks like a class A object.

Figure 18-17. *A reference conversion returns a different type associated to the object.*

Implicit Reference Conversions

Just as there are implicit numeric conversions that the language will automatically perform for you, there are also implicit reference conversions. These are illustrated in Figure 18-18.

- All reference types have an implicit conversion to type `object`.

- Any interface can be implicitly converted to an interface from which it is derived.

- A class can be implicitly converted to

  — Any class in the chain from which it is derived

  — Any interface that it implements

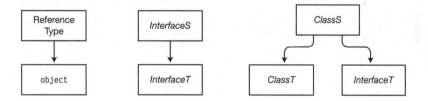

Figure 18-18. *Implicit conversions for classes and interfaces*

A delegate can be implicitly converted to the .NET BCL classes and interfaces shown in Figure 18-19. An array, *ArrayS*, with elements of type *Ts*, can be implicitly converted to the following:

- The .NET BCL class and interfaces shown in Figure 18-19.

- Another array, *ArrayT*, with elements of type *Tt*, if *all* of the following are true:

  — Both arrays have the same number of dimensions.

  — The element types, *Ts* and *Tt*, are reference types—not value types.

  — There is an *implicit* conversion between types *Ts* and *Tt*.

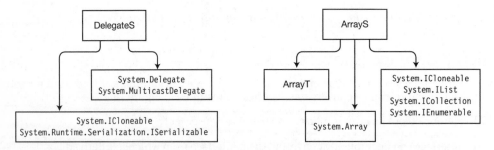

Figure 18-19. *Implicit conversions for delegates and arrays*

Explicit Reference Conversions

Explicit reference conversions are reference conversions from a general type to a more specialized type.

- Explicit conversions include

  — Conversions from an object to any reference type

  — Conversions from a base class to a class derived from it

- The explicit reference conversions are illustrated by reversing each of the arrows in Figures 18-18 and 18-19.

If this type of conversion were allowed without restriction, you could easily attempt to reference members of a class that are not actually in memory. The compiler, however, *does* allow these types of conversions. But when the system encounters them at run time, it raises an exception.

For example, the code in Figure 18-20 converts the reference of base class A to its derived class B and assigns it to variable myVar2.

- If myVar2 were to attempt to access Field2, it would be attempting to access a field in the "B part" of the object, which doesn't exist—causing a memory fault.

- The runtime will catch this inappropriate cast and raise an InvalidCastException exception. Notice, however, that it does *not cause* a compile error.

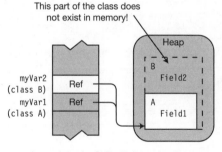

```
class A {
    public int Field1 }

class B: A {
    public int Field2 }


class Program {
    static void Main( )
    {
        A myVar1 = new A();
        B myVar2 = (B)myVar1;
    }
}
```

Unsafe—raises an exception at run time.

This part of the class does not exist in memory!

At run time, the CLR will determine that the conversion is unsafe and raise an exception.

Figure 18-20. *Invalid casts raise runtime exceptions.*

Valid Explicit Reference Conversions

There are three situations in which an explicit reference conversion will succeed at run time—that is, not raise an InvalidCastException exception.

The first case is where the explicit conversion is unnecessary—that is, where the language would have performed an implicit conversion for you anyway. For example, in the code that follows, the explicit conversion is unnecessary because there is always an implicit conversion from a derived class to one of its base classes.

```
class A { }
class B: A { }
   ...
B myVar1 = new B();
A myVar2 = (A) myVar1;      // Cast is unnecessary; A is the base class of B.
```

The second case is where the source reference is null. For example, in the following code, even though it would normally be unsafe to convert a reference of a base class to that of a derived class, the conversion is allowed because the value of the source reference is null.

```
class A { }
class B: A { }
   ...
A myVar1 = null;
B myVar2 = (B) myVar1;      // Allowed because myVar1 is null
```

The third case is where the *actual data* pointed to by the source reference could safely be converted implicitly. The following code shows an example, and Figure 18-21 illustrates the code.

- The implicit conversion in the second line makes myVar2 "think" that it is pointing to data of type A, while it is actually pointing to a data object of type B.

- The explicit conversion in the third line is casting a reference of a base class to a reference of one of its derived classes. Normally this would raise an exception. In this case, however, the object being pointed to actually is a data item of type B.

```
B myVar1 = new B();
A myVar2 = myVar1;     // Implicitly cast myVar1 to type A.
B myVar3 = (B)myVar2;  // This cast is fine because the data is of type B.
```

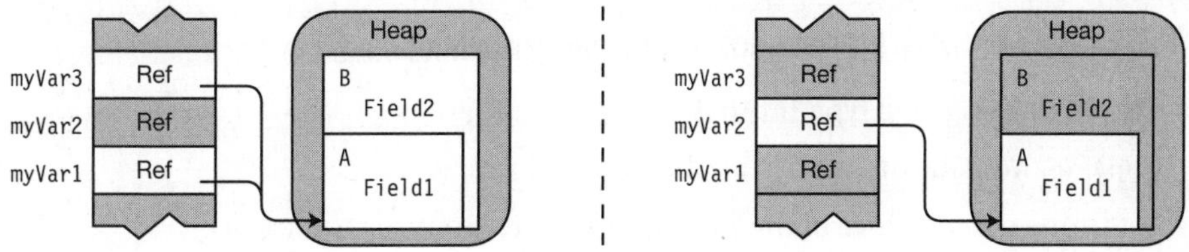

Figure 18-21. *Casting to a safe type*

Boxing Conversions

All C# types, including the value types, are derived from type object. Value types, however, are efficient, lightweight types that do not, by default, include their object component in the heap. When the object component is needed, however, you can use *boxing*, which is an implicit conversion that takes a value type value, creates from it a full reference type object in the heap, and returns a reference to the object.
For example, Figure 18-22 shows three lines of code.

- The first two lines of code declare and initialize value type variable i and reference type variable oi.

- In the third line of code, you want to assign the value of variable i to oi. But oi is a reference type variable and must be assigned a reference to an object in the heap. Variable i, however, is a value type and doesn't have a reference to an object in the heap.

- The system therefore boxes the value of i by doing the following:

  — Creating an object of type int in the heap

  — Copying the value of i to the int object

  — Returning the reference of the int object to oi to store as its reference

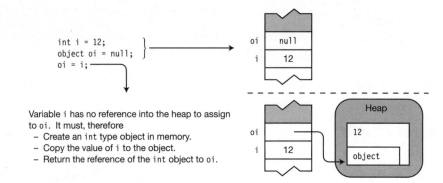

Figure 18-22. *Boxing creates a full reference type object from a value type.*

Boxing Creates a Copy

A common misunderstanding about boxing is that it somehow acts upon the item being boxed. It doesn't. It returns a reference type *copy* of the value. After the boxing procedure, there are two copies of the value—the value type original and the reference type copy—each of which can be manipulated separately.

For example, the following code shows the separate manipulation of each copy of the value. Figure 18-23 illustrates the code.

- The first line defines value type variable i and initializes its value to 10.

- The second line creates reference type variable oi and initializes it with the boxed copy of variable i.

- The last three lines of code show i and oi being manipulated separately.

```
int i = 10;                      // Create and initialize value type
     Box i and assign its reference to oi.
                   ↓
object oi = i;                   // Create and initialize     reference type
Console.WriteLine("i: {0}, io: {1}", i, oi);

i  = 12;
oi = 15;
Console.WriteLine("i: {0}, io: {1}", i, oi);
```

This code produces the following output:

```
i: 10, io: 10

i: 12, io: 15
```

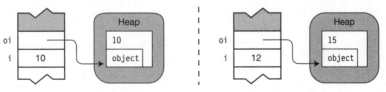

Figure 18-23. *Boxing creates a copy that can be manipulated separately.*

The Boxing Conversions

Figure 18-24 shows the boxing conversions. Any value type *ValueTypeS* can be implicitly converted to any of types object, System.ValueType, or *InterfaceT*, if *ValueTypeS* implements *InterfaceT*.

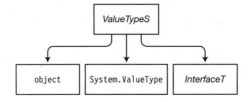

Figure 18-24. *Boxing is the implicit conversion of value types to reference types.*

Unboxing Conversions

Unboxing is the process of converting a boxed object back to its value type.

- Unboxing is an explicit conversion.

- The system performs the following steps when unboxing a value to *ValueTypeT*:

  — It checks that the object being unboxed is actually a boxed value of type *ValueTypeT* .

  — It copies the value of the object to the variable.

  For example, the following code shows an example of unboxing a value.

- Value type variable i is boxed and assigned to reference type variable oi.

- Variable oi is then unboxed, and its value is assigned to value type variable j.

```
static void Main()
{
    int i = 10;
       Box i and assign its reference to oi.
                 ↓
    object oi = i;
          Unbox oi and assign its value to j.
                 ↓
    int j = (int) oi;
    Console.WriteLine("i: {0},   oi: {1},   j: {2}", i,  oi, j);
}
```

This code produces the following output:

```
i: 10,   oi: 10,   j: 10
```

Attempting to unbox a value to a type other than the original type raises an `InvalidCastException` exception.

The Unboxing Conversions

Figure 18-25 shows the unboxing conversions.

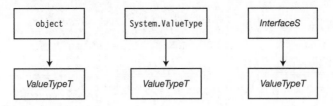

Figure 18-25. *The unboxing conversions*

User-Defined Conversions

Besides the standard conversions, you can also define both implicit and explicit conversions for your own classes and structs.

The syntax for user-defined conversions is shown following.

- The syntax is the same for both implicit and explicit conversion declarations, except for the keywords implicit and explicit.

- The modifiers public and static are required.

```
      Required              Operator    Keyword              Source
         ↓                     ↓           ↓                    ↓
public static implicit operator  TargetType ( SourceType  Identifier )
{                          ↑
              Implicit or explicit
    ...
    return ObjectOfTargetType;
}
```

For example, the following shows an example of the syntax of a conversion method that converts an object of type Person to an int:

```
public static implicit operator int(Person p)
{
    return p.Age;
}
```

Constraints on User-Defined Conversions

There are some important constraints on user-defined conversions. The most important are the following:

- You can only define user-defined conversions for classes and structs.

- You cannot redefine standard implicit or explicit conversions.

- The following is true for source type *S* and target type *T:*

    — *S* and *T* must be different types.

    — *S* and *T* cannot be related by inheritance. That is, *S* cannot be derived from *T*, and *T* cannot be derived from *S*.

    — Neither *S* nor *T* can be an interface type or the type object.

    — The conversion operator must be a member of either *S* or *T*.

- You cannot declare two conversions, one implicit and the other explicit, with the same source and target types.

Example of a User-Defined Conversion

The following code defines a class called Person that contains a person's name and age. The class also defines two implicit conversions. The first converts a Person object to an int value. The target int value is the age of the person. The second converts an int to a Person object.

```
class Person
{
   public string Name;
   public int    Age;
   public Person(string name, int age)
   {
      Name = name;
      Age = age;
   }

   public static implicit operator int(Person p)    // Convert Person to int.
   {
      return p.Age;
   }

   public static implicit operator Person(int i)    // Convert int to Person.
   {
      return new Person("Nemo", i);
   }
}

class Program
{
   static void Main( )
   {
      Person bill = new Person( "bill", 25);

      Convert a Person object to an int.
                ↓
      int age = bill;
      Console.WriteLine("Person Info: {0}, {1}", bill.Name, age);

           Convert an int to a Person object.
                   ↓
      Person anon = 35;
      Console.WriteLine("Person Info: {0}, {1}", anon.Name, anon.Age);
   }
}
```

This code produces the following output:

```
Person Info: bill, 25
Person Info: Nemo, 35
```

If you had defined the same conversion operators as explicit rather than implicit, then you would have needed to use cast expressions to perform the conversions, as shown here:

```
                        Explicit
    ...                    ↓
public static explicit operator int( Person p )
{
    return p.Age;
}

...

static void Main( )
{
        ...   Requires cast expression
                    ↓
    int age = (int) bill;
        ...
```

Evaluating User-Defined Conversions

The user-defined conversions discussed so far have directly converted the source type to an object of the target type in a single step, as shown in Figure 18-26.

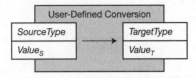

Figure 18-26. *Single-step user-defined conversion*

But user-defined conversions can have up to three steps in the full conversion. Figure 18-27 illustrates these stages, which include the following:

- The preliminary standard conversion

- The user-defined conversion

- The following standard conversion

There is *never* more than a single user-defined conversion in the chain.

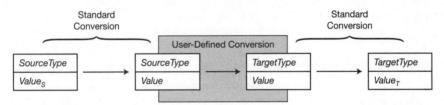

Figure 18-27. *Multistep user-defined conversion*

Example of a Multistep User-Defined Conversion

The following code declares class Employee, which is derived from class Person.

- Several sections ago, the code sample declared a user-defined conversion from class Person to int. So if there is a standard conversion from Employee to Person and one from int to float, you can convert from Employee to float.

  — There is a standard conversion from Employee to Person, since Employee is derived from Person.

  — There is a standard conversion from int to float, since that is an implicit numeric conversion.

- Since all three parts of the chain exist, you can convert from Employee to float. Figure 18-28 illustrates how the compiler performs the conversion.

```
class Employee : Person { }

class Person
{
   public string Name;
   public int    Age;

   // Convert a Person object to an int.
   public static implicit operator int(Person p)
   {
       return p.Age;
   }
}

class Program
{
   static void Main( )
   {
      Employee bill = new Employee();
      bill.Name = "William";
      bill.Age  = 25;
          Convert an Employee to a float.
                  ↓
   float fVar = bill;

      Console.WriteLine("Person Info: {0}, {1}", bill.Name, fVar);
   }
}
```

This code produces the following output:

```
Person Info: William, 25
```

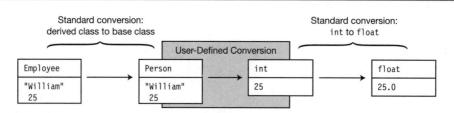

Figure 18-28. *Conversion of Employee to float*

The is Operator

As shown previously, some conversion attempts are not successful and raise an InvalidCastException exception at run time. Instead of blindly attempting a conversion, you can use the is operator to check whether a conversion would complete successfully.

The syntax of the is operator is the following, where *Expr* is the source expression:

```
      Returns a bool
            ↓
_____
Expr is TargetType
```

The operator returns true if *Expr* can be successfully converted to the target type through any of the following:

- A reference conversion

- A boxing conversion

- An unboxing conversion

For example, in the following code, you use the is operator to check whether variable bill of type Employee can be converted to type Person, and then you take the appropriate action.

```
class Employee : Person { }
class Person
{
   public string Name = "Anonymous";
   public int Age     = 25;
}

class Program
{
   static void Main()
   {
      Employee bill = new Employee();
      Person p;

      // Check if variable bill can be converted to type Person
      if( bill is Person )
      {
         p = bill;
         Console.WriteLine("Person Info: {0}, {1}", p.Name, p.Age);
      }
   }
}
```

The is operator can be used only for reference conversions and boxing and unboxing conversions. It *cannot* be used for user-defined conversions.

The as Operator

The as operator is like the cast operator, except that it does not raise an exception. If the conversion fails, rather than raising an exception, it returns null.

The syntax of the as operator is the following, where

- *Expr* is the source expression.

- *TargetType* is the target type, which must be a reference type.

```
       Returns a reference
              ↓
Expr as TargetType
```

Since the as operator returns a reference expression, it can be used as the source for an assignment.

For example, variable bill of type Employee is converted to type Person, using the as operator, and assigned to variable p of type Person. You then check to see whether p is null before using it.

```
class Employee : Person { }

class Person
{
   public string Name = "Anonymous";
   public int Age      = 25;
}

class Program
{
   static void Main()
   {
      Employee bill = new Employee();
      Person p;

      p = bill as Person;
      if( p != null )
      {
         Console.WriteLine("Person Info: {0}, {1}", p.Name, p.Age);
      }
   }
}
```

Like the is operator, the as operator can be used only for reference conversions and boxing conversions. It *cannot* be used for user-defined conversions or conversions to a value type.

CHAPTER 19

■ ■ ■

Generics

What Are Generics?

With the language constructs you've learned so far, you can build powerful objects of many different types. You do this mostly by declaring classes that encapsulate the behavior you want and then creating instances of those classes.

All the types used in the class declarations so far have been specific types—either programmer-defined or supplied by the language or the BCL. There are times, however, when a class would be more useful if you could "distill" or "refactor" out its actions and apply them not just to the data types for which they are coded but for other types as well.

Generics allow you to do just that. You can refactor your code and add an additional layer of abstraction so that, for certain kinds of code, the data types are not hard-coded. This is particularly designed for cases in which there are multiple sections of code performing the same instructions, but on different data types.

That might sound pretty abstract, so we'll start with an example that should make things clearer.

A Stack Example

Suppose first that you have created the following code, which declares a class called `MyIntStack`, which implements a stack of `ints`. It allows you to push `ints` onto the stack and pop them off. This, by the way, isn't the system stack.

```
class MyIntStack                        // Stack for ints
{
   int   StackPointer = 0;
   int[] StackArray;                    // Array of int
    ↑                    int
   int                    ↓
   public void Push( int x )            // Input type: int
   {
     ...
   }      int
          ↓
   public int Pop()                     // Return type: int
   {
     ...
   }

     ...
}
```

Suppose now that you would like the same functionality for values of type float. There are several ways you could achieve this. One way is to perform the following steps to produce the subsequent code:

- Cut and paste the code for class MyIntStack.

- Change the class name to MyFloatStack.

- Change the appropriate int declarations to float declarations throughout the class declaration.

```
class MyFloatStack                      // Stack for floats
{
   int   StackPointer = 0;
   float [] StackArray;                 // Array of float
    ↑                    float
   float                   ↓
   public void Push( float x )          // Input type: float
   {
      ...
   }
           float
             ↓
   public float Pop()                   // Return type: float
   {
      ...
   }

   ...

}
```

This method certainly works, but it's error-prone, and has the following drawbacks:

- You need to inspect every part of the class carefully to determine which type declarations need to be changed and which should be left alone.

- You need to repeat the process for each new type of stack class you need (long, double, string, and so on).

- After the process, you end up with multiple copies of nearly identical code, taking up additional space.

- Debugging and maintaining the parallel implementations is inelegant and error-prone.

Generics in C#

With C# 2.0, Microsoft introduced the *generics* features, which offer more elegant ways of using a set of code with more than one type. Generics allow you to declare *type-parameterized* code, which you can instantiate with different types. This means you can write the code with "placeholders for types" and then supply the *actual* types when you create an instance of the class.

By this point in the text, you should be very familiar with the concept that a type is not an object but a template for an object. In the same way, a generic type is not a type but a template for a type. Figure 19-1 illustrates this point.

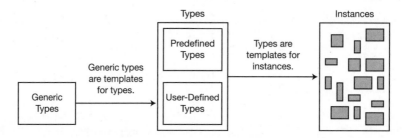

Figure 19-1. *Generic types are templates for types.*

C# provides five kinds of generics: classes, structs, interfaces, delegates, and methods. Notice that the first four are types, and methods are members.

Figure 19-2 shows how generic types fit in with the other types covered.

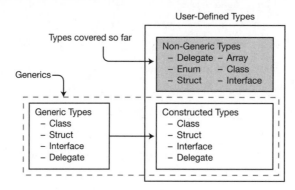

Figure 19-2. *Generics and user-defined types*

Continuing with the Stack Example

In the stack example, with classes `MyIntStack` and `MyFloatStack`, the bodies of the declarations of the classes are identical except at the positions dealing with the type of the value held by the stack.

- In `MyIntStack`, these positions are occupied by type `int`.

- In `MyFloatStack`, they are occupied by `float`.

You can create a generic class from `MyIntStack` by doing the following:

- Take the `MyIntStack` class declaration, and instead of substituting `float` for `int`, substitute the type placeholder T.

- Change the class name to `MyStack`.

- Place the string `<T>` after the class name.

The result is the following generic class declaration. The string consisting of the angle brackets with the T means that T is a placeholder for a type. (It doesn't have to be the letter T—it can be any identifier.) Everywhere throughout the body of the class declaration where T is located, an actual type will need to be substituted by the compiler.

```
class MyStack <T>
{
   int StackPointer = 0;
   T [] StackArray;
   ↑
                  ↓
   public void Push(T x ) {...}

        ↓
   public T Pop() {...}
      ...
}
```

Generic Classes

Now that you've seen a generic class, let's look at generic classes in more detail and see how they're created and used.

As you know, there are two steps for creating and using your own regular, nongeneric classes: declaring the class and creating instances of the class. But generic classes are not actual classes but templates for classes—so you must first construct actual class types from them. You can then create references and instances from these constructed class types.

Figure 19-3 illustrates the process at a high level. If it's not all completely clear yet, don't worry—we'll cover each part in the following sections.

1. Declare a class, using placeholders for some of the types.

2. Provide *actual* types to substitute in for the placeholders. This gives you an actual class definition, with all the "blanks" filled in.

3. Create instances from the "filled-in" class definition.

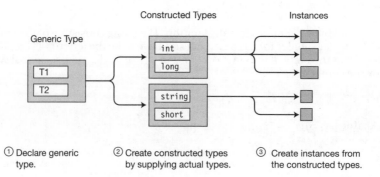

Figure 19-3. *Creating instances from a generic type*

Declaring a Generic Class

Declaring a simple generic class is much like declaring a regular class, with the following differences:

- Place a matching set of angle brackets after the class name.

- Between the angle brackets, place a comma-separated list of the placeholder strings that represent the types, to be supplied on demand. These are called *type parameters*.

- Use the type parameters throughout the body of the declaration of the generic class to represent the types that should be substituted in.

For example, the following code declares a generic class called SomeClass. The type parameters are listed between the angle brackets and then used throughout the body of the declaration as if they were real types.

```
                  Type parameters
                        ↓
class SomeClass < T1, T2 >
{   Normally, types would be used in these positions.
              ↓                   ↓
    public T1 SomeVar  = new T1();
    public T2 OtherVar = new T2();
}         ↑                 ↑
       Normally, types would be used in these positions.
```

There is no special keyword that flags a generic class declaration. Instead, the presence of the type parameter list, demarcated with angle brackets, distinguishes a generic class declaration from a regular class declaration.

Creating a Constructed Type

You *cannot* create class objects directly from a generic class. First, you need to tell the compiler what actual types should be substituted for the placeholders (the type parameters). The compiler takes those actual types and creates a template from which it creates actual class objects.

To construct a class type from a generic class, list the class name and supply real types between the angle brackets, in place of the type parameters. The real types being substituted for the type parameters are called *type arguments*.

```
            Type arguments
                 ↓
 SomeClass< short, int >
```

The compiler takes the type arguments and substitutes them for their corresponding type parameters throughout the body of the generic class, producing the *constructed type*—from which actual class instances are created.

Figure 19-4 shows the declaration of generic class SomeClass on the left. On the right, it shows the constructed class created by using the type arguments short and int.

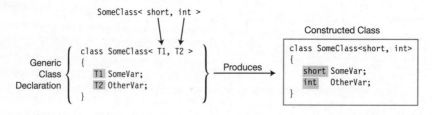

Figure 19-4. *Supplying type arguments for all the type parameters of a generic class produces a constructed class from which actual class objects can be created.*

Figure 19-5 illustrates the difference between type parameters and type arguments.

- Generic class declarations have type parameters, which act as placeholders for types.

- Type arguments are the actual types you supply when creating a constructed type.

Figure 19-5. *Type parameters versus type arguments*

Creating Variables and Instances

A constructed class type is used just like a regular type in creating references and instances. For example, the following code shows the creation of two class objects.

- The first line shows the creation of an object from a regular, nongeneric class. This is a form that you should be completely familiar with by now.

- The second line of code shows the creation of an object from generic class SomeClass, instantiated with types short and int. The form is exactly analogous to the line above it, with the constructed class forms in place of a regular class name.

- The third line is the same semantically as the second line, but rather than listing the constructed type on both sides of the equals sign, it uses the var keyword to make the compiler use type inference.

```
MyNonGenClass        myNGC = new MyNonGenClass        ();
   Constructed class                Constructed class
         ↓                                ↓
  _____                _____
SomeClass<short, int>  mySc1 = new SomeClass<short  int>();
var                    mySc2 = new SomeClass<short, int>();
```

As with nongeneric classes, the reference and the instance can be created separately, as shown in Figure 19-6. The figure also shows that what is going on in memory is the same as for a nongeneric class.

- The first line below the generic class declaration allocates a reference in the stack for variable myInst. Its value is null.

- The second line allocates an instance in the heap and assigns its reference to the variable.

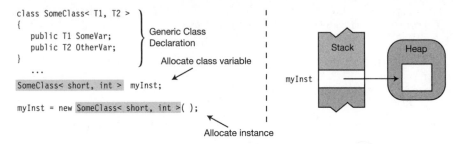

Figure 19-6. *Using a constructed type to create a reference and an instance*

Many different class types can be constructed from the same generic class. Each one is a separate class type, just as if it had its own separate nongeneric class declaration.

For example, the following code shows the creation of two types from generic class SomeClass. The code is illustrated in Figure 19-7.

- One type is constructed with types short and int.

- The other is constructed with types int and long.

```
class SomeClass< T1, T2 >                              // Generic class
{
   ...
}

class Program
{
   static void Main()
   {
      var first  =  new SomeClass<short, int >();    // Constructed type
      var second =  new SomeClass<int,   long>();    // Constructed type

         ...
```

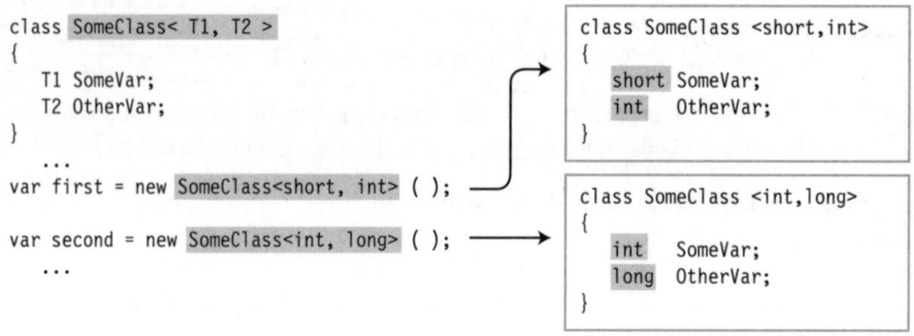

Figure 19-7. *Two constructed classes created from a generic class*

The Stack Example Using Generics

The following code shows the stack example implemented using generics. Method Main defines two variables: stackInt and stackString. The two constructed types are created using int and string as the type arguments.

```csharp
class MyStack<T>
{
   T[] StackArray;
   int StackPointer = 0;

   public void Push(T x)
   {
      if ( !IsStackFull )
         StackArray[StackPointer++] = x;
   }

   public T Pop()
   {
      return ( !IsStackEmpty )
         ? StackArray[--StackPointer]
         : StackArray[0];
   }

   const int MaxStack = 10;
   bool IsStackFull  { get{ return StackPointer >= MaxStack; } }
   bool IsStackEmpty { get{ return StackPointer <= 0; } }

   public MyStack()
   {
      StackArray = new T[MaxStack];
   }

   public void Print()
   {
      for (int i = StackPointer -1; i >= 0 ; i--)
         Console.WriteLine("   Value: {0}", StackArray[i]);
   }
}
```

```
class Program
{
   static void Main()
   {
      var    stackInt = new MyStack<int>();
      var stackString = new MyStack<string>();

      stackInt.Push(3);
      stackInt.Push(5);
      stackInt.Push(7);

      stackInt.Print();

      stackString.Push("Generics are great!");
      stackString.Push("Hi there!");

      stackString.Print();
   }
}
```

This code produces the following output:

```
Value: 7
Value: 5
Value: 3
Value: Hi there!
Value: Generics are great!
```

Comparing the Generic and Nongeneric Stack

Table 19-1 summarizes some of the differences between the initial nongeneric version of the stack and the final generic version of the stack. Figure 19-8 illustrates some of these differences.

Table 19-1. *Differences Between the Nongeneric and Generic Stacks*

	Nongeneric	**Generic**
Source Code Size	Larger: You need a new implementation for each type.	Smaller: You need only one implementation regardless of the number of constructed types.
Executable Size	The compiled version of each stack is present, regardless of whether it is used.	Only types for which there is a constructed type are present in the executable.
Ease of Writing	Easier to write because it's more concrete.	Harder to write because it's more abstract.
Difficulty to Maintain	More error-prone to maintain, since all changes need to be applied for each applicable type.	Easier to maintain, because modifications are needed in only one place.

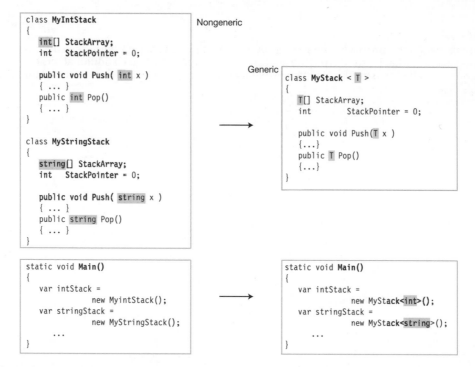

Figure 19-8. *Nongeneric stack versus generic stack*

Constraints on Type Parameters

In the generic stack example, the stack did not do anything with the items it contained other than store them and pop them. It didn't try to add them, compare them, or do anything else that would require using operations of the items themselves. There's good reason for that. Since the generic stack doesn't know the type of the items it will be storing, it can't know what members these types implement.

All C# objects, however, are ultimately derived from class object, so the one thing the stack can be sure of about the items it's storing is that they implement the members of class object. These include methods ToString, Equals, and GetType. Other than that, it can't know what members are available.

As long as your code doesn't access the objects of the types it handles (or as long as it sticks to the members of type object), your generic class can handle any type. Type parameters that meet this constraint are called *unbounded type parameters*. If, however, your code tries to use any other members, the compiler will produce an error message.

For example, the following code declares a class called Simple with a method called LessThan that takes two variables of the same generic type. LessThan attempts to return the result of using the less-than operator. But not all classes implement the less-than operator, so you can't just substitute any class for T. The compiler, therefore, produces an error message.

```
class Simple<T>
{
    static public bool LessThan(T i1, T i2)
    {
        return i1 < i2;                      // Error
    }
    ...
}
```

To make generics more useful, therefore, you need to be able to supply additional information to the compiler about what kinds of types are acceptable as arguments. These additional bits of information are called *constraints*. Only types that meet the constraints can be substituted for the given type parameter.

Where Clauses

Constraints are listed as where clauses.

- Each type parameter that has constraints has its own where clause.

- If a parameter has multiple constraints, they are listed in the where clause, separated by commas.

The syntax of a where clause is the following:

```
          Type parameter              Constraint list
               ↓                            ↓
where   TypeParam : constraint, constraint, ...
  ↑                 ↑
Keyword           Colon
```

The important points about where clauses are the following:

- They're listed after the closing angle bracket of the type parameter list.

- They're not separated by commas or any other token.

- They can be listed in any order.

- The token where is a contextual keyword, so you can use it in other contexts.

For example, the following generic class has three type parameters. T1 is unbounded. For T2, only classes of type Customer, or classes *derived from* Customer, can be used as type arguments. For T3, only classes that implement interface IComparable can be used as type arguments.

```
           Unbounded   With constraints
               ↓         ↓         No separators
class MyClass < T1, T2, T3 >        ↓
                  where T2: Customer              // Constraint for T2
                  where T3: IComparable           // Constraint for T3
{                                    ↑
   ...                            No separators
}
```

Constraint Types and Order

There are five types of constraints. These are listed in Table 19-2.

Table 19-2. *Types of Constraints*

Constraint Type	Description
ClassName	Only classes of this type, or classes derived from it, can be used as the type argument.
class	Any reference type, including classes, arrays, delegates, and interfaces, can be used as the type argument.
struct	Any value type can be used as the type argument.
InterfaceName	Only this interface, or types that implement this interface, can be used as the type argument.
new()	Any type with a parameterless public constructor can be used as the type argument. This is called the *constructor constraint*.

The where clauses can be listed in any order. The constraints in a where clause, however, must be placed in a particular order, as shown in Figure 19-9.

- There can be at most one primary constraint, and if there is one, it must be listed first.

- There can be any number of *InterfaceName* constraints.

- If the constructor constraint is present, it must be listed last.

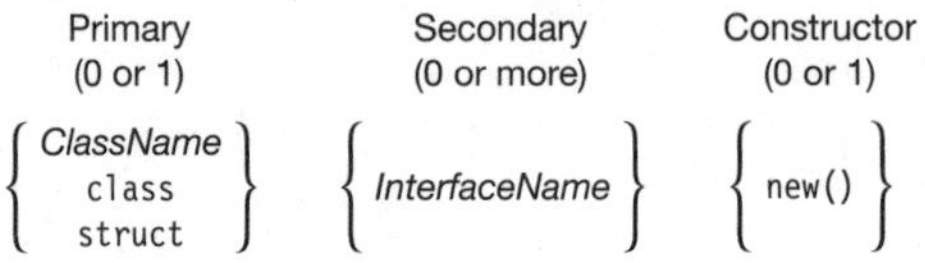

Figure 19-9. *If a type parameter has multiple constraints, they must be in this order.*

The following declarations show examples of where clauses:

```
class SortedList<S>
        where S: IComparable<S> { ... }

class LinkedList<M,N>
        where M : IComparable<M>
        where N : ICloneable     { ... }

class MyDictionary<KeyType, ValueType>
        where KeyType : IEnumerable,
        new()                    { ... }
```

Generic Methods

Unlike the other generics, a method is not a type but a member. You can declare generic methods in both generic and nongeneric classes, and in structs and interfaces, as shown in Figure 19-10.

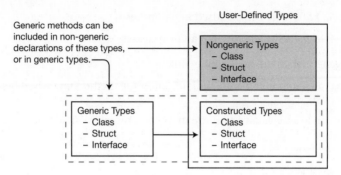

Figure 19-10. *Generic methods can be declared in generic and nongeneric types.*

Declaring a Generic Method

Generic methods have a type parameter list and optional constraints.

- Generic methods have two parameter lists:

  — The *method parameter* list, enclosed in parentheses

  — The *type parameter* list, enclosed in angle brackets

- To declare a generic method, do the following:

  — Place the type parameter list immediately after the method name and before the method parameter list.

  — Place any constraint clauses after the method parameter list.

```
                 Type parameter list        Constraint clauses
                         ↓                          ↓
public void PrintData<S, T> ( S p, T t ) where S: Person
{                                 ↑
   ...                    Method parameter list
}
```

■ **Note** Remember that the type parameter list goes after the method name and before the method parameter list.

Invoking a Generic Method

To invoke a generic method, supply type arguments with the method invocation, as shown here:

```
            Type arguments
               ↓
  MyMethod<short, int>();
  MyMethod<int, long >();
```

Figure 19-11 shows the declaration of a generic method called DoStuff, which takes two type parameters. Below it are two places where the method is called, each with a different set of type parameters. Each of these constructed instances produces a different version of the method, as shown on the right of the figure.

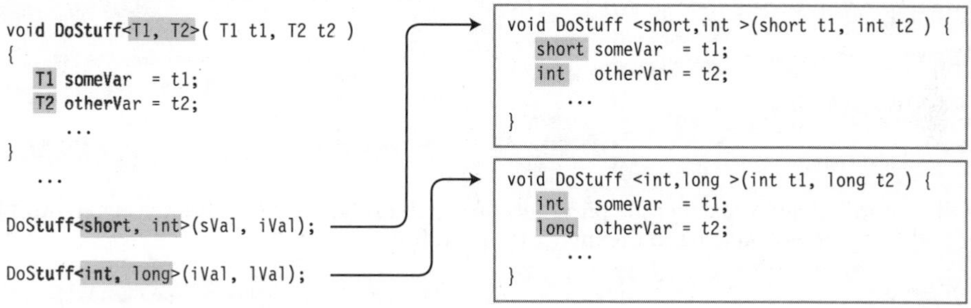

Figure 19-11. *A generic method with two instantiations*

Inferring Types

If you are passing parameters into a method, the compiler can sometimes infer from the types of the *method parameters* the types that should be used as the *type parameters* of the generic method. This can make the method calls simpler and easier to read.

For example, the following code declares MyMethod, which takes a method parameter of the same type as the type parameter.

```
public void MyMethod <T> (T myVal) { ... }
                      ↑    ↑
               Both are of type T
```

If you invoke MyMethod with a variable of type int, as shown in the following code, the information in the type parameter of the method invocation is redundant, since the compiler can see from the method parameter that it's an int.

```
int myInt = 5;
MyMethod <int> (myInt);
          ↑       ↑
       Both are ints
```

Since the compiler can infer the type parameter from the method parameter, you can omit the type parameter and its angle brackets from the invocation, as shown here:

```
MyMethod(myInt);
```

Example of a Generic Method

The following code declares a generic method called ReverseAndPrint in a nongeneric class called Simple. The method takes as its parameter an array of any type. Main declares three different array types. It then calls the method twice with each array. The first time it calls the method with a particular array, it explicitly uses the type parameter. The second time, the type is inferred.

```
class Simple                                        // Non-generic class
{
   static public void ReverseAndPrint<T>(T[] arr)   // Generic method
   {
      Array.Reverse(arr);
      foreach (T item in arr)                        // Use type argument T.
         Console.Write("{0}, ", item.ToString());
      Console.WriteLine("");
   }
}

class Program
{
   static void Main()
   {
      // Create arrays of various types.
      var intArray    = new int[]    { 3, 5, 7, 9, 11 };
      var stringArray = new string[] { "first", "second", "third" };
      var doubleArray = new double[] { 3.567, 7.891, 2.345 };

      Simple.ReverseAndPrint<int>(intArray);         // Invoke method
      Simple.ReverseAndPrint(intArray);              // Infer type and invoke

      Simple.ReverseAndPrint<string>(stringArray);   // Invoke method
      Simple.ReverseAndPrint(stringArray);           // Infer type and invoke

      Simple.ReverseAndPrint<double>(doubleArray);   // Invoke method
      Simple.ReverseAndPrint(doubleArray);           // Infer type and invoke
   }
}
```

This code produces the following output:

```
11, 9, 7, 5, 3,
3, 5, 7, 9, 11,
third, second, first,
first, second, third,
2.345, 7.891, 3.567,
3.567, 7.891, 2.345,
```

Extension Methods with Generic Classes

Extension methods are described in detail in Chapter 7 and work just as well with generic classes. They allow you to associate a static method in one class with a different generic class and to invoke the method as if it were an instance method on a constructed instance of the class.

As with nongeneric classes, an extension method for a generic class must satisfy the following constraints:

- It must be declared static.

- It must be the member of a static class.

- It must contain as its first parameter type the keyword this, followed by the name of the generic class it extends.

The following code shows an example of an extension method called Print on a generic class called Holder<T>:

```
static class ExtendHolder
{
    public static void Print<T>(this Holder<T> h)
    {
        T[] vals = h.GetValues();
        Console.WriteLine("{0},\t{1},\t{2}", vals[0], vals[1], vals[2]);
    }
}

class Holder<T>
{
    T[] Vals = new T[3];

    public Holder(T v0, T v1, T v2)
    { Vals[0] = v0; Vals[1] = v1; Vals[2] = v2; }

    public T[] GetValues() { return Vals; }
}

class Program
{
    static void Main(string[] args) {
        var intHolder    = new Holder<int>(3, 5, 7);
        var stringHolder = new Holder<string>("a1", "b2", "c3");
        intHolder.Print();
        stringHolder.Print();
    }
}
```

This code produces the following output:

```
3,      5,      7
a1,     b2,     c3
```

Generic Structs

Like generic classes, generic structs can have type parameters and constraints. The rules and conditions for generic structs are the same as those for generic classes.

For example, the following code declares a generic struct called PieceOfData, which stores and retrieves a piece of data, the type of which is determined when the type is constructed. Main creates objects of two constructed types—one using int and the other using string.

```
struct PieceOfData<T>                                // Generic struct
{
   public PieceOfData(T value) { _data = value; }
   private T _data;
   public  T Data
   {
      get { return _data; }
      set { _data = value; }
   }
}

class Program
{
   static void Main()                 Constructed type
   {                                         ↓
      var intData    = new PieceOfData<int>(10);
      var stringData = new PieceOfData<string>("Hi there.");
                                            ↑
                                  Constructed type
      Console.WriteLine("intData    = {0}", intData.Data);
      Console.WriteLine("stringData = {0}", stringData.Data);
   }
}
```

This code produces the following output:

```
intData    = 10
stringData = Hi there.
```

Generic Delegates

Generic delegates are very much like nongeneric delegates, except that the type parameters determine the characteristics of what methods will be accepted.

- To declare a generic delegate, place the type parameter list in angle brackets after the delegate name and before the delegate parameter list.

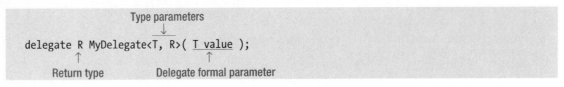

- Notice that there are two parameter lists: the delegate formal parameter list and the type parameter list.

- The scope of the type parameters includes the following:

    — The return type

    — The formal parameter list

    — The constraint clauses

The following code shows an example of a generic delegate. In Main, generic delegate MyDelegate is instantiated with an argument of type string and initialized with method PrintString.

```
delegate void MyDelegate<T>(T value);              // Generic delegate

class Simple
{
   static public void PrintString(string s)        // Method matches delegate
   {
      Console.WriteLine(s);
   }

   static public void PrintUpperString(string s)   // Method matches delegate
   {
      Console.WriteLine("{0}", s.ToUpper());
   }
}

class Program
{
   static void Main( )
   {
      var myDel =                                   // Create inst of delegate
         new MyDelegate<string>(Simple.PrintString);
      myDel += Simple.PrintUpperString;            // Add a method.

      myDel("Hi There.");                          // Call delegate
   }
}
```

This code produces the following output:

```
Hi There.
HI THERE.
```

Another Generic Delegate Example

Since the LINQ feature of C# 3.0 uses generic delegates extensively, it's worth showing another example before we get there. I'll cover LINQ itself, and more about its generic delegates, in Chapter 21.

The following code declares a generic delegate named Func, which takes methods with two parameters and that return a value. The method return type is represented as TR, and the method parameter types are represented as T1 and T2.

```
                             Delegate parameter type
                          ↓    ↓         ↓      ↓
public delegate TR Func<T1, T2, TR>(T1 p1, T2 p2);  // Generic delegate
                       ↑                ↑
class Simple        Delegate return type
{
    static public string PrintString(int p1, int p2) // Method matches delegate
    {
        int total = p1 + p2;
        return total.ToString();
    }
}

class Program
{
    static void Main()
    {
        var myDel =                                   // Create inst of delegate
            new Func<int, int, string>(Simple.PrintString);

        Console.WriteLine("Total: {0}", myDel(15, 13));  // Call delegate
    }
}
```

This code produces the following output:

```
Total: 28
```

Generic Interfaces

Generic interfaces allow you to write interfaces where the formal parameters and return types of interface members are generic type parameters. Generic interface declarations are similar to nongeneric interface declarations but have the type parameter list in angle brackets after the interface name.

For example, the following code declares a generic interface called IMyIfc.

- Simple is a generic class that implements generic interface IMyIfc.

- Main instantiates two objects of the generic class: one with type int and the other with type string.

```
          Type parameter
               ↓
interface IMyIfc<T>                      // Generic interface
{
    T ReturnIt(T inValue);
}
     Type parameter    Generic interface
            ↓                 ↓
class Simple<S> : IMyIfc<S>              // Generic class
{
    public S ReturnIt(S inValue)        // Implement generic interface
    { return inValue; }
}

class Program
{
    static void Main()
    {
        var trivInt    = new Simple<int>();
        var trivString = new Simple<string>();

        Console.WriteLine("{0}", trivInt.ReturnIt(5));
        Console.WriteLine("{0}", trivString.ReturnIt("Hi there."));
    }
}
```

This code produces the following output:

```
5
Hi there.
```

An Example Using Generic Interfaces

The following example illustrates two additional capabilities of generic interfaces:

- Like other generics, instances of a generic interface instantiated with different type parameters are different interfaces.

- You can implement a generic interface in a *nongeneric type*.

For example, the following code is similar to the last example, but in this case, Simple is a *nongeneric* class that implements a generic interface. In fact, it implements two instances of IMyIfc. One instance is instantiated with type int and the other with type string.

```
interface IMyIfc<T>                          // Generic interface
{
    T ReturnIt(T inValue);
}
            Two different interfaces from the same generic interface
                    ↓              ↓
class Simple : IMyIfc<int>, IMyIfc<string>   // Non-generic class
{
    public int ReturnIt(int inValue)         // Implement interface using int
    { return inValue; }

    public string ReturnIt(string inValue)   // Implement interface using string
    { return inValue; }
}

class Program
{
    static void Main()
    {
        Simple trivial = new Simple();

        Console.WriteLine("{0}", trivial.ReturnIt(5));
        Console.WriteLine("{0}", trivial.ReturnIt("Hi there."));
    }
}
```

This code produces the following output:

```
5
Hi there.
```

Generic Interface Implementations Must Be Unique

When implementing an interface in a generic type, there must be no possible combination of type arguments that would create a duplicate interface in the type.

For example, in the following code, class Simple uses two instantiations of interface IMyIfc.

- The first one is a constructed type, instantiated with type int.

- The second one has a type parameter rather than an argument.

There's nothing wrong in itself with the second interface, since it's perfectly fine to use a generic interface. The problem here, though, is that it allows a possible conflict, because if int is used as the type argument to replace S in the second interface, then Simple would have two interfaces of the same type—which is not allowed.

```
interface IMyIfc<T>
{
   T ReturnIt(T inValue);
}
                          Two interfaces
                     _____↓_____↓_____
class Simple<S> : IMyIfc<int>, IMyIfc<S>      // Error!
{
   public int ReturnIt(int inValue)   // Implement first interface.
   {
      return inValue;
   }

   public S ReturnIt(S inValue)        // Implement second interface,
   {                                   // but if it's int, it would be
      return inValue;                  // the same as the one above.
   }
}
```

■ **Note** The names of generic interfaces do not clash with nongeneric interfaces. For example, in the preceding code, we could have also declared a nongeneric interface named IMyIfc.

Covariance and Contravariance in Generics

As you've seen throughout this chapter, when you create an instance of a generic type, the compiler takes the generic type declaration and the type arguments and creates a constructed type. A mistake that people commonly make, however, is to assume that you can assign a delegate of a derived type to a variable of a delegate of a base type. In the following sections, we'll look at this topic, which is called variance. There are three types of variance—*covariance*, *contravariance*, and *invariance*.

We'll start by reviewing something you've already learned: every variable has a type assigned to it, and you can assign an object of a more derived type to a variable of one of its base types. This is called *assignment compatibility*. The following code demonstrates assignment compatibility with a base class Animal and a class Dog derived from Animal. In Main, you can see that the code creates an object of type Dog and assigns it to variable a2 of type Animal.

```
class Animal
{
    public int NumberOfLegs = 4;
}

class Dog : Animal
{
}

class Program
{
    static void Main( )
    {
        Animal a1 = new Animal( );
        Animal a2 = new Dog( );

        Console.WriteLine( "Number of dog legs: {0}", a2.NumberOfLegs );
    }
}
```

Figure 19-12 illustrates assignment compatibility. In this figure, the boxes showing the Dog and Animal objects also show their base classes.

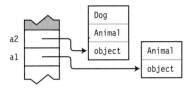

Figure 19-12. *Assignment compatibility means that you can assign a reference of a more derived type to a variable of a less derived type.*

Now let's look at a more interesting case by expanding the code in the following ways as shown following:

- This code adds a generic delegate named Factory, which takes a single type parameter T, takes no method parameters, and returns an object of type T.

- I've added a method named MakeDog that takes no parameters and returns a Dog object. This method, therefore, matches delegate Factory if we use Dog as the type parameter.

- The first line of Main creates a delegate object whose type is delegate Factory<Dog> and assigns its reference to variable dogMaker, of the same type.

- The second line attempts to assign a delegate of type delegate Factory<Dog> to a delegate type variable named animalMaker of type delegate Factory<Animal>.

This second line in Main, however, causes a problem, and the compiler produces an error message saying that it can't implicitly convert the type on the right to the type on the left.

```
class Animal      { public int Legs = 4; }  // Base class
class Dog : Animal { }                      // Derived class

delegate T Factory<T>( );          ← delegate Factory

class Program
{
   static Dog MakeDog( )           ← Method that matches delegate Factory
   {
      return new Dog( );
   }

   static void Main( )
   {
      Factory<Dog>    dogMaker    = MakeDog;    ← Create delegate object
      Factory<Animal> animalMaker = dogMaker;   ← Attempt to assign delegate object

      Console.WriteLine( animalMaker( ).Legs.ToString( ) );
   }
}
```

It seems to make sense that a delegate constructed with the base type should be able to hold a delegate constructed with the derived type. So why does the compiler give an error message? Doesn't the principle of assignment compatibility hold?

The principle *does* hold, but it doesn't apply in this situation! The problem is that although Dog derives from Animal, delegate Factory<Dog> does *not* derive from delegate Factory<Animal>. Instead, both delegate objects are peers, deriving from type delegate, which derives from type object, as shown in Figure 19-13. Neither delegate is derived from the other, so assignment compatibility doesn't apply.

Figure 19-13. *Assignment compatibility doesn't apply because the two delegates are unrelated by inheritance.*

Although the mismatch of delegate types doesn't allow assigning one type to the variable of another type, it's too bad in this situation, because in the example code, any time we would execute delegate animalMaker, the calling code would expect to have a reference to an Animal object returned. If it returned a reference to a Dog object instead, that would be perfectly fine since a reference to a Dog is a reference to an Animal, by assignment compatibility.

Looking at the situation more carefully, we can see that for any generic delegate, if a type parameter is used *only as an output value*, then the same situation applies. In all such situations, you would be able to use a constructed delegate type created with a derived class, and it would work fine, since the invoking code would always be expecting a reference to the base class—which is exactly what it would get.

This constant *relation* between the use of a derived type only as an output value, and the validity of the constructed delegate, is called *covariance*, and is now explicitly allowed in C# 4.0. To let the compiler know that this is what you intend, you must mark the type parameter in the delegate declaration with the out keyword.

For example, if we change the delegate declaration in the example by adding the out keyword, as shown here, the code compiles and works fine.

```
delegate T Factory<out T>( );
                    ↑
            Keyword specifying covariance
               of the type parameter
```

Figure 19-14 illustrates the components of covariance in this example:

- The variable on the stack on the left is of type delegate T Factory<out T>(), where type variable T is of class Animal.

- The actual constructed delegate in the heap, on the right, was declared with a type variable of class Dog, which is derived from class Animal.

- This is acceptable because when the delegate is called, the calling code receives an object of type Dog, instead of the expected object of type Animal. The calling code can freely operate on the Animal part of the object as it expects to do.

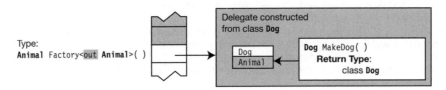

Figure 19-14. *The covariant relation allows a more derived type to be in return and out positions.*

The following code illustrates a related situation. In this example, there's a delegate, named Action1, which takes a single type parameter, and a single method parameter whose type is that of the type parameter, and it returns no value.

The code also contains a method called ActOnAnimal, whose signature and void return type match the delegate declaration.

The first line in Main creates a constructed delegate using type Animal and method ActOnAnimal, whose signature and void return type match the delegate declaration. In the second line, however, the code attempts to assign the reference to this delegate to a stack variable named dog1, of type delegate Action1<Dog>.

```
class Animal { public int NumberOfLegs = 4; }
class Dog : Animal { }

class Program              Keyword for Contravariance
{                                   ↓
    delegate void Action1<in T>( T a );

    static void ActOnAnimal( Animal a ) { Console.WriteLine( a.NumberOfLegs ); }

    static void Main( )
    {
        Action1<Animal> act1 = ActOnAnimal;
        Action1<Dog>    dog1 = act1;
        dog1( new Dog() );
    }
}
```

This code produces the following output:

```
4
```

Like the previous situation, by default, you can't assign the two incompatible types. But also like the previous situation, there are situations where the assignment would work perfectly fine.

As a matter of fact, this is true whenever the type parameter is used *only as an input parameter* to the method in the delegate. The reason for this is that even though the invoking code passes in a reference to a more derived class, the method in the delegate is only expecting a reference to a less derived class—which of course it receives and knows how to manipulate.

This relation, allowing a more derived object where a less derived object is expected, is called *contravariance* and is now explicitly allowed in C# 4.0. To use it, you must use the in keyword with the type parameter, as shown in the code.

Figure 19-15 illustrates the components of contravariance in line 2 of `Main`.

- The variable on the stack on the left is of type delegate `void Action1<in T>(T p)`, where the type variable is of class `Dog`.

- The actual constructed delegate, on the right, is declared with a type variable of class `Animal`, which is a base class of class `Dog`.

- This works fine because when the delegate is called, the calling code passes in an object of type `Dog`, to method `ActOnAnimal`, which is expecting an object of type `Animal`. The method can freely operate on the `Animal` part of the object as it expects to do.

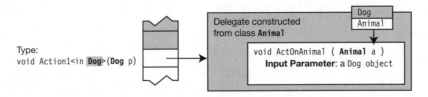

Figure 19-15. *The contravariant relation allows more derived types to be allowed as input parameters.*

Figure 19-16 summarizes the differences between covariance and contravariance in a generic delegate.

- The top figure illustrates covariance.

  — The variable on the stack on the left is of type delegate F<out T>( ) where the type variable is of a class named Base.

  — The actual constructed delegate, on the right, was declared with a type variable of class Derived, which is derived from class Base.

  — This works fine because when the delegate is called, the method returns a reference to an object of the derived type, which is also a reference to the base class, which is exactly what the calling code is expecting.

- The bottom figure illustrates contravariance.

  — The variable on the stack on the left is of type delegate void F<in T>(T p), where the type parameter is of class Derived.

  — The actual constructed delegate, on the right was declared with a type variable of class Base, which is a base class of class Derived.

  — This works fine because when the delegate is called, the calling code passes in an object of the derived type, to the method which is expecting an object of the base type. The method can operate freely on the base part of the object as it expects to do.

Covariance

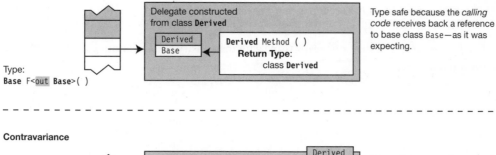

Contravariance

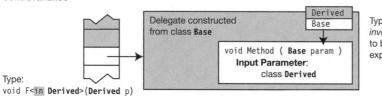

Figure 19-16. *A comparison of covariance and contravariance*

Covariance and Contravariance in Interfaces

You should now have an understanding of covariance and contravariance as it applies to delegates. The same principles apply to interfaces, including the syntax using the out and in keywords in the interface declaration.

The following code shows an example of using covariance with an interface. The things to note about the code are the following:

- The code declares a generic interface with type parameter T. The out keyword specifies that the type parameter is covariant.

- Generic class SimpleReturn implements the generic interface.

- Method DoSomething shows how a method can take an *interface* as a parameter. This method takes as its parameter a generic IMyIfc interface constructed with type Animal.

The code works in the following way:

- The first two lines of Main create and initialize a constructed instance of generic class SimpleReturn, using class Dog.

- The next line assigns that object to a variable on the stack that is declared of constructed interface type IMyIfc<Animal>. Notice several things about this declaration:

  — The type on the left of the assignment is an interface type—not a class.

  — Even though the interface types don't exactly match, the compiler allows them because of the covariant out specifier in the interface declaration.

- Finally, the code calls method DoSomething with the constructed covariant class that implements the interface.

```
class Animal { public string Name; }
class Dog: Animal{ };
                    Keyword for Covariance
                        ↓
interface IMyIfc<out T>
{
    T GetFirst();
}

class SimpleReturn<T>: IMyIfc<T>
{
    public T[] items = new T[2];
    public T GetFirst() { return items[0]; }
}

class Program
{
    static void DoSomething(IMyIfc<Animal> returner)
    {
        Console.WriteLine(returner.GetFirst().Name);
    }

    static void Main( )
    {
        SimpleReturn<Dog> dogReturner = new SimpleReturn<Dog>();
        dogReturner.items[0] = new Dog() { Name = "Avonlea" };

        IMyIfc<Animal> animalReturner = dogReturner;

        DoSomething(dogReturner);
    }
}
```

This code produces the following output:

```
Avonlea
```

More About Variance

The previous two sections explained explicit covariance and contravariance. There is also a situation where the compiler automatically recognizes that a certain constructed delegate is covariant or contravariant and makes the type coercion automatically. That happens when the object hasn't yet had a type assigned to it. The following code shows an example.

The first line of Main creates a constructed delegate of type Factory<Animal> from a method where the return type is a Dog object, not an Animal object. In creating this delegate, the method name on the right side of the assignment operator doesn't yet have a type, and the compiler can determine that the method fits the type of the delegate except that its return type is of type Dog rather than type Animal. The compiler is smart enough to realize that this is a covariant relation and creates the constructed type and assigns it to the variable.

Compare that with the assignments in the third and fourth lines of Main. In these cases, the expressions on the right side of the equals sign already have a type and therefore need the out specifier in the delegate declaration to signal the compiler to allow them to be covariant.

```
class Animal { public int Legs = 4; }          // Base class
class Dog : Animal { }                          // Derived class

class Program
{
    delegate T Factory<out T>();

    static Dog MakeDog() { return new Dog(); }

    static void Main()
    {
        Factory<Animal> animalMaker1 = MakeDog;        // Coerced implicitly

        Factory<Dog>    dogMaker     = MakeDog;
        Factory<Animal> animalMaker2 = dogMaker;       // Requires the out specifier

        Factory<Animal> animalMaker3
                = new Factory<Dog>(MakeDog);           // Requires the out specifier
    }
}
```

This implicit coercion implementing covariance and contravariance has been available without the in/out keywords since before C# 4.0.

Other important things you should know about variance are the following:

- As you've seen, variance deals with the issue of where it's safe to substitute a base type for a derived type, and vice versa. Variance, therefore, applies only to reference types, since value types can't be derived from.

- Explicit variance, using the in and out keywords applies only to delegates and interfaces—not classes, structs, or methods.

- Delegate and interface type parameters that don't include either the in or out keyword are called *invariant*. These types cannot be used covariantly or contravariantly.

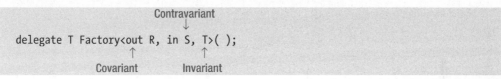

CHAPTER 20

Enumerators and Iterators

Enumerators and Enumerable Types

In Chapter 14, you saw that you can use a foreach statement to cycle through the elements of an array. In this chapter, you'll take a closer look at arrays and see why they can be processed by foreach statements. You'll also look at how you can add this capability to your own user-defined classes. Later in the chapter, I'll explain the use of iterators.

Using the foreach Statement

When you use a foreach statement with an array, the statement presents you with each element in the array, one by one, allowing you to read its value.

For example, the following code declares an array with four elements and then uses a foreach loop to print out the values of the items:

```
int[] arr1 = { 10, 11, 12, 13 };              // Define the array.

foreach (int item in arr1)                     // Enumerate the elements.
   Console.WriteLine("Item value:  {0}", item);
```

This code produces the following output:

```
Item value:   10
Item value:   11
Item value:   12
Item value:   13
```

Why does this work, apparently magically, with arrays? The reason is that an array can produce, upon request, an object called an *enumerator*. The enumerator is an object that can return the elements of the array, one by one, in order, as they are requested. The enumerator "knows" the order of the items and keeps track of where it is in the sequence. It then returns the current item when it is requested.

For types that have enumerators, there must be a way of retrieving them. The standard way of retrieving an object's enumerator in .NET is to call the object's GetEnumerator method. Types that implement a GetEnumerator method are called *enumerable types*, or just *enumerables*. Arrays are enumerables.

Figure 20-1 illustrates the relationship between enumerables and enumerators.

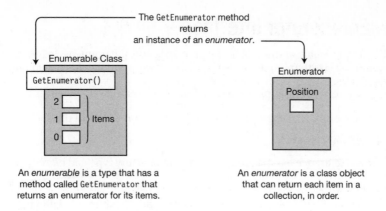

Figure 20-1. *Overview of enumerators and enumerables*

The foreach construct is designed to work with enumerables. As long as the object it is given to iterate over is an enumerable type, such as an array, it will perform the following actions:

- Get the object's enumerator by calling its GetEnumerator method

- Request each item from the enumerator and make it available to your code as the *iteration variable*, which your code can read (but not change).

```
                    Must be enumerable
                           ↓
foreach( Type VarName in EnumerableObject )
{
   ...
}
```

Types of Enumerators

There are three variations on enumerators. They all work essentially the same way, with only slight differences. I'll discuss all three types. You can implement enumerators using the following:

- The IEnumerator/IEnumerable interfaces—called the *nongeneric interface* form

- The IEnumerator<T>/IEnumerable<T> interfaces—called the *generic interface* form

- The form that uses no interfaces

Using the IEnumerator Interface

This section will start by looking at the first in the preceding list: the nongeneric interface form. This form of enumerator is a class that implements the IEnumerator interface. It's called *nongeneric* because it does not use C# generics.

The IEnumerator interface contains three function members: Current, MoveNext, and Reset.

- Current is a property that returns the item at the current position in the sequence.

  — It is a read-only property.

  — It returns a reference of type object, so an object of any type can be returned.

- MoveNext is a method that advances the enumerator's position to the next item in the collection. It also returns a Boolean value, indicating whether the new position is a valid position or is beyond the end of the sequence.

  — If the new position is valid, the method returns true.

  — If the new position isn't valid (that is, it's beyond the end), the method returns false.

  — The initial position of the enumerator is *before* the first item in the sequence. MoveNext must be called *before* the first access of Current.

- Reset is a method that resets the position to the initial state.

Figure 20-2 illustrates a collection of three items, which is shown on the left of the figure, and its enumerator, which is shown on the right. In the figure, the enumerator is an instance of a class called ArrEnumerator.

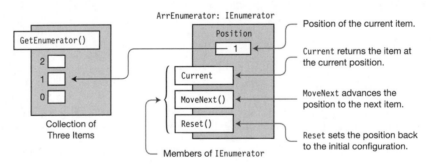

Figure 20-2. *The enumerator for a small collection*

The enumerator class is usually declared as a nested class of the class for which it is an enumerator. A *nested class* is declared inside the declaration of another class. Nested classes are described in detail in Chapter 25.

The way the enumerator keeps track of the current item in the sequence is entirely implementation-dependent. It might be implemented as a reference to an object, an index value, or something else entirely. In the case of the built-in single-dimensional array type, it's simply the index of the item.

Figure 20-3 illustrates the states of an enumerator for a collection of three items. The states are labeled 1 through 5.

- Notice that in state 1, the initial position of the enumerator is -1 (that is, before the first element of the collection).

- Each transition between states is caused by a call to MoveNext, which advances the position in the sequence. Each call to MoveNext between states 1 and 4 returns true. In the transition between states 4 and 5, however, the position ends up beyond the last item in the collection, so the method returns false.

- In the final state, any further calls to MoveNext return false.

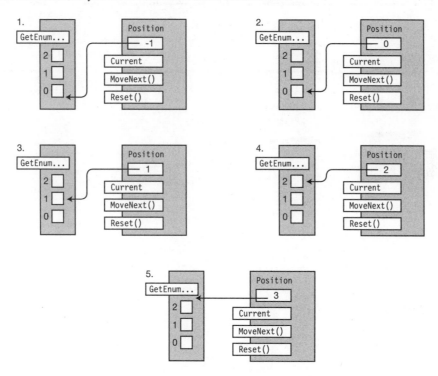

Figure 20-3. *The states of an enumerator*

Given a collection's enumerator, you should be able to simulate a foreach loop by cycling through the items in the collection using the MoveNext and Current members. For example, you know that arrays are enumerable, so the following code does *manually* what the foreach statement does *automatically*. In fact, the C# compiler generates exactly this code when you write a foreach loop.

```csharp
static void Main()
{
    int[] MyArray = { 10, 11, 12, 13 };               // Create an array.

    IEnumerator ie = MyArray.GetEnumerator();         // Get its enumerator.
    while ( ie.MoveNext() )                            // Move to the next item.
    {
        int i = (int) ie.Current;                     // Get the current item.
        Console.WriteLine("{0}", i);                  // Write it out.
    }
}
```

This code produces the following output:

```
10
11
12
13
```

Declaring an IEnumerator Enumerator

To create a nongeneric interface enumerator class, you must declare a class that implements the IEnumerator interface. The IEnumerator interface has the following characteristics:

- It is a member of the System.Collections namespace.

- It contains the three members Current, MoveNext, and Reset.

The following code shows the outline of a nongeneric enumerator class. It does not show how the position is maintained. Notice that Current returns a reference to an object.

```
using System.Collections;                     // Include the namespace.

class MyEnumerator: IEnumerator
{              Returns a reference to an object
                              ↓
   public object Current    { get; }          // Current

   public bool MoveNext()   { ... }           // MoveNext

   public void Reset()      { ... }           // Reset
      ...
}
```

For example, the following code implements an enumerator class that lists an array of color names:

```
using System.Collections;

class ColorEnumerator: IEnumerator
{                               ↑
   string[] Colors;         Implements IEnumerator
   int Position = -1;

   public object Current                                // Current
   {
      get
      {
         if (Position == -1)
            throw new InvalidOperationException();
         if (Position == Colors.Length)
            throw new InvalidOperationException();

         return Colors[Position];
      }
   }

   public bool MoveNext()                               // MoveNext
   {
      if (Position < Colors.Length - 1)
      {
         Position++;
         return true;
      }
      else
         return false;
   }

   public void Reset()                                  // Reset
   {
      Position = -1;
   }

   public ColorEnumerator(string[] theColors)           // Constructor
   {
      Colors = new string[theColors.Length];
      for (int i = 0; i < theColors.Length; i++)
         Colors[i] = theColors[i];
   }
}
```

The IEnumerable Interface

The IEnumerable interface has only a single member, method GetEnumerator, which returns an enumerator for the object.

Figure 20-4 shows class MyClass, which has three items to enumerate, and implements the IEnumerable interface by implementing the GetEnumerator method.

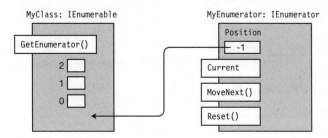

Figure 20-4. *The GetEnumerator method returns an enumerator object for the class.*

The following code shows the form for the declaration of an enumerable class:

```
using System.Collections;
                   Implements the IEnumerable interface
                              ↓
class MyClass : IEnumerable
{
    public IEnumerator GetEnumerator { ... }
    ...          ↑
}        Returns an object of type IEnumerator
```

The following code gives an example of an enumerable class that uses enumerator class ColorEnumerator from the previous example. Remember that ColorEnumerator implements IEnumerator.

```
using System.Collections;

class MyColors: IEnumerable
{
    string[] Colors = { "Red", "Yellow", "Blue" };

    public IEnumerator GetEnumerator()
    {
        return new ColorEnumerator(Colors);
    }                        ↑
}                 An instance of the enumerator class
```

Example Using IEnumerable and IEnumerator

Putting the MyColors and ColorEnumerator examples together, you can add a class called Program with a Main method that creates an instance of MyColors and uses it in a foreach loop.

```csharp
using System;
using System.Collections;

namespace ColorCollectionEnumerator
{
   class ColorEnumerator: IEnumerator
   {
      string[] Colors;
      int Position = -1;

      public ColorEnumerator(string[] theColors)              // Constructor
      {
         Colors = new string[theColors.Length];
         for (int i = 0; i < theColors.Length; i++)
            Colors[i] = theColors[i];
      }

      public object Current                                    // Current
      {
         get
         {
            if (Position == -1)
            {
               throw new InvalidOperationException();
            }
            if (Position == Colors.Length)
            {
               throw new InvalidOperationException();
            }

            return Colors[Position];
         }
      }

      public bool MoveNext()                                   // MoveNext
      {
         if (Position < Colors.Length - 1)
         {
            Position++;
            return true;
         }
         else
            return false;
      }

      public void Reset()                                      // Reset
      { Position = -1; }
   }
```

```
class MyColors: IEnumerable
{
    string[] Colors = { "Red", "Yellow", "Blue" };

    public IEnumerator GetEnumerator()
    {
        return new ColorEnumerator(Colors);
    }
}

class Program
{
    static void Main()
    {
        MyColors mc = new MyColors();
        foreach (string color in mc)
            Console.WriteLine(color);
    }
}
```

This code produces the following output:

```
Red
Yellow
Blue
```

The Noninterface Enumerator

You've just seen how to use the IEnumerable and IEnumerator interfaces to create useful enumerables and enumerators. But there are several drawbacks to this method.

First, remember that the object returned by Current is of type object. For value types, this means that before they are returned by Current, they must be boxed to turn them into objects. They must then be unboxed again after they have been received from Current. This can exact a substantial performance penalty if it needs to be done on large amounts of data.

Another drawback of the nongeneric interface method is that you've lost type safety. The values being enumerated are being handled as objects and so can be of any type. This eliminates the safety of compile-time type checking.

You can solve these problems by making the following changes to the enumerator/enumerable class declarations.

- For the enumerator class

  — Do *not* derive the class from IEnumerator.

  — Implement MoveNext just as before.

  — Implement Current just as before but have as its return type the type of the items being enumerated.

  — You do not have to implement Reset.

- For the enumerable class

  — Do not derive the class from IEnumerable.

  — Implement GetEnumerator as before, but have its return type be the type of the enumerator class.

Figure 20-5 shows the differences. The nongeneric interface code is on the left, and the noninterface code is on the right. With these changes, the foreach statement will be perfectly happy to process your collection, but without the drawbacks just listed.

```
class SibEnumerator : IEnumerator        class SibEnumerator
{                                        {
   ...                                      ...
   public object Current                    public string Current
      { get { ... } }                          { get { ... } }

   public bool MoveNext()                   public bool MoveNext()
   { ... }                                  { ... }

   public void Reset()
   { ... }
}                                        }

class Siblings : IEnumerable             class Siblings
{                                        {
   ...                                      ...
   public IEnumerator GetEnumerator()       public SibEnumerator GetEnumerator()
   { ... }                                  { ... }
}                                        }
```

Figure 20-5. *Comparing interface-based and non-interface-based enumerators*

One possible problem with the noninterface enumerator implementation is that types from other assemblies might expect enumeration to be implemented using the interface method. If these objects attempt to get an enumeration of your class objects using the interface conventions, they won't be able to find them.

To solve this problem, you can implement both forms in the same classes. That is, you can create implementations for Current, MoveNext, Reset, and GetEnumerator at the class level and also create *explicit* interface implementations for them. With both sets of implementations, the type-safe, more efficient implementation will be called by foreach and other constructs that can use the noninterface implementations, while the other constructs will call the explicit interface implementations. An even better way, however, is to use the generic forms, which I describe next.

The Generic Enumeration Interfaces

The third form of enumerator uses the generic interfaces IEnumerable<T> and IEnumerator<T>. They are called generic because they use C# generics. Using them is very similar to using the nongeneric forms. Essentially, the differences between the two are the following:

- With the nongeneric interface form

    — The GetEnumerator method of interface IEnumerable returns an enumerator class instance that implements IEnumerator.

    — The class implementing IEnumerator implements property Current, which returns a reference of type object, which you must then cast to the actual type of the object.

- With the generic interface form

    — The GetEnumerator method of interface IEnumerable<T> returns an instance of a class that implements IEnumerator<T>.

    — The class implementing IEnumerator<T> implements property Current, which returns an instance of the actual type, rather than a reference to the base class object.

The most important point to notice, though, is that the nongeneric interface implementations are not type-safe. They return references to type object, which must then be cast to the actual types. With the *generic interfaces*, however, the enumerator is type-safe, returning references to the actual types. Of the three forms of enumerations, this is the one you should implement and use. The others are for legacy code developed before C# 2.0 when generics were introduced.

The IEnumerator<T> Interface

The IEnumerator<T> interface uses generics to return an actual derived type, rather than a reference to an object.

The IEnumerator<T> interface derives from two other interfaces: the nongeneric IEnumerator interface and the IDisposable interface. It must therefore implement their members.

- You've already seen the nongeneric IEnumerator interface and its three members.

- The IDisposable interface has a single, void, parameterless method called Dispose, which can be used to free unmanaged resources being held by the class. (The Dispose method was described in Chapter 6.)

- The IEnumerator<T> interface itself has a single property, Current, which returns an instance of type T or derived from T—rather than a reference of type object.

- Since both IEnumerator<T> and IEnumerator have a member named Current, you should explicitly implement the IEnumerator version and implement the generic version in the class itself, as shown in Figure 20-6.

Figure 20-6 illustrates the implementation of the interface.

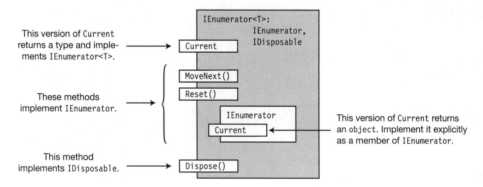

Figure 20-6. *Implementing the IEnumerator<T> interface*

The declaration of the class implementing the interface should look something like the pattern in the following code, where T is the type returned by the enumerator:

```
using System.Collections;
using System.Collections.Generic;

class MyGenEnumerator: IEnumerator< T >
{
   public T Current  { get {…} }                // IEnumerator<T>--Current
                          Explicit implementation
                                   ↓
   object IEnumerator.Current { get { ... } }    // IEnumerator--Current

   public bool MoveNext() { ... }                // IEnumerator--MoveNext

   public void Reset()    { ... }                // IEnumerator--Reset

   public void Dispose() { ... }                 // IDisposable--Dispose
      ...
}
```

For example, the following code implements the ColorEnumerator example using the generic enumerator interface:

```csharp
using System.Collections;
using System.Collections.Generic;     Substitute type string for T
                                                  ↓
class ColorEnumerator : IEnumerator<string>
{
    string[] Colors;
    int Position = -1;
        Returns the type argument type
              ↓
    public string Current                       // Current--generic
    {
        get { return Colors[Position]; }
    }
                 Explicit implementation
                        ↓
    object IEnumerator.Current                   // Current--nongeneric
    {
        get { return Colors[Position]; }
    }

    public bool MoveNext()                       // MoveNext
    {
        if (Position < Colors.Length - 1)
        {
            Position++;
            return true;
        }
        else
            return false;
    }

    public void Reset()                          // Reset
    { Position = -1; }

    public void Dispose() { }

    public ColorEnumerator(string[] colors)      // Constructor
    {
        Colors = new string[colors.Length];

        for (int i = 0; i < colors.Length; i++)
            Colors[i] = colors[i];
    }
}
```

The IEnumerable<T> Interface

The generic IEnumerable<T> interface is very similar to the nongeneric version, IEnumerable. The generic version derives from IEnumerable, so it must also implement the IEnumerable interface.

- Like IEnumerable, the generic version also contains a single member, a method called GetEnumerator. This version of GetEnumerator, however, returns a class object implementing the generic IEnumerator<T> interface.

- Since the class must implement two GetEnumerator methods, you should explicitly implement the nongeneric version and implement the generic version at the class level, as shown in Figure 20-7.

Figure 20-7 illustrates the implementation of the interface.

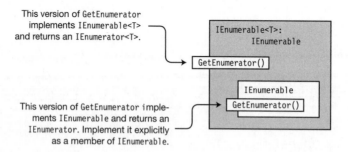

Figure 20-7. *Implementing the IEnumerable<T> interface*

The following code shows a pattern for implementing the generic interface. T is the type returned by the enumerator.

```
using System.Collections;
using System.Collections.Generic;

class MyGenEnumerable: IEnumerable<T>
{
    public IEnumerator<T> GetEnumerator() { ... }      // IEnumerable<T> version
                        Explicit implementation
                       ─────────────────────
                                ↓
    IEnumerator IEnumerable.GetEnumerator() { ... }    // IEnumerable version
        ...
}
```

The following code shows the use of the generic enumerable interface:

```
using System.Collections;
using System.Collections.Generic;
                        Substitute actual type for T
                                ↓
class MyColors : IEnumerable<string>
{
    string[] Colors = { "Red", "Yellow", "Blue" };
                    Substitute actual type for T
                            ↓
    public IEnumerator<string> GetEnumerator()       // IEnumerable<T> version
    {
        return new ColorEnumerator(Colors);
    }
                        Explicit implementation
                       ──────────────────────
                                ↓
    IEnumerator IEnumerable.GetEnumerator()          // IEnumerable version
    {
        return new ColorEnumerator(Colors);
    }
}
```

Iterators

Enumerable classes and enumerators are used extensively in the .NET collection classes, so it's important that you know how they work. But now that you know how to create your own enumerable classes and enumerators, you might be pleased to learn that, starting with C# 2.0, the language got a much simpler way of creating enumerators and enumerables. In fact, the compiler will create them for you. The construct that produces them is called an *iterator*. You can use the enumerators and enumerables generated by iterators wherever you would use manually coded enumerators or enumerables.

Before I explain the details, let's take a look at two examples. The following method declaration implements an iterator that produces and returns an enumerator.

- The iterator returns a generic enumerator that returns three items of type string.

- The yield return statements declare that *this is the next item in the enumeration.*

```
        Return a generic enumerator.
                 ↓
public IEnumerator<string> BlackAndWhite()              // Version 1
{
   yield return "black";                                // yield return
   yield return "gray";                                 // yield return
   yield return "white";                                // yield return
}
```

The following method declaration is another version that produces the same result:

```
        Return a generic enumerator.
                 ↓
public IEnumerator<string> BlackAndWhite()              // Version 2
{
   string[] theColors = { "black", "gray", "white" };

   for (int i = 0; i < theColors.Length; i++)
      yield return theColors[i];                        // yield return
}
```

I haven't explained the yield return statement yet, but on inspecting these code segments, you might have the feeling that something is different about this code. It doesn't seem quite right. What exactly does the yield return statement do?

For example, in the first version, if the method returns on the first yield return statement, then the last two statements can never be reached. If it doesn't return on the first statement but continues through to the end of the method, then what happens to the values? And in the second version, if the yield return statement in the body of the loop returns on the first iteration, then the loop will *never* get to any subsequent iterations.

And besides all that, an enumerator doesn't just return all the elements in one shot—it returns a new value with each access of the Current property. So, how does this give you an enumerator? Clearly this code is different from anything shown before.

Iterator Blocks

An *iterator block* is a code block with one or more `yield` statements. Any of the following three types of code blocks can be iterator blocks:

- A method body

- An accessor body

- An operator body

    Iterator blocks are treated differently than other blocks. Other blocks contain sequences of statements that are treated *imperatively*. That is, the first statement in the block is executed, followed by the subsequent statements, and eventually control leaves the block.

    An iterator block, on the other hand, is not a sequence of imperative commands to be executed at one time. Instead, it's declarative; it describes the behavior of the enumerator class you want the compiler to build for you. The code in the iterator block describes how to enumerate the elements.

    Iterator blocks have two special statements:

- The `yield return` statement specifies the next item in the sequence to return.

- The `yield break` statement specifies that there are no more items in the sequence.

    The compiler takes this description of how to enumerate the items and uses it to build an enumerator class, including all the required method and property implementations. The resulting class is nested inside the class where the iterator is declared.

    You can have the iterator produce either an enumerator or an enumerable depending on the return type you use for the iterator block, as shown in Figure 20-8.

```
public IEnumerator<string> IteratorMethod()          public IEnumerable<string> IteratorMethod()
{                                                    {
    ...                                                  ...
    yield return ...;                                    yield return ...;
}                                                    }
```
      An iterator that produces an enumerator   An iterator that produces an enumerable

Figure 20-8. *You can have an iterator block produce either an enumerator or an enumerable depending on the return type you specify.*

Using an Iterator to Create an Enumerator

The following code illustrates how to use an iterator to create an enumerable class.

- MyClass uses iterator method BlackAndWhite to produce an enumerator for the class.

- MyClass also implements method GetEnumerator, which in turn calls BlackAndWhite, and returns the enumerator that BlackAndWhite returns to it.

- Notice that in Main, you can use an instance of the class directly in the foreach statement since the class is enumerable.

```csharp
class MyClass
{
   public IEnumerator<string> GetEnumerator()
   {
      return BlackAndWhite();                        // Returns the enumerator.
   }
            Returns an enumerator
                    ↓
   public IEnumerator<string> BlackAndWhite()  // Iterator
   {
      yield return "black";
      yield return "gray";
      yield return "white";
   }
}

class Program
{
   static void Main()
   {
      MyClass mc = new MyClass();
                    Use the instance of MyClass.
                          ↓
      foreach (string shade in mc)
         Console.WriteLine(shade);
   }
}
```

This code produces the following output:

```
black
gray
white
```

Figure 20-9 shows the code for MyClass on the left and the resulting objects on the right. Notice how much is built for you automatically by the compiler.

- The iterator's code is shown on the left side of the figure and shows that its return type is IEnumerator<string>.

- On the right side of the figure, the diagram shows that the nested class implements IEnumerator<string>.

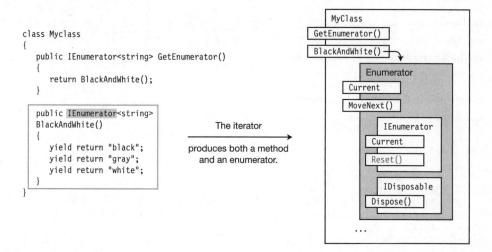

Figure 20-9. *An iterator block that produces an enumerator*

Using an Iterator to Create an Enumerable

The previous example created a class comprising two parts: the iterator that produced the enumerator and the GetEnumerator method that returned that enumerator. In this example, the iterator is used to create an *enumerable* rather than an *enumerator*. There are some important differences between this example and the last:

- In the previous example, iterator method BlackAndWhite returned an IEnumerator<string>, and MyClass implemented method GetEnumerator by returning the object created by BlackAndWhite.

- In this example, the iterator method BlackAndWhite returns an IEnumerable<string> rather than an IEnumerator<string>. MyClass, therefore, implements its GetEnumerator method by first calling method BlackAndWhite to get the enumerable object and then calling that object's GetEnumerator method and returning its results.

- Notice that in the foreach statement in Main, you can either use an instance of the class or call BlackAndWhite directly, since it returns an enumerable. Both ways are shown.

```
class MyClass
{
    public IEnumerator<string> GetEnumerator()
    {
        IEnumerable<string> myEnumerable = BlackAndWhite(); // Get enumerable
        return myEnumerable.GetEnumerator();                // Get enumerator
    }            Returns an enumerable
                            ↓
    public IEnumerable<string> BlackAndWhite()
    {
        yield return "black";
        yield return "gray";
        yield return "white";
    }
}

class Program
{
    static void Main()
    {
        MyClass mc = new MyClass();
                        Use the class object.
                               ↓
        foreach (string shade in mc)
            Console.Write("{0}  ", shade);
                               Use the class iterator method.
                                        ↓
        foreach (string shade in mc.BlackAndWhite())
            Console.Write("{0}  ", shade);
    }
}
```

This code produces the following output:

```
black   gray   white   black   gray   white
```

Figure 20-10 illustrates the generic enumerable produced by the enumerable iterator in the code.

- The iterator's code is shown on the left side of the figure and shows that its return type is IEnumerable<string>.

- On the right side of the figure, the diagram shows that the nested class implements both IEnumerator<string> and IEnumerable<string>.

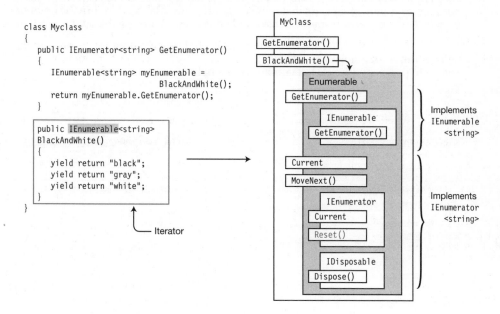

Figure 20-10. *The compiler produces a class that is both an enumerable and an enumerator. It also produces the method, BlackAndWhite, that returns the Enumerable object.*

Common Iterator Patterns

The previous two sections showed that you can create an iterator to return either an *enumerable* or an *enumerator*. Figure 20-11 summarizes how to use the common iterator patterns.

- When you implement an iterator that returns an enumerator, you must make the *class* enumerable by implementing GetEnumerator so that it returns the enumerator returned by the iterator. This is shown on the left of the figure.

- In a class, when you implement an iterator that returns an enumerable, you can either make this class itself enumerable or not by either making it implement GetEnumerator or not.

  — If you implement GetEnumerator, make it call the iterator method to get an instance of the automatically generated class that implements IEnumerable. Next, return the enumerator built by GetEnumerator from this IEnumerable object, as shown on the right of the figure.

  — If you don't make the class itself enumerable by not implementing GetEnumerator, you can still use the enumerable returned by the iterator, by calling the iterator method directly, as shown in the second foreach statement on the right.

```
class MyClass
{
    public IEnumerator<string> GetEnumerator()
    {
        return IteratorMethod();
    }


    public IEnumerator<string> IteratorMethod()
    {
        ...
        yield return ...;
    }
}
    ...

Main
{
    MyClass mc = new MyClass();

    foreach( string x in mc )
        ...
```

```
class MyClass
{
    public IEnumerator<string> GetEnumerator()
    {
        return IteratorMethod().GetEnumerator();
    }


    public IEnumerable<string> IteratorMethod()
    {
        ...
        yield return ...;
    }
}
    ...

Main
{
    MyClass mc = new MyClass();

    foreach( string x in mc )
        ...

    foreach( string x in mc.IteratorMethod() )
        ...
```

The enumerator iterator pattern   The enumerable iterator pattern

Figure 20-11. *The common iterator patterns*

Producing Enumerables and Enumerators

The previous examples used iterators that returned either an IEnumerator<T> or an IEnumerable<T>. You can also create iterators that return the nongeneric versions as well. The return types you can specify are the following:

- IEnumerator<T> (generic—substitute an actual type for T)

- IEnumerable<T> (generic—substitute an actual type for T)

- IEnumerator (nongeneric)

- IEnumerable (nongeneric)

For the two enumerator types, the compiler generates a nested class that contains the implementation of either the nongeneric or the generic enumerator, with the behavior specified by the iterator block.

For the two enumerable types, it does even more. It produces a nested class that is both enumerable and the enumerator. The class, therefore, implements both the enumerator interface and the GetEnumerator method. Notice that GetEnumerator is implemented as part of the *nested* class—*not* as part of the *enclosing* class.

Producing Multiple Enumerables

In the following example, class ColorCollection has two enumerable iterators—one enumerating the items in forward order and the other enumerating them in reverse order. Notice that although it has two methods that return enumerables, the class itself is not enumerable since it doesn't implement GetEnumerator.

```csharp
using System;
using System.Collections.Generic;                    // You need this namespace.

namespace ColorCollectionIterator
{
   class ColorCollection
   {
      string[] Colors={"Red", "Orange", "Yellow", "Green", "Blue", "Purple"};

      public IEnumerable<string> Forward() {          // Enumerable iterator
         for (int i = 0; i < Colors.Length; i++)
            yield return Colors[i];
      }

      public IEnumerable<string> Reverse() {          // Enumerable iterator
         for (int i = Colors.Length - 1; i >= 0; i--)
            yield return Colors[i];
      }
   }
```

```
class Program
{
    static void Main()
    {
        ColorCollection cc = new ColorCollection();
                        Return enumerable to the foreach statement
                                       ↓
        foreach (string color in cc.Forward())
            Console.Write("{0} ", color);
        Console.WriteLine();

          Return enumerable to the foreach statement
                           ↓
        foreach (string color in cc.Reverse())
            Console.Write("{0} ", color);
        Console.WriteLine();

        // Skip the foreach and manually use the enumerable and enumerator.
        IEnumerable<string> ieable = cc.Reverse();
        IEnumerator<string> ieator = ieable.GetEnumerator();

        while (ieator.MoveNext())
            Console.Write("{0} ", ieator.Current);
        Console.WriteLine();
    }
}
}
```

This code produces the following output:

```
Red Orange Yellow Green Blue Purple
Purple Blue Green Yellow Orange Red
Purple Blue Green Yellow Orange Red
```

Producing Multiple Enumerators

The previous example used iterators to produce a class with two enumerables. This example shows two things. First, it uses iterators to produce a class with two enumerators. Second, it shows how iterators can be implemented as *properties* rather than methods.

The code declares two properties that define two different enumerators. The GetEnumerator method returns one or the other of the two enumerators, depending on the value of the Boolean variable ColorFlag. If ColorFlag is true, the Colors enumerator is returned. Otherwise, the BlackAndWhite enumerator is returned.

```csharp
class MyClass: IEnumerable<string>
{
   bool ColorFlag = true;

   public MyClass(bool flag)              // Constructor
   {
      ColorFlag = flag;
   }

   IEnumerator<string> BlackAndWhite      // Property--enumerator iterator
   {
      get
      {
         yield return "black";
         yield return "gray";
         yield return "white";
      }
   }

   IEnumerator<string> Colors             // Property--enumerator iterator
   {
      get
      {
         string[] theColors = { "blue", "red", "yellow" };
         for (int i = 0; i < theColors.Length; i++)
            yield return theColors[i];
      }
   }
```

```
    public IEnumerator<string> GetEnumerator()  // GetEnumerator
    {
        return ColorFlag
                ? Colors                        // Return Colors enumerator
                : BlackAndWhite;                // Return BlackAndWhite enumerator
    }

    System.Collections.IEnumerator
    System.Collections.IEnumerable.GetEnumerator()
    {
        return ColorFlag
                ? Colors                        // Return Colors enumerator
                : BlackAndWhite;                // Return BlackAndWhite enumerator
    }
}

class Program
{
    static void Main()
    {
        MyClass mc1 = new MyClass( true );      // Call constructor with true
        foreach (string s in mc1)
            Console.Write("{0}  ", s);
        Console.WriteLine();

        MyClass mc2 = new MyClass( false );     // Call constructor with false
        foreach (string s in mc2)
            Console.Write("{0}  ", s);
        Console.WriteLine();
    }
}
```

This code produces the following output:

```
blue   red   yellow
black  gray  white
```

Behind the Scenes with Iterators

The following are some other important things to know about iterators:

- Iterators require the System.Collections.Generic namespace, so you should include it with a using directive.

- In the compiler-generated enumerators, the Reset method is not supported. It is implemented, since it is required by the interface, but the implementation throws a System.NotSupportedException exception if it is called. Notice that the Reset method is shown grayed out in Figure 20-9.

Behind the scenes, the enumerator class generated by the compiler is a state machine with four states:

Before: The initial state before the first call to MoveNext.

Running: The state entered when MoveNext is called. While in this state, the enumerator determines and sets the position for the next item. It exits the state when it encounters a yield return, a yield break, or the end of the iterator body.

Suspended: The state where the state machine is waiting for the next call to MoveNext.

After: The state where there are no more items to enumerate.

If the state machine is in either the *before or suspended states* and there is a call to the MoveNext method, it goes into the running state. In the *running* state, it determines the next item in the collection and sets the position.

If there are more items, the state machine goes into the *suspended* state. If there are no more items, it goes into the *after* state, where it remains. Figure 20-12 shows the state machine.

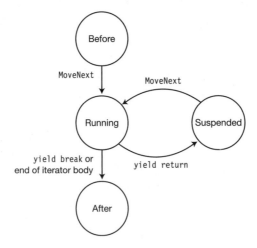

Figure 20-12. *An iterator state machine*

CHAPTER 21

Introduction to LINQ

What Is LINQ?

In a relational database system, data is organized into nicely normalized tables and accessed with a very simple but powerful query language—SQL. SQL can work with any set of data in a database because the data is organized into tables, following strict rules.

In a program, as opposed to a database, however, data is stored in class objects or structs that are all vastly different. As a result, there's been no general query language for retrieving data from data structures. The method of retrieving data from objects has always been custom-designed as part of the program. LINQ, however, makes it easy to query collections of objects.

The following are the important high-level characteristics of LINQ:

- LINQ stands for *Language Integrated Query* and is pronounced *link*.

- LINQ is an extension of the .NET Framework that allows you to query collections of data in a manner similar to using SQL to query databases.

- With LINQ you can query data from databases, collections of program objects, XML documents, and more.

The following code shows a simple example of using LINQ. In this code, the data source being queried is simply an array of ints. The definition of the query is the statement with the from and select keywords. Although the query is *defined* in this statement, it is actually performed and used in the foreach statement at the bottom.

```
static void Main()
{
   int[] numbers = { 2, 12, 5, 15 };          // Data source

   IEnumerable<int> lowNums =                  // Define and store the query.
                   from n in numbers
                   where n < 10
                   select n;

   foreach (var x in lowNums)                  // Execute the query.
       Console.Write("{0}, ", x);
}
```

This code produces the following output:

```
2, 5,
```

LINQ Providers

In the previous example, the data source was simply an array of ints, which is an in-memory object of the program. LINQ, however, can work with many different types of data sources, such as SQL databases, XML documents, and a host of others. For every data source type, however, under the covers there must be a module of code that implements the LINQ queries in terms of that data source type. These code modules are called *LINQ providers*. The important points about LINQ providers are the following:

- Microsoft provides LINQ providers for a number of common data source types, as shown in Figure 21-1.

- You can use any LINQ-enabled language (C# in our case) to query any data source type for which there is a LINQ provider.

- New LINQ providers are constantly being produced by third parties for all sorts of data source types.

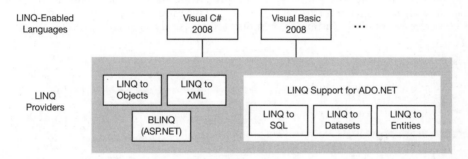

Figure 21-1. *The architecture of LINQ, the LINQ-enabled languages, and LINQ providers*

There are entire books dedicated to LINQ in all its forms and subtleties, but that's clearly beyond the scope of this chapter. Instead, this chapter will introduce you to LINQ and explain how to use it with program objects (LINQ to Objects) and XML (LINQ to XML).

Anonymous Types

Before getting into the details of LINQ's querying features, I'll start by covering a language feature that allows you to create unnamed class types. These are called, not surprisingly, *anonymous types*.

In Chapter 6 we covered *object initializers*, which is the construct that allows you to initialize the fields and properties of a new class instance when using an object-creation expression. Just to remind you, this kind of object-creation expression consists of three components: the keyword new, the class name or constructor, and the object initializer. The object initializer consists of a comma-separated list of member initializers between a set of curly braces.

Creating a variable of an anonymous type uses the same form—but without the class name or constructor. The following line of code shows the object-creation expression form of an anonymous type:

```
                         Object initializer
                              ↓
new { FieldProp = InitExpr, FieldProp = InitExpr, ...}
                      ↑                      ↑
              Member initializer      Member initializer
```

The following code shows an example of creating and using an anonymous type. It creates a variable called student, with an anonymous type that has three string properties and one int property. Notice in the WriteLine statement that the instance's members are accessed just as if they were members of a named type.

```
static void Main( )
{
    var student = new {LName="Jones", FName="Mary", Age=19, Major="History"};
      ↑                                            ↑
  Must use var                              Object initializer
    Console.WriteLine("{0} {1}, Age {2}, Major: {3}",
          student.FName, student.LName, student.Age, student.Major);
}
```

This code produces the following output:

```
Mary Jones, Age 19, Major: History
```

Important things to know about anonymous types are the following:

- Anonymous types can be used only with local variables—not with class members.

- Since an anonymous type doesn't have a name, you must use the var keyword as the variable type.

When the compiler encounters the object initializer of an anonymous type, it creates a new class type with a private name that it constructs. For each member initializer, it infers its type and creates a private variable of that type in the new class, and it creates a read/write property to access the variable. The property has the same name as the member initializer. Once the anonymous type is constructed, the compiler creates an object of that type.

Besides the assignment form of member initializers, anonymous type object initializers also allow two other forms: simple identifiers and member access expressions. These two forms are called *projection initializers*. The following variable declaration shows all three forms. The first member initializer is in the assignment form. The second is an identifier, and the third is a member access expression.

```
var student = new { Age = 19, Major, Other.Name };
```

For example, the following code uses all three types. Notice that the projection initializers must be defined before the declaration of the anonymous type. Major is a local variable, and Name is a static field of class Other.

```
class Other
{
    static public string Name = "Mary Jones";
}

class Program
{
    static void Main()
    {
        string Major = "History";
                        Assignment form        Identifier
                             ↓                     ↓
        var student = new { Age = 19, Other.Name, Major};
                                         ↑
                              Member access
        Console.WriteLine("{0}, Age {1}, Major: {2}",
                    student.Name, student.Age, student.Major);
    }
}
```

This code produces the following output:

```
Mary Jones, Age 19, Major: History
```

The projection initializer form of the object initializer just shown has exactly the same result as the assignment form shown here:

```
var student = new { Age = Age, Name = Other.Name, Major = Major};
```

Although your code cannot see the anonymous type, it's visible to object browsers. If the compiler encounters another anonymous type with the same parameter names, with the same inferred types, and in the same order, it will reuse the type and create a new instance—not create a new anonymous type.

Query Syntax and Method Syntax

There are two syntactic forms you can use when writing LINQ queries—query syntax and method syntax.

- *Query syntax* is a *declarative form* that looks very much like an SQL statement. Query syntax is written in the form of *query expressions*.

- *Method syntax* is an *imperative form*, which uses standard method invocations. The methods are from a set called the *standard query operators*, which will be described later in the chapter.

- You can also combine both forms in a single query.

   Microsoft recommends using query syntax because it's more readable, more clearly states your query intentions, and is therefore less error-prone. There are some operators, however, that can be written only using method syntax.

■ **Note** Queries expressed using query syntax are translated by the C# compiler into method invocation form. There is no difference in runtime performance between the two forms.

The following code shows all three query forms. In the method syntax part, you might find that the parameter of the Where method looks a bit odd. It's a lambda expression, as was described in Chapter 15. I'll cover its use in LINQ a bit later in the chapter.

```
static void Main( )
{
   int[] numbers = { 2, 5, 28, 31, 17, 16, 42 };

   var numsQuery = from n in numbers                  // Query syntax
                   where n < 20
                   select n;

   var numsMethod = numbers.Where(x => x < 20);       // Method syntax

   int numsCount = (from n in numbers                 // Combined
                    where n < 20
                    select n).Count();

   foreach (var x in numsQuery)
      Console.Write("{0}, ", x);
   Console.WriteLine();

   foreach (var x in numsMethod)
      Console.Write("{0}, ", x);
   Console.WriteLine();

   Console.WriteLine(numsCount);
}
```

This code produces the following output:

```
2, 5, 17, 16,
2, 5, 17, 16,
4
```

Query Variables

LINQ queries can return two types of results: an *enumeration*, which lists the items that satisfy the query parameters; or a single value, called a *scalar*, which is some form of summary of the results that satisfied the query.

In the following example code, the following happens:

- The first statement creates an array of ints and initializes it with three values.

- The second statement returns an IEnumerable object, which can be used to enumerate the results of the query.

- The third statement executes a query and then calls a method (Count) that returns the count of the items returned from the query. We'll cover operators that return scalars, such as Count, later in the chapter.

```
int[] numbers = { 2, 5, 28 };

IEnumerable<int> lowNums = from n in numbers        // Returns an enumerator
                          where n < 20
                          select n;

int numsCount          = (from n in numbers        // Returns an int
                          where n < 20
                          select n).Count();
```

The variable on the left of the equals sign is called the *query variable*. Although the types of the query variables are given explicitly in the example statements, you could also have had the compiler infer the types of the query variables by using the var keyword in place of the type names.

It's important to understand the contents of query variables. After executing the preceding code, query variable lowNums does *not* contain the results of the query. Instead, it contains an object of type IEnumerable<int>, which can perform the query if it's called upon to do so later in the code. Query variable numsCount, however, contains an actual integer value, which can have been obtained only by actually running the query.

The differences in the timing of the execution of the queries can be summarized as follows:

- If a query expression returns an enumeration, the query is not executed until the enumeration is processed.

  — If the enumeration is processed multiple times, the query is executed multiple times.

  — If the data changes between the time the enumeration is produced and the time the query is executed, the query is run on the new data.

- If the query expression returns a scalar, the query is executed immediately, and the result is stored in the query variable.

Figure 21-2 illustrates this for the enumerable query. Variable lowNums contains a reference to the enumerable that can enumerate the query results from the array.

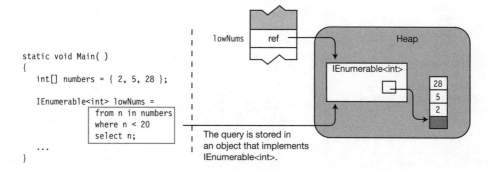

Figure 21-2. *The compiler creates an object that implements IEnumerable<int> and stores the query in the object.*

The Structure of Query Expressions

A query expression consists of a `from` clause followed by a query body, as illustrated in Figure 21-3. Some of the important things to know about query expressions are the following:

- The clauses must appear in the order shown.

  — The two parts that are required are the `from` clause and the `select...group` clause.

  — The other clauses are optional.

- In a LINQ query expression, the `select` clause is at the end of the expression. This is different than SQL, where the `SELECT` statement is at the beginning of a query. One of the reasons for using this position in C# is that it allows Visual Studio's IntelliSense to give you more options while you're entering code.

- There can be any number of `from...let...where` clauses, as illustrated in the figure.

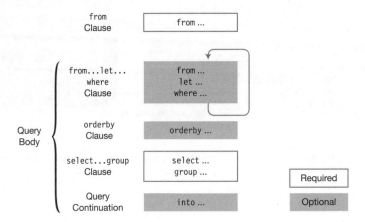

Figure 21-3. *The structure of a query statement consists of a from clause followed by a query body.*

The from Clause

The from clause specifies the data collection that is to be used as the data source. It also introduces the iteration variable. The important points about the from clause are the following:

- The *iteration variable* sequentially represents each element in the data source.

- The syntax of the from clause is shown following, where

  — *Type* is the type of the elements in the collection. This is optional, because the compiler can infer the type from the collection.

  — *Item* is the name of the *iteration variable*.

  — *Items* is the name of the collection to be queried. The collection must be enumerable, as described in Chapter 13.

```
Iteration variable declaration
            ↓
from Type Item in Items
```

The following code shows a query expression used to query an array of four ints. Iteration variable item will represent each of the four elements in the array and will be either selected or rejected by the where and select clauses following it. This code leaves out the optional type (int) of the iteration variable.

```
int[] arr1 = {10, 11, 12, 13};
              Iteration variable
                     ↓
var query = from item in arr1
            where item < 13      ← Uses the iteration variable
            select item;         ← Uses the iteration variable

foreach( var item in query )
   Console.Write("{0}, ", item );
```

This code produces the following output:

```
10, 11, 12,
```

Figure 21-4 shows the syntax of the from clause. The type specifier is optional, since it can be inferred by the compiler. There can be any number of optional join clauses.

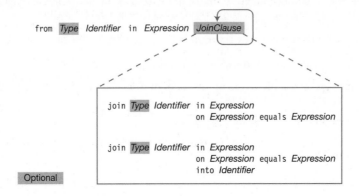

Figure 21-4. *The syntax of the from clause*

Although there is a strong similarity between the LINQ from clause and the foreach statement, there are several major differences:

- The foreach statement executes its body at the point in the code where it is encountered. The from clause, on the other hand, does not execute anything. It creates an enumerable object that's stored in the query variable. The query itself might or might not be executed later in the code.

- The foreach statement imperatively specifies that the items in the collection are to be considered in order, from the first to the last. The from clause declaratively states that each item in the collection must be considered but does not assume an order.

The join Clause

The join clause in LINQ is much like the JOIN clause in SQL. If you're familiar with joins from SQL, then joins in LINQ will be nothing new for you conceptually, except for the fact that you can now perform them on collections of objects as well as database tables. If you're new to joins or need a refresher, then the next section should help clear things up for you.

The first important things to know about a join are the following:

- A join operation takes two collections and creates a new temporary collection of objects, where each object contains all the fields from an object from both initial collections.

- Use a join to combine data from two or more collections.

The syntax for a join is shown here. It specifies that the second collection is to be joined with the collection in the previous clause.

```
Keyword         Keyword         Keyword     Keyword
   ↓               ↓               ↓           ↓
join Identifier in Collection2 on Field1 equals Field2
                     ↑                    ↑
            Specify additional collection    The fields to compare
               and ID to reference it            for equality
```

Figure 21-5 illustrates the syntax for the join clause.

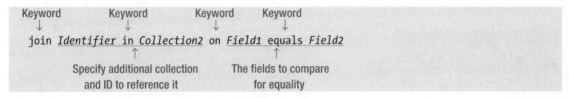

```
join Type Identifier in Expression
          on Expression equals Expression


join Type Identifier in Expression
          on Expression equals Expression
          into Identifier
```

Figure 21-5. *Syntax for the join clause*

The following annotated statement shows an example of the join clause:

```
              First collection and ID
                      ↓
                              Item from first collection   Item from second
                                        ↓                      ↓
var query = from s in students
            join c in studentsInCourses on s.StID equals c.StID
                    ↑                              ↑
            Second collection and ID        Fields to compare
```

What Is a Join?

A join in LINQ takes two collections and creates a new collection where each element has members from the elements of the two original collections.

For example, the following code declares two classes: Student and CourseStudent.

- Objects of type Student contain a student's last name and student ID number.

- Objects of type CourseStudent represent a student that is enrolled in a course and contain the course name and a student ID number.

```
public class Student
{
    public int     StID;
    public string  LastName;
}

public class CourseStudent
{
    public string  CourseName;
    public int     StID;
}
```

Figure 21-6 shows the situation in a program where there are three students and three courses, and the students are enrolled in various courses. The program has an array called students, of Student objects, and an array called studentsInCourses, of CourseStudent objects, which contains one object for every student enrolled in each course.

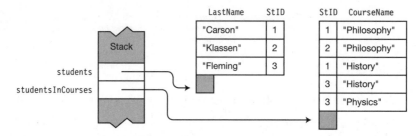

Figure 21-6. *Students enrolled in various courses*

Suppose now that you want to get the last name of every student in a particular course. The students array has the last names, and the studentsInCourses array has the course enrollment information. To get the information, you must combine the information in the arrays, based on the student ID field, which is common to objects of both types. You can do this with a join on the StID field.

Figure 21-7 shows how the join works. The left column shows the students array, and the right column shows the studentsInCourses array. If we take the first student record and compare its ID with the student ID in each studentsInCourses object, we find that two of them match, as shown at the top of the center column. If we then do the same with the other two students, we find that the second student is taking one course, and the third student is taking two courses.

The five grayed objects in the middle column represent the join of the two arrays on field StID. Each object contains three fields: the LastName field from the Students class, the CourseName field from the CourseStudent class, and the StID field common to both classes.

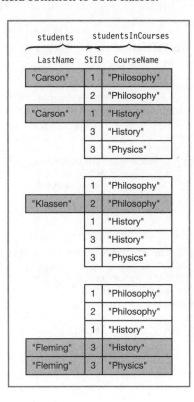
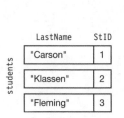
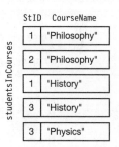

Figure 21-7. *Two arrays of objects and their join on field StId*

The following code puts the whole example together. The query finds the last names of all the students taking the history course.

```
class Program
{
    public class Student {                              // Declare classes.
        public int    StID;
        public string LastName;
    }

    public class CourseStudent {
        public string CourseName;
        public int    StID;
    }
                                                       // Initialize arrays.
    static CourseStudent[] studentsInCourses = new CourseStudent[] {
        new CourseStudent { CourseName = "Art",     StID = 1 },
        new CourseStudent { CourseName = "Art",     StID = 2 },
        new CourseStudent { CourseName = "History", StID = 1 },
        new CourseStudent { CourseName = "History", StID = 3 },
        new CourseStudent { CourseName = "Physics", StID = 3 },
    };

    static Student[] students = new Student[] {
        new Student { StID = 1, LastName = "Carson"  },
        new Student { StID = 2, LastName = "Klassen" },
        new Student { StID = 3, LastName = "Fleming" },
    };

    static void Main( )
    {
        // Find the last names of the students taking history.
        var query = from s in students
                    join c in studentsInCourses on s.StID equals c.StID
                    where c.CourseName == "History"
                    select s.LastName;

        // Display the names of the students taking history.
        foreach (var q in query)
            Console.WriteLine("Student taking History:  {0}", q);
    }
}
```

This code produces the following output:

```
Student taking History:  Carson
Student taking History:  Fleming
```

The from . . . let . . . where Section in the Query Body

The optional from...let...where section is the first section of the query body. It can have any number of any of the three clauses that comprise it—the from clause, the let clause, and the where clause. Figure 21-8 summarizes the syntax of the three clauses.

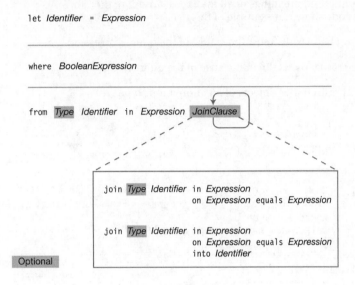

Figure 21-8. *The syntax of the from . . . let . . . where clause*

The from Clause

You saw that a query expression starts with a required from clause, which is followed by the query body. The body itself can start with any number of additional from clauses, where each subsequent from clause specifies an additional source data collection and introduces a new iteration variable for use in further evaluations. The syntax and meanings of all the from clauses are the same.

The following code shows an example of this use.

- The first from clause is the required clause of the query expression.

- The second from clause is the first clause of the query body.

- The select clause creates objects of an anonymous type.

```
static void Main()
{
    var groupA = new[] { 3, 4, 5, 6 };
    var groupB = new[] { 6, 7, 8, 9 };

    var someInts = from a in groupA              ← Required first from clause
                   from b in groupB              ← First clause of query body
                   where a > 4 && b <= 8
                   select new {a, b, sum = a + b};  ← Object of anonymous type

    foreach (var a in someInts)
        Console.WriteLine(a);
}
```

This code produces the following output:

```
{ a = 5, b = 6, sum = 11 }
{ a = 5, b = 7, sum = 12 }
{ a = 5, b = 8, sum = 13 }
{ a = 6, b = 6, sum = 12 }
{ a = 6, b = 7, sum = 13 }
{ a = 6, b = 8, sum = 14 }
```

The let Clause

The let clause takes the evaluation of an expression and assigns it to an identifier to be used in other evaluations. The syntax of the let clause is the following:

```
let Identifier = Expression
```

For example, the query expression in the following code pairs each member of array groupA with each element of array groupB. The where clause eliminates each set of integers from the two arrays where the sum of the two is not equal to 12.

```
static void Main()
{
    var groupA = new[] { 3, 4, 5, 6 };
    var groupB = new[] { 6, 7, 8, 9 };

    var someInts = from a in groupA
                   from b in groupB
                   let sum = a + b          ← Store result in new variable
                   where sum == 12
                   select new {a, b, sum};

    foreach (var a in someInts)
        Console.WriteLine(a);
}
```

This code produces the following output:

```
{ a = 3, b = 9, sum = 12 }
{ a = 4, b = 8, sum = 12 }
{ a = 5, b = 7, sum = 12 }
{ a = 6, b = 6, sum = 12 }
```

The where Clause

The where clause eliminates items from further consideration if they don't meet the specified condition. The syntax of the where clause is the following:

```
where BooleanExpression
```

Important things to know about the where clause are the following:

- A query expression can have any number of where clauses, as long as they are in the from...let...where section.

- An item must satisfy all the where clauses to avoid elimination from further consideration.

The following code shows an example of a query expression that contains two where clauses. The where clauses eliminate each set of integers from the two arrays where the sum of the two is not greater than or equal to 11, and the element from groupA is not the value 4. Each set of elements selected must satisfy the conditions of *both* where clauses.

```
static void Main()
{
   var groupA = new[] { 3, 4, 5, 6 };
   var groupB = new[] { 6, 7, 8, 9 };

   var someInts = from int a in groupA
                  from int b in groupB
                  let sum = a + b
                  where sum >= 11          ← Condition 1
                  where a == 4             ← Condition 2
                  select new {a, b, sum};

   foreach (var a in someInts)
      Console.WriteLine(a);
}
```

This code produces the following output:

```
{ a = 4, b = 7, sum = 11 }
{ a = 4, b = 8, sum = 12 }
{ a = 4, b = 9, sum = 13 }
```

The orderby Clause

The orderby clause takes an expression and returns the result items in order according to the expression.

Figure 21-9 shows the syntax of the orderby clause. The optional keywords ascending and descending set the direction of the order. *Expression* is generally a field of the items.

- The default ordering of an orderby clause is ascending. You can, however, explicitly set the ordering of the elements to either ascending or descending, using the ascending and descending keywords.

- There can be any number of orderby clauses, and they must be separated by commas.

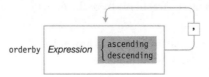

Figure 21-9. *The syntax of the orderby clause*

The following code shows an example of student records ordered by the ages of the students. Notice that the array of student information is stored in an array of anonymous types.

```
static void Main( ) {
   var students = new []        // Array of objects of an anonymous type
   {
      new { LName="Jones",   FName="Mary",   Age=19, Major="History" },
      new { LName="Smith",   FName="Bob",    Age=20, Major="CompSci" },
      new { LName="Fleming", FName="Carol",  Age=21, Major="History" }
   };

   var query = from student in students
               orderby student.Age       ← Order by Age.
               select student;

   foreach (var s in query) {
      Console.WriteLine("{0}, {1}:  {2} - {3}",
            s.LName, s.FName, s.Age, s.Major);
   }
}
```

This code produces the following output:

```
Jones, Mary:  19 - History
Smith, Bob:  20 - CompSci
Fleming, Carol:  21 - History
```

The select . . . group Clause

There are two types of clauses that make up the select...group section—the select clause and the group...by clause. While the clauses that precede the select...group section specify the data sources and which objects to choose, the select...group section does the following:

- The select clause specifies which parts of the chosen objects should be selected. It can specify any of the following:

  — The entire data item

  — A field from the data item

  — A new object comprising several fields from the data item (or any other value, for that matter).

- The group...by clause is optional and specifies how the chosen items should be grouped. We'll cover the group...by clause later in the chapter.

Figure 21-10 shows the syntax for the select...group clause.

```
select  Expression
_____

group  Expression1  by  Expression2
```

Figure 21-10. *The syntax of the select . . . group clause*

The following code shows an example of using the select clause to select the entire data item. First, the program creates an array of objects of an anonymous type. The query expression then uses the select statement to select each item in the array.

```
using System;
using System.Linq;
class Program {
    static void Main() {
        var students = new[]          // Array of objects of an anonymous type
        {
            new { LName="Jones",   FName="Mary",  Age=19, Major="History" },
            new { LName="Smith",   FName="Bob",   Age=20, Major="CompSci" },
            new { LName="Fleming", FName="Carol", Age=21, Major="History" }
        };

        var query = from s in students
                    select s;

        foreach (var q in query)
            Console.WriteLine("{0}, {1}: Age {2}, {3}",
                              q.LName, q.FName, q.Age, q.Major);
    }
}
```

This code produces the following output:

```
Jones, Mary: Age 19, History
Smith, Bob: Age 20, CompSci
Fleming, Carol: Age 21, History
```

You can also use the select clause to choose only particular fields of the object. For example, the select clause in the following code selects only the last name of the student.

```
var query = from s in students
            select s.LName;

foreach (var q in query)
    Console.WriteLine(q);
```

When you substitute these two statements for the corresponding two statements in the preceding full example, the program produces the following output:

```
Jones
Smith
Fleming
```

Anonymous Types in Queries

The result of a query can consist of items from the source collections, fields from the items in the source collections, or anonymous types.

You can create an anonymous type in a select clause by placing curly braces around a comma-separated list of fields you want to include in the type. For example, to make the code in the previous section select just the names and majors of the students, you could use the following syntax:

```
select new { s.LastName, s.FirstName, s.Major };
                          ↑
                   Anonymous type
```

The following code creates an anonymous type in the select clause and uses it later in the WriteLine statement.

```
using System;
using System.Linq;

class Program {
   static void Main()
   {
      var students = new[]        // Array of objects of an anonymous type
      {
         new { LName="Jones",   FName="Mary",  Age=19, Major="History" },
         new { LName="Smith",   FName="Bob",   Age=20, Major="CompSci" },
         new { LName="Fleming", FName="Carol", Age=21, Major="History" }
      };

      var query = from s in students
                  select new { s.LName, s.FName, s.Major };
                             ↑
                   Create anonymous type
      foreach (var q in query)
         Console.WriteLine("{0} {1} -- {2}",
                           q.FName, q.LName, q.Major );
   }                                ↑
}                        Access fields of anonymous type
```

This code produces the following output:

```
Mary Jones -- History
Bob Smith -- CompSci
Carol Fleming -- History
```

The group Clause

The group clause groups the selected objects according to some criterion. For example, with the array of students in the previous examples, the program could group the students according to their majors.

The important things to know about the group clause are the following:

- When items are included in the result of the query, they're placed in groups according to the value of a particular field. The value on which items are grouped is called the *key*.

- Unlike the select clause, the group clause *does not return an enumerable that can enumerate the items* from the original source. Instead, it returns an enumerable that enumerates the *groups of items* that have been formed.

- The groups themselves are enumerable and can enumerate the actual items.

An example of the syntax of the group clause is the following:

```
group student by student.Major;
  ↑              ↑
Keyword        Keyword
```

For example, the following code groups the students according to their majors:

```
static void Main( )
{
   var students = new[]        // Array of objects of an anonymous type
   {
      new { LName="Jones",   FName="Mary",  Age=19, Major="History" },
      new { LName="Smith",   FName="Bob",   Age=20, Major="CompSci" },
      new { LName="Fleming", FName="Carol", Age=21, Major="History" }
   };

   var query = from student in students
               group student by student.Major;

   foreach (var s in query)            // Enumerate the groups.
   {
      Console.WriteLine("{0}", s.Key);
                                ↑
                          Grouping key
      foreach (var t in s)             // Enumerate the items in the group.
         Console.WriteLine("     {0}, {1}", t.LName, t.FName);
   }
}
```

This code produces the following output:

```
History
      Jones, Mary
      Fleming, Carol
CompSci
      Smith, Bob
```

Figure 21-11 illustrates the object that is returned from the query expression and stored in the query variable.

- The object returned from the query expression is an enumerable that enumerates the groups resulting from the query.

- Each group is distinguished by a field called Key.

- Each group is itself enumerable and can enumerate its items.

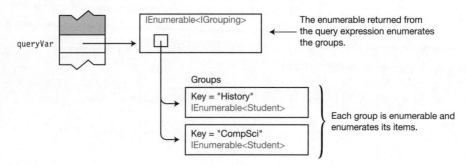

Figure 21-11. *The group clause returns a collection of collections of objects rather than a collection of objects.*

Query Continuation

A query continuation clause takes the result of one part of a query and assigns it a name so that it can be used in another part of the query. Figure 21-12 shows the syntax for query continuation.

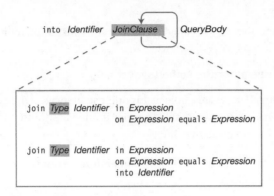

Figure 21-12. *The syntax of the query continuation clause*

For example, the following query joins groupA and groupB and names the join groupAandB. It then performs a simple select from groupAandB.

```
static void Main()
{
   var groupA = new[] { 3, 4, 5, 6 };
   var groupB = new[] { 4, 5, 6, 7 };

   var someInts = from a in groupA
                  join b in groupB on a equals b
                  into groupAandB                  ← Query continuation
                  from c in groupAandB
                  select c;

   foreach (var a in someInts)
      Console.Write("{0}  ", a);
}
```

This code produces the following output:

4   5   6

The Standard Query Operators

The standard query operators comprise a set of methods called an application programming interface (API) that lets you query any .NET array or collection. Important characteristics of the standard query operators are the following:

- The collection objects queried are called *sequences* and must implement the IEnumerable<T> interface, where T is a type.

- The standard query operators use method syntax.

- Some operators return IEnumerable objects (or other sequences), while others return scalars. Operators that return scalars execute their queries immediately and return a value instead of an enumerable object to be iterated over later.

For example, the following code shows the use of operators Sum and Count, which return ints. Notice the following about the code:

- The operators are used as methods *directly on the sequence objects*, which in this case is array numbers.

- The return type is not an IEnumerable object but an int.

```
class Program
{
    static int[] numbers = new int[] {2, 4, 6};

    static void Main( )
    {
        int total   = numbers.Sum();
        int howMany = numbers.Count();
          ↑               ↑       ↑
        Scalar          Sequence Operator
        object
        Console.WriteLine("Total: {0}, Count: {1}", total, howMany);
    }
}
```

This code produces the following output:

```
Total: 12, Count: 3
```

There are 47 standard query operators that fall into 14 different categories. These categories are shown in Table 21-1.

Table 21-1. *Categories of the Standard Query Operators*

Name	Number of Operators	Description
Restriction	1	Returns a subset of the objects of the sequence, based on selection criteria
Projection	2	Selects which parts of the objects of a sequence are finally returned
Partitioning	4	Skips or returns objects from a sequence
Join	2	Returns an IEnumerable object that joins two sequences, based on some criterion
Concatenation	1	Produces a single sequence from two separate sequences
Ordering	2	Orders a sequence based on supplied criteria
Grouping	1	Groups a sequence based on supplied criteria
Set	4	Performs set operations on a sequence
Conversion	7	Converts sequences to various forms such as arrays, lists, and dictionaries
Equality	1	Compares two sequences for equality
Element	9	Returns a particular element of a sequence
Generation	3	Generates sequences
Quantifiers	3	Returns Boolean values specifying whether a particular predicate is true about a sequence
Aggregate	7	Returns a single value representing characteristics of a sequence

Query Expressions and the Standard Query Operators

As mentioned at the beginning of the chapter, every query expression can also be written using method syntax with the standard query operators. The set of standard query operators is a set of methods for performing queries. The compiler translates every query expression into standard query operator form.

Clearly, since all query expressions are translated into the standard query operators—the operators can perform everything done by query expressions. But the operators also give additional capabilities that aren't available in query expression form. For example, operators Sum and Count, which were used in the previous example, can be expressed only using the method syntax.

The two forms, query expressions and method syntax, however, can be combined. For example, the following code shows a query expression that also uses operator Count. Notice that the query expression part of the statement is inside parentheses, which is followed by a dot and the name of the method.

```
static void Main()
{
    var numbers = new int[] { 2, 6, 4, 8, 10 };

    int howMany = (from n in numbers
                    where n < 7
                    select n).Count();
                        ↑           ↑
              Query expression    Operator

    Console.WriteLine("Count: {0}", howMany);
}
```

This code produces the following output:

Count: 3

Signatures of the Standard Query Operators

The standard query operators are methods declared in class System.Linq.Enumerable. These methods, however, aren't just any methods—they are extension methods that extend generic class IEnumerable<T>.

Extension methods were covered in Chapters 7 and 19, but the most important thing to remember about them is that they are public, static methods that, although defined in one class, are designed to add functionality to a *different* class—the one listed as the first formal parameter. This formal parameter must be preceded by the keyword this.

For example, the following are the signatures of three of the operators: Count, First, and Where. At first glance, the signatures of the operators can be somewhat intimidating. Notice the following about the signatures:

- Since the operators are generic methods, they have a generic parameter (T) associated with their names.

- Since the operators are *extension methods* that extend IEnumerable<T>, they must satisfy the following syntactic requirements:

  — They must be declared public and static.

  — They must have the this extension indicator before the first parameter.

  — They must have IEnumerable<T> as the first parameter type.

```
        Always                    Name and              First
     public, static            generic param         parameter
    ┌──────┴──────┐               ┌─┴─┐             ┌───┴───┐

    public static       int     Count<T>(  this IEnumerable<T> source );
    public static        T      First<T>(  this IEnumerable<T> source );
    public static IEnumerable<T> Where<T>( this IEnumerable<T> source, ... );
                         ↑                      ↑
                      Return                Extension
                       type                 indicator
```

For example, the following code shows the use of operators Count and First. Both operators take only a single parameter—the reference to the IEnumerable<T> object.

- The Count operator returns a single value, which is the count of all the elements in the sequence.

- The First operator returns the first element of the sequence.

The first two times the operators are used in this code, they are called directly, just like normal methods, passing the name of the array as the first parameter. In the following two lines, however, they are called using the extension method syntax, as if they were method members of the array, which is enumerable. Notice that in this case no parameter is supplied. Instead, the array name has been moved from the parameter list to before the method name. There it is used as if it contained a declaration of the method.

The direct syntax calls and the extension syntax calls are completely equivalent in effect—only their syntax is different.

```
using System.Linq;
   ...
static void Main( )
{
   int[] intArray = new int[] { 3, 4, 5, 6, 7, 9 };
                              Array as parameter
                                     ↓
   var count1    = Enumerable.Count(intArray);    // Called directly
   var firstNum1 = Enumerable.First(intArray);    // Called directly

   var count2    = intArray.Count();              // Called as extension
   var firstNum2 = intArray.First();              // Called as extension
                         ↑
              Array as extended object
   Console.WriteLine("Count: {0}, FirstNumber: {1}", count1, firstNum1);
   Console.WriteLine("Count: {0}, FirstNumber: {1}", count2, firstNum2);
}
```

This code produces the following output:

```
Count: 6, FirstNumber: 3
Count: 6, FirstNumber: 3
```

Delegates As Parameters

As you just saw in the previous section, the first parameter of every operator is a reference to an IEnumerable<T> object. The parameters following it can be of any type. Many operators take *generic delegates* as parameters. (Generic delegates were explained in Chapter 19.) The most important thing to recall about generic delegates as parameters is the following:

- Generic delegates are used to supply user-defined code to the operator.

To explain this, I'll start with an example showing several ways you might use the Count operator. The Count operator is overloaded and has two forms. The first form, which was used in the previous example, has a single parameter, as shown here:

```
public static int Count<T>(this IEnumerable<T> source);
```

Like all extension methods, you can use it in the standard static method form or in the form of an instance method on an instance of the class it extends, as shown in the following two lines of code:

```
var count1 = Linq.Enumerable.Count(intArray);        // Static method form

var count2 = intArray.Count();                       // Instance method form
```

In these two instances, the query counts the number of ints in the given integer array. Suppose, however, that you only want to count the odd elements of the array. To do that, you must supply the Count method with code that determines whether an integer is odd.

To do this, you would use the second form of the Count method, which is shown following. It has a generic delegate as its second parameter. At the point it is invoked, you must supply a delegate object that takes a single input parameter of type T and returns a Boolean value. The return value of the delegate code must specify whether the element should be included in the count.

```
public static int Count<T>(this IEnumerable<T> source,
                                   Func<T, bool> predicate );
                                        ↑
                                   Generic delegate
```

For example, the following code uses the second form of the Count operator to instruct it to include only those values that are odd. It does this by supplying a lambda expression that returns true if the input value is odd and false otherwise. (Lambda expressions were covered in Chapter 15.) At each iteration through the collection, Count calls this method (represented by the lambda expression) with the current value as input. If the input is odd, the method returns true, and Count includes the element in the total.

```
static void Main()
{
    int[] intArray = new int[] { 3, 4, 5, 6, 7, 9 };

    var countOdd = intArray.Count(n => n % 2 == 1);
                                  ↑
                   Lambda expression identifying the odd values
    Console.WriteLine("Count of odd numbers: {0}", countOdd);
}
```

This code produces the following output:

```
Count of odd numbers: 4
```

The LINQ Predefined Delegate Types

Like the Count operator from the previous example, many of the LINQ operators require you to supply code that directs how the operator performs its operation. You can do this by using delegate objects as parameters.

Remember from Chapter 15 that you can think of a delegate object as an object that contains a method or list of methods with a particular signature and return type. When the delegate is invoked, the methods it contains are invoked in sequence.

LINQ defines two families of generic delegate types for use with the standard query operators. These are the Func delegates and the Action delegates. Each set has 17 members.

- The delegate objects you create for use as actual parameters must be of these delegate types or of these forms.

- TR represents the return type and is always *last* in the list of type parameters.

The first four generic Func delegates are listed here. The first form takes no method parameters and returns an object of the return type. The second takes a single method parameter and returns a value, and so forth. Notice that the return type parameter has the out keyword, making it covariant. It can therefore accept the type declared or any type derived from that type. The input parameters have the in keyword, making them contravariant. They, therefore, can accept the declared type, or any type derived from that type.

```
public delegate TR Func<out TR>                        ( );
public delegate TR Func<in T1, out TR >                ( T1 a1 );
public delegate TR Func<in T1, in T2, out TR >         ( T1 a1, T2 a2 );
public delegate TR Func<in T1, in T2, in T3, out TR>( T1 a1, T2 a2, T3 a3 );
                ↑                    ↑                        ↑
            Return type      Type parameters          Method parameters
```

With this in mind, if you look again at the declaration of Count, which follows, you can see that the second parameter must be a delegate object that takes a single value of some type T as the method parameter and returns a value of type bool.

```
public static int Count<T>(this IEnumerable<T> source,
                              Func<T, bool> predicate );
                                    ↑    ↑
                          Parameter type  Return type
```

A parameter delegate that produces a Boolean value is called a *predicate*.

The first four Action delegates are the following. They're the same as the Func delegates except that they have no return value and hence no return value type parameter. All their type parameters are contravariant.

```
public delegate void Action                         ( );
public delegate void Action<in T1>                  ( T1 a1 );
public delegate void Action<in T1, in T2>           ( T1 a1, T2 a2 );
public delegate void Action<in T1, in T2, in T3>( T1 a1, T2 a2, T3 a3 );
```

Example Using a Delegate Parameter

Now that you better understand Count's signature and LINQ's use of generic delegate parameters, you'll be better able to understand a full example.

The following code first declares method IsOdd, which takes a single parameter of type int and returns a bool value stating whether the input parameter was odd. Method Main does the following:

- It declares an array of ints as the data source.

- It creates a delegate object called MyDel of type Func<int, bool>, and it uses method IsOdd to initialize the delegate object. Notice that you don't need to declare the Func delegate type because, as you saw, it's already predefined by LINQ.

- It calls Count using the delegate object.

```
class Program
{
    static bool IsOdd(int x)     // Method to be used by the delegate object
    {
        return x % 2 == 1;       // Return true if x is odd.
    }

    static void Main()
    {
        int[] intArray = new int[] { 3, 4, 5, 6, 7, 9 };

        Func<int, bool> myDel = new Func<int, bool>(IsOdd); // Delegate object
        var countOdd = intArray.Count(myDel);               // Use delegate

        Console.WriteLine("Count of odd numbers: {0}", countOdd);
    }
}
```

This code produces the following output:

```
Count of odd numbers: 4
```

Example Using a Lambda Expression Parameter

The previous example used a separate method and a delegate to attach the code to the operator. This required declaring the method, declaring the delegate object, and then passing the delegate object to the operator. This works fine and is exactly the right approach to take if either of the following conditions is true:

- If the method must be called from somewhere else in the program than just in the place it's used to initialize the delegate object

- If the code in the method body is more than just a statement or two long

If neither of these conditions is true, however, you probably want to use a more compact and localized method of supplying the code to the operator, using a lambda expression as described in Chapter 15.

We can modify the previous example to use a lambda expression by first deleting the IsOdd method entirely and placing the equivalent lambda expression directly at the declaration of the delegate object. The new code is shorter and cleaner and looks like this:

```
class Program
{
   static void Main()
   {
      int[] intArray = new int[] { 3, 4, 5, 6, 7, 9 };
                                        Lambda expression
                                              ↓
      var countOdd = intArray.Count( x => x % 2 == 1 );

      Console.WriteLine("Count of odd numbers: {0}", countOdd);
   }
}
```

Like the previous example, this code produces the following output:

```
Count of odd numbers: 4
```

We could also have used an anonymous method in place of the lambda expression, as shown following. This is more verbose, though, and since lambda expressions are equivalent semantically and are less verbose, there's little reason to use anonymous methods anymore.

```
class Program
{
   static void Main( )
   {
      int[] intArray = new int[] { 3, 4, 5, 6, 7, 9 };
                             Anonymous method
                                     ↓
      Func<int, bool> myDel = delegate(int x)
                              {
                                  return x % 2 == 1;
                              };
      var countOdd = intArray.Count(myDel);

      Console.WriteLine("Count of odd numbers: {0}", countOdd);
   }
}
```

LINQ to XML

Extensible Markup Language (XML) is an important method of storing and exchanging data. LINQ adds features to the language that make working with XML much easier than previous methods such as XPath and XSLT. If you're familiar with these methods, you might be pleased to hear that LINQ to XML simplifies the creation, traversal, and manipulation of XML in a number of ways, including the following:

- You can create an XML tree in a top-down fashion, with a single statement.

- You can create and manipulate XML in-memory without having an XML document to contain the tree.

- You can create and manipulate string nodes without having a Text subnode.

Although I won't give a complete treatment of XML, I will start by giving a very brief introduction to it before describing some of the XML manipulation features supplied by LINQ.

Markup Languages

A *markup language* is a set of tags placed in a document to give information *about the information* in the document. That is, the markup tags are not the data of the document—they contain data *about* the data. Data about data is called *metadata*.

A markup language is a defined set of tags designed to convey particular types of metadata about the contents of a document. HTML, for example, is the most widely known markup language. The metadata in its tags contains information about how a web page should be rendered in a browser and how to navigate among the pages using the hypertext links.

While most markup languages contain a predefined set of tags, XML contains only a few defined tags, and the rest are defined by the programmer to represent whatever kinds of metadata are required by a particular document type. As long as the writer and reader of the data agree on what the tags mean, the tags can contain whatever useful information the designers want.

XML Basics

Data in an XML document is contained in an XML tree, which consists mainly of a set of nested elements.

The *element* is the fundamental constituent of an XML tree. Every element has a name and can contain data. Some can also contain other, nested elements. Elements are demarcated by opening and closing tags. Any data contained by an element must be between its opening and closing tags.

- An opening tag starts with an open angle bracket, followed by the element name, followed optionally by any attributes, followed by a closing angle bracket.

```
<PhoneNumber>
```

- A closing tag starts with an open angle bracket, followed by a slash character, followed by the element name, followed by a closing angle bracket.

```
</PhoneNumber>
```

- An element with no content can be represented by a single tag that starts with an open angle bracket, followed by the name of the element, followed by a slash, and is terminated with a closing angle bracket.

```
<PhoneNumber />
```

The following XML fragment shows an element named `EmployeeName` followed by an empty element named `PhoneNumber`.

```
<EmployeeName>Sally Jones</EmployeeName>
           ↑              ↑              ↑
      Opening tag     Content      Closing tag
<PhoneNumber />        ← Element with no content
```

Other important things to know about XML are the following:

- XML documents must have a single root element that contains all the other elements.

- XML tags must be properly nested.

- Unlike HTML tags, XML tags are case sensitive.

- XML *attributes* are name/value pairs that contain additional metadata about an element. The value part of an attribute must always be enclosed in quotation marks, which can be either double quotation marks or single quotation marks.

- Whitespace within an XML document is maintained. This is unlike HTML, where whitespace is consolidated to a single space in the output.

The following XML document is an example of XML that contains information about two employees. This XML tree is extremely simple in order to show the elements clearly. The important things to notice about the XML tree are the following:

- The tree contains a root node of type `Employees` that contains two child nodes of type `Employee`.

- Each `Employee` node contains nodes containing the name and phone numbers of an employee.

```
<Employees>
   <Employee>
      <Name>Bob Smith</Name>
      <PhoneNumber>408-555-1000</PhoneNumber>
      <CellPhone />
   </Employee>
   <Employee>
      <Name>Sally Jones</Name>
      <PhoneNumber>415-555-2000</PhoneNumber>
      <PhoneNumber>415-555-2001</PhoneNumber>
   </Employee>
</Employees>
```

Figure 21-13 illustrates the hierarchical structure of the sample XML tree.

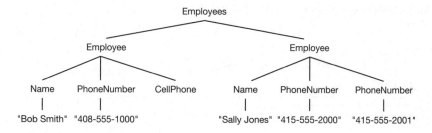

Figure 21-13. *Hierarchical structure of the sample XML tree*

The XML Classes

LINQ to XML can be used to work with XML in two ways. The first way is as a simplified XML manipulation API. The second way is to use the LINQ query facilities you've seen throughout the earlier part of this chapter. I'll start by introducing the LINQ to XML API.

The LINQ to XML API consists of a number of classes that represent the components of an XML tree. The three most important classes you'll use are XElement, XAttribute, and XDocument. There are other classes as well, but these are the main ones.

In Figure 21-13, you saw that an XML tree is a set of nested elements. Figure 21-14 shows the classes used to build an XML tree and how they can be nested.

For example, the figure shows the following:

- An XDocument node can have the following as its direct child nodes:

  — At most, one of each of the following node types: an XDeclaration node, an XDocumentType node, and an XElement node

  — Any number of XProcessingInstruction nodes

- If there is a top-level XElement node under the XDocument, it is the root of the rest of the elements in the XML tree.

- The root element can in turn contain any number of nested XElement, XComment, or XProcessingInstruction nodes, nested to any level.

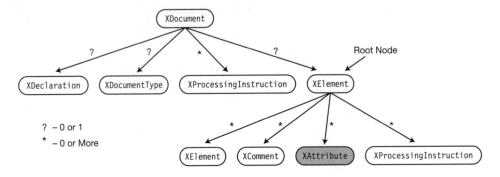

Figure 21-14. *The containment structure of XML nodes*

Except for the XAttribute class, most of the classes used to create an XML tree are derived from a class called XNode and are referred to generically in the literature as "XNodes." Figure 21-14 shows the XNode classes in white clouds, while the XAttribute class is shown in a gray cloud.

Creating, Saving, Loading, and Displaying an XML Document

The best way to demonstrate the simplicity and usage of the XML API is to show simple code samples. For example, the following code shows how simple it is to perform several of the important tasks required when working with XML.

It starts by creating a simple XML tree consisting of a node called Employees, with two subnodes containing the names of two employees. Notice the following about the code:

- The tree is created with a single statement that creates all the nested elements in place in the tree. This is called *functional construction*.

- Each element is created in place using an object creation expression, using the constructor of the type of the node.

After creating the tree, the code saves it to a file called EmployeesFile.xml, using XDocument's Save method. It then reads the XML tree back from the file using XDocument's static Load method and assigns the tree to a new XDocument object. Finally, it uses WriteLine to display the structure of the tree held by the new XDocument object.

```
using System;
using System.Xml.Linq;                        // Required namespace

class Program {
    static void Main( ) {
        XDocument employees1 =
            new XDocument(                     // Create the XML document.
                new XElement("Employees",      // Create the root element.
                    new XElement("Name", "Bob Smith"),     // Create element
                    new XElement("Name", "Sally Jones")    // Create element
                )
            );

        employees1.Save("EmployeesFile.xml");          // Save to a file

        // Load the saved document into a new variable.
        XDocument employees2 = XDocument.Load("EmployeesFile.xml");
                                    ↑
                              Static method
        Console.WriteLine(employees2);                 // Display document
    }
}
```

This code produces the following output:

```
<Employees>
  <Name>Bob Smith</Name>
  <Name>Sally Jones</Name>
</Employees>
```

Creating an XML Tree

In the previous example, you saw that you can create an XML document in-memory by using constructors for XDocument and XElement. In the case of both constructors

- The first parameter is the name of the object.

- The second and following parameters contain the nodes of the XML tree. The second parameter of the constructor is a params parameter, and so can have any number of parameters.

For example, the following code produces an XML tree and displays it using the Console.WriteLine method:

```csharp
using System;
using System.Xml.Linq;                              // This namespace is required.

class Program
{
    static void Main( ) {
        XDocument employeeDoc =
            new XDocument(                          // Create the document.
                new XElement("Employees",           // Create the root element.

                    new XElement("Employee",        // First employee element
                        new XElement("Name", "Bob Smith"),
                        new XElement("PhoneNumber", "408-555-1000") ),

                    new XElement("Employee",        // Second employee element
                        new XElement("Name", "Sally Jones"),
                        new XElement("PhoneNumber", "415-555-2000"),
                        new XElement("PhoneNumber", "415-555-2001") )
                )
            );
        Console.WriteLine(employeeDoc);             // Displays the document
    }
}
```

This code produces the following output:

```
<Employees>
  <Employee>
    <Name>Bob Smith</Name>
    <PhoneNumber>408-555-1000</PhoneNumber>
  </Employee>
  <Employee>
    <Name>Sally Jones</Name>
    <PhoneNumber>415-555-2000</PhoneNumber>
    <PhoneNumber>415-555-2001</PhoneNumber>
  </Employee>
</Employees>
```

Using Values from the XML Tree

The power of XML becomes evident when you traverse an XML tree and retrieve or modify values. Table 21-2 shows the main methods used for retrieving data.

Table 21-2. *Methods for Querying XML*

Method Name	Class	Return Type	Description
Nodes	Xdocument XElement	IEnumerable<object>	Returns all the children of the current node, regardless of their type
Elements	Xdocument XElement	IEnumerable<XElement>	Returns all the current node's XElement child nodes or all the child nodes with a specific name
Element	Xdocument XElement	XElement	Returns the current node's first XElement child node or the first child node with a specific name
Descendants	XElement	IEnumerable<XElement>	Returns all the descendant XElement nodes or all the descendant XElement nodes with a specific name, regardless of their level of nesting below the current node
DescendantsAndSelf	XElement	IEnumerable<XElement>	Same as Descendants but also includes the current node
Ancestors	XElement	IEnumerable<XElement>	Returns all the ancestor XElement nodes or all the ancestor XElement nodes above the current node that have a specific name
AncestorsAndSelf	XElement	IEnumerable<XElement>	Same as Ancestors but also includes the current node
Parent	XElement	XElement	Returns the parent node of the current node

Some of the important things to know about the methods in Table 21-2 are the following:

- Nodes: The Nodes method returns an object of type IEnumerable<object>, because the nodes returned might be of different types, such as XElement, XComment, and so on. You can use the type parameterized method OfType<*type*> to specify what type of nodes to return. For example, the following line of code retrieves only the XComment nodes:

```
IEnumerable<XComment> comments = xd.Nodes().OfType<XComment>();
```

- Elements: Since retrieving XElements is such a common requirement, there is a shortcut for expression Nodes().OfType<XElement>()—the Elements method.

  — Using the Elements method with no parameters returns all the child XElements.

  — Using the Elements method with a single name parameter returns only the child XElements with that name. For example, the following line of code returns all the child XElement nodes with the name *PhoneNumber*.

```
IEnumerable<XElement> empPhones = emp.Elements("PhoneNumber");
```

- Element: This method retrieves just the first child XElement of the current node. Like the Elements method, it can be called with either one or no parameters. With no parameters, it gets the first child XElement node. With a single name parameter, it gets the first child XElement node of that name.

- Descendants and Ancestors: These methods work like the Elements and Parent methods, but instead of returning the immediate child elements or parent element, they include the elements below or above the current node, regardless of the difference in nesting level.

The following code illustrates the `Element` and `Elements` methods:

```
using System;
using System.Collections.Generic;
using System.Xml.Linq;

class Program {
    static void Main( ) {
        XDocument employeeDoc =
            new XDocument(
                new XElement("Employees",
                    new XElement("Employee",
                        new XElement("Name", "Bob Smith"),
                        new XElement("PhoneNumber", "408-555-1000")),
                    new XElement("Employee",
                        new XElement("Name", "Sally Jones"),
                        new XElement("PhoneNumber", "415-555-2000"),
                        new XElement("PhoneNumber", "415-555-2001"))
                    )
            );                      Get first child XElement named "Employees"
                                                    ↓
        XElement root = employeeDoc.Element("Employees");
        IEnumerable<XElement> employees = root.Elements();

        foreach (XElement emp in employees)
        {                              Get first child XElement named "Name"
                                                    ↓
            XElement empNameNode = emp.Element("Name");
            Console.WriteLine(empNameNode.Value);
                                       Get all child elements named "PhoneNumber"
                                                    ↓
            IEnumerable<XElement> empPhones = emp.Elements("PhoneNumber");
            foreach (XElement phone in empPhones)
                Console.WriteLine("   {0}", phone.Value);
        }
    }
}
```

This code produces the following output:

```
Bob Smith
   408-555-1000
Sally Jones
   415-555-2000
   415-555-2001
```

Adding Nodes and Manipulating XML

You can add a child element to an existing element using the Add method. The Add method allows you to add as many elements as you like in a single method call, regardless of the node types you are adding.

For example, the following code creates a simple XML tree and displays it. It then uses the Add method to add a single node to the root element. Following that, it uses the Add method a second time to add three elements—two XElements and an XComment. Notice the results in the output:

```
using System;
using System.Xml.Linq;

class Program
{
   static void Main()
   {
      XDocument xd = new XDocument(              // Create XML tree
         new XElement("root",
            new XElement("first")
         )
      );

      Console.WriteLine("Original tree");
      Console.WriteLine(xd); Console.WriteLine(); // Display the tree.

      XElement rt = xd.Element("root");          // Get the first element.

      rt.Add( new XElement("second"));           // Add a child element.

      rt.Add( new XElement("third"),             // Add three more children.
              new XComment("Important Comment"),
              new XElement("fourth"));

      Console.WriteLine("Modified tree");
      Console.WriteLine(xd);                     // Display modified tree
   }
}
```

This code produces the following output:

```
<root>
  <first />
</root>

<root>
  <first />
  <second />
  <third />
  <!--Important Comment-->
  <fourth />
</root>
```

The `Add` method places the new child nodes after the existing child nodes, but you can place the nodes before and between the child nodes as well, using the `AddFirst`, `AddBeforeSelf`, and `AddAfterSelf` methods.

Table 21-3 lists some of the most important methods for manipulating XML. Notice that some of the methods are applied to the parent node and others to the node itself.

Table 21-3. *Methods for Manipulating XML*

Method Name	Call From	Description
Add	Parent	Adds new child nodes after the existing child nodes of the current node
AddFirst	Parent	Adds new child nodes before the existing child nodes of the current node
AddBeforeSelf	Node	Adds new nodes before the current node at the same level
AddAfterSelf	Node	Adds new nodes after the current node at the same level
Remove	Node	Deletes the currently selected node and its contents
RemoveNodes	Node	Deletes the currently selected XElement and its contents
SetElement	Parent	Sets the contents of a node
ReplaceContent	Node	Replaces the contents of a node

Working with XML Attributes

Attributes give additional information about an XElement node. They're placed in the opening tag of the XML element.

When you functionally construct an XML tree, you can add attributes by just including XAttribute constructors within the scope of the XElement constructor. There are two forms of the XAttribute constructor; one takes a name and a value, and the other takes a reference to an already existing XAttribute.

The following code adds two attributes to root. Notice that both parameters to the XAttribute constructor are strings; the first specifies the name of the attribute, and the second gives the value.

```
XDocument xd = new XDocument(
                        Name      Value
    new XElement("root",  ↓        ↓
            new XAttribute("color", "red"),        // Attribute constructor
            new XAttribute("size", "large"),       // Attribute constructor
        new XElement("first"),
        new XElement("second")
    )
);

Console.WriteLine(xd);
```

This code produces the following output. Notice that the attributes are placed inside the opening tag of the element.

```
<root color="red" size="large">
  <first />
  <second />
</root>
```

To retrieve an attribute from an XElement node, use the Attribute method, supplying the name of the attribute as the parameter. The following code creates an XML tree with a node with two attributes—color and size. It then retrieves the values of the attributes and displays them.

```csharp
static void Main( )
{
   XDocument xd = new XDocument(                         // Create XML tree
      new XElement("root",
         new XAttribute("color", "red"),
         new XAttribute("size", "large"),
         new XElement("first")
      )
   );

   Console.WriteLine(xd); Console.WriteLine();           // Display XML tree

   XElement rt = xd.Element("root");                     // Get the element.

   XAttribute color = rt.Attribute("color");            // Get the attribute.
   XAttribute size =  rt.Attribute("size");             // Get the attribute.

   Console.WriteLine("color is {0}", color.Value);      // Display attr. value
   Console.WriteLine("size  is {0}", size.Value);       // Display attr. value
}
```

This code produces the following output:

```
<root color="red" size="large">
  <first />
</root>

color is red
size  is large
```

To remove an attribute, you can select the attribute and use the Remove method or use the SetAttributeValue method on its parent and set the attribute value to null. The following code demonstrates both methods:

```
static void Main( ) {
    XDocument xd = new XDocument(
        new XElement("root",
            new XAttribute("color", "red"),
            new XAttribute("size", "large"),
            new XElement("first")
        )
    );

    XElement rt = xd.Element("root");            // Get the element.

    rt.Attribute("color").Remove();             // Remove the color attribute.
    rt.SetAttributeValue("size", null);         // Remove the size attribute.

    Console.WriteLine(xd);
}
```

This code produces the following output:

```
<root>
  <first />
</root>
```

To add an attribute to an XML tree or change the value of an attribute, you can use the
SetAttributeValue method, as shown in the following code:

```
static void Main( ) {
   XDocument xd = new XDocument(
      new XElement("root",
         new XAttribute("color", "red"),
         new XAttribute("size", "large"),
         new XElement("first")));

   XElement rt = xd.Element("root");            // Get the element.

   rt.SetAttributeValue("size",  "medium");     // Change attribute value
   rt.SetAttributeValue("width", "narrow");     // Add an attribute.

   Console.WriteLine(xd); Console.WriteLine();
}
```

This code produces the following output:

```
<root color="red" size="medium" width="narrow">
  <first />
</root>
```

Other Types of Nodes

Three other types of nodes used in the previous examples are XComment, XDeclaration, and XProcessingInstruction. They're described in the following sections.

XComment

Comments in XML consist of text between the <!-- and --> tokens. The text between the tokens is ignored by XML parsers. You can insert text in an XML document using the XComment class, as shown in the following line of code:

```
new XComment("This is a comment")
```

XDeclaration

XML documents start with a line that includes the version of XML used, the type of character encoding used, and whether the document depends on external references. This is information about the XML, so it's actually metadata about the metadata! This is called the *XML declaration* and is inserted using the XDeclaration class. The following shows an example of an XDeclaration statement:

```
new XDeclaration("1.0", "utf-8", "yes")
```

XProcessingInstruction

An XML processing instruction is used to supply additional data about how an XML document should be used or interpreted. Most commonly, processing instructions are used to associate a style sheet with the XML document.

You can include a processing instruction using the XProcessingInstruction constructor, which takes two string parameters—a target and a data string. If the processing instruction takes multiple data parameters, those parameters must be included in the second parameter string of the XProcessingInstruction constructor, as shown in the following constructor code. Notice that in this example, the second parameter is a verbatim string, and literal double quotes inside the string are represented by sets of two contiguous double quote marks.

```
new XProcessingInstruction( "xml-stylesheet",
                            @"href=""stories"", type=""text/css""")
```

The following code uses all three constructs:

```
static void Main( )
{
   XDocument xd = new XDocument(
      new XDeclaration("1.0", "utf-8", "yes"),
      new XComment("This is a comment"),
      new XProcessingInstruction("xml-stylesheet",
                                 @"href=""stories.css"" type=""text/css"""),
      new XElement("root",
         new XElement("first"),
         new XElement("second")
      )
   );
}
```

This code produces the following output in the output file. Using a `WriteLine` of xd, however, would not show the declaration statement, even though it is included in the document file.

```
<?xml version="1.0" encoding="utf-8" standalone="yes"?>
<!--This is a comment-->
<?xml-stylesheet href="stories.css" type="text/css"?>
<root>
  <first />
  <second />
</root>
```

Using LINQ Queries with LINQ to XML

You can combine the LINQ XML API with LINQ query expressions to produce simple yet powerful XML tree searches.

The following code creates a simple XML tree, displays it to the screen, and then saves it to a file called SimpleSample.xml. Although there's nothing new in this code, we'll use this XML tree in the following examples.

```
static void Main( )
{
   XDocument xd = new XDocument(
      new XElement("MyElements",
         new XElement("first",
            new XAttribute("color", "red"),
            new XAttribute("size",  "small")),
         new XElement("second",
            new XAttribute("color", "red"),
            new XAttribute("size",  "medium")),
         new XElement("third",
            new XAttribute("color", "blue"),
            new XAttribute("size",  "large"))));

   Console.WriteLine(xd);                    // Display XML tree
   xd.Save("SimpleSample.xml");              // Save XML tree
}
```

This code produces the following output:

```
<MyElements>
  <first color="red" size="small" />
  <second color="red" size="medium" />
  <third color="blue" size="large" />
</MyElements>
```

The following example code uses a simple LINQ query to select a subset of the nodes from the XML tree and then displays them in several ways. This code does the following:

- It selects from the XML tree only those elements whose names have five characters. Since the names of the elements are *first*, *second*, and *third*, only node names *first* and *third* match the search criterion, and therefore those nodes are selected.

- It displays the names of the selected elements.

- It formats and displays the selected nodes, including the node name and the values of the attributes. Notice that the attributes are retrieved using the Attribute method, and the values of the attributes are retrieved with the Value property.

```
static void Main( )
{
    XDocument xd = XDocument.Load("SimpleSample.xml"); // Load the document.
    XElement rt = xd.Element("MyElements");            // Get the root element.

    var xyz = from e in rt.Elements()                 // Select elements whose
              where e.Name.ToString().Length == 5     // names have 5 chars.
              select e;

    foreach (XElement x in xyz)                        // Display the
        Console.WriteLine(x.Name.ToString());          // selected elements.

    Console.WriteLine();
    foreach (XElement x in xyz)
        Console.WriteLine("Name: {0}, color: {1}, size: {2}",
                          x.Name,
                          x.Attribute("color").Value,
                          x.Attribute("size") .Value);
                                 ↑                ↑
}               Get the attribute.    Get the attribute's value.
```

This code produces the following output:

```
first
third

Name: first, color: red, size: small
Name: third, color: blue, size: large
```

The following code uses a simple query to retrieve all the top-level elements of the XML tree and creates an object of an anonymous type for each one. The first use of the WriteLine method shows the default formatting of the anonymous type. The second WriteLine statement explicitly formats the members of the anonymous type objects.

```csharp
using System;
using System.Linq;
using System.Xml.Linq;

static void Main( )
{
    XDocument xd = XDocument.Load("SimpleSample.xml"); // Load the document.
    XElement rt = xd.Element("MyElements");            // Get the root element.

    var xyz = from e in rt.Elements()
              select new { e.Name, color = e.Attribute("color") };
                         ↑
    foreach (var x in xyz)      Create an anonymous type.
        Console.WriteLine(x);                          // Default formatting

    Console.WriteLine();
    foreach (var x in xyz)
        Console.WriteLine("{0,-6},   color: {1, -7}", x.Name, x.color.Value);
}
```

This code produces the following output. The first three lines show the default formatting of the anonymous type. The last three lines show the explicit formatting specified in the format string of the second WriteLine method.

```
{ Name = first, color = color="red" }
{ Name = second, color = color="red" }
{ Name = third, color = color="blue" }

first ,   color: red
second,   color: red
third ,   color: blue
```

From these examples, you can see that you can easily combine the XML API with the LINQ query facilities to produce powerful XML querying capabilities.

CHAPTER 22

■ ■ ■

Introduction to Asynchronous Programming

- Processes, Threads, and Asynchronous Programming
- Parallel Loops
- The BackgroundWorker Class
- Asynchronous Programming Patterns
- BeginInvoke and EndInvoke
- Timers

Processes, Threads, and Asynchronous Programming

In this chapter, we're going to introduce four methods you can use to add multithreading to your programs. This chapter is a bit different from the previous chapters in that it goes beyond just the language features. Instead, we'll also include classes from the BCL and include some programming techniques. In spite of the fact that these things are a bit beyond just the language features, I want to do this because it's imperative that we as programmers increase our use of multiprocessing in our code—and I think a first book on C# is a good place to start.

When you start a program, the system creates a new *process* in memory. A process is the set of resources that comprise a running program. These include the virtual address space, file handles, and a host of other things required for the program to run.

Inside the process, the system creates a kernel object, called a *thread*, which represents the actual executing program. (*Thread* is short for "thread of execution.") Once the process is set up, the system starts execution of the thread at the first statement in method Main.

Some important things to know about threads are the following:

- By default, a process contains only a single thread, which executes from the beginning of the program to the end.

- A thread can spawn other threads so that at any time, a process might have multiple threads in various states, executing different parts of the program.

- If there are multiple threads in a process, they all share the process's resources.

- It's threads, not processes, that are the units scheduled by the system for execution on the processor.

All the sample programs shown so far in this book have used only a single thread and have executed sequentially from the first statement in the program to the last. This is called *synchronous programming*. *Asynchronous programming* refers to programs that spawn multiple threads, which are, at least conceptually, executed at the same time. (They might not *actually* be executed at the same time.)

If the program is running on a multiprocessor system, the different threads might actually be executing at the same time on different processors. This can considerably improve performance, and as multicore processors become the norm, we need to write our programs to take advantage of this opportunity.

On a single-processor system, though, clearly only one instruction can be executed by the processor at a time. In this case, the operating system coordinates the threads so that the processor is shared among them. Each thread gets the processor for a short time, called a *time slice*, before being kicked off the processor and sent to the back of the line. This round-robin sharing of the processor lets all the threads work their ways through the code.

Multithreading Considerations

Using multiple threads in a program, called *multithreading*, or just *threading*, creates program overhead and additional program complexity. Here are some examples:

- There are time and resource costs in both creating and destroying threads.

- The time required for scheduling threads, loading them onto the processor, and storing their states after each time slice is pure overhead.

- Since the threads in a process all share the same resources and heap, it adds additional programming complexity to ensure that they're not stepping on each other's work.

- Debugging multithreaded programs can be quite difficult, since the timing on each run of the program can be different, producing different results. And the act of running the program in a debugger blows the timing out of the water.

In spite of these considerations, the benefits of threading can outweigh its costs, as long as it's used wisely—and not overused. For example, you've already seen that on a multiprocessor system, if the different threads can be placed on different processors, it can result in a much more efficient execution.

To help alleviate some of the costs associated with creating and destroying threads, the CLR maintains a *thread pool* for each process. Initially, a process's thread pool is empty, but after a thread is created and used by a process and then the thread completes its execution, it isn't destroyed but instead added to the process's thread pool. Later, if the process needs another thread, the CLR recycles one from the pool, saving a significant amount of time.

Another common example where multithreading is crucial is in *graphical user interface* (*GUI*) programming, where users expect a quick response any time they click a button or use the keyboard. In this case, if the program needs to perform an operation that's going to take any appreciable time, it should perform that operation on another thread, leaving the main thread available to respond to the user's input. It would be totally unacceptable to have the program unresponsive during that time.

The Complexity of Multithreading

Although multithreading is conceptually easy, getting all the details right can be frustratingly difficult on nontrivial programs. The areas that need to be considered are the following:

- *Communicating between the threads*: There are few built-in mechanisms for communicating between threads, so this is often done simply using their shared memory, since the memory space is visible and accessible by all threads in the same process.

- *Coordinating threads*: Although it's easy to create threads, you also need to be able to coordinate their actions. For example, a thread might need to wait for one or more other threads to complete before it can continue its execution.

- *Synchronization of resource usage*: Since all the threads in a process share the same resources and memory, you need to make sure that the different threads aren't accessing and changing them at the same time, causing state inconsistencies.

The System.Threading namespace contains classes and types that you can use to build complex multithreaded systems. These include the Thread class itself and classes such as Mutex, Semaphore, and Monitor, which are used to synchronize resource usage. The use, complexities, and nuances of this tricky subject are beyond the scope of this text, and you'd be better advised to settle down with an in-depth book on the subject.

Parallel Loops

.NET 4.0 has introduced a new library, called the Task Parallel Library, which greatly simplifies parallel programming. This is a huge advance and includes a large amount of material—far more than I can cover in this chapter. So unfortunately, I've had to settle by just whetting your appetite by introducing just two of its very simple constructs that you can learn and use quickly and easily. These are the `Parallel.For` loop and the `Parallel.ForEach` loop. These constructs are in the `System.Threading.Tasks` namespace.

By this point in the book I'm sure you're quite familiar with C#'s standard for and foreach loops. These are common and tremendously powerful constructs. Many times when using these constructs, each iteration depends on a calculation or action in the previous iteration. But this isn't always the case. When the iterations are independent, it would be a huge advantage if you could put different iterations on different processors and process them in parallel. This is exactly what the `Parallel.For` and `Parallel.ForEach` constructs do.

These constructs are in the form of methods with input parameters. There are 12 overloads of the `Parallel.For` method, but the simplest has the following signature:

- The *fromInclusive* parameter is the first integer in the iteration series.

- The *toExclusive* parameter is an integer that is *one greater than the last index* in the iteration series. That is, it's the same as comparing on the expression index < *ToExclusive*.

- The *body* is a delegate that takes a single input parameter. The code of *body* is executed once per iteration.

```
void Parallel.For( int fromInclusive, int toExclusive, Action body );
```

The following code is an example using the `Parallel.For` construct. It iterates from 0 to 15 and prints out the iteration index and the square of the index. Notice that it fits the requirement that each iteration is independent of any other iteration. Notice also that you must use the `System.Threading.Tasks` namespace.

```
using System;
using System.Threading.Tasks;          // Must use this namespace

namespace ExampleParallelFor
{
   class Program
   {
      static void Main( )
      {
         Parallel.For( 0, 15, i =>
            Console.WriteLine( "The square of {0} is {1}", i, i * i ));
      }
   }
}
```

One run of this code on a PC with a two-core processor produced the following output. Notice that you're not guaranteed any particular order of the iterations.

```
The square of 0 is 0
The square of 7 is 49
The square of 8 is 64
The square of 9 is 81
The square of 10 is 100
The square of 11 is 121
The square of 12 is 144
The square of 13 is 169
The square of 3 is 9
The square of 4 is 16
The square of 5 is 25
The square of 6 is 36
The square of 14 is 196
The square of 1 is 1
The square of 2 is 4
```

Another example is the following code. This program fills an integer array, in parallel, with the square of the iteration index.

```
class Program
{
    static void Main()
    {
        const int maxValues = 50;
        int[] squares = new int[maxValues];

        Parallel.For( 0, maxValues, i => squares[i] = i * i );
    }
}
```

Unlike the previous example, even though the iterations might be executed in parallel and in any order, the end result is an array containing the first 50 squares.

The other parallel loop construct is the `Parallel.ForEach` method. There are more than a dozen overloads for this method, but the simplest is the following:

- The TSource is the type of object in the collection.

- The *source* is the collection of TSource objects.

- The *body* is the lambda expression to be applied to each element of the collection.

```
static ParallelLoopResult ForEach<TSource>( IEnumerable<TSource> source,
                                            Action<TSource> body)
```

An example of using the `Parallel.ForEach` method is the following code. In this case, TSource is string, and the *source* is a string[ ].

```
using System;
using System.Threading.Tasks;

namespace ParallelForeach1
{
    class Program
    {
        static void Main()
        {
            string[] squares = new string[]
                    { "We", "hold", "these", "truths", "to", "be", "self-evident",
                      "that", "all", "men", "are", "created", "equal"};

            Parallel.ForEach( squares,
                i => Console.WriteLine( string.Format("{0} has {1} letters", i, i.Length) ));
        }
    }
}
```

One run of this code on a PC with a two-core processor produced the following output, but the order might change each time:

```
"We" has 2 letters
"equal" has 5 letters
"truths" has 6 letters
"to" has 2 letters
"be" has 2 letters
"that" has 4 letters
"hold" has 4 letters
"these" has 5 letters
"all" has 3 letters
"men" has 3 letters
"are" has 3 letters
"created" has 7 letters
"self-evident" has 12 letters
```

The BackgroundWorker Class

Although much of asynchronous programming is complex, the BackgroundWorker class makes it simple to perform a task in the background on a separate thread. This class was designed primarily for GUI programming (Windows Forms and WPF) to allow them to offload time-consuming tasks from the main thread to a background thread. Figure 22-1 illustrates the key members of the class. The following is an overview of these members:

- The first two properties shown in the figure are used to set whether the background task can report its progress to the main thread and whether it supports cancellation from the main thread. You use the third property to find out whether the background task is running.

- The class has three events, which are used to signal different program events and states. You need to write event handlers for these events to take whatever actions are appropriate for your program.

  — The DoWork event is raised when the background thread starts.

  — The ProgressChanged event is raised when the background task reports progress.

  — The RunWorkerCompleted event is raised when the background worker exits.

- The three methods are used to initiate actions or change state.

  — Calling the RunWorkerAsync method retrieves a background thread that executes the DoWork event handler.

  — Calling the CancelAsync method sets the CancellationPending property to true, potentially, although not necessarily, canceling the thread. It is the responsibility of the DoWork event handler to inspect this property to determine whether it should stop its processing.

  — The ReportProgress method can be called by the DoWork event handler (from the *background thread*) when it wants to report its progress to the main thread.

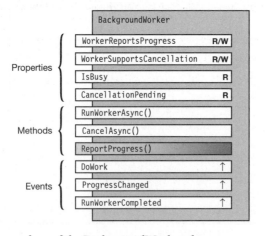
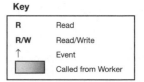

Figure 22-1. *The key members of the BackgroundWorker class*

To use a BackgroundWorker class object, you need to write the following event handlers. The first is required since it contains the code you want to be executed by the background thread, but the other two are optional, depending on the needs of your program.

- The handler attached to the DoWork event contains the code you want executed in the background on a separate thread.
  — In Figure 22-2, this handler is named DoTheWork and is in a gradient-shaded box to illustrate that it's executed in the separate thread.
  — The DoWork event is raised when the main thread calls the RunWorkerAsync method.

- The handler attached to the ProgressChanged event should contain the code to be executed on the main thread when the background task reports its progress.
  — The ProgressChanged event is raised when *the background process* calls the ReportProgress method.
  — Calling the ReportProgress method is how the background thread communicates with the main thread.

- The handler attached to the RunWorkerCompleted event should contain the code to be executed on the main thread after the background thread completes the execution of the DoWork event handler.

Figure 22-2 shows the structure of your program, with the event handlers attached to the events of the BackgroundWorker object.

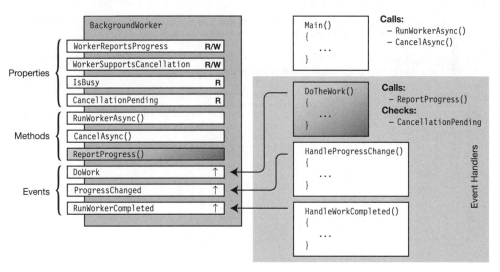

Figure 22-2. *Your code supplies event handlers for the events that control the flow through execution of the tasks.*

The delegates for these event handlers are the following. Each takes an object reference as the first parameter and a specialized subclass of the EventArgs class as the second parameter.

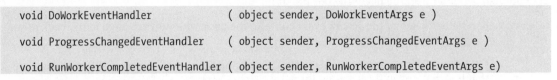

```
void DoWorkEventHandler              ( object sender, DoWorkEventArgs e )

void ProgressChangedEventHandler     ( object sender, ProgressChangedEventArgs e )

void RunWorkerCompletedEventHandler ( object sender, RunWorkerCompletedEventArgs e)
```

Figure 22-3 illustrates the structure of the EventArg classes used by these event handlers.

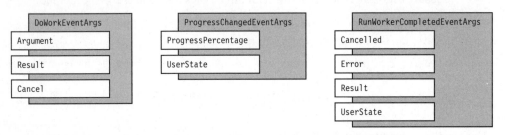

Figure 22-3. *The EventArg classes used by the BackgroundWorker event handlers*

When you have the event handlers written and attached to their events, you can use the class by doing the following:

- Start by creating an object of the BackgroundWorker class and configuring it.
  - If you want the worker thread to communicate progression to the main thread, then set the WorkerReportsProgress property to true.
  - If you want to be able to cancel the worker thread from the main thread, then set the WorkerSupportsCancellation property to true.
- Now that the object is configured, you can start it by calling the object's RunWorkerAsync method. This retrieves a background thread that raises the DoWork event and executes the event's handler in the background.

Now you have both the main thread and the background thread running. While the background thread is running, you can continue processing on the main thread.

- In the main thread, if you've enabled the WorkerSupportsCancellation property, then you can call the object's CancelAsync method. *This does not cancel the background thread!* Instead, it sets the object's CancellationPending property to true that needs to be checked by the DoWork event handler code running on the background thread.

- The background thread, in the meantime, continues to perform its computational tasks, as well as doing the following:

  — If the WorkerReportsProgress property is true and the background thread has progress to report to the main thread, then it must call the BackgroundWorker object's ReportProgress method. When the background thread calls the ReportProgress method, this raises the ProgressChanged event in the main thread, which runs the corresponding event handler.

  — If the WorkerSupportsCancellation property is enabled, then the DoWork event handler code should regularly check the CancellationPending property to determine whether it has been canceled. If so, it should exit.

  — If the background thread finishes its processing without being canceled, it can return a result to the main thread by setting the Result field in the DoWorkEventArgs parameter shown previously, in Figure 22-3.

- When the background thread exits, the RunWorkerCompleted event is raised, and its handler is executed on the main thread. The RunWorkerCompletedEventArgs parameter can contain information from the now completed background thread, such as the return value and whether the thread was canceled.

Example Code Using the BackgroundWorker Class

Although the BackgroundWorker class was designed for GUI programming, I'll start by showing its use with a console program since that's what we've used throughout the book. In the next section, I'll show an example with a GUI program.

This program creates a background thread that sums a sequence of numbers. Several times during the process it checks to see whether it has been canceled. If it finds it's been canceled, it cleans up and exits. Otherwise, if it goes to completion, it stores the total in the Result field and exits.

Meanwhile, the main thread sums its own sequence of numbers and reports its total, along with the result from the background thread.

```
using System;
using System.ComponentModel;                    // Must have this namespace
using System.Threading;                         // Must have this namespace

namespace ConsoleBackgroundWorker
{
    class DoBackgroundwork
    {
        BackgroundWorker bgWorker = new BackgroundWorker();

        public long BackgroundTotal    { get; private set; }
        public bool CompletedNormally { get; private set; }

        // Constructor
        public DoBackgroundwork()
        {
            // Set BackgroundWorker properties
            bgWorker.WorkerReportsProgress       = true;
            bgWorker.WorkerSupportsCancellation = true;

            // Connect handlers to BackgroundWorker object.
            bgWorker.DoWork                += DoWork_Handler;
            bgWorker.ProgressChanged       += ProgressChanged_Handler;
            bgWorker.RunWorkerCompleted += RunWorkerCompleted_Handler;
        }

        public void StartWorker()
        {
            if ( !bgWorker.IsBusy )
                bgWorker.RunWorkerAsync();
        }

        // This just calculates the sum of the integers from 0 to the input value.
        public static long CalculateTheSequence( long value )
        {
            long total = 0;
            for ( int i=0; i < value; i++ )
                total += i;
            return total;
        }
```

```csharp
public void DoWork_Handler( object sender, DoWorkEventArgs args )
{
   BackgroundWorker worker = sender as BackgroundWorker;

   // Do the background calculation
   long total = 0;
   for ( int i = 1; i <= 5; i++ )
   {
      // Each time through the loop, check to see if we've been cancelled
      if ( worker.CancellationPending )
      {
         args.Cancel = true;
         worker.ReportProgress( -1 );
         break;
      }
      else
      {
         // If we haven't been cancelled, then continue the calculation.
         total += CalculateTheSequence( i * 10000000 );
         worker.ReportProgress( i * 20 );

         // Slow the program down to a more comfortable output rate
         // just for this demo.
         Thread.Sleep( 300 );
      }
   }

   args.Result = total;        // Store the result and exit.
}

// Handle input from background thread.
private void ProgressChanged_Handler
            ( object sender, ProgressChangedEventArgs args )
{
   string output
        = args.ProgressPercentage == -1
            ? "              Cancelled"
            : string.Format("              {0}%", args.ProgressPercentage );

   Console.WriteLine( output );
}

// On completion of background thread, summarize and store the result.
private void RunWorkerCompleted_Handler
            ( object sender, RunWorkerCompletedEventArgs args )
{
   CompletedNormally = !args.Cancelled;
   BackgroundTotal   =  args.Cancelled
                           ? 0
                           : (long) args.Result;   // Cast from object
}
```

```csharp
      public void Cancel()
      {
         if( bgWorker.IsBusy )
            bgWorker.CancelAsync();
      }
   }

   class Program
   {
      static void Main()
      {
         GiveInstructionsToTheUser();
         OutputTheSummaryHeaders();

         // Create and Start the background worker
         DoBackgroundwork bgw = new DoBackgroundwork();
         bgw.StartWorker();

         // Start the computation on the main thread.  Each time through the loop,
         // check to see whether the user has cancelled the background thread.
         // After the calculation, add a short sleep, just to slow the program
         // down enough so the main thread doesn't run faster than the background.
         long mainTotal = 0;
         for ( int i = 0; i < 5; i++ )
         {
            if ( Program.CheckForCancelInput() )
               bgw.Cancel();

            mainTotal += DoBackgroundwork.CalculateTheSequence( 100000000 );
            Thread.Sleep( 200 );
            Console.WriteLine( "     {0}%", (i+1) * 20 );
         }

         SummarizeResults( bgw, mainTotal );
         Console.ReadLine();
      }

      private static void GiveInstructionsToTheUser()
      {
         Console.WriteLine( "Press <Enter> to start background worker." );
         Console.WriteLine( "Press <Enter> again to cancel background worker." );
         Console.ReadLine();
      }

      private static void OutputTheSummaryHeaders()
      {
         Console.WriteLine( "   Main    Background" );
         Console.WriteLine( "--------------------" );
      }
```

```
      private static void SummarizeResults( DoBackgroundwork bgw, long mainTotal )
      {
         if ( bgw.CompletedNormally )
         {
            Console.WriteLine( "\nBackground completed Normally" );
            Console.WriteLine( "Background total = {0}", bgw.BackgroundTotal );
         }
         else
         {
            Console.WriteLine( "\nBackground        Cancelled" );
         }

         Console.WriteLine( "Main total       = {0}", mainTotal );
      }

      private static bool CheckForCancelInput()
      {
         bool doCancel = Console.KeyAvailable;
         if ( doCancel )
            Console.ReadKey();
         return doCancel;
      }
   }
}
```

This code produces the following results when allowed to run to completion.

```
Press <Enter> to start background worker.
Press <Enter> again to cancel background worker.

   Main    Background
---------------------
            20%
            40%
   20%
            60%
   40%
            80%
   60%
            100%
   80%
   100%

Background completed Normally
Background total = 2749999925000000
Main total       = 24999999750000000
```

Example of the BackgroundWorker Class in a WPF Program

Since the BackgroundWorker class is primarily used with GUI programming, the following program shows its use in a simple WPF program rather than the console programs we've used throughout the text. WPF is Microsoft's replacement for the Windows Forms GUI programming framework. For further information about WPF programming, please see my book *Illustrated WPF*, also published by Apress.

This program produces the window shown on the left in Figure 22-4. When you click the Process button, it starts the background thread, which reports to the main thread every half second and increments the progress bar at the top by 10 percent. At completion, it shows the dialog box on the right of Figure 22-4.

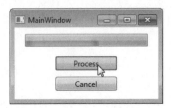 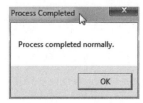

Figure 22-4. *The example WPF program using the BackgroundWorker class*

To create this WPF program in Visual Studio 2010, do the following:

1. Select the File ➤ New ➤ Project menu item, which pops up the New Project window.

2. In the pane on the left of the window, open the Installed Templates section, if it's not already open.

3. Under the C# category, click the Windows entry. This populates the center pane with the installed Windows program templates.

4. Click WPF Application, and then at the bottom of the window enter **SimpleWorker** in the Name text box. Below that, select a location, and click the OK button.

There are only two files you'll modify—MainWindow.xaml and MainWindow.xaml.cs. Modify your MainWindow.xaml file to match the following listing:

```
<Window x:Class="SimpleWorker.MainWindow"
        xmlns="http://schemas.microsoft.com/winfx/2006/xaml/presentation"
        xmlns:x="http://schemas.microsoft.com/winfx/2006/xaml"
        Title="MainWindow" Height="150  " Width="250">
    <StackPanel>
        <ProgressBar Name="progressBar" Height="20" Width="200" Margin="10"/>
        <Button Name="btnProcess" Width="100" Click="btnProcess_Click"
                Margin="5">Process</Button>
        <Button Name="btnCancel" Width="100" Click="btnCancel_Click"
                Margin="5">Cancel</Button>
    </StackPanel>
</Window>
```

Modify your `MainWindow.xaml.cs` file to match the following listing:

```
using System.Windows;
using System.ComponentModel;
using System.Threading;

namespace SimpleWorker
{
    public partial class MainWindow : Window
    {
        BackgroundWorker bgWorker = new BackgroundWorker();

        public MainWindow()
        {
            InitializeComponent();

            // Set BackgroundWorker properties
            bgWorker.WorkerReportsProgress     = true;
            bgWorker.WorkerSupportsCancellation = true;

            // Connect handlers to BackgroundWorker object.
            bgWorker.DoWork             += DoWork_Handler;
            bgWorker.ProgressChanged    += ProgressChanged_Handler;
            bgWorker.RunWorkerCompleted += RunWorkerCompleted_Handler;
        }

        private void btnProcess_Click( object sender, RoutedEventArgs e )
        {
            if ( !bgWorker.IsBusy )
                bgWorker.RunWorkerAsync();
        }

        private void ProgressChanged_Handler( object sender,
                                              ProgressChangedEventArgs args )
        {
            progressBar.Value = args.ProgressPercentage;
        }
```

```csharp
   private void DoWork_Handler( object sender, DoWorkEventArgs args )
   {
      BackgroundWorker worker = sender as BackgroundWorker;

      for ( int i = 1; i <= 10; i++ )
      {
         if ( worker.CancellationPending )
         {
            args.Cancel = true;
            break;
         }
         else
         {
            worker.ReportProgress( i * 10 );
            Thread.Sleep( 500 );
         }
      }
   }

   private void RunWorkerCompleted_Handler( object sender,
                                            RunWorkerCompletedEventArgs args )
   {
      progressBar.Value = 0;

      if ( args.Cancelled )
         MessageBox.Show( "Process was cancelled.", "Process Cancelled" );
      else
         MessageBox.Show( "Process completed normally.", "Process Completed" );
   }

   private void btnCancel_Click( object sender, RoutedEventArgs e )
   {
      bgWorker.CancelAsync();
   }
}
}
```

Asynchronous Programming Patterns

In Chapter 15, we covered the topic of delegates, and you saw that when a delegate object is invoked, it invokes the methods contained in its invocation list. This is done synchronously, just as if the methods had been called by the program.

If a delegate object has only a single method (which I'll call the *referenced method*) in its invocation list, it can execute that method asynchronously. The delegate class has two methods, called BeginInvoke and EndInvoke, that are used to do this. You use these methods in the following way:

- When you call the delegate's BeginInvoke method, it starts its referenced method executing on a separate thread from the thread pool and then returns immediately to the initial thread. The initial thread then continues on while the referenced method executes in parallel.

- When your program wants to retrieve the results of the completed asynchronous method, it either checks the IsCompleted property of the IAsyncResult returned by BeginInvoke or calls the delegate's EndInvoke method to wait for the delegate to finish.

Figure 22-5 shows the three standard patterns for using this process. In all three patterns, the initial thread initiates an asynchronous method call and then does some additional processing. The patterns differ, however, in the ways in which the initial thread receives the information that the spawned thread has completed.

- In the *wait-until-done* pattern, after spawning the asynchronous method and doing some additional processing, the initial thread halts and waits for the spawned thread to finish before continuing.

- In the *polling* pattern, the initial thread checks periodically whether the spawned thread has completed, and if not, it continues additional processing.

- In the *callback* pattern, the initial thread continues execution without waiting or checking whether the spawned thread has completed. Instead, when the referenced method in the spawned thread finishes, it calls a callback method, which handles the results of the asynchronous method before calling EndInvoke.

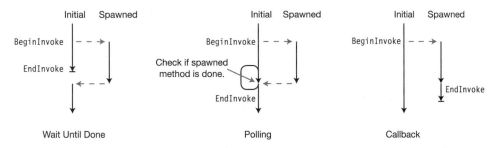

Figure 22-5. *The standard patterns for asynchronous method calls*

BeginInvoke and EndInvoke

Before we look at examples of these asynchronous programming patterns, let's take a closer look at the `BeginInvoke` and `EndInvoke` methods. Some of the important things to know about `BeginInvoke` are the following:

- When calling `BeginInvoke`, the actual parameters in the parameter list consist of the following:
  - The parameters required by the referenced method
  - Two additional parameters, called the `callback` parameter and the `state` parameter
- `BeginInvoke` retrieves a thread from the thread pool and starts the referenced method running on the new thread.
- `BeginInvoke` returns to the calling thread a reference to an object implementing the `IAsyncResult` interface. This interface reference contains information about the current state of the asynchronous method. The initial thread then continues execution.

The following code shows an example of calling a delegate's `BeginInvoke` method. The first line declares a delegate type called `MyDel`. The next line declares a method called `Sum`, which matches the delegate.

- The following line declares a delegate object called `del`, of the delegate type `MyDel`, and initializes its invocation list with the `Sum` method.
- Finally, the last line of code calls the `BeginInvoke` method of the delegate object and supplies it with the two delegate parameters 3 and 5 and the two `BeginInvoke` parameters `callback` and `state`, which are set to `null` in this example. When executed, the `BeginInvoke` method performs two actions:
  - It gets a thread from the thread pool and starts method `Sum` running on the new thread, supplying it with 3 and 5 as its actual parameters.
  - It collects information about the state of the new thread and makes it available through a reference to an interface of type `IAsyncResult`, which it returns to the calling thread. The calling thread, in this example, stores it in a variable called `iar`.

```
delegate long MyDel( int first, int second ); // Delegate declaration
   ...
static long Sum(int x, int y){ ... }           // Method matching delegate
   ...
MyDel del = new MyDel(Sum);                     // Create delegate object
IAsyncResult iar = del.BeginInvoke( 3, 5, null, null );
        ↑                    ↑             ↑       ↑
 Information about    Invoke delegate   Delegate  Extra
   new thread         asynchronously    params   params
```

You use the EndInvoke method to retrieve the values returned by the asynchronous method call and to release resources used by the thread. EndInvoke has the following characteristics:

- It takes as a parameter the reference to the IAsyncResult returned by the BeginInvoke method and finds the thread it refers to.

- If the thread pool thread has exited, EndInvoke does the following:

  — It cleans up the exited thread's loose ends and disposes of its resources.

  — It finds the value returned by the referenced method and returns that value as its return value.

- If the thread pool thread is still running when EndInvoke is called, the calling thread stops and waits for it to finish before cleaning up and returning the value. Because EndInvoke cleans up after the spawned thread, you must make sure that an EndInvoke is called for each BeginInvoke.

- If the asynchronous method triggers an exception, the exception is raised when EndInvoke is called.

The following line of code shows an example of calling EndInvoke to retrieve the value from an asynchronous method. You must always include the reference to the IAsyncResult object as a parameter.

```
                    Delegate object
                          ↓
    long result = del.EndInvoke( iar );
         ↑                        ↑
    Return value             IAsyncResult
    from async method           object
```

EndInvoke supplies all the output from the asynchronous method call, including ref and out parameters. If a delegate's referenced method has ref or out parameters, they must be included in EndInvoke's parameter list before the reference to the IAsyncResult object, as shown here:

```
    long result = del.EndInvoke(out someInt, iar);
         ↑                         ↑        ↑
    Return value                  Out    IAsyncResult
    from async method          parameter   object
```

615

The Wait-Until-Done Pattern

Now that you understand the BeginInvoke and EndInvoke delegate methods, we can look at the asynchronous programming patterns. The first one we'll look at is the wait-until-done pattern. In this pattern, the initial thread initiates an asynchronous method call, does some additional processing, and then stops and waits until the spawned thread finishes. It's summarized as follows:

```
IAsyncResult iar = del.BeginInvoke( 3, 5, null, null );
    // Do additional work in the calling thread, while the method
    // is being executed asynchronously in the spawned thread.
    ...
long result = del.EndInvoke( iar );
```

The following code shows a full example of this pattern. This code uses the Sleep method of the Thread class to suspend itself for 100 milliseconds (1/10 of a second). The Thread class is in the System.Threading namespace.

```
using System;
using System.Threading;                         // For Thread.Sleep()

delegate long MyDel( int first, int second );   // Declare delegate type

class Program {
   static long Sum(int x, int y)                // Declare method for async
   {
      Console.WriteLine("                       Inside Sum");
      Thread.Sleep(100);

      return x + y;
   }

   static void Main( ) {
      MyDel del = new MyDel(Sum);

      Console.WriteLine( "Before BeginInvoke" );
      IAsyncResult iar = del.BeginInvoke(3, 5, null, null); // Start async
      Console.WriteLine( "After  BeginInvoke" );

      Console.WriteLine( "Doing stuff" );

      long result = del.EndInvoke( iar );    // Wait for end and get result
      Console.WriteLine( "After  EndInvoke: {0}", result );
   }
}
```

This code produces the following output:

```
Before BeginInvoke
After  BeginInvoke
Doing stuff
                     Inside Sum
After  EndInvoke: 8
```

The AsyncResult Class

Now that you've seen BeginInvoke and EndInvoke in action in their simplest forms, it's time to take a closer look at IAsyncResult, which is an integral part of using these methods.

BeginInvoke returns a reference to an IAsyncResult interface that is inside a class object of type AsyncResult. The AsyncResult class represents the state of the asynchronous method. Figure 22-6 shows a representation of some of the important parts of the class. The important things to know about the class are the following:

- When you call a delegate object's BeginInvoke method, the system creates an object of the class AsyncResult. It doesn't, however, return a reference to the class object. Instead, it returns a reference to the *interface* contained in the object—IAsyncResult.

- An AsyncResult object contains a property called AsyncDelegate, which returns a reference to the delegate that was invoked to start the asynchronous method. This property, however, is part of the class object but not part of the interface.

- The IsCompleted property returns a Boolean value indicating whether the asynchronous method has completed.

- The AsyncState property returns a reference to the object that was listed as the state parameter in the BeginInvoke method invocation. It returns a reference of type object. I'll explain this in the section on the callback pattern.

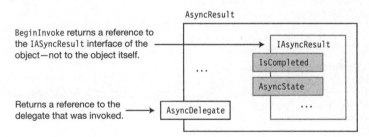

Figure 22-6. *An AsyncResult class object*

The Polling Pattern

In the polling pattern, the initial thread initiates an asynchronous method call, does some additional processing, and then uses the IsCompleted method of the IAsyncResult object to check periodically whether the spawned thread has completed. If the asynchronous method has completed, the initial thread calls EndInvoke and continues. Otherwise, it does some additional processing and checks again later. The "processing" in this example just consists of counting from 0 to 10,000,000.

```
delegate long MyDel(int first, int second);

class Program
{
    static long Sum(int x, int y)
    {
        Console.WriteLine("                    Inside Sum");
        Thread.Sleep(100);

        return x + y;
    }

    static void Main()
    {
        MyDel del = new MyDel(Sum);   Spawn async method
                                          ↓
        IAsyncResult iar = del.BeginInvoke(3, 5, null, null); // Start async.
        Console.WriteLine("After BeginInvoke");
        Check whether the async method is done.
                            ↓
        while ( !iar.IsCompleted )
        {
            Console.WriteLine("Not Done");

            // Continue processing, even though in this case it's just busywork.
            for (long i = 0; i < 10000000; i++)
                ;                                      // Empty statement
        }
        Console.WriteLine("Done");
                        Call EndInvoke to get result and clean up.
                              ↓
        long result = del.EndInvoke(iar);
        Console.WriteLine("Result: {0}", result);
    }
}
```

This code produces the following output:

```
After BeginInvoke
Not Done
                Inside Sum
Not Done
Not Done
Done
Result: 8
```

The Callback Pattern

In the previous two patterns, wait-until-done and polling, the initial thread continues with its flow of control only after it knows that the spawned thread has completed. It then retrieves the results and continues.

The callback pattern is different in that once the initial thread spawns the asynchronous method, it goes on its way without synchronizing with it again. When the asynchronous method call completes, the system invokes a user-supplied method to handle its results and to call the delegate's EndInvoke method. This user-defined method is called a *callback method*, or just a *callback*.

The two extra parameters at the end of the BeginInvoke parameter list are used with the callback method as follows:

- The first of the two parameters, the callback parameter, is the name of the callback method.

- The second parameter, the state parameter, can be either null or a reference to an object you want passed into the callback method. You'll be able to access this object through the method's IAsyncResult parameter using its AsyncState property. The type of this parameter is object.

The Callback Method

The signature and return type of the callback method must be of the form described by the AsyncCallback delegate type. This form requires that the method take a single parameter of type IAsyncResult and have a void return type, as shown here:

```
void AsyncCallback( IAsyncResult iar )
```

There are several ways you can supply the callback method to the BeginInvoke method. Since the callback parameter in BeginInvoke is a delegate of type AsyncCallback, you can supply it as a delegate, as shown in the first code statement that follows. Or you can just supply the name of the callback method and let the compiler create the delegate for you. Both forms are semantically equivalent.

```
                          Create a delegate with the callback method.
IAsyncResult iar1 =                       ↓
    del.BeginInvoke(3, 5, new AsyncCallback(CallWhenDone), null);
                                 Just use the callback method's name.
                                             ↓
IAsyncResult iar2 = del.BeginInvoke(3, 5, CallWhenDone, null);
```

The second BeginInvoke parameter is used to send an object to the callback method. It can be an object of any type, but the parameter is of type object, so inside the callback method you'll have to cast it to the correct type.

Calling EndInvoke Inside the Callback Method

Inside the callback method, your code should call the delegate's EndInvoke method and take care of handling the output results of the asynchronous method execution. To call the delegate's EndInvoke method, though, you need a reference to the delegate object, which is in the initial thread—not here in the spawned thread.

If you're not using BeginInvoke's state parameter for anything else, you can use it to send the delegate reference to the callback method, as shown here:

```
        Delegate object              Send delegate object as state param
              ↓                                    ↓
IAsyncResult iar = del.BeginInvoke(3, 5, CallWhenDone, del);
```

Otherwise, you can extract the delegate's reference from the IAsyncResult object sent into the method as the parameter. This is shown in the following code and illustrated in Figure 22-7.

- The single parameter to the callback method is a reference to the IAsyncResult interface of the asynchronous method that has just completed. Remember that the IAsyncResult interface object is inside the AsyncResult class object.

- Although the IAsyncResult interface doesn't have a reference to the delegate object, the AsyncResult class object enclosing it *does* have a reference to the delegate object. So, the first line inside the example method body gets a reference to the class object by casting the interface reference to the class type. Variable ar now has a reference to the class object.

- With the reference to the class object, you can now use the AsyncDelegate property of the class object and cast it to the appropriate delegate type. This gives you the delegate reference, which you can then use to call EndInvoke.

```
using System.Runtime.Remoting.Messaging;      // Contains AsyncResult class

void CallWhenDone( IAsyncResult iar )
{
    AsyncResult ar = (AsyncResult) iar;       // Get class object reference
    MyDel del = (MyDel) ar.AsyncDelegate;     // Get reference to delegate

    long Sum = del.EndInvoke( iar );          // Call EndInvoke
       ...
}
```

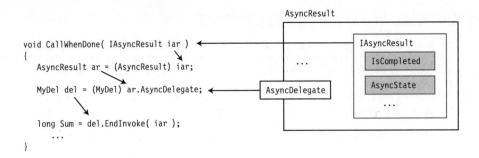

Figure 22-7. *Extracting the delegate's reference inside the callback method*

The following code puts it all together and is an example of using the callback pattern.

```csharp
using System;
using System.Runtime.Remoting.Messaging;        // To access the AsyncResult type
using System.Threading;

delegate long MyDel(int first, int second);

class Program
{
   static long Sum(int x, int y)
   {
      Console.WriteLine("                           Inside Sum");
      Thread.Sleep(100);
      return x + y;
   }

   static void CallWhenDone(IAsyncResult iar)
   {
      Console.WriteLine("                           Inside CallWhenDone.");
      AsyncResult ar = (AsyncResult) iar;
      MyDel del = (MyDel)ar.AsyncDelegate;

      long result = del.EndInvoke(iar);
      Console.WriteLine
         ("                           The result is: {0}.", result);
   }

   static void Main()
   {
      MyDel del = new MyDel(Sum);

      Console.WriteLine("Before BeginInvoke");
      IAsyncResult iar =
         del.BeginInvoke(3, 5, new AsyncCallback(CallWhenDone), null);

      Console.WriteLine("Doing more work in Main.");
      Thread.Sleep(500);
      Console.WriteLine("Done with Main. Exiting.");
   }
}
```

This code produces the following output:

```
Before BeginInvoke
Doing more work in Main.
                     Inside Sum
                     Inside CallWhenDone.
                     The result is: 8.
Done with Main. Exiting.
```

Timers

Timers provide another way to run an asynchronous method on a regular, recurring basis. Although there are several Timer classes available in the .NET BCL, I'll describe the one in the System.Threading namespace.

The important things to know about this timer class are the following:

- The timer uses a callback method that is called each time the timer expires. The callback method must be in the form of the TimerCallback delegate, which has the following form. It takes a single parameter of type object and has a void return type.

```
void TimerCallback( object state )
```

- When the timer expires, the system sets up the callback method on a thread from the thread pool, supplies the state object as its parameter, and starts it running.

- You can set a number of the timer's characteristics, including the following:

  - The dueTime is the amount of time before the first call of the callback method. If dueTime is set to the special value Timeout.Infinite, the timer will not start. If it's set to 0, the callback is called immediately.

  - The period is the amount of time between each successive call of the callback method. If it's value is set to Timeout.Infinite, the callback won't be called after the first time.

  - The state is either null or a reference to an object to be passed to the callback method each time it's executed.

The constructor for the Timer class takes as parameters the name of the callback method, the dueTime, the period, and the state. There are several constructors for Timer; the one that's probably the most commonly used has the following form:

```
Timer( TimerCallback callback, object state, uint dueTime, uint period)
```

The following code statement shows an example of the creation of a Timer object:

```
                             Name of          Call first time after
                            the callback       2000 milliseconds
                                ↓                     ↓
Timer myTimer = new Timer ( MyCallback, someObject, 2000, 1000 );
                                ↑                     ↑
                           Object to pass        Call every
                           to the callback    1000 milliseconds
```

Once a Timer object is created, you can change its dueTime or period using the Change method.

The following code shows an example of using a timer. The Main method creates the timer so that it will call the callback for the first time after two seconds and once every second after that. The callback method simply prints out a message, including the number of times it's been called.

```
using System;
using System.Threading;

namespace Timers
{
    class Program
    {
        int TimesCalled = 0;

        void Display (object state)
        {
            Console.WriteLine("{0} {1}",(string)state, ++TimesCalled);
        }

        static void Main( )
        {
            Program p = new Program();              First callback at
                                                     2 seconds
            Timer myTimer = new Timer                    ↓
                (p.Display, "Processing timer event", 2000, 1000);
            Console.WriteLine("Timer started.");         ↑
                                                    Repeat every
            Console.ReadLine();                      second
        }
    }
}
```

This code produces the following output before being terminated after about five seconds:

```
Timer started.
Processing timer event 1
Processing timer event 2
Processing timer event 3
Processing timer event 4
```

There are several other timer classes supplied by the .NET BCL, each having its own uses. The other timer classes are the following:

- `System.Windows.Forms.Timer`: This class is used in Windows Forms applications to periodically place `WM_TIMER` messages into the program's message queue. When the program gets the message from the queue, it processes the handler *synchronously* on the main user interface thread. This is extremely important in Windows Forms applications.

- `System.Timers.Timer`: This class is more extensive and contains a number of members for manipulating the timer through properties and methods. It also has a member event called `Elapsed`, which is raised when each period expires. This timer can run on either a user interface thread or a worker thread.

CHAPTER 23

Preprocessor Directives

What Are Preprocessor Directives?

The source code specifies the definition of a program. The *preprocessor directives* instruct the compiler how to treat the source code. For example, under certain conditions, you might want the compiler to ignore portions of the code, and under other conditions, you might want that code compiled. The preprocessor directives give you those options and several others.

In C and C++ there is an actual preprocessor phase, in which the preprocessor goes through the source code and prepares an output stream of text to be processed by the subsequent compilation phase. In C# there is no actual preprocessor. The "preprocessor" directives are handled by the compiler. The term, however, remains.

General Rules

Some of the most important syntactic rules for preprocessor directives are the following:

- Preprocessor directives must be on lines separate from C# code.

- Unlike C# statements, preprocessor directives are not terminated with a semicolon.

- Every line containing a preprocessor directive must start with the # character.

  — There can be space before the # character.

  — There can be space between the # character and the directive.

- End-of-line comments are allowed.

- Delimited comments are *not* allowed in a preprocessor directive line.

Here are some examples illustrating the rules:

```
                    No semicolon
                        ↓
    #define PremiumVersion          // OK

Space before
    ↓
      #define BudgetVersion         // OK
  #     define MediumVersion        // OK
  ↑
Space between               Delimited comments are not allowed.
                                        ↓
    #define PremiumVersion      /* all bells & whistles */
                               End-of-line comments are fine.
                                        ↓
    #define BudgetVersion      // Stripped-down version
```

The preprocessor directives are listed in Table 23-1.

Table 23-1. *Preprocessor Directives*

Directive	Summary of Meaning
#define identifier	Defines a compilation symbol
#undef identifier	Undefines a compilation symbol
#if expression	If the expression is true, compiles the following section
#elif expression	If the expression is true, compiles the following section
#else	If the previous #if or #elif expression is false, compiles the following section
#endif	Marks the end of an #if construct
#region name	Marks the beginning of a region of code; has no compilation effect
#endregion name	Marks the end of a region of code; has no compilation effect
#warning message	Displays a compile-time warning message
#error message	Displays a compile-time error message
#line indicator	Changes the line numbers displayed in compiler messages
#pragma text	Specifies information about the program context

The #define and #undef Directives

A *compilation symbol* is an identifier that has only two possible states. It is either *defined* or *undefined*. A compilation symbol has the following characteristics:

- It can be any identifier except true or false. This includes C# keywords and identifiers declared in your C# code—both of which are fine.

- It has no value. Unlike in C and C++, it does not represent a string.

As shown in Table 23-1:

- The #define directive declares a compilation symbol.

- The #undef directive undefines a compilation symbol.

```
#define PremiumVersion
#define EconomyVersion
  ...
#undef PremiumVersion
```

The #define and #undef directives can be used only at the top of a source file, before any C# code is listed. After the C# code has started, the #define and #undef directives can no longer be used.

```
using System;                    // First line of C# code
#define PremiumVersion           // Error

namespace Eagle
{
   #define PremiumVersion        // Error
   ...
```

The scope of a compilation symbol is limited to a single source file. Redefining a symbol that is already defined is perfectly fine—as long as it's before any C# code, of course.

```
#define AValue
#define BValue

#define AValue                   // Redefinition is fine.
```

Conditional Compilation

Conditional compilation allows you to mark a section of source code to be either compiled or skipped, depending on whether a particular compilation symbol is defined.

There are four directives for specifying conditional compilation:

- `#if`

- `#else`

- `#elif`

- `#endif`

A *condition* is a simple expression that returns either `true` or `false`.

- A condition can consist of a single compilation symbol or an expression of symbols and operators, as summarized in Table 23-2. Subexpressions can be grouped with parentheses.

- The literals `true` and `false` can also be used in conditional expressions.

Table 23-2. *Conditions Used in the #if and #elif Directives*

Parameter Type	Meaning	Evaluation
Compilation symbol	Identifier, defined (or not) using the #define directive	True: If the symbol has been defined using a #define directive False: Otherwise
Expression	Constructed using symbols and the operators !, ==, !=, &&, ||	True: If the expression evaluates to true False: Otherwise

The following are examples of conditional compilation conditions:

```
        Expression
           ↓
      _____
#if !DemoVersion
  ...
#endif            Expression
                     ↓
          _____
#if (LeftHanded && OemVersion) || FullVersion
  ...
#endif

#if true    // The following code segment will always be compiled.
  ...
#endif
```

The Conditional Compilation Constructs

The #if and #endif directives are the matching demarcations of a conditional compilation construct. Whenever there is an #if directive, there must also be a matching #endif.

Figure 23-1 illustrates the #if and #if...#else constructs.

- If the condition in the #if construct evaluates to true, the code section following it is compiled. Otherwise, it is skipped.

- In the #if...#else construct, if the condition evaluates to true, *CodeSection1* is compiled. Otherwise, *CodeSection2* is compiled.

Figure 23-1. *The #if and #else constructs*

For example, the following code illustrates a simple #if...#else construct. If the symbol RightHanded is defined, the code between the #if and the #else will be compiled. Otherwise, the code between the #else and the #endif will be compiled.

```
...
#if RightHanded
    // Code implementing right-handed functionality
    ...
#else
    // Code implementing left-handed functionality
    ...
#endif
```

Figure 23-2 illustrates the #if...#elif and #if...#elif...#else constructs.

- In the #if...#elif construct, if *Cond1* evaluates to true, *CodeSection1* is compiled, and compilation continues after the #endif.

  — Otherwise, if *Cond2* evaluates to true, *CodeSection2* is compiled, and compilation continues after the #endif.

  — This continues until either a condition evaluates to true or all the conditions have returned false. If that's the case, none of the code sections in the construct are compiled, and compilation continues after the #endif.

- The #if...#elif...#else construct works the same way, except that if no condition is true, then the code section after the #else is then compiled, and compilation continues after the #endif.

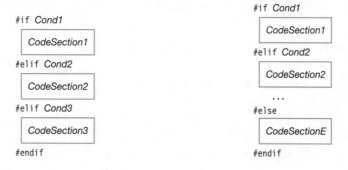

Figure 23-2. *The #elif construct*

The following code demonstrates the #if...#elif...#else construct. The string containing the description of the version of the program is set to various values, depending on which compilation symbol is defined.

```
#define DemoVersionWithoutTimeLimit
      ...
   const int intExpireLength = 30;
   string strVersionDesc = null;
   int    intExpireCount = 0;

#if   DemoVersionWithTimeLimit
   intExpireCount = intExpireLength;
   strVersionDesc = "This version of Supergame Plus will expire in 30 days";

#elif DemoVersionWithoutTimeLimit
   strVersionDesc = "Demo Version of Supergame Plus";

#elif OEMVersion
   strVersionDesc = "Supergame Plus, distributed under license";

#else
   strVersionDesc = "The original Supergame Plus!!";

#endif

   Console.WriteLine( strVersionDesc );
      ...
```

Diagnostic Directives

Diagnostic directives produce user-defined compile-time warning and error messages.

The following is the syntax of the diagnostic directives. The messages are strings, but notice that unlike normal C# strings, they do not have to be enclosed in quotation marks.

```
#warning Message
```

```
#error Message
```

When the compiler reaches a diagnostic directive, it writes out the associated message. The diagnostic directive messages are listed by the compiler along with any compiler-generated warning and error messages.

For example, the following code shows an #error directive and a #warning directive.

- The #error directive is inside an #if construct so that it will be generated only if the conditions on the #if directive are met.

- The #warning directive is a reminder to the programmer to come back and clean up a section of code.

```
#define RightHanded
#define LeftHanded

#if RightHanded && LeftHanded
#error Can't build for both RightHanded and LeftHanded
#endif

#warning Remember to come back and clean up this code!
```

Line Number Directives

Line number directives can do several things, including the following:

- Change the apparent line numbers reported by the compiler's warning and error messages

- Change the apparent file name of the source file being compiled

- Hide a sequence of lines from the interactive debugger

The syntax for the #line directives is the following:

```
#line integer        // Sets line number of next line to value of integer
#line "filename"     // Sets the apparent filename
#line default        // Restores real line number and filename

#line hidden         // Hides the following code from stepping debugger
#line                // Stops hiding from debugger
```

The #line directive with an integer parameter causes the compiler to consider that value to be the line number of the following line of code. Numbering of the subsequent lines continues, based on that line number.

- To change the apparent file name, use the file name, inside double quotes, as the parameter. The double quotes are required.

- To return to true line numbering and the true file name, use default as the parameter.

- To hide a segment of code from the step-through-code feature of the interactive debugger, use hidden as the parameter. To stop hiding, use the directive with no parameter. This feature has, so far, mostly been used in ASP.NET and WPF for hiding compiler-generated code.

The following code shows examples of the line number directives:

```
#line 226
      x = y + z; // Now considered by the compiler to be line 226
      ...

#line 330 "SourceFile.cs" // Changes the reported line number and filename
      var1 = var2 + var3;
      ...

#line default               // Restores true line numbers and filename
```

Region Directives

The region directive allows you to mark, and optionally name, a section of code. The characteristics of the #region directive are the following:

- It is placed on the line above the section of code you want to mark.

- It can take an optional string of text following it on the line, which serves as its name.

- It must be terminated by an #endregion directive, further down in the code.

Although region directives are ignored by the compiler, they can be used by source code tools. Visual Studio, for example, allows you to easily hide or display regions.

As an example, the following code has a region called Constructors, which encloses the two constructors of class MyClass. In Visual Studio, you could collapse this region to a single line when you didn't want to see it in the code and then expand it again when you needed to work on it or add another constructor.

```
#region Constructors
   MyClass()
   {
      ...
   }

   MyClass(string s)
   {
      ...
   }
#endregion
```

Regions can be nested, as shown in Figure 23-3.

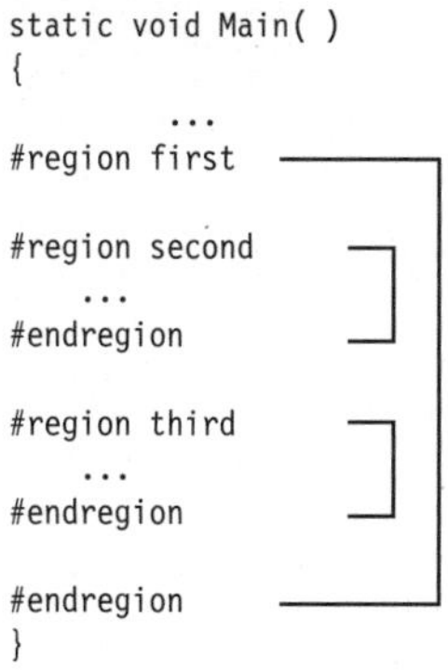

```
static void Main( )
{
      ...
#region first

#region second
   ...
#endregion

#region third
   ...
#endregion

#endregion
}
```

Figure 23-3. *Nested regions*

637

The #pragma warning Directive

The #pragma warning directive allows you to turn off warning messages and to turn them back on.

- To turn off warning messages, use the disable form with a comma-separated list of warning numbers you want to turn off.

- To turn warning messages back on, use the restore form with a list of the warning numbers you want to turn back on.

For example, the following code turns off two warning messages: 618 and 414. Further down in the code, it turns on messages for 618 but leaves the messages for 414 turned off.

```
                          Warning messages to turn off
                                    ↓
#pragma warning disable 618, 414
    ...        Messages for the listed warnings are off in this section of code.
#pragma warning restore 618
```

If you use either form without a warning number list, the command then applies to all warnings. For example, the following code turns off, and then restores, all warning messages.

```
#pragma warning disable
    ...        All warning messages are turned off in this section of code.

#pragma warning restore
    ...        All warning messages are turned back on in this section of code.
```

CHAPTER 24

■ ■ ■

Reflection and Attributes

Metadata and Reflection

Most programs are written to work on data. They read, write, manipulate, and display data. (Graphics are a form of data.) The types that you as the programmer create and use are designed for these purposes, and it is you, at design time, who must understand the characteristics of the types you use.

For some types of programs, however, the data they manipulate is not numbers, text, or graphics but information about programs and program types.

- Data about programs and their types is called *metadata* and is stored in the programs' assemblies.

- A program can look at the metadata of other assemblies or of itself, while it's running. When a running program looks at its own metadata, or that of other programs, it's called *reflection*.

An object browser is an example of a program that displays metadata. It can read assemblies and display the types they contain, along with all the characteristics and members.

This chapter will look at how your programs can reflect on data using the Type class and how you can add metadata to your types using *attributes*.

■ **Note** To use reflection, you must use the System.Reflection namespace.

The Type Class

Throughout this text I've described how to declare and use the types available in C#. These include the predefined types (int, long, string, and so on), types from the BCL (Console, IEnumerable, and so on), and user-defined types (MyClass, MyDel, and so on). Every type has its own members and characteristics.

The BCL declares an abstract class called Type, which is designed to contain the characteristics of a type. Using objects of this class allows you to get information about the types your program is using.

Since Type is an abstract class, it cannot have actual instances. Instead, at run time, the CLR creates instances of a class *derived* from Type (RuntimeType) that contains the type information. When you access one of these instances, the CLR returns a reference, not of the derived type but of the base class Type. For simplicity's sake, though, throughout the rest of the chapter, I'll call the object pointed at by the reference an object of type Type, although technically it's an object of a derived type that is internal to the BCL.

Important things to know about Type are the following:

- For every type used in a program, the CLR creates a Type object that contains the information about the type.

- Every type used in a program is associated with a separate Type object.

- Regardless of the number of instances of a type that are created, there is only a single Type object associated with all the instances.

Figure 24-1 shows a running program with two MyClass objects and an OtherClass object. Notice that although there are two instances of MyClass, there is only a single Type object representing it.

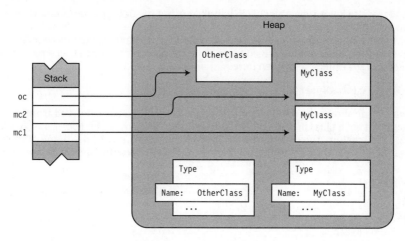

Figure 24-1. *The CLR instantiates objects of type Type for every type used in a program.*

You can get almost anything you need to know about a type from its Type object. Table 24-1 lists some of the more useful members of the class.

Table 24-1. *Selected Members of Class System.Type*

Member	Member Type	Description
Name	Property	Returns the name of the type.
Namespace	Property	Returns the namespace containing the type declaration.
Assembly	Property	Returns the assembly in which the type is declared. If the type is generic, it returns the assembly in which the type is defined.
GetFields	Method	Returns a list of the type's fields.
GetProperties	Method	Returns a list of the type's properties.
GetMethods	Method	Returns a list of the type's methods.

Getting a Type Object

There are several ways to get a Type object. We'll look at using the GetType method and using the typeof operator.

Type object contains a method called GetType, which returns a reference to an instance's Type object. Since every type is ultimately derived from object, you can call the GetType method on an object of any type to get its Type object, as shown here:

```
Type t = myInstance.GetType();
```

The following code shows the declarations of a base class and a class derived from it. Method Main creates an instance of each class and places the references in an array called bca for easy processing. Inside the outer foreach loop, the code gets the Type object and prints out the name of the class. It then gets the fields of the class and prints them out. Figure 24-2 illustrates the objects in memory.

```csharp
using System;
using System.Reflection;                        // Must use this namespace

class BaseClass
{ public int BaseField = 0; }

class DerivedClass : BaseClass
{ public int DerivedField = 0; }

class Program
{
   static void Main( )
   {
      var bc = new BaseClass();
      var dc = new DerivedClass();
      BaseClass[] bca = new BaseClass[] { bc, dc };

      foreach (var v in bca)
      {
         Type t = v.GetType();                    // Get the type.

         Console.WriteLine("Object type : {0}", t.Name);

         FieldInfo[] fi = t.GetFields();          // Get the field info.
         foreach (var f in fi)
            Console.WriteLine("      Field : {0}", f.Name);
         Console.WriteLine();
      }
   }
}
```

This code produces the following output:

```
Object type : BaseClass
      Field : BaseField

Object type : DerivedClass
      Field : DerivedField
      Field : BaseField
```

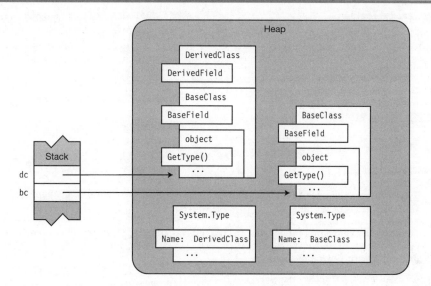

Figure 24-2. *The base class and derived class objects along with their Type objects*

You can also use the typeof operator to get a Type object. Just supply the name of the type as the operand, and it returns a reference to the Type object, as shown here:

```
Type t = typeof( DerivedClass );
         ↑              ↑
      Operator    Type you want the Type object for
```

The following code shows a simple example of using the typeof operator:

```
using System;
using System.Reflection;                          // Must use this namespace

namespace SimpleReflection
{
    class BaseClass
    { public int MyFieldBase; }

    class DerivedClass : BaseClass
    { public int MyFieldDerived; }

    class Program
    {
        static void Main( )
        {
            Type tbc = typeof(DerivedClass);                  // Get the type.
            Console.WriteLine("Result is {0}.", tbc.Name);

            Console.WriteLine("It has the following fields:");  // Use the type.
            FieldInfo[] fi = tbc.GetFields();
            foreach (var f in fi)
                Console.WriteLine("   {0}", f.Name);
        }
    }
}
```

This code produces the following output:

```
Result is DerivedClass.
It has the following fields:
   MyFieldDerived
   MyFieldBase
```

What Is an Attribute?

An *attribute* is a language construct that allows you to add metadata to a program's assembly. It's a special type of class for storing information about program constructs.

- The program construct to which you apply an attribute is called its *target*.

- Programs designed to retrieve and use metadata, such as object browsers, are said to be *consumers* of the attributes.

- There are attributes that are predefined in .NET, and you can also declare custom attributes.

Figure 24-3 is an overview of the components involved in using attributes and illustrates the following points about them:

- You *apply* attributes to program constructs in the source code.

- The compiler takes the source code and produces metadata from the attributes and places that metadata in the assembly.

- Consumer programs can access the metadata of the attributes along with the metadata for the rest of the components of the program. Notice that the compiler both produces and consumes attributes.

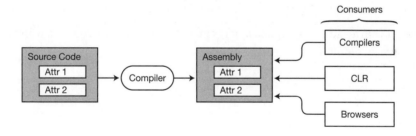

Figure 24-3. *The components involved with creating and using attributes*

By convention, attribute names use Pascal casing and end with the suffix `Attribute`. When applying an attribute to a target, you can leave off the suffix. For example, for attributes `SerializableAttribute` and `MyAttributeAttribute`, you can use the short names `Serializable` and `MyAttribute` when applying them to a construct.

Applying an Attribute

The purpose of an attribute is to tell the compiler to emit a certain set of metadata about a program construct to the assembly. You do this by *applying* the attribute to the construct.

- You apply an attribute by placing an *attribute section* immediately before the construct.

- An *attribute section* consists of square brackets enclosing an attribute name and sometimes a parameter list.

For example, the following code shows the headings of two classes. The first few lines of code show an attribute named Serializable applied to class MyClass. Notice that Serializable has no parameter list. The second class declaration has an attribute called MyAttribute, which has a parameter list with two string parameters.

```
[ Serializable ]                                    // Attribute
public class MyClass
{ ...

[ MyAttribute("Simple class", "Version 3.57") ]    // Attribute with parameters
public class MyOtherClass
{ ...
```

Some important things to know about attributes are the following:

- Most attributes apply only to the construct immediately following the attribute section or sections.

- A construct with an attribute applied to it is said to be *decorated*, or *adorned*, with the attribute. Both terms are common.

Predefined, Reserved Attributes

Before looking at how you can define your own attributes, this section describes two attributes predefined and reserved by .NET: the Obsolete and Conditional attributes.

The Obsolete Attribute

The Obsolete attribute allows you to mark a program construct as obsolete and to display a helpful warning message when the code is compiled. The following code shows an example of its use:

```
class Program        Apply attribute
{                          ↓
    [Obsolete("Use method SuperPrintOut")]   // Apply attribute to method
    static void PrintOut(string str)
    {
        Console.WriteLine(str);
    }

    static void Main(string[] args)
    {
        PrintOut("Start of Main");           // Invoke obsolete method
    }
}
```

Notice that method Main calls PrintOut even though it's marked as obsolete. In spite of this, the code compiles and runs fine and produces the following output:

```
Start of Main
```

During compilation, though, the compiler produces the following CS0618 warning message to inform you that you're using an obsolete construct:

```
'AttrObs.Program.PrintOut(string)' is obsolete: 'Use method SuperPrintOut'
```

Another overload of the Obsolete attribute takes a second parameter of type bool. This parameter specifies whether use of the target should be flagged as an error instead of just a warning. The following code specifies that it should be flagged as an error:

```
                        Flag as an error
                              ↓
[ Obsolete("Use method SuperPrintOut", true) ]  // Apply attribute to method
static void PrintOut(string str)
{ ...
```

The Conditional Attribute

The Conditional attribute allows you to either include or exclude all the *invocations* of a particular method. To use the Conditional attribute, apply it to the method declaration, along with a compilation symbol as a parameter.

- If the compilation symbol is defined, the compiler includes the code for all the invocations of the method, the way it would for any normal method.

- If the compilation symbol is *not* defined, the compiler *omits* all the method invocations throughout the code.

The CIL code defining the method itself is always included in the assembly. It's just the invocations that are either inserted or omitted.

For example, in the following code, the Conditional attribute is applied to the declaration of a method called TraceMessage. The attribute has a single parameter, which in this case is the string DoTrace.

- When the compiler is compiling the code, it checks whether there is a compilation symbol named DoTrace defined.

- If DoTrace is defined, the compiler includes all the calls to method TraceMessage, as usual.

- If there is no DoTrace compilation symbol defined, it doesn't output code for any of the calls to TraceMessage.

```
                 Compilation symbol
                        ↓
[Conditional( "DoTrace" )]
static void TraceMessage(string str)
{
    Console.WriteLine(str);
}
```

Example of the Conditional Attribute

The following code shows a full example of using the Conditional attribute.

- Method Main contains two calls to method TraceMessage.

- The declaration for method TraceMessage is decorated with the Conditional attribute, which has the compilation symbol DoTrace as its parameter. So if DoTrace is defined, the compiler will include the code for all the calls to TraceMessage.

- Since the first line of code defines a compilation symbol named DoTrace, the compiler will include the code for both calls to TraceMessage.

```
#define DoTrace
using System;
using System.Diagnostics;

namespace AttributesConditional
{
    class Program
    {
        [Conditional( "DoTrace" )]
        static void TraceMessage(string str)
        { Console.WriteLine(str); }

        static void Main( )
        {
            TraceMessage("Start of Main");
            Console.WriteLine("Doing work in Main.");
            TraceMessage("End of Main");
        }
    }
}
```

This code produces the following output:

```
Start of Main
Doing work in Main.
End of Main
```

If you comment out the first line so that DoTrace is not defined, the compiler will not insert the code for the two calls to TraceMessage. This time, when you run the program, it produces the following output:

```
Doing work in Main.
```

Predefined Attributes

The .NET Framework predefines a number of attributes that are understood and interpreted by the compiler and the CLR. Table 24-2 lists some of these. The table uses the short names, without the "Attribute" suffix. For example, the full name of CLSCompliant is CLSCompliantAttribute.

Table 24-2. *Important Attributes Defined in .NET*

Attribute	Meaning
CLSCompliant	Declares that the publicly exposed members should be checked by the compiler for compliance with the CLS. Compliant assemblies can be used by any .NET-compliant language.
Serializable	Declares that the construct can be serialized.
NonSerialized	Declares that the construct cannot be serialized.
Obsolete	Declares that the construct should not be used. The compiler also produces a compile-time warning or error message, if the construct is used.
DLLImport	Declares that the implementation is unmanaged code.
WebMethod	Declares that the method should be exposed as part of an XML web service.
AttributeUsage	Declares what types of program constructs the attribute can be applied to. This attribute is applied to attribute declarations.

More About Applying Attributes

The simple attributes shown so far have used a single attribute applied to a method. This section describes other types of attribute usage.

Multiple Attributes

You can apply multiple attributes to a single construct.

- Multiple attributes can be listed in either of the following formats:

  — Separate attribute sections stacked on top of each other

  — A single attribute section, with the attributes separated by commas

- You can list the attributes in any order.

For example, the following two sections of code show the two ways of applying multiple attributes. The sections of code are equivalent.

```
[ Serializable ]                                        // Stacked
[ MyAttribute("Simple class", "Version 3.57") ]

[ MyAttribute("Simple class", "Version 3.57"), Serializable ]   // Commas
              ↑                                 ↑
          Attribute                         Attribute
```

Other Types of Targets

Besides classes, you can also apply attributes to other program constructs such as fields and properties. The following declaration shows an attribute on a field, and multiple attributes on a method:

```
[MyAttribute("Holds a value", "Version 3.2")]          // On a field
public int MyField;

[Obsolete]                                              // On a method
[MyAttribute("Prints out a message.", "Version 3.6")]
public void PrintOut()
{
    ...
```

You can also explicitly label attributes to apply to a particular target construct. To use an explicit target, place the target type, followed by a colon, at the beginning of the attribute section. For example, the following code decorates the *method* with an attribute and also applies an attribute to the *return value*.

```
Explicit target
     ↓
[method: MyAttribute("Prints out a message.", "Version 3.6")]
[return: MyAttribute("This value represents ...", "Version 2.3")]
public long ReturnSetting()
{
    ...
```

The C# language defines ten standard attribute targets, which are listed in Table 24-3. Most of the target names are self-explanatory, but type covers classes, structs, delegates, enums, and interfaces. The typevar target name specifies type parameters to constructs that use generics.

Table 24-3. *Attribute Targets*

event	field
method	param
property	return
type	typevar
assembly	module

Global Attributes

You can also use an explicit target to set attributes at the assembly and module level, by using the assembly and module target names. (Assemblies and modules were explained in Chapter 10.) Some important points about assembly-level attributes are the following:

- Assembly-level attributes must be placed outside any namespace scope and are usually placed in the AssemblyInfo.cs file.

- The AssembyInfo.cs file usually contains metadata about the company, product, and copyright information.

The following are lines from an AssemblyInfo.cs file:

```
[assembly: AssemblyTitle("SuperWidget")]
[assembly: AssemblyDescription("Implements the SuperWidget product.")]
[assembly: AssemblyConfiguration("")]
[assembly: AssemblyCompany("McArthur Widgets, Inc.")]
[assembly: AssemblyProduct("Super Widget Deluxe")]
[assembly: AssemblyCopyright("Copyright © McArthur Widgets 2010")]
[assembly: AssemblyTrademark("")]
[assembly: AssemblyCulture("")]
```

Custom Attributes

You've probably noticed that the syntax for applying an attribute is very different from anything you've seen so far. From that, you might get the impression that attributes are an entirely different type of construct. They're not—they're just a special kind of class.

Some important points about attribute classes are the following:

- User-defined attribute classes are called *custom attributes*.

- All attribute classes are derived from class System.Attribute.

Declaring a Custom Attribute

Declaring an attribute class is, for the most part, the same as declaring any other class. There are, however, several things to be aware of:

- To declare a custom attribute, do the following:

  — Declare a class derived from System.Attribute.

  — Give it a name ending with the suffix Attribute.

- For security, it's generally suggested that you declare your attribute classes as sealed.

For example, the following code shows the beginning of the declaration of attribute MyAttributeAttribute:

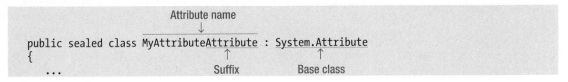

Since an attribute holds information about the target, the public members of an attribute class generally consist only of the following:

- Fields

- Properties

- Constructors

Using Attribute Constructors

Attributes, like other classes, have constructors. Every attribute must have at least one public constructor.

- As with other classes, if you don't declare a constructor, the compiler will produce an implicit, public, parameterless constructor for you.

- Attribute constructors, like other constructors, can be overloaded.

- When declaring the constructor, you must use the full class name, including the suffix. You can use the shortened name only when *applying* an attribute.

For example, with the following constructor, the compiler would produce an error message if the name did not include the suffix:

```
                        Suffix
                          ↓
public MyAttributeAttribute(string desc, string ver)
{
   Description   = desc;
   VersionNumber = ver;
}
```

Specifying the Constructor

When you apply an attribute to a target, you are specifying which constructor should be used to create the instance of the attribute. The parameters listed in the attribute application are the actual parameters for the constructor.

For example, in the following code, MyAttribute is applied to a field and to a method. For the field, the declaration specifies a constructor with a single string parameter. For the method, it specifies a constructor with two string parameters.

```
[MyAttribute("Holds a value")]              // Constructor with one string
public int MyField;

[MyAttribute("Version 1.3", "Sal Martin")]  // Constructor with two strings
public void MyMethod()
{ ...
```

Other important points about attribute constructors are the following:

- When applying an attribute, the actual parameters for the constructor must be constant expressions whose values can be determined at compile time.

- If you apply an attribute constructor with no parameters, you can leave off the parentheses. For example, both classes in the following code use the parameterless constructor for the attribute MyAttr. The meanings of the two forms are the same.

```
[MyAttr]
class SomeClass ...

[MyAttr()]
class OtherClass ...
```

Using the Constructor

You cannot call the constructor explicitly. An instance of an attribute is created, and a constructor called, only when an attribute consumer accesses the attribute. This is very different from other class instances, which are created at the position where you use an object-creation expression. Applying an attribute is a declarative statement that does not determine when an object of the attribute class should be constructed.

Figure 24-4 compares the use of a constructor for a regular class and the use of a constructor with attributes.

- The imperative statement says, in effect, "Create a new class object here."

- The declarative statement says, "This attribute is associated with this target, and in case the attribute needs to be constructed, use this constructor."

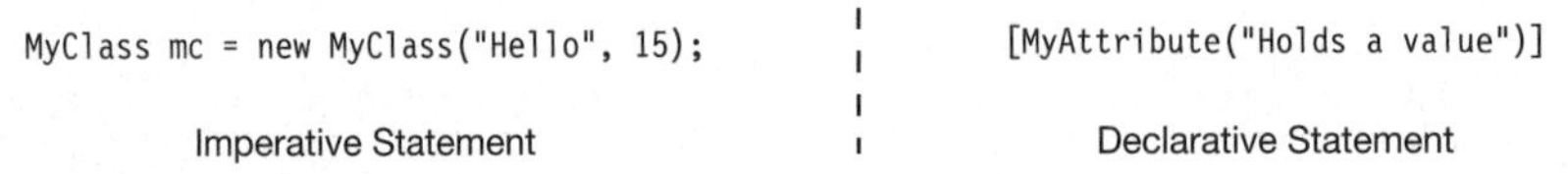

```
MyClass mc = new MyClass("Hello", 15);          [MyAttribute("Holds a value")]

        Imperative Statement                         Declarative Statement
```

Figure 24-4. *Comparing the use of constructors*

Positional and Named Parameters in Constructors

Like the methods and constructors of regular classes, the attribute constructors can also use positional and named parameters.

The following code shows the application of an attribute using a positional parameter and two named parameters:

```
        Positional parameter          Named parameter       Named parameter
                 ↓                           ↓                     ↓
[MyAttribute("An excellent class", Reviewer="Amy McArthur", Ver="0.7.15.33")]
                                        ↑                        ↑
                                   Equals sign              Equals sign
```

The following code shows the declaration of the attribute class, as well as its application on class MyClass. Notice that the constructor *declaration* lists only a single formal parameter. And yet, by using named parameters, you can give the constructor three actual parameters. The two named parameters set the values of fields Ver and Reviewer.

```
public sealed class MyAttributeAttribute : System.Attribute
{
    public string Description;
    public string Ver;
    public string Reviewer;

    public MyAttributeAttribute(string desc)  // Single formal parameters
    { Description = desc; }
}                                Three actual parameters
                                          ↓
[MyAttribute("An excellent class", Reviewer="Amy McArthur", Ver="7.15.33")]
class MyClass
{ ... }
```

■ **Note** If the constructor requires any positional parameters, they must be placed before any named parameters.

Restricting the Usage of an Attribute

You've seen that you can apply attributes to classes. But attributes *themselves* are classes, and there is one important predefined attribute that you can apply to your custom attributes. It's the AttributeUsage attribute. You can use it to restrict the usage of an attribute to a specific set of target types.

For example, if you want your custom attribute MyAttribute to be applied only to methods, you could use the following form of AttributeUsage:

```
                        Only to methods
                             ↓

[ AttributeUsage( AttributeTarget.Method ) ]
public sealed class MyAttributeAttribute : System.Attribute
{ ...
```

AttributeUsage has three important public properties, which are listed in Table 24-4. The table shows the names of the properties and their meanings. For the second two properties, it also shows their default values.

Table 24-4. *Public Properties of AttributeUsage*

Name	Meaning	Default
ValidOn	Stores a list of the types of targets to which the attribute can be applied. The first parameter of the constructor must be an enum value of type AttributeTarget.	
Inherited	A Boolean value that specifies whether the attribute can be inherited by derived classes of the decorated type.	true
AllowMultiple	A Boolean value that specifies whether the target can have multiple instances of the attribute applied to it.	false

The Constructor for AttributeUsage

The constructor for AttributeUsage takes a single, positional parameter that specifies which target types are allowed for the attribute. It uses this parameter to set the ValidOn property. The acceptable target types are members of the AttributeTarget enumeration. Table 24-5 shows the complete set of the members of the AttributeTarget enumeration.

You can combine the usage types by using the bitwise OR operator. For example, the attribute declared in the following code can be applied only to methods and constructors.

```
                                            Targets
                                               ↓
[ AttributeUsage( AttributeTarget.Method | AttributeTarget.Constructor ) ]
public sealed class MyAttributeAttribute : System.Attribute
{ ...
```

Table 24-5. *Members of Enum AttributeTarget*

All	Assembly	Class	Constructor
Delegate	Enum	Event	Field
GenericParameter	Interface	Method	Module
Parameter	Property	ReturnValue	Struct

When you apply AttributeUsage to an attribute declaration, the constructor will have at least the one required parameter, which contains the target types to be stored in ValidOn. You can also optionally set the Inherited and AllowMultiple properties by using named parameters. If you don't set them, they'll have their default values, as shown in Table 24-4.

As an example, the next code block specifies the following about MyAttribute:

- MyAttribute must be applied only to classes.

- MyAttribute is not inherited by classes derived from classes to which it is applied.

- There cannot be multiple instances of MyAttribute applied to the same target.

```
[ AttributeUsage( AttributeTarget.Class,          // Required, positional
                  Inherited = false,              // Optional, named
                  AllowMultiple = false ) ]       // Optional, named
public sealed class MyAttributeAttribute : System.Attribute
{ ...
```

Suggested Practices for Custom Attributes

The following practices are strongly suggested when writing custom attributes:

- The attribute class should represent some state of the target construct.

- If the attribute *requires* certain fields, include a constructor with positional parameters to collect that data, and let optional fields be initialized with named parameters, as needed.

- Don't implement public methods or other function members other than properties.

- For additional security, declare the attribute class as sealed.

- Use the AttributeUsage attribute on your attribute declaration to explicitly specify the set of attribute targets.

The following code illustrates these guidelines:

```
[AttributeUsage( AttributeTargets.Class )]
public sealed class  ReviewCommentAttribute : System.Attribute
{
   public string Description   { get; set; }
   public string VersionNumber { get; set; }
   public string ReviewerID    { get; set; }

   public ReviewCommentAttribute(string desc, string ver)
   {
      Description   = desc;
      VersionNumber = ver;
   }
}
```

Accessing an Attribute

At the beginning of the chapter, you saw that you can access information about a type using its Type object. You can access custom attributes in the same way. There are two methods of Type that are particularly useful in this: IsDefined and GetCustomAttributes.

Using the IsDefined Method

You can use the IsDefined method of the Type object to determine whether a particular attribute is applied to a particular class.

For example, the following code declares an attributed class called MyClass and also acts as its own attribute consumer by accessing an attribute declared and applied in the program itself. At the top of the code are declarations of the attribute ReviewComment and the class MyClass, to which it is applied. The code does the following:

- First, Main creates an object of the class. It then retrieves a reference to the Type object by using the GetType method, which it inherited from its base class, object.

- With the reference to the Type object, it can call the IsDefined method to find out whether attribute ReviewComment is applied to this class.

  — The first parameter takes a Type object of the *attribute* you are checking for.

  — The second parameter is of type bool and specifies whether to search the inheritance tree of MyClass to find the attribute.

```
[AttributeUsage(AttributeTargets.Class)]
public sealed class ReviewCommentAttribute : System.Attribute
{ ... }

[ReviewComment("Check it out", "2.4")]
class MyClass {  }

class Program {
   static void Main() {
      MyClass mc = new MyClass(); // Create an instance of the class.
      Type t = mc.GetType();      // Get the Type object from the instance.
      bool isDefined =            // Check the Type for the attribute.
         t.IsDefined(typeof(ReviewCommentAttribute), false);

      if( isDefined )
         Console.WriteLine("ReviewComment is applied to type {0}", t.Name);
   }
}
```

This code produces the following output:

```
ReviewComment is applied to type MyClass
```

Using the GetCustomAttributes Method

The GetCustomAttributes method returns an array of the attributes applied to a construct.

- The actual object returned is an array of objects, which you must then cast to the correct attribute type.

- The Boolean parameter specifies whether to search the inheritance tree to find the attribute.

  ```
  object[] AttArr = t.GetCustomAttributes(false);
  ```

- When the GetCustomAttributes method is called, an instance of each attribute associated with the target is created.

The following code uses the same attribute and class declarations as the previous example. But in this case, it doesn't just determine whether an attribute is applied to the class. Instead, it retrieves an array of the attributes applied to the class and cycles through them, printing out their member values.

```
static void Main()
{
    Type t = typeof(MyClass);
    object[] AttArr = t.GetCustomAttributes(false);

    foreach (Attribute a in AttArr)
    {
        ReviewCommentAttribute attr = a as ReviewCommentAttribute;
        if (null != attr)
        {
            Console.WriteLine("Description     : {0}", attr.Description);
            Console.WriteLine("Version Number : {0}", attr.VersionNumber);
            Console.WriteLine("Reviewer ID     : {0}", attr.ReviewerID);
        }
    }
}
```

This code produces the following output:

```
Description     : Check it out
Version Number : 2.4
Reviewer ID     :
```

CHAPTER 25

■ ■ ■

Other Topics

Overview

In this chapter, I'll cover a number of other topics that are important in using C# but that don't fit neatly into one of the other chapters. These include string handling, nullable types, the Main method, documentation comments, and nested types.

Strings

0s and 1s are fine for internal computation, but for human-readable input and output, we need strings of characters. The BCL provides a number of classes that make string handling easy.

The C# predefined type string represents the .NET class System.String. The most important things to know about strings are the following:

- Strings are arrays of Unicode characters.

- Strings are immutable—they cannot be changed.

The string type has many useful string-manipulation members, including those that allow you to determine their length, change their case, concatenate strings, and perform many other useful tasks. Table 25-1 shows some of the most useful members.

Table 25-1. *Useful Members of the string Type*

Member	Type	Meaning
Length	Property	Returns the length of the string
Concat	Static method	Returns a string that is the concatenation of its argument strings
Contains	Method	Returns a bool value indicating whether the argument is a substring of the object string
Format	Static method	Returns a formatted string
Insert	Method	Takes as parameters a string and a position and creates and returns a new copy of the object string, with the parameter string inserted at the given position.
Remove	Method	Returns a copy of the object string in which a substring has been removed
Replace	Method	Returns a copy of the object string in which a substring has been replaced
Substring	Method	Retrieves a substring from the object string
ToUpper	Method	Returns a copy of the object string in which the alphabetic characters are all uppercase
ToLower	Method	Returns a copy of the object string in which the alphabetic characters are all lowercase

The names of many of the methods in Table 25-1 sound as if they are changing the string object. Actually, they're not changing the strings but returning new copies. For a string, any "change" allocates a new immutable string.

For example, the following code declares and initializes a string called s. The first WriteLine statement calls the ToUpper method on s, which returns a copy of the string in all uppercase. The last line prints out the value of s, showing that it is unchanged.

```
string s = "Hi there.";

Console.WriteLine("{0}", s.ToUpper());          // Print uppercase copy
Console.WriteLine("{0}", s);                    // String is unchanged
```

This code produces the following output:

```
HI THERE.
Hi there.
```

Using Class StringBuilder

The StringBuilder class helps you dynamically and efficiently produce strings without too many copies being made.

- The StringBuilder class is a member of the BCL, in namespace System.Text.

- A StringBuilder object is a *mutable* array of Unicode characters.

For example, the following code declares and initializes a StringBuilder and prints its resulting string value. The fourth line changes the actual object by replacing part of the internal array of characters. Now when you print its string value by implicitly calling ToString, you can see that, unlike an object of type string, the StringBuilder object has actually been changed.

```
using System.Text;

StringBuilder sb = new StringBuilder("Hi there.");
Console.WriteLine("{0}", sb);          // Print string
sb.Replace("Hi", "Hello");             // Replace a substring
Console.WriteLine("{0}", sb);          // Print changed string
```

This code produces the following output:

```
Hi there.
Hello there.
```

When a StringBuilder object is created based on a given string, the class allocates a buffer longer than the actual current string length. As long as the changes made to the string can fit in the buffer, no new memory is allocated. If changes to the string require more space than is available in the buffer, a new, larger buffer is allocated, and the characters are copied to it. Like the original buffer, this new buffer also has extra space.

To get the string corresponding to the StringBuilder content, you simply call its ToString method.

Formatting Numeric Strings

Throughout the text, the sample code has used the WriteLine method to display values. Each time, it used the simple substitution marker consisting of curly braces surrounding an integer. Many times, however, you'll want to present the output of a text string in a format more appropriate than just a plain number. For example, you might want to display a value as currency or as a fixed-point value with a certain number of decimal places. You can do these things by using format strings.

For example, the following code consists of two statements that print out the value 500. The first line prints out the number without any additional formatting. In the second line, the format string specifies that the number should be formatted as currency.

```
Console.WriteLine("The value: {0}."   , 500);      // Print out number
Console.WriteLine("The value: {0: C}.", 500);      // Format as currency
                               ↑
                         Format as currency
```

This code produces the following output:

```
The value: 500.
The value: $500.00.
```

The difference between the two statements is that the format item includes additional information in the form of a format specifier. The syntax for a format specifier consists of three fields inside the set of curly braces: the index, the alignment specifier, and the format specifier. Figure 25-1 shows the syntax.

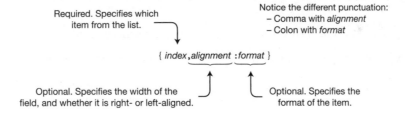

Figure 25-1. *Syntax for a format item*

The first thing in the format item is the index. As you well know by now, the index specifies which item from the list following the format string should be formatted. The index is required, and the numbering of the list items starts at 0.

The Alignment Specifier

The alignment specifier represents the *minimum width* of the field in terms of characters. The alignment specifier has the following characteristics:

- It is optional and separated from the index with a comma.

- It consists of a positive or negative integer.

  — The integer represents the minimum number of characters to use for the field.

  — The sign represents either right or left alignment. Positive specifies right alignment; negative specifies left alignment.

```
                Index—use 0th item in the list
                          ↓
    Console.WriteLine("{0, 10}", 500);
                            ↑
    Alignment specifier—right-align in a field of ten characters
```

For example, the following code shows two format items, formatting the value of int variable myInt. In the first case, the value of myInt is displayed as a right-aligned string of ten characters. In the second case, it's left-aligned. The format items are between two vertical bars, just to show in the output their limits on each side.

```
int myInt = 500;
Console.WriteLine("|{0, 10}|", myInt);            // Aligned right
Console.WriteLine("|{0,-10}|", myInt);            // Aligned left
```

This code produces the following output; there are ten characters between the vertical bars:

```
|       500|
|500       |
```

The actual representation of the value might take more or fewer characters than specified in the alignment specifier:

- If the representation takes fewer characters than specified in the alignment specifier, the remaining characters are padded with spaces.

- If the representation takes more characters than specified, the alignment specifier is ignored, and the representation uses as many characters as are needed.

The Format Component

The format component specifies the form that the numeric representation should take. For example, should it be represented as currency, in decimal format, in hexadecimal format, or in fixed-point notation?

The format component has two parts, as shown in Figure 25-2:

- The *format specifier* is a single alphabetic character, from a set of nine built-in character formats. The character can be uppercase or lowercase. The case is significant for some specifiers but not for others.

- The *precision specifier* is optional and consists of one or two digits. Its actual meaning depends on the format specifier.

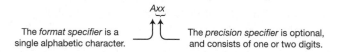

Figure 25-2. *Standard format specifier string*

The following code shows an example of the syntax of the format string component:

```
                   Index—use 0th item in the list
                              ↓
Console.WriteLine("{0: F4}", 12.345678);
                        ↑
               Format component—fixed-point, four decimal places
```

The following code shows examples of different format strings:

```
double myDouble = 12.345678;
Console.WriteLine("{0,-10:G} -- General",                      myDouble);
Console.WriteLine("{0,-10} -- Default, same as General",       myDouble);
Console.WriteLine("{0,-10:F4} -- Fixed Point, 4 dec places",   myDouble);
Console.WriteLine("{0,-10:C} -- Currency",                     myDouble);
Console.WriteLine("{0,-10:E3} -- Sci. Notation, 3 dec places", myDouble);
Console.WriteLine("{0,-10:x} -- Hexadecimal integer",          1194719 );
```

This code produces the following output:

```
12.345678  -- General
12.345678  -- Default, same as General
12.3457    -- Fixed Point, 4 dec places
$12.35     -- Currency
1.235E+001 -- Sci. Notation, 3 dec places
123adf     -- Hexadecimal integer
```

Standard Numeric Format Specifiers

The Regional and Language Options applet of the Windows Control Panel can affect the resulting formats of some of the specifiers. For example, the currency symbol of the country or region specified will be used by the currency format specifier. You can do the same in code by creating a CultureInfo and assigning it to the Thread.CurrentThread.CurrentCulture property.

Table 25-2 summarizes the nine standard numeric format specifiers. The first column lists the name of the specifier followed by the specifier characters. If the specifier characters have different output depending on their case, they are marked *case sensitive*.

Table 25-2. *Standard Numeric Format Specifiers*

Name and Characters	Meaning
Currency C, c	Formats the value as a currency, using a currency symbol. Precision specifier: The number of decimal places. Sample: `Console.WriteLine("{0 :C}", 12.5);` Output: $12.50
Decimal D, d	A string of decimal digits, with a negative sign, if appropriate. Can be used only with integral types. Precision specifier: The minimum number of digits to use in the output string. If the number has fewer digits, it will be padded with 0s on the left. Sample: `Console.WriteLine("{0 :D4}", 12);` Output: 0012
Fixed-point F, f	A string of decimal digits with a decimal point. Can also include a negative sign, if appropriate. Precision specifier: The number of decimal places. Sample: `Console.WriteLine("{0 :F4}", 12.3456789);` Output: 12.3457
General G, g	A compact fixed-point representation or a scientific notation representation, depending on the value. This is the default, if no specifier is listed. Precision specifier: Depends on the value. Sample: `Console.WriteLine("{0 :G4}", 12.3456789);` Output: 12.35
Hexadecimal X, x Case sensitive	A string of hexadecimal digits. The hex digits A through F will match the case of the specifier. Precision specifier: The minimum number of digits to use in the output string. If the number has fewer digits, it will be padded with 0s on the left. Sample: `Console.WriteLine("{0 :x}", 180026);` Output: 2bf3a

Number N, n	Similar to fixed-point representation but includes separators between each group of three digits, starting at the decimal point and going left. Precision specifier: The number of decimal places. Sample: `Console.WriteLine("{0 :N2}", 12345678.54321);` Output: `12,345,678.54`
Percent P, p	A string that represents percent. The number is multiplied by 100. Precision specifier: The number of decimal places Sample: `Console.WriteLine("{0 :P2}", 0.1221897);` Output: `12.22 %`
Round-trip R, r	The output string is chosen so that if the string is converted back to a numeric value using a `Parse` method, the result will be the original value. Precision specifier: Ignored. Sample: `Console.WriteLine("{0 :R}", 1234.21897);` Output: `1234.21897`
Scientific E, e Case sensitive	Scientific notation with a mantissa and an exponent. The exponent is preceded by the letter E. The E will be the same case as the specifier. Precision specifier: The number of decimal places. Sample: `Console.WriteLine("{0 :e4}", 12.3456789);` Output: `1.2346e+001`

Parsing Strings to Data Values

Strings are arrays of Unicode characters. For example, string `"25.873"` is six characters long and is *not* a number. Although it looks like a number, you cannot perform arithmetic functions on it. "Adding" two strings produces their concatenation.

- *Parsing* allows you to take a string that represents a value and convert it into an actual value.

- All the predefined, simple types have a static method called `Parse`, which takes a string value representing the type and converts it into an actual value of the type.

- If the string cannot be parsed, the system raises an exception.

The following statement shows an example of the syntax of using a `Parse` method. Notice that `Parse` is static, so you need to invoke it by using the name of the target type.

```
double d1 = double.Parse("25.873");
              ↑              ↑
          Target type   String to be converted
```

The following code shows an example of parsing two strings to values of type `double` and then adding them:

```
static void Main()
{
   string s1 = "25.873";
   string s2 = "36.240";

   double d1 = double.Parse(s1);
   double d2 = double.Parse(s2);

   double total = d1 + d2;
   Console.WriteLine("Total:  {0}", total);
}
```

This code produces the following output:

```
Total:  62.113
```

■ **Note** A common misconception about `Parse` is that since it operates on a string, it is thought of as a member of the `string` class. It is not. `Parse` is not a single method at all but a number of methods implemented by the *target* types.

The disadvantage of the Parse methods is that they throw an exception if they can't successfully parse the string to the target type. Exceptions are expensive operations, and you should try to programmatically avoid them if you can. The TryParse method allows you to do that. The important things to know about TryParse are the following:

- Every built-in type that has a Parse method also has a TryParse method (and you should use the TryParse).

- The TryParse method takes two parameters and returns a bool.

  — The first parameter is the string you're trying to parse.

  — The second is an out parameter of a reference to a variable of the target type.

  — If the TryParse succeeds, it returns true. Otherwise, it returns false.

The following code shows an example of using a TryParse method:

```
class Program
{
    static void Main( )
    {
        bool success;
        string parseResultSummary;

        string stringFirst = "28";
        int intFirst;              Input string      Output variable
                                        ↓                ↓
        success = int.TryParse( stringFirst, out intFirst );

        parseResultSummary = success
                            ? "was successfully parsed"
                            : "was not successfully parsed";
        Console.WriteLine( "String {0} {1}", stringFirst, parseResultSummary );

        string stringSecond = "vt750";
        int intSecond;             Input string      Output variable
                                        ↓                ↓
        success = int.TryParse( stringSecond, out intSecond );

        parseResultSummary = success
                            ? "was successfully parsed"
                            : "was not successfully parsed";
        Console.WriteLine( "String {0} {1}", stringSecond, parseResultSummary );
    }
}
```

This code produces the following output:

```
String 28 was successfully parsed
String vt750 was not successfully parsed
```

More About the Nullable Types

In Chapter 3 you got an introduction to nullable types. As you'll remember, nullable types allow you to create a value type variable that can be marked as valid or invalid, effectively letting you set a value type variable to "null." I wanted to introduce nullable types in Chapter 3 with the other built-in types, but now that you know more about C#, it's a good time to cover their more intricate aspects.

Just to review, a nullable type is always based on another type, called the *underlying type*, that has already been declared.

- You can create a nullable type from any value type, including the predefined, simple types.

- You cannot create a nullable type from a reference type or another nullable type.

- You do not explicitly declare a nullable type in your code. Instead, you declare a *variable of a nullable type*. The compiler implicitly creates the nullable type for you.

To create a variable of a nullable type, simply add a question mark to the end of the name of the underlying type, in the variable declaration.

For example, the following code declares a variable of the nullable int type. Notice that the suffix is attached to the *type* name—not the variable name.

```
        Suffix
          ↓
  int? myNInt = 28;
    ↑
The name of the nullable type includes the suffix.
```

With this declaration statement, the compiler takes care of both producing the nullable type and the variable of that type. Figure 25-3 shows the structure of this nullable type. It contains the following:

- An instance of the underlying type

- Several important read-only properties:

  — Property HasValue is of type bool and indicates whether the value is valid.

  — Property Value is the same type as the underlying type and returns the value of the variable—if the variable is valid.

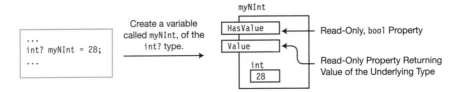

Figure 25-3. *A nullable type contains an object of the underlying type in a struct, with two read-only properties.*

You can use the two read-only properties explicitly as follows. Reading a variable of a nullable type returns its value. You must, however, make sure that the variable is not null. Attempting to read the value of a null variable produces an exception.

```
int? myInt1 = 15;
Explicitly use the property.
                ↓
if (myInt1.HasValue )
    Console.WriteLine("{0}", myInt1.Value);
                                    ↑
                        Explicitly use the property.
```

A better method, however, is to use the shortcut forms, as shown in the following code.

- To check whether a nullable type has a value, you can compare it to null.

- Like any variable, to retrieve its value, you can just use its name.

```
        Compare to null
            ↓
if ( myInt1 != null )
    Console.WriteLine("{0}", myInt1);
                            ↑
                    Use variable name
```

Both sets of code produce the following output:

15

The Null Coalescing Operator

The standard arithmetic and comparison operators also handle nullable types. There is also a special operator called the null *coalescing operator*, which returns a non-null value to an expression, in case a nullable type variable is null.

The null coalescing operator consists of two contiguous question marks and has two operands:

- The first operand is a variable of a nullable type.

- The second is a non-nullable value of the same underlying type.

- If, at run time, the first operand evaluates to null, the second operand is returned as the result of the operation.

```
                          Null coalescing operator
int? myI4 = null;                    ↓
Console.WriteLine("myI4: {0}", myI4 ?? -1);

myI4 = 10;
Console.WriteLine("myI4: {0}", myI4 ?? -1);
```

This code produces the following output:

```
myI4: -1
myI4: 10
```

The equality comparison operators, == and !=, have an interesting characteristic you need to be aware of. If you compare two values of the same nullable type and both are null, the equality comparison operators consider them equal. For example, in the following code, the two nullable ints are set to null. The equality comparison operator declares them equal.

```
int? i1 = null, i2 = null;              // Both are null.

if (i1 == i2)                           // Operator returns true.
    Console.WriteLine("Equal");
```

Using Nullable User-Defined Types

So far, you've seen nullable forms of the predefined, simple types. You can also create nullable forms of user-defined value types. These bring up additional issues that don't come up when using the simple types.

The main issue is access to the members of the encapsulated underlying type. A nullable type doesn't directly expose any of the members of the underlying type. For example, take a look at the following code and its representation in Figure 25-4. The code declares a struct (which is a value type) called MyStruct, with two public fields.

- Since the fields of the struct are public, they can easily be accessed in any instance of the struct, as shown on the left of the figure.

- The nullable version of the struct, however, exposes the underlying type only through the Value property and doesn't *directly* expose any of its members. Although the members are public to the struct, they are not public to the nullable type, as shown on the right of the figure.

```
struct MyStruct                              // Declare a struct.
{
   public int X;                             // Field
   public int Y;                             // Field
   public MyStruct(int xVal, int yVal)       // Constructor
   { X = xVal;   Y = yVal; }
}

class Program {
   static void Main()
   {
      MyStruct? mSNull = new MyStruct(5, 10);
      ...
```

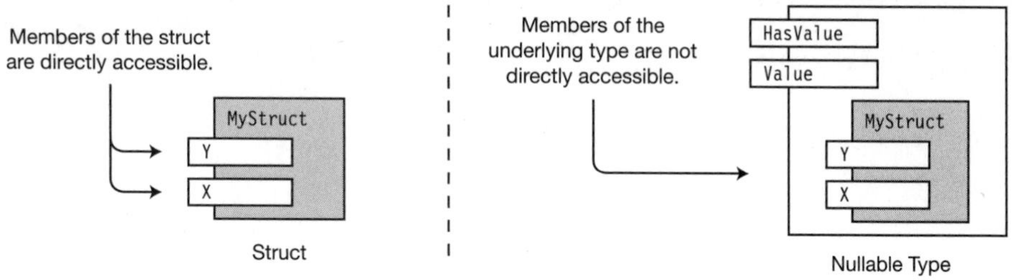

Figure 25-4. *The accessibility of the members of a struct is different from that of the nullable type.*

For example, the following code uses this struct and creates variables of both the struct and the corresponding nullable type. In the third and fourth lines of code, the values of the struct's variables are read directly. In the fifth and sixth lines, they must be read from the value returned by the nullable's Value property.

```
MyStruct  mSStruct = new MyStruct(6, 11);      // Variable of struct
MyStruct? mSNull   = new MyStruct(5, 10);      // Variable of nullable type
                                     Struct access
                                           ↓

Console.WriteLine("mSStruct.X: {0}", mSStruct.X);
Console.WriteLine("mSStruct.Y: {0}", mSStruct.Y);

Console.WriteLine("mSNull.X: {0}",   mSNull.Value.X);
Console.WriteLine("mSNull.Y: {0}",   mSNull.Value.Y);
                                           ↑
                                 Nullable type access
```

Nullable<T>

Nullable types are implemented by using a .NET type called System.Nullable<T>, which uses the C# generics feature.

The question mark syntax of C# nullable types is just shortcut syntax for creating a variable of type Nullable<T>, where T is the underlying type. Nullable<T> takes the underlying type, embeds it in a structure, and provides the structure with the properties, methods, and constructors of the nullable type.

You can use either the generics syntax of Nullable<T> or the C# shortcut syntax. The shortcut syntax is easier to write and to understand and is less prone to errors.

The following code uses the Nullable<T> syntax with struct MyStruct, declared in the preceding example, to create a variable called mSNull of type Nullable<MyStruct>:

```
Nullable<MyStruct> mSNull = new Nullable<MyStruct>();
```

The following code uses the question mark syntax but is semantically equivalent to the Nullable<T> syntax:

```
MyStruct? mSNull = new MyStruct();
```

Method Main

Every C# program must have one entry point—a method that must be called Main.

In the sample code throughout this text, I've used a version of Main that takes no parameters and returns no value. There are, however, four forms of Main that are acceptable as the entry point to a program. These forms are the following:

- `static void Main()`   `{...}`

- `static void Main( string[] args) {...}`

- `static int  Main()`   `{...}`

- `static int  Main( string[] args) {...}`

The first two forms don't return a value to the execution environment when the program terminates. The second two forms return an int value. A return value, if one is used, is generally used to report success or failure of the program, where 0 is generally used to indicate success.

The second and fourth forms allow you to pass actual parameters, also called *arguments*, from the command line into the program, when it starts. Some important characteristics of command-line arguments are the following:

- There can be zero or more command-line arguments. Even if there are no arguments, the args parameter is not null. Instead, it is an array with no elements.

- The arguments are separated by spaces or tabs.

- Each argument is interpreted by the program as a string, but you don't need to enclose them in quotation marks on the command line.

For example, the following program, called CommandLineArgs, accepts command-line arguments and prints out each argument supplied:

```csharp
class Program
{
   static void Main(string[] args)
   {
      foreach (string s in args)
         Console.WriteLine(s);
   }
}
```

The following command line executes program CommandLineArgs with five arguments:

```
CommandLineArgs Jon Peter Beth Julia Tammi
       ↑                     ↑
   Executable            Arguments
     Name
```

679

The preceding program and command line produce the following output:

```
Jon
Peter
Beth
Julia
Tammi
```

Other important things to know about `Main` are the following:

- `Main` must always be declared `static`.

- `Main` can be declared in either a class or a struct.

A program can contain only one declaration of the four acceptable entry point forms of `Main`. You can, however, legally declare other methods named `Main`, as long as they don't have any of the four entry point forms—but doing this is inviting confusion.

Accessibility of Main

`Main` can be declared `public` or `private`:

- If `Main` is declared `private`, other assemblies cannot access it, and only the execution environment can start the program.

- If `Main` is declared `public`, other assemblies can call it.

The execution environment, however, *always* has access to `Main`, regardless of its declared access level or the declared access level of the class or struct in which it is declared.

By default, when Visual Studio creates a project, it creates a program outline where `Main` is implicitly private. You can always add the `public` modifier if you need to do so.

Documentation Comments

The dcumentation comments feature allows you to include documentation of your program in the form of XML elements. Visual Studio even assists you in inserting the elements and will read them from your source file and copy them to a separate XML file for you. This section does not cover the topic of XML but presents the overall process of using documentation comments.

Figure 25-5 gives an overview of using XML comments. This includes the following steps:

- You can use Visual Studio to produce the source file with the embedded XML. Visual Studio can automatically insert most of the important XML elements.

- Visual Studio reads the XML from the source code file and copies the XML code to a new file.

- Another program, called a documentation compiler, can take the XML file and produce various types of documentation files from it.

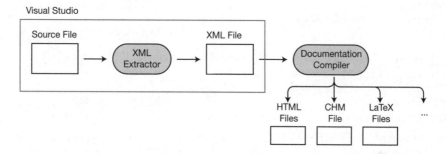

Figure 25-5. *The XML comments process*

Earlier versions of Visual Studio contained an elementary documentation compiler, but it was removed before the release of Visual Studio 2005. Microsoft has developed a new documentation compiler called Sandcastle, which they already use to generate the .NET Framework documentation. You can learn more about it and download it for free from http://sandcastle.codeplex.com.

Inserting Documentation Comments

Documentation comments start with three consecutive forward slashes.

- The first two slashes indicate to the compiler that this is an end-of-line comment and should be ignored in the parsing of the program.

- The third slash indicates that it's a documentation comment.

For example, in the following code, the first four lines show documentation comments about the class declaration. They use the `<summary>` XML tag. Above the declaration of the field are three lines documenting the field—again using the `<summary>` tag.

```
/// <summary>        ← Open XML tag for the class
/// This is class MyClass, which does the following wonderful things, using
/// the following algorithm. ... Besides those, it does these additional
/// wonderful things.
/// </summary>       ← Close XML tag
class MyClass                                    // Class declaration
{
    /// <summary>     ← Open XML tag for the field
    /// Field1 is used to hold the value of ...
    /// </summary>    ← Close XML tag
    public int Field1 = 10;                      // Field declaration
    ...
```

Each XML element is inserted by Visual Studio automatically when you type three slashes above the declaration of a language feature, such as a class or a class member.

For example, the following code shows two slashes above the declaration of class `MyClass`:

```
//
class MyClass
{ ...
```

As soon as you add the third slash, Visual Studio immediately expands the comment to the following code, without your having to do anything. You can then type anything you want on the documentation comment lines between the tags.

```
/// <summary>        Automatically inserted
///                  Automatically inserted
/// </summary>       Automatically inserted
class MyClass
{ ...
```

Using Other XML Tags

In the preceding examples, you saw the use of the summary XML tag. There are also a number of other tags that C# recognizes. Table 25-3 lists some of the most important.

Table 25-3. *Documentation Code XML Tags*

Tag	Meaning
<code>	Format the enclosing lines in a font that looks like code.
<example>	Mark the enclosing lines as an example.
<param>	Mark a parameter for a method or constructor and allow a description.
<remarks>	Describe a type declaration.
<returns>	Describe a return value.
<seealso>	Create a *See Also* entry in the output document.
<summary>	Describe a type or a type member.
<value>	Describe a property.

Nested Types

Types are usually declared directly inside a namespace. You can, however, also declare types inside a class or struct declaration.

- Types declared inside another type declaration are called *nested types*. Like all type declarations, nested types are templates for an instance of the type.

- A nested type is declared like a member of the *enclosing type*.

  — A nested type can be any type.

  — An enclosing type can be either a class or a struct.

For example, the following code shows class MyClass, with a nested class called MyCounter.

```
class MyClass                    // Enclosing class
{
    class MyCounter              // Nested class
    {
        ...
    }
    ...
}
```

Declaring a type as a nested type often makes sense if it's only meant to be used as a helper for the enclosing type.

Don't be confused by the term *nested*. Nested refers to the location of the *declaration*—not the location of any *instances*. Although a nested type's declaration is inside the enclosing type's declaration, objects of the nested type are not necessarily enclosed in objects of the enclosing type. Objects of the nested type—if any are created at all—are located wherever they would have been located had they not been declared inside another type.

For example, Figure 25-6 shows objects of types MyClass and MyCounter, as outlined in the preceding code. The figure additionally shows a field called Counter, in class MyClass, that is a reference to an object of the nested class, which is located elsewhere in the heap.

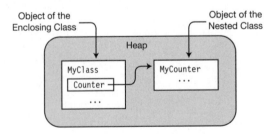

Figure 25-6. *Nesting refers to the location of the declaration, not the location of the object.*

Example of a Nested Class

The following code fleshes out classes MyClass and MyCounter into a full program. MyCounter implements an integer counter that starts at 0 and can be incremented using the ++ operator. When the constructor for MyClass is called, it creates an instance of the nested class and assigns the reference to the field. Figure 25-7 illustrates the structure of the objects in the code.

```csharp
class MyClass
{
   class MyCounter                                       // Nested class
   {
      private int _Count = 0;
      public int Count                                   // Read-only property
      {
         get { return _Count; }
      }

      public static MyCounter operator++( MyCounter current )
      {
         current._Count++;
         return current;
      }
   }

   private MyCounter counter;                            // Field of nested class

   public MyClass() { counter = new MyCounter(); }      // Constructor

   public int Incr()     { return (counter++).Count; }  // Increment method
   public int GetValue() { return counter.Count; }      // Get counter value
}

class Program
{
   static void Main( )
   {
      MyClass mc = new MyClass();                        // Create object

      mc.Incr(); mc.Incr(); mc.Incr();                   // Increment it.
      mc.Incr(); mc.Incr(); mc.Incr();                   // Increment it.

      Console.WriteLine("Total: {0}", mc.GetValue());    // Print its value.
   }
}
```

This code produces the following output:

```
Total:  6
```

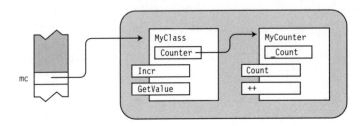

Figure 25-7. *Objects of a nested class and its enclosing class*

Visibility and Nested Types

In Chapter 7, you learned that classes, and types in general, can have an access level of either `public` or `internal`. Nested types, however, are different in that they have *member accessibility* rather than *type accessibility*. Therefore, the following are true:

- A nested type declared inside a class can have any of the five class member accessibility levels `public`, `protected`, `private`, `internal`, or `protected internal`.

- A nested type declared inside a struct can have one of the three struct member accessibility levels `public`, `internal`, or `private`.

In both cases, the default access level of a nested type is `private`, which means it cannot be seen outside the enclosing type.

The relationship between the members of the enclosing class and the nested class is a little less straightforward and is illustrated in Figure 25-8. The nested type has complete access to the members of the enclosing type, regardless of their declared accessibility, including members that are `private` and `protected`.

The relationship, however, is not symmetrical. Although the members of the enclosing type can always see the nested type declaration and create variables and instances of it, they do not have complete access to its members. Instead, their access is limited to the declared access of the nested class members—just as if the nested type were a separate type. That is, they can access the `public` and `internal` members but cannot access the `private` or `protected` members of the nested type.

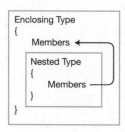

Members of the nested type have
complete access permission to members
of the enclosing type.

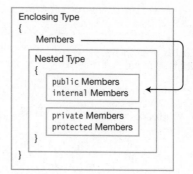

Members of the enclosing type have access
permission only to public and internal members
of the nested type.

Figure 25-8. *Accessibility between nested type members and enclosing type members*

You can summarize this relationship as follows:

- The members of a nested type always have full access rights to members of the enclosing type.

- The members of an enclosing type

  — Always have access to the nested type itself

  — Only have the *declared access* rights to members of the nested type

The visibility of nested types can also affect the inheritance of base members. If the enclosing class is a derived class, a nested type can hide a base class member with the same name. Use the new modifier with the declaration of the nested class to make the hiding explicit.

A this reference within a nested type refers to the *object of the nested type*—not the object of the enclosing type. If an object of the nested type needs access to the enclosing type, it must have a reference to it. You can have the enclosing object supply its this reference as a parameter to the nested type's constructor, as shown in the following code:

```
class SomeClass                              // Enclosing class
{
   int Field1 = 15, Field2 = 20;            // Fields of enclosing class
   MyNested mn = null;                      // Reference to nested class

   public void PrintMyMembers()
   {
      mn.PrintOuterMembers();               // Call method in nested class
   }

   public SomeClass()                       // Constructor
   {
      mn = new MyNested(this);              // Create instance of nested class
   }                     ↑
                Pass in the reference to the enclosing class.
   class MyNested                           // Nested class declaration
   {
      SomeClass sc = null;                  // Reference to enclosing class

      public MyNested(SomeClass SC)         // Constructor of the nested class
      {
         sc = SC;                           // Store reference to enclosing class
      }

      public void PrintOuterMembers()
      {
         Console.WriteLine("Field1: {0}", sc.Field1);   // Enclosing field
         Console.WriteLine("Field2: {0}", sc.Field2);   // Enclosing field
      }
   }                                        // End of nested class
}

class Program {
   static void Main( ) {
      SomeClass MySC = new SomeClass();
      MySC.PrintMyMembers();
   }
}
```

This code produces the following output:

```
Field1: 15
Field2: 20
```

Interoperating with COM

Although this text doesn't cover COM programming, C# 4.0 added several syntactic changes to the language specifically to make COM programming easier. One of these changes is called the "omit ref" feature and allows you to call a COM method without using the ref keyword, when you don't need to use the value passed back by the method.

For example, if Microsoft Word is installed on the machine your program is running on, you can use Word's spell checker functionality in your own program. The method you would use to do this is the CheckSpelling method on the Document class, which is in the Microsoft.Office.Tools.Word namespace. This method has 12 parameters, and all of them are ref parameters. This means previously you would have had to supply reference variables for each of the parameters, even if you didn't need to use them to pass data to the method or to receive data back from the method. Omitting the ref keyword *only works with COM methods*—with anything else, you'll still get a compile error.

This code might look something like the following. Notice the following about this code:

- I'm only using the second and third parameters, which are Booleans, but I have to create two variables, ignoreCase and alwaysSuggest of type object to hold the values, since the method requires ref parameters.

- I've created an object variable called optional for the other ten parameters.

```
object ignoreCase    = true;
object alwaysSuggest = false;          Objects to hold Boolean variables
object optional      = Missing.Value;   ↓              ↓
tempDoc.CheckSpelling( ref optional,  ref ignoreCase, ref alwaysSuggest,
    ref optional, ref optional, ref optional, ref optional, ref optional,
    ref optional, ref optional, ref optional, ref optional );
```

With the "omit ref" feature we can clean this up considerably, since we don't have to use the ref keyword on those parameters from which we don't need the output, and we can use inline bools for the two parameters we care about. The simplified code looks like the following:

```
                         bool    bool
object optional = Missing.Value;  ↓     ↓
tempDoc.CheckSpelling( optional, true, false,
    optional, optional, optional, optional,
    optional, optional, optional, optional, optional );
```

If, beyond the "omit ref" feature, we add the fact that the parameters are optional, we can use the option parameters feature of C# 4.0. This looks like the following, which is much less cumbersome than the original:

```
tempDoc.CheckSpelling( Missing.Value, true, false );
```

The following code includes this method in a complete program. To compile this code, you need to have Visual Studio Tools for Office installed on your machine, and you must add a reference in your project to the `Microsoft.Office.Interop.Word` assembly. For the compiled code to run, you must have Microsoft Word installed on your machine.

```
using System;
using System.Reflection;
using Microsoft.Office.Interop.Word;

class Program
{
    static void Main()
    {
        Console.WriteLine( "Enter a string to spell-check:" );
        string stringToSpellCheck = Console.ReadLine();

        string spellingResults;
        int errors = 0;
        if ( stringToSpellCheck.Length == 0 )
            spellingResults = "No string to check";
        else
        {
            Microsoft.Office.Interop.Word.Application app =
                       new Microsoft.Office.Interop.Word.Application();

            Console.WriteLine( "\nChecking the string for misspellings ..." );
            app.Visible = false;

            Microsoft.Office.Interop.Word._Document tempDoc = app.Documents.Add( );

            tempDoc.Words.First.InsertBefore( stringToSpellCheck );
            Microsoft.Office.Interop.Word.ProofreadingErrors
                                spellErrorsColl = tempDoc.SpellingErrors;
            errors = spellErrorsColl.Count;

            //1.  Before C# 4.0
            //object ignoreCase    = true;
            //object alwaysSuggest = false;
            //object optional      = Missing.Value;
            //tempDoc.CheckSpelling( ref optional, ref ignoreCase, ref alwaysSuggest,
            //    ref optional, ref optional, ref optional, ref optional, ref optional,
            //    ref optional, ref optional, ref optional, ref optional );
```

```
            //2. Using the "omit ref" feature of C# 4.0
            object optional = Missing.Value;
            tempDoc.CheckSpelling(
                optional, true, false, optional, optional, optional,
                optional, optional, optional, optional, optional, optional );

            //3. Using "omit ref" and optional parameters
            //tempDoc.CheckSpelling( Missing.Value, true, false );

            app.Quit(false);

            spellingResults = errors + " errors found";
        }

        Console.WriteLine( spellingResults );
        Console.WriteLine( "\nPress <Enter> to exit program." );
        Console.ReadLine();
    }
}
```

When you run this code, it produces a console window, shown in Figure 25-9, that asks you to enter a string that you want run through the spell checker. When it receives the string, it opens Word and runs the spell checker on it. When that happens, you'll see Word's spell checker window appear, as shown in Figure 25-10.

Figure 25-9. *The console window that asks for the string to send to Word's spell checker*

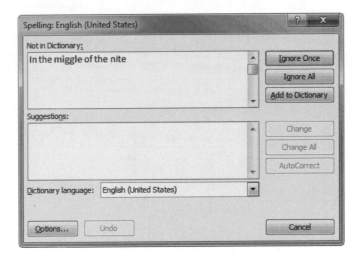

Figure 25-10. *Word's spell checker created using COM calls from the console program*

Index

■ ■ ■

You Need the Companion eBook

Your purchase of this book entitles you to buy the companion PDF-version eBook for only $10. Take the weightless companion with you anywhere.

We believe this Apress title will prove so indispensable that you'll want to carry it with you everywhere, which is why we are offering the companion eBook (in PDF format) for $10 to customers who purchase this book now. Convenient and fully searchable, the PDF version of any content-rich, page-heavy Apress book makes a valuable addition to your programming library. You can easily find and copy code—or perform examples by quickly toggling between instructions and the application. Even simultaneously tackling a donut, diet soda, and complex code becomes simplified with hands-free eBooks!

Once you purchase your book, getting the $10 companion eBook is simple:

❶ Visit **www.apress.com/promo/tendollars/**.

❷ Complete a basic registration form to receive a randomly generated question about this title.

❸ Answer the question correctly in 60 seconds, and you will receive a promotional code to redeem for the $10.00 eBook.

THE EXPERT'S VOICE™

233 Spring Street, New York, NY 10013

Offer valid through 6/11.